Indonesia at the Crossroads: Transformation and Challenges

Indonesia at the Crossroads: Transformation and Challenges

Editors:
Okamoto Masaaki and Jafar Suryomenggolo

Kyoto University Press

Indonesia at the Crossroads: Transformation and Challenges

Published in 2022 jointly by:
UGM Press
Jl. Sendok, Karanggayam CT VIII Caturtunggal Depok, Sleman, D.I. Yogyakarta, 55281, Indonesia
Telephone/Fax.: (0274) 561037
Email: gmupress@ugm.ac.id and ugmpress@ugm.ac.id
Web: ugmpress.ugm.ac.id

Kyoto University Press
69 Yoshida Konoe-cho Sakyo-ku, Kyoto 606-8315, Japan
Telephone: +81-75-761-6182 Fax: +81-75-761-6190
Email: sales@kyoto-up.or.jp
Web: https://www.kyoto-up.or.jp

Trans Pacific Press Co., Ltd
2-2-15-2F Hamamatsu-cho, Minato-ku, Tokyo105-0013, Japan
Telephone: +81-50-5371-9475
Email: info@transpacificpress.com
Web: https://www.transpacificpress.com

© UGM Press, Kyoto University Press, and Trans Pacific Press

Editors: Okamoto Masaaki, Jafar Suryomenggolo
Language editor: Irfan, Karl Smith
Cover design: Pram's | **Cover images**: Ata | **Typesetting**: Rio

ISBN:
Distributors:

(USA and Canada)
Independent Publishers Group (IPG)
814 N. Franklin Street Chicago, IL 60610, USA
Telephone inquiries: +1-312-337-0747
Order placement: 800-888-4741 (domestic only)
Fax: +1-312-337-5985
Email: frontdesk@ipgbook.com
Web: http://www.ipgbook.com

(Japan)
For purchase orders in Japan, please contact any distributor in Japan.

(Europe, Oceania, Middle East and Africa)
EUROSPAN
Gray's Inn House,127 Clerkenwell Road London,
EC1R 5DB United Kingdom
Telephone: +44-(0)20-7240-0856
Email: info@eurospan.co.uk
Web: https://www.eurospangroup.com/

(Southeast Asia, except Indonesia)
Alkem Company Pte Ltd
1, Sunview Road #01-27, Eco-Tech@ Sunview,
Singapore 627615
Telephone: +65 6265 6666
Email: enquiry@alkem.com.sg

No part of this publication may be reproduced or transmitted in any form or by any means, electronic or mechanical, including photocopying, recording, or any information storage and retrieval system, without the written permission of UGM Press, Kyoto University Press or Trans Pacific Press.

Table of Contents

Table of Contents v

List of Tables vii

List of Figures ix

Acknowledgments xii

Introduction 1
Jafar Suryomenggolo and *Okamoto Masaaki*

Part 1: Governance and Social Dynamics

Chapter 1: Managing Multiculturalism in 21st Century
Indonesia amid Ethnic and Religious Diversity 29
Thung Ju Lan

Chapter 2: Post-*Reformasi* Dynamism of the Urban Landscape:
A Visual Report of the Street Art of Yogyakarta 56
Brigitta Isabella

Chapter 3: Religious Intolerance after *Reformasi*: Violence
against the Shia Community in Sampang Regency, Madura 86
Kayane Yuka

Chapter 4: The Uneasy Road to Peace: Papuanization
and the Politics of Recognition 110
Rosita Dewi

Part 2: Paths to Equality

Chapter 5: The Dynamic of Education Outcome
in Decentralized Indonesia (2000–2014) 149
Abdul Wahid Fajar Amin

Chapter 6: Understanding Metropolitan Poverty:
The Profile of Poverty in Jabodetabek 210
Asep Suryahadi and *Cecilia Marlina*

Chapter 7: Between Land Tenure Security and Agricultural
Production: Problems of Farmland Liquidation in Rural Java 235
Ernoiz Antriyandarti and *Susi Wuri Ani*

Chapter 8: Fiscal Policy and Infrastructure Development:
A Reflection of the Two Decades after the 1997 Financial Crisis .. 259
Maxensius Tri Sambodo and *Latif Adam*

Part 3: Structural Challenges

Chapter 9: Corruption and Anti-Corruption:
Major Challenges to Reform 291
Adnan Topan Husodo

Chapter 10: Beyond the Enclave? Human Rights Promotion
Strategies in Post-*Reformasi* Indonesia 311
Suh Jiwon

Chapter 11: Return Strategy of the State: Re-taming Private Security
Providers in Democratized Indonesia 334
Okamoto Masaaki

Chapter 12: Intelligence Apparatus after Suharto:
A Troubled Reform 361
Muhamad Haripin and *Diandra Megaputri Mengko*

Concluding Remarks 394
Jafar Suryomenggolo and *Okamoto Masaaki*

Index 399
Contributors 406

List of Tables

Table 4.1.	Policy approach to Papua 1942–2004	118
Table 5.1.	Share of education expenditures by level of government and level of education in 2009.	158
Table 5.2.	Distribution of population, pupils, education institutions and average distance between schools by level of education and age in 2002–2014.	159
Table 5.3.	Reasons for not continuing to secondary school.	162
Table 5.4.	Determinants of school enrolment for lower- and upper-secondary level education.	164
Table 5.4.	Determinants of school enrolment for lower- and upper-secondary level education. (continued)	165
Table 5.5.	T-test for gender disparity at the regency level in 2002 and 2014.	188
Table 5.6.	School enrolment, school institution, average distance of school, and poverty rate in Madura Island in 2002–2014.	189
Table 5.7.	Reasons for not continuing school in regencies in Madura in 2014.	192
Table 6.1.	Poverty rates in the cities and regencies of Jabodetabek in 2014.	217
Table 6.2.	The correlates of poverty in Jabodetabek and Indonesia (in marginal effects after logit).	221
Table 6.3.	Education level of the poor population in Jabodetabek and Indonesia in 2014 (percent).	223
Table 6.4.	Employment sector of the poor population in Jabodetabek and Indonesia in 2014 (percent of total population).	227
Table 6.5.	Job sector of people who work in a family business without pay	229
Table 7.1.	Crop rotation in the study areas.	245
Table 7.2.	Occupations of farm household heads in study areas.	249
Table 7.3.	Farmland liquidation in the study areas.	250
Table 7.4.	Rice farming analysis in the study areas.	251
Table 8.1.	Growth and contribution to GDP by sector in 1993–1999.	264

Table 9.1. Corruption cases of high-ranking public officials from state auxiliary bodies.. 299

Table 9.2. Corruption Perception Index Indonesia in 2000–2016...................... 300

Table 9.3. Political corruption cases handled by the KPK in 2004–2017. 303

Table 10.1. Steps taken based on the human rights court law. 316

Table 12.1. Terrorist Incidents in Indonesia in 1999–2017. 366

Table 12.2. Director of National Intelligence Agency in post-Suharto Indonesia. 374

List of Figures

Figure 2.1.　　Left: *Giyanto's* mural in original condition, Right: Giyanto's mural painted over by PSIM's Blue Soldiers. Credit: Subandi Giyanto. 62

Figure 2.2.　　The AXIS mural on the Kewek Bridge wall. Credit: Elanto Wijoyono, from his personal blog. 68

Figure 2.3.　　Street artists and bikers painting the Kewek Bridge walls white. Credit: Anti-Tank. 70

Figure 2.4.　　The Jogja Ora Didol mural on the abandoned building in Jokteng Wetan. Credit: Selamatkan Bumi. 74

Figure 2.5.　　Censorship of Anti-Tank's poster in several locations. Credit: Brigitta Isabella (left) and Anti-Tank (center and right). 76

Figure 2.6.　　Banners with intolerant messages in front of the abandoned building. Credit: Brigitta Isabella. 78

Figure 2.7.　　The first winner of Jogokaryan Mosque's mural competition in 2012. Credit: Brigitta Isabella. 80

Figure 2.8.　　Anti-Tank's poster of Gus Dur in several locations in Yogyakarta. Credit: Anti-Tank. 80

Figure 4.1.　　Number of families migrating from Java to Papua through the government transmigration program in 1967–1997. 117

Figure 4.2.　　The structure of the Papua Customary Council (DAP). 125

Figure 4.3.　　Percentage of Papuan members of the DPRD in several regencies in Papua Province in 2009–2014. 136

Figure 4.4.　　Local government heads in Papua and West Papua Provinces (Papuan and non-Papuan). 137

Figure 5.1.　　Indonesia's education system in the decentralization period................156

Figure 5.2.　　Indonesia's net enrolment rate —primary and secondary education.....161

Figure 5.3.　　Lower-secondary enrolment rates by province in 2002–2014...............170

Figure 5.4. Disparities in regional enrolment rates in 2002–2014 (provincial data)....................172

Figure 5.5. Regional disparities in lower-secondary enrolment rates in 2002–2014 (regency level data) 173

Figure 5.6. Regional patterns in secondary enrolment in 2014...............175

Figure 5.7. Upper-secondary enrolment rates by province in 2002–2014..............178

Figure 5.8. Regional disparities in upper-secondary enrolment rates by regency in 2002–2014.....................180

Figure 5.9. Aceh's enrolment rates compared to Indonesia by regency in 2006–2014 183

Figure 5.10. Gender disparities in secondary education by regency in 2014 186

Figure 6.1. Map of Jabodetabek metropolitan area.....................212

Figure 6.2. Poverty rates in Jabodetabek, all urban areas, and Indonesia, 2004–2014. 216

Figure 6.3. Poverty map of Jabodetabek at village level in 2015 (percent)............218

Figure 7.1. Percent of GDP contribution by sector. 236

Figure 7.2. GDP contribution by agricultural sector. 236

Figure 7.3. Income gap between the agricultural and non-agricultural sectors 237

Figure 7.4. Rice production (in tonnes) in 1993–2015. 238

Figure 7.5. Area under paddy cultivation (in hectares) in 2003–2015....................239

Figure 7.6. Farmland in Cilacap.....................246

Figure 7.7. Farmland in Grobogan.....................246

Figure 7.8. Farmland in Lamongan.....................247

Figure 7.9. Farmland in Jember.....................247

Figure 8.1. Infrastructure spending as a percentage of total central government spending.....................261

Figure 8.2. Gross domestic product (GDP), capital expenditure, and tax ratio in Indonesia.....................266

Figure 8.3. Development spending for selected sectors (in billion IDR)...............268

Figure 8.4.	Percent of overall central government spending allocated to subsidies	269
Figure 9.1.	Corruption trend analysis: Suspected and convicted corruption perpetrators in 2010–2016.	295
Figure 12.1.	Indonesia's intelligence structure 2004–present.	369

Acknowledgments

This book originated from a November 10, 2017 workshop on "Two Decades after 1998 *Reformasi*: Achievements and Challenges" at the National Graduate Institute for Policy Studies (GRIPS), Tokyo, sponsored by GRIPS Emerging State Project under the Grant-in-Aid research project No. 25101004 of the Japan Society for Promotion of Sciences.

Most of the contributors to this book presented their papers at that workshop, with later contributions from Kayane Yuka, Rosita Dewi, and Muhammad Haripin and Diandra Megaputri Mengko. Amalinda Savirani, Dian Ekowati, Douglas Kammen, Iqra Anugrah, Nurul Ilmi Idrus, and Ito Takeshi gave excellent presentations at the workshop, but did not contribute their papers to the book.

We thank all contributors for their hard work and patience throughout the process. We would like to extend our thanks to three anonymous readers for their constructive comments and suggestions. We would also like to thank Jackie Imamura, Agung Wicaksono, Shitara Narumi, I Wayan Mustika, Suzuki Tetsuya, and the staff of UGM Press and Kyoto University Press for their editorial support. And we thank Devin Sukardi for preparing the index and Ata for the use of his painting for the book's cover

Much has changed in Indonesia as the proofs of this book were being corrected and the final printing was stalled due to the ongoing COVID-19 pandemic. It goes without saying that the analysis in this book is limited within a time frame up until the end of 2019. In its report published in early July 2020, the World Bank has raised Indonesia's status from lower-middle income to upper-middle income countries. Despite this fact, we acknowledge Indonesia faces new issues pertaining to the government's measures in response to the pandemic, and the strong resistance from civil society against the government's effort to deregulate the economy.

Finally, the publication of this book was supported by JSPS KAKENHI Grant Number 19KK0032, 19H01446, 17KT0004, 17H02239.

August 17, 2020

Okamoto Masaaki (Kyoto, Japan)

Jafar Suryomenggolo (Paris, France)

Introduction

Jafar Suryomenggolo and Okamoto Masaaki

Contemporary Indonesia is full of contradictions. It is a country whose citizens celebrate Muslim, Christian, Buddhist, Hindu, and Confucian religious days as official public holidays, yet there is a constant tension between religious communities in the public sphere. It is a country where around 94% of the adult population has one or more smart phones and 64% spend one-third of the time on the internet checking Facebook, Instagram, tweeting, and so on.[1] This is despite only 88% of the population having access to electricity, a smaller proportion than in neighboring countries. During the last ten years, the adult literacy rate in Indonesia has increased and remained steady at above 95%, yet it ranks 60th out of 61 countries in terms of reading interest. Indonesia has recently established a universal health care system, yet there is just one medical doctor for every 5,000 people. Its geography supports the world's second highest level of biodiversity, yet it was the world's fourth largest emitter of greenhouse gases in 2015. These are but a few examples that illuminate the complexities of Indonesia today.

Indonesia entered the 21st century after a quick yet bloody regime change in 1998. After the anti-communist purge of 1965–1966 and the subsequent overthrow of the Sukarno regime, Indonesia was ruled by the "New Order" authoritarian regime with General Suharto as president until 1998. For 32 years, the regime kept a firm grip on power with the strong

---

1   See "*Digital* 2020 Indonesia," a report by We Are Social (2020).

backing of the military. It controlled the parliament and political parties, suppressing grassroots protests and any budding social movements. The regime fell amid the 1997 Asian financial crisis which hit the Indonesian economy hard and exposed the widespread corruption within the regime. Democratic transition in 1998 was marked by public anxieties and mass violence (Anderson, 2001; Aragon, 2001), including anti-Chinese riots and ethnic conflicts in some parts of the country. Nonetheless, Indonesia proceeded to establish democratic institutions, manage an ambitious decentralization project,[2] and hold four direct presidential elections (2004, 2009, 2014, and 2019) rather peacefully. With various institutional changes during the 1998–2004 period, Indonesia consolidated its democracy. With a population of approximately 270 million people as of 2020, Indonesia has become the world's third largest democracy.

A growing body of literature on Indonesia's democratization has emerged during the last decade, providing analysis of its failures and achievements from various perspectives. Marcus Mietzner and Edward Aspinall (2010) categorize works on Indonesian democracy into three groups. The first group (the majority) questions the substance of Indonesian democracy, the second group sees Indonesian democracy as successful from a comparative perspective, and the third group takes a middle position between these two groups. These differences of opinion on Indonesian democracy are certainly based on scholars' perceptions and/or ideologies and academic/institutional backgrounds, as well as the indicators used in their studies. They are also based on the intended audience. The following paragraphs are not meant as a comprehensive survey of the literature, but rather as an illustration of the development and diversity of opinions.

In an edited volume, Anthony Reid argues for Indonesia's "new prominence in the world" (Reid, 2012). He notes that Indonesia has successfully managed to hold three popular elections, achieved high economic growth during the first decade of the 21st century, and, in acknowledgement of Indonesia's position in the world, was admitted as

---

2   Aspinall and Fealy (2003: 3) note that Indonesia's decentralization program is "one of the most radical decentralization programs attempted anywhere in the world."

a member of the G20 in 2009. He argues that Indonesia's success story is proof of its potential and that the world should seriously consider Indonesia as a rising power. The volume focuses on the country's achievements, and sectors in which it can improve its performance (economically, socially, and culturally) on the world stage. In a similar vein, Aspinall (2013) also notes Indonesia's successful democratic integration, which provides an interesting comparative case. Indonesia's experience is different from Yugoslavia and the Soviet Union, for example, in that "ethnic identities were only weakly articulated" (Aspinall, 2013: 145) and the democratic institutions that were established soon after the collapse of the New Order were relatively strong. These two studies illustrate how Indonesia's democratization has been viewed in a positive light, as a force that will find its way to bring Indonesians to a better future despite the challenges (and no matter how major they are).

Olle Törnquist (2013) offers a different perspective on Indonesia's democratization, noting that democratic actors have failed to unify and push for real reform from below, with some of them having "opted instead for linking up with the traditional politicians and largely became co-opted" (Törnquist, 2013: 28). His observation challenges existing positive assessments, and his proposed "qualitative surveys" to understand democracy from below are an important analytical tool in assessing the quality of Indonesia's democratization. Törnquist rightly questions if Indonesian democracy is substantial and if the hopes and demands that the *Reformasi* movement raised have been realized. Parallel to this, Sidel (2015) offers a "comparative regional perspective" through analysis of Susilo Bambang Yudhoyono's presidency. He provides a thought-provoking description of Yudhoyono's incompetence as a national leader who came to power precisely because of popular elections in a democratized Indonesia. These two studies expose how "traditional" political actors have co-opted Indonesia's *Reformasi*. These actors know how to manipulate the mechanisms behind Indonesia's newly established democratic institutions and are willing to sacrifice democratic ideals for their own advantages.

From this perspective, democratization has failed to deliver real political change or economic equality.

Despite the differences, competing assessments of Indonesia's democratization are all written with the aim of introducing and promoting Indonesia as an object of study. They are part of academic debate on contemporary Indonesia and act as signposts of what scholars and students of Indonesia are noting, discussing, and producing in the English language. Ironically, at the same time, there is a noticeable decline in Indonesian studies in the West (the United States, Europe, and Australia). This is partly due to budget cuts that have hit universities and research institutes, and the failure to attract (Western) graduate students. It seems that debates around Indonesia's democratization matter only to specialists, failing to reach broader audiences of general readers, policy-makers, and business communities in the West.

Perspectives from the Region

In discussions of contemporary Indonesia beyond the issue of democratization, it is important to note the publication of *Producing Indonesia,* a volume consisting of 25 papers in the fields of anthropology, art history, history, language and literature, government and political science, and ethnomusicology edited by Eric Tagliacozzo (2014). With its longue durée perspective, it claims to analyze the last 150 years of knowledge production about Indonesia. However, in a review of the volume, Bambang Purwanto (2015: 368) correctly points out that, "[t]he absence of any contribution by a Japanese scholar also illustrates the limitations of most essays regarding the uniqueness of the Asian perspective on Indonesian studies."

Purwanto's review highlights two related matters. First, it reflects the crisis of Indonesian studies in universities in the West. In a time of institutional restructuring, there is a strong demand for Western academics working on Indonesia to show (and claim) their contributions to international audiences in order to maintain funding for Indonesian studies in their universities.

In contrast, Japanese scholars do not have a strong need or pretension to write for an "international audience" due to the sizeable domestic readership they write for and share their knowledge with. Although Japanese scholars in general are increasingly required to publish papers and books in English, Indonesian studies in the Japanese language have their own market in Japan: Indonesia is the most important country in the Southeast Asia region, not solely because of its sheer size, but also because it is tightly linked to Japan's economic and international relations interests. As policy makers and business communities unceasingly seek information, Indonesia continues to be a major object of study by Japanese scholars and Indonesian studies continues to attract new generations of students. This type of domestic-oriented approach may not be solely limited to Japan. Korea also has a limited domestic market for Indonesian studies. Naturally, Indonesia has its own large market in the Indonesian language, which is the most important for any scholar of Indonesian studies to access in order to provoke discussions and contribute to various debates.

Purwanto's observation also reflects the challenge of accessing the contributions of Japanese scholars to Indonesian studies due to the language barrier. Most works are written in Japanese, which only a handful of Western specialists of Indonesia (and Indonesians) can read. Although there are efforts to overcome the language barrier through academic exchanges, joint seminars, and translation of academic works, these efforts are not enough to capture the depth of the discussions and contributions that Japanese scholars make to Indonesian studies.[3] It is important to note that Japanese specialists of Indonesia have a wide range of opinions and perspectives that enrich debates in the field.[4] For example,

---

3   For examples of translation project of the Japanese scholarship on Indonesia, see Nagazumi (1986), Shiraishi (1994), Masuhara (2015).

4   As in the United States, the development of Indonesian studies in post-war Japan is part of the rise of area studies (especially, Southeast Asian studies) and the Cold-War situation. The Japan Society for Southeast Asian Studies (previously the Japan Society for Southeast Asian History) was established in 1966 and its membership has been increasing from 52 in 1967 to 316 in 1989, 592 in 2000 and 635 in 2008 (Kitagawa, 2002: 67; Sasagawa, 2008: 57).

Jun Honna (2013) writes about power struggles among the political elites after democratization, and how democratization is perceived through military eyes. Kawamura (2015) examines Yudhoyono's presidency from an economic perspective, and how Joko Widodo's leadership is expected to deliver positive economic indicators. These are just two examples of works written by Japanese scholars with diverse audiences in mind.

In this context, this book is our modest attempt to fill gaps with two objectives. First, it aims to present viewpoints (although not entirely within Purwanto's notion of an "Asian perspective") from scholars based in the region (in this case, Japan, Korea, and Indonesia), who usually, and primarily, write in their national languages. While these scholars build upon previous studies written in English, Indonesian, and Japanese, they approach the topic differently from studies published in English. While this book is not the first to bring scholars from the region together, it highlights the need to advance discussions and various forms of collaboration among researchers of Indonesia in the region. As a work of collaboration, this book takes English as the language of exchange, while not specifically intending to contribute (or respond) to the on-going debate(s) in the English language. Some of our authors are trained in Western higher-educational institutions (in Australia and the United States), which gives them insight and knowledge on the development of Indonesian studies in English. While it enriches their contributions to this book, they primarily focus on the topic of their study. Publishing this book in the region is also an effort to promote collaborations between scholars within the region.

Second, it seeks to stimulate dialogue between academics and those working in the field. Our contributors come from different professional backgrounds; they are scholars, field researchers, and non-government organization (NGO) workers. Dialogue among them is important to uncover how issues are viewed and experienced from different perspectives, and how praxis informs academic debates. Importantly, such dialogue is meant to sustain ongoing debates about Indonesia and the study of Indonesia abroad as multi-disciplinary, not limited to theoretical discussions, and inclusive of practical and mundane issues. We believe that contributing to the study of Indonesia is not a privilege belonging to academics alone. Field researchers, professionals, and NGO workers have contributed their thoughts and time to the development of the study—and will continue to do so.

This book brings together 12 original chapters to discuss the achievements and challenges of Indonesia's transformation after 1998. It examines how state institutions and civil society manage the complexities of Indonesia's transformations to develop common ground upon which to reach a national consensus. Unlike the pre-1998 New Order regime that resorted to repression and violence to impose a national "consensus," the post-1998 Indonesian state can be sanctioned by the populace and therefore must justify its policies and actions to avoid losing stability and legitimacy. State institutions are now expected to forge convivial relationships with different actors under the rhetoric of "good governance" and meet increasingly complex and diverse demands from society. Meanwhile, various actors are ready to take advantage of the country's fragile democracy and exploit still infant state institutions for their own interests. It is in this context that Indonesia's state institutions and civil society, while having different agendas of their own, have evolved to make democracy work.[5]

The following paragraphs identify key issues of Indonesia's transformation to provide further context for the contributions of each chapter of this book. While they are by no means an exhaustive discussion of the current situation in Indonesia, they offer some background by which to better understand the diversity of perspectives and approaches of each chapter.

---

5 State-society interactions are complex, and Indonesia's situation, especially after 1998, cannot be described as a "simplistic image of a staged confrontation between the sovereign and the subjugated" (Abélès, 2017: 62).

Ambitions, Efforts, and Challenges

The Asian economic crisis hit Indonesia hardest in Southeast Asia, but the newly democratized Indonesia's economic indicators have become steadier since the early 2000s. Indonesia's gross domestic product (GDP) increased from USD 510 billion in 2008 to USD 888 billion in 2014, and GDP per capita steadily increased from USD 7,511 per year in 2008 to USD 10,517 in 2014. During the period 2008–2015, its economy grew by more than 4% annually, the highest steady rate in Southeast Asia. Indonesia is now transitioning from a lower-middle income country to an upper-middle level one.[6] According to a study of 124 countries, this transition takes a median of 28 years, while transition from the upper-middle level to the high-income level takes a median of 14 years (Felipe et al., 2012). Indonesia has so far spent 25 years in the lower-middle income level, putting it "at risk of falling into the trap [of being stuck at that level] in the coming years" (Felipe et al., 2012: 4, 46). If Indonesia's average growth rate of per capita income fails to reach more than 4.7% per annum, it could end up like Sri Lanka and the Philippines, both of which have remained stagnant in the lower-middle income "trap."

To avoid this outcome, Badan Perencanaan Pembangunan Nasional (Bappenas—National Development Planning Agency) has set a target for Indonesia to escape the middle-income trap by 2034, with an economic growth requirement of 6.4% per annum. Bappenas highlights Indonesia's "infrastructure deficit" as a priority problem to address, and suggests infrastructure development as a way to graduate to the next level.[7] Considered a major factor for economic growth, infrastructure development has been a substantial part of the Joko Widodo administration's macroeconomic policy (2014–present).[8] The emphasis on infrastructure development indicates

---

6 Shiraishi (2014) suggests that the politics of economic growth has been the major policy of each of the post-1998 presidents, seeking to produce a national consensus.

7 Spending on infrastructure development accounted for 49% of Indonesia's GDP in 1995, and only 38% in 2012.

8 The government claims that during 2014–2019, it has built 3,400 km of national roads, 940 km of toll roads, and a number of new airports and seaports. It plans to develop 4,479 km of toll roads by 2030 in addition to the 1,500 km of toll road projects that are to be completed by 2024.

that Indonesia is embracing a new style of developmentalism, which is a narrow version of its old developmental model, which subordinated various political goals (including environmental protection) in order to achieve rapid economic growth (Warburton, 2016). Infrastructure allocation in the state budget has more than doubled since the Yudhoyono presidency (2010–2014), when the total amount was USD 51 billion, to a projection of USD 129 billion during Joko Widodo's first term (2015–2019). Despite the increase, the government budget is not able to fully support its infrastructure development aims; it could only cover 41.3% of the required investment needs of USD 359 billion during 2015–2019. Public private partnerships (PPP) and equity financing are expected to fill this gap.

In the meantime, Indonesia is facing the impacts of a population shift. In 1999, 40.7% of the population lived in urban areas; by 2011 this had risen to 50.7%, reaching 55% in 2018. Indonesia has become urbanized. In a 2015 report, the World Bank notes that the sharp increase in Indonesia's urban population density between 2000 and 2010 is the largest increase in the urban population density of any country in the East Asia region. This current urbanization is putting more pressure on over-crowded cities than at any other time in the country's history. Urban housing is such an important issue that it has entered local and national politics, becoming a hot topic of debate during direct local head elections in urban areas and the recent 2019 national election. Urbanization also impacts rural areas: the decline in young agricultural workers, similar to Thailand and Malaysia, requires Indonesia to adapt to the effects on productivity of an aging agricultural workforce.

Another issue is inequality, which has steadily increased since Indonesia recovered from the 1998 economic crisis. Although Indonesia's Gini ratio declined during 2010–2015, economic inequality continues to be a challenge.[9] The *reforma agraria dan perhutanan social* (agrarian reform and social forest) program was enacted as part of the main program of

---

9   It is interesting to note that a 2014 World Bank survey of more than 3,000 Indonesian households found that people underestimate the level of inequality, that "the actual level of inequality is far higher than most respondents believe" (Wolrd Bank, 2015: 11).

Joko Widodo and Jusuf Kalla's administration (2014–2019) to address rural poverty. In its master plan of 2015–2019, this administration set a redistribution target of 12.7 million hectares for social forest and 9 million hectares for agrarian reform. This is an ambitious project, supported with limited institutional capacities and budget by the Ministry of Economic Affairs.[10] NGO activists involved in the project have pointed to the lack of coordination among government agencies to settle land disputes and set parameters, particularly given that the program does not have strong legal footing, which has resulted in an increase in the number of land disputes. Related to that, there have been numerous cases of the criminalization of farmers, small landowners, and forest conservation activists who have criticized and opposed the government's developmental plans, expansion of oil palm plantations, establishment of cement factories, and so on.

Reformasi has paved the way for the reconfiguration and improvement of Indonesia's institutions to support economic growth. However, like Thailand, which failed to regulate the redistribution of wealth after democratization, Indonesia is now faced with the double challenges of uncontainable urbanization and rising inequality – which are common issues in 'compressed development' (Whittaker et al., 2020). As such, there is a danger that Indonesia's ambitions and efforts to graduate from the middle-income trap will be undermined by its own feeble capabilities to manage these challenges.

Accommodation, Inclusion, and Contestation

Notwithstanding these issues, since 2004, the government has been trying to respond to the political demands of civil society. A number of NGO activists and representatives have been appointed to government posts; some have become "Presidential Staff." This practice illustrates that the NGO movement in Indonesia is no longer marginalized as it was during the New Order regime. The state needs the participation of NGO activists

---

10   To be fair, in the three years of Jokowi's administration (2014–2017), the social forest program has redistributed 700,000 hectares, in contrast to a total of 300,000 hectares during the New Order through to the Yudhoyono presidency.

not merely to legitimize its control over society, but also to develop the state's institutions, to speak in the language of society, and to meet social and economic demands effectively (Priyono et al., 2003). We have yet to see, however, whether and how their involvement in the government will bring important changes in executive power.

The political opening brought about by democratization has also allowed members of the middle class to enter formal politics both at the national and local levels. As a result, post-1998 political leadership, despite coming from diverse professions, is dominated by men with middle class backgrounds. This is a stark contrast to the democratic experiences of 1950s Indonesia. Despite rhetoric to defend the interests of *wong cilik* (the underprivileged), hardly any current parliamentary members have a working class or peasant background, or represent these classes.

It is also important to note that the percentage of women in the national parliament and local legislative bodies is still below the mandated 30% quota. Although direct elections provide structural opportunities for women to enter politics, their participation is still constricted under the oligarchical male-dominated atmosphere.

Meanwhile, political life in Indonesia as a newly democratized country is often characterized by various forms of illegality (Aspinall and van Klinken, 2011; Morishita, 2015), the opportunism of local actors (Nordholt and van Klinken, 2007), and money politics and thuggery (Hadiz, 2010; Wilson, 2015). Local politicians, both newcomers and experienced players, take great pains to emphasize their roots in their respective constituencies. In some areas, such as Banten, there is a strong influence of family ties in local politics (Okamoto, 2015). In these areas, corruption is so rampant that even basic infrastructure is poorly maintained.

Addressing the geospatial spread of inequality is also a challenge for a country as diverse as Indonesia. Regional disparity has slowly reduced, but the gap remains quite wide. A typical example of this is the gap in "economic importance" between the Western part of Indonesia (Java and Sumatra Islands) and the Eastern part of Indonesia (including Kalimantan,

Bali, Sulawesi, Halmahera, Papua). Indonesia adopted two decentralization strategies to try to close this gap. The first was a radical transfer of authority and money to the local governments (province, regency and city) and the second was a further decentralization to the village level. While these decentralization projects have numerous flaws and problems, including decentralized corruption, a rise in clan politics, and a tendency to enrich natural-resource rich areas at the expense of others, they also provide more opportunities for initiatives and empowerment to grow from the local level.

At the national level, the various administrations since 1998 have all taken a common approach to political contestation. That is, through various party coalitions, the ruling government negotiates a share of executive power by offering leaders from different political parties (including the opposition) positions with decision-making power in the cabinet. Each of Indonesia's presidents since 1998 has created a government party coalition with more than 70% of total votes. Although no coalition has ever been completely solid, this large-scale coalition approach mitigated many potential political conflicts at the national level. Elitist accommodation and compromise through quid pro quo exchanges of money and favor became the stabilizing force in politics. This model is not limited to national politics, but defines local politics as well.

This coalition and cartel politics both at the national and local levels does not always guarantee political stability, however. Especially since democratization, there is a view that Indonesian Islam is at a conservative turning point (van Bruinessen, 2013) and that Indonesian society has become polarized between conservatives and non-conservatives and thus faces a deepening instability. The most conspicuous case of this trend was a series of staunch campaigns against the incumbent Chinese protestant governor of Jakarta, Basuki Tjahaja Purnama (Ahok) running for re-election in 2017. An allegedly incorrect citation of the Quran by Ahok sparked anger among conservative Muslims and triggered massive rallies demanding his arrest and blocking his re-election. The anti-Ahok campaign was so effective that he lost the election and was sentenced to jail for two years for blasphemy against Islam. Many scholars and journalists interpreted this event as foreshadowing the possibility of the politicization of religious identities and expressed fear that the direct local head elections in 2018 and the direct presidential election in 2019 might deepen this trend. It turned out that the religious identity was politicized in both elections but did not lead to detrimental conflicts, however. As the fact that the incumbent president, Jokowi chose Ma'ruf Amin, one of the most anti-Ahok Islamic leaders as his vice-presidential candidate, shows that the politics of compromise and cartel still prevails among the national elites and that politics has, so far, prevented the deepening of social cleavages.

A newly established independent anti-corruption agency, Komisi Pemberantasan Korupsi (Corruption Eradication Commission or KPK), has arrested mayors, regency heads, provincial governors, MPs, and the chairmen of the Regional Representative Council and the National Parliament. However, the commission can only deal with a limited number of cases and is in constant danger of being disbanded due to strong antipathy and opposition from the police, the public prosecutor, and politicians threatened by its power and authority.

This book discusses some of these important issues in detail, illustrating how democracy has taken root in Indonesia over the last two decades, and what Indonesians have done to overcome the accompanying problems. All of these chapters were written before the COVID-19 pandemic seriously shook up every aspect of economic, social and political life in Indonesia, but the issues addressed in the chapters remain unchanged.

Structure of the Book

This book is divided into three parts. Part One, "Governance and Social Dynamics," consists of four chapters that describe the changes in institutions and social conditions after democratization in 1998. Each chapter addresses an issue that is pertinent to understanding how democracy has shaped and altered the public spaces where Indonesians gather, interact, and engage, within the state's definition of the nation. It begins with Thung Ju Lan, who provides an overview of the development of the construction of the nation, and is followed by three chapters that use local cases to reflect on social changes.

Thung Ju Lan considers the complexities of managing Indonesia's plural societies as a nation-state. She underlines how Indonesia's social and cultural diversity, in particular in terms of ethnicity and religion, defines the political realm. However, the problematic interpretation of culture is reflected in the relationship between the so-called national and local cultures, which in practice embodies the difficulties of accommodating and embracing all ethnic groups, each with their own culture, within the nationalistic and democratic framework. Democratization has introduced a legal framework, such as Law Number 29 Year 1999 and Law Number 40 Year 2008 on the elimination of all forms of racial discrimination, to facilitate institutional changes in respecting diversity. In the meantime, multiculturalism has become a means to maintain Indonesia's unity as a *negara kesatuan* (united state). Thung identifies the limitations of multiculturalism, and stresses that Indonesia as a nation-state is an on-going project in itself. In that regard, she suggests some ways to encourage pluralism in the government's public policy.

Brigitta Isabella discusses the cultural practices of democracy after 1998 based on observations of the walls along Yogyakarta's street. Changes to this landscape reflect the dynamics of the city's cultural production and its local politics. At the same time, the logics of the market, as in all Indonesian cities, have shaped Yogyakarta's urban landscape, especially in terms of land ownership in the city. Isabella shows how three prominent walls (of the Lempuyangan flyover, the Kewek Bridge, and of an abandoned building near the Kraton) have become sites of contestation between various groups, including young people, artists, NGO workers, local government officers, (organized) thugs, fundamentalist groups, and others. Her detailed observations reveal the symbolic struggles between various actors as they publicize different messages and interrupt each other, how a dominant power tries to discipline the cultural landscape of the city, and why it fails. The chapter is a study of Indonesia's changing political situation (from state-centered to decentered power relations) and the struggles of various actors over public space.

Kayane Yuka invites us to understand the political process of religious intolerance after 1998 by focusing on the violence against the Shia community in Sampang Regency (Madura, East Java) during 2011–2012. She describes how the violence started from a conflict in the context of local politics in Madura, and developed into a mass persecution against the Shia community that resulted in the burning of houses and expulsion of hundreds from the village. She details the involvement of both local and national political elites in the persecution, showing how violence against the Shia community was politically justified and propagated at the national level. She describes how Tajul Muluk (Ali Murtadha), a leader in the local community, was charged with blasphemy and sentenced to two years in prison, and then follows the trajectory of how anti-Shia campaigns have been consolidated and used by various political actors to fit their own agendas. Kayane concludes that religious intolerance is still a delicate issue after 1998, especially when minority protections remain weak and law enforcement institutions fail to perform their duties to maintain independence and deliver justice.

Finally, Rosita Dewi explores the important topic of governing from the center in times of decentralization. She discusses the progress of the post-1998 Indonesian state's approach to Papua by focusing on "papuanization" as regulated under Law Number 21 Year 2001 on special autonomy for Papua. While on paper the policy aims to expand the participation of local Papuans in the government, she traces how the Dutch colonial government had a similar policy, known as *papoeanisering*, after World War II. Under the Dutch policy, many young Papuans were employed in the government service, and a special Regional Council was established to prepare for self-determination. After 1962, the Indonesian government (under Soekarno) administered Papua though its *transmigrasi* program. Subsequently, Papua was controlled by the military under Suharto from 1967 to 1998. Democratization brought crucial changes to the state's approach to Papua through the politics of recognition. While Rosita Dewi acknowledges some social and cultural improvements for the Papuans under the state's new policy, she also notes a new set of problems that have emerged in local politics, especially in terms of claims to political representation, and suggests that the pitfalls of identity politics could represent a new version of a divide and rule approach to Papua.

Part Two, "Paths to Equality," consists of four chapters that examine the economic background of Indonesia's development policies for addressing poverty, inequality, and productivity, which are critical to the country's ability to escape from the middle-income trap. Although each chapter discusses its own specific topic—educational outcomes, poverty-eradication programs, agrarian policy, and infrastructure development— they use economic analyses to understand what *Reformasi* has achieved and its limitations. Each chapter is richly informed with data from the local level, not relying on the economic models and prescriptions often found in reports from the central government and international financial institutions.

Abdul Wahid Fajar Amin analyses an important result of the decentralization program that began in 1999: changes to the education sector. Local governments gained the authority to administer educational institutions (particularly at the elementary and lower-secondary levels) in their region. Educational outcomes are an important indicator for the human development index (HDI), and the central government is keen to see improvements across the country. Amin notes that elementary and secondary school enrolment rates have been steady since 2003, with a net elementary enrolment rate of 95%. Based on a panel data set that covered 450 regencies for the 2002–2014 period, his analysis shows patterns of educational outcomes by clustering regions into categories. Although regional and gender disparities are apparent, they are masked by the high overall national enrolment rate. He finds that income per capita, household expenditure on education, and local government expenditure on education are significant factors that increase enrolment rates. He suggests that local governments, especially those with rich natural resources, should increase their educational expenditure to improve educational outcomes, ultimately increasing social welfare and equality.

Asep Suryahadi and Cecilia Marlina begin their analysis by comparing the stagnant poverty rate (6% since the early 2000s) in the Jabodetabek (Jakarta, Bogor, Depok, Tangerang, South Tangerang and Bekasi) metropolitan area to the central government's national poverty alleviation program that brought the national poverty rate down (from 24% in 1999 to 11% in 2013). Although the poverty rate in Jabodetabek is lower than the national level, population in the area has increased sharply due to urbanization. Based on household survey data, Suryahadi and Marlina create a poverty profile of Jabodetabek to determine the significant demographic features that correlate with poverty. They find that in Jabodetabek, tertiary education attainment is important to employment (especially, in the formal sector), which enables people to avoid poverty. They also find that improvement in basic facilities is still relevant to tackle the problems of poverty in Jabodetabek. Based on these findings, they conclude that the national poverty alleviation program is inadequate and suggest that policy makers consider local situations to more fully address poverty.

While Suryahadi and Marlina focus on poverty in the urban setting, Ernoiz Antriyandarti and Susi Wuri Ani focus on income and production in the rural setting. They examine the conditions of rice production as part of the nation's self-sufficiency program. They note that agricultural land holdings, as a result of the provision of Law Number 5 Year 1960 on Basic Agrarian Law, are relatively small, limiting production and generally reducing the global competitiveness of Indonesia's rice sector. Meanwhile, the income gap between agricultural and non-agricultural sectors has been widening since 2004. To better understand productivity and the economies of scale, Antriyandarti dan Wuri Ani conducted field research in four main rice-production centers (Cilacap and Grobongan in Central Java, and Jember and Lamongan in East Java). They find that farmers are reluctant to transfer or lease their land to the market, regardless of the pay-off. To maintain productivity, they suggest farm liquidation as a way to increase farm size and thus labor efficiency in Java. They also find that farm liquidation can be encouraged through off-farm job development: by engaging in off-farm jobs, small holder-farmers will lease out their farmland and earn higher incomes, allowing medium and large-scale farmers to expand their production capacities. Thus, farmland liquidation is a technical solution to improve rice production and maintain farmer income.

Maxensius Tri Sambodo and Latif Adam review fiscal policy and infrastructure development after the 1997 economic crisis. Studies in developmental economics have noted that infrastructure development correlates positively to economic growth, and is considered to be a key factor in improving a country's competitiveness. Each of the post-1998 presidents has implemented fiscal policy to promote infrastructure development, with differing degrees of concentration. Although generally economic growth has been quite high, investment in infrastructure development has remained relatively low. Indeed, until 2004 development expenditures were lower than those during the New Order period. There has been an urgent need to invest in and improve infrastructure development, especially after the fiscal decentralization of 2001. Sambodo and Adam note the basic challenge to this need: the lack of government funds to support it. The government has established several mechanisms to introduce creative financing, for example encouraging PPP since 2005, and forming an infrastructure guarantee agency in 2010. In evaluating the PPP schemes, Sambodo and Adam observe that the government's efforts have been slow, and its achievements are below target. They conclude that strong macroeconomic stability and long-term support are important for accelerating infrastructure development and maintaining economic growth.

Part Three, "Structural Challenges," consists of four chapters that discuss corruption, human rights practices, and security and military reforms. All papers acknowledge the institutional development the government of Indonesia has achieved since 1998. Beyond that, they also note the challenges that could impede democracy taking root in Indonesian society. Corruption and human rights issues are tightly linked to each other, and together they are important indicators of how democracy manages—or fails—to deliver an accountable government. Democratization has also shaped security issues in Indonesia during the last twenty years.

Adnan Topan Husodo examines anti-corruption reform—an important part of the democratization agenda—to better understand why corruption is still a major issue in Indonesia. While the government has established a number of new institutions, including Komisi Pemberantasan Korupsi (KPK—Corruption Eradication Commission), and ratified the United Nation's Convention against Corruption (UNCAC) in 2006, the results have been minimal. Husodo identifies some major problems within the system and in the implementation of reforms. Notwithstanding the KPK's corruption cases against a number of high-ranking public officials, the commission is constantly challenged by institutions and actors wishing to undermine its authority and prevent investigation and monitoring of all public offices, including members of the parliament. The impact of oligarchical power on political parties also limits the progress of the reform. The reform has concentrated on legal and administrative procedures, and implementation lacks serious political commitment from state institutions. In that regard, Husodo suggests that, to sustain anti-corruption efforts, the government must have a strong willingness to promote public sector reform and build trust with civil society.

Suh Jiwon discusses the contradictions in the state's human rights practices and promotion strategies. Since 1998 Indonesia has ratified eight major United Nations human rights treaties and established several supporting institutions, such as the Directorate for Human Rights, Komisi Nasional Hak Asasi Manusia (Komnas HAM—National Commission of Human Rights), and others. By focusing on four areas of study—the Human Rights Court, the military court, "human rights cities," and the war on drugs—Suh outlines the development of human rights practices and promotions after 1998 and more importantly, their contradictions. She shows how these contradictions are rooted in the late New Order strategy of creating "human rights enclaves" within the state apparatus to defend itself against accusations of human rights violations from the outside world, while at the same time allowing it to maintain repressive practices. This strategy continues today, as commitment to human rights is made on paper only, and government action remains confined within these "enclaves." The state's outward "solutions" to human rights issues allow it to continue to use violence with impunity. As such, there is a strong need to move beyond enclaves and promotion toward a genuine respect for human rights backed by concrete actions.

Okamoto Masaaki analyzes the transformation of the relationship between the state (security forces) and the private security providers from the New Order period to the democratic consolidation period. He starts with a detailed account of the use of non-state actors by the military during the New Order regime through cooptation and mobilization. The fall of the regime in 1998 ended the state's repressive security approach, and during the early years of democratization vigilante groups took advantage of the state's limited security capacities to dominate the society by offering protection and private security. Based on this description, Okamoto argues that the Indonesian state has always tried to nurture and forge relationships with private security providers for the state's benefit. The Indonesian state after the democratic consolidation has started to re-tame the private security actors through various methods: professionalizing, cultivating, weeding out, indoctrinating, and making them more visible or exposed to the state. As such, Okamoto concludes that providing protection and security remains a sensitive issue for Indonesia.

Finally, Muhamad Haripin and Dianda Megaputri Mengko examine institutional reform in Badan Intelijen Negara (BIN—National Intelligence

Agency). They note how intelligence reform in Indonesia, like any post-authoritarian state, tends to present a challenging and intricate dilemma of maintaining public freedom and protecting national security. During the New Order period (1966–1998), BIN was active as the regime's notorious surveillance instrument. Since 1998, like many government institutions, it has had to reorient its identity towards a professional and non-partisan agency. Haripin and Mengko explain that internal reform has been inadequate and initiatives from external sources are poorly implemented, as patronage politics remains the norm in the agency. Based on this description, they suggest that the role of BIN in the contemporary security environment (especially on counter-terrorism) remains ambiguous, and its continuing expansion may obstruct the development of a safe public sphere in Indonesia.

All chapters of this book discuss how *Reformasi* has changed the structure of the Indonesian state and affected the daily lives of its citizens, to what extend Indonesia's economy has developed beyond economic indicators, and how certain issues continue to exist despite the institutional changes and the relative freedom Indonesians now have. Indeed, the last twenty years of democratization has transformed Indonesia as a nation-state.

Indonesia's experiences may provide a lesson for other emerging nations in managing their economic and political development, in particular in dealing with the challenges of 'compressed development'. Indonesia has yet to graduate from the middle-income trap, but its experience in formulating macroeconomic policy shows that developing physical infrastructure (such as building roads and ports) should be accompanied with investment in social infrastructure (such as strengthening education) and environmental protection.[11] Its experience in reducing the poverty gap

---

11   To meet the rapidly growing demands for energy to support development projects, Indonesia still relies on fossil fuel-based power generations. Between 2007–2017, on average, the share of energy consumption in the country's industries was dominated by fuel oil (32.9%), followed by gas (31.3%), coal and briquette (23.7%) and biomass (11.8%). Indonesia's power sector CO2 emissions is projected to double in the period 2015–2024, primarily due to growth in coal-fired generation. Coal-fired power plants will still dominate Indonesia's electricity supply in 2045.

shows that it is important to design a national poverty alleviation program, but also to address specific local needs. While Indonesia is still grappling with economic inequality, its experience shows that it is necessary to develop universal access to social insurance and health care in order to protect the majority of its population against economic risks.

Indonesia's reform experience might inform other post-authoritarian societies embarking on democratization projects. The transition to democracy is not an easy one; Indonesia has experienced numerous ethnic conflicts in the process. Supported by democratic institutions and a vibrant civil society, Indonesians are now more equipped to engage in public discussions to manage and solve these issues. Consultation with civil society is now a prerequisite in drafting and approving laws. While recognizing the different context and challenges of other cases, Indonesia's democratization provides at least two comparative lessons. First, the involvement of civil society is necessary to ensure that democracy works at all levels. It is not a state project, but rather an ideal demanded, crafted, and realized by the society. Second, while structural challenges like corruption and human right violations persist, economic development has been the major theme to maintain national consensus and support the development of democracy in the country. As a major theme, it ties the dreams and hopes of the majority, if not all, of Indonesians, across the political spectrum.

Reformasi as a national project to cultivate democracy and realize improved welfare for all Indonesians will continue to progress. It will provide more inspirations and further reflection on how Indonesia has changed in the first two decades of the 21st century. The lessons learnt from the two decades after *Reformasi* are quite valuable when all Indonesians deal with COVID-19 and the post-pandemic restoration period. There will be more academic debates to come as part of our efforts to understand the complexity of Indonesia's democratization and its implications. We hope that this volume will contribute to advancing those debates toward improving Indonesian democracy.

References

Abélès, Marc. 2017. *Thinking Beyond the State*. Ithaca: Cornell University Press.

Anderson, Benedict (ed.). 2001. *Violence and the State in Suharto's Indonesia*. Ithaca: Southeast Asia Program, Cornell University.

Aragon, Lorraine. 2001. "Communal Violence in Poso, Central Sulawesi: Where People Eat Fish and Fish Eat People". *Indonesia* 72: 45–80.

Aspinall, Edward. 2013. "How Indonesia Survived: Comparative Perspectives on State Disintegration and Democratic Integration". In *Democracy and Islam in Indonesia*, edited by Mirjam Kunkler and Alfred Stephan, pp. 126-1146. New York: Columbia University Press.

Aspinall, Edward and Gerry van Klinken. 2011. "The State and Illegality in Indonesia". In *The State and Illegality in Indonesia*, edited by Edward Aspinall and Gerry van Klinken, pp. 1-28. Leiden: KITLV Press.

Aspinall, Edward and Greg Fealy. 2003. "Introduction: Decentralization, Democratization and the Rise of the Local". In *Local Power and Politics in Indonesia: Decentralization and Democratization*, edited by Edward Aspinall and Greg Fealy, pp. 1-11. Singapore: ISEAS.

Felipe, Jesus. et al. 2012. "Tracking the Middle-Income Trap: What Is it, Who Is in It, and Why?". Working Paper no. 715. New York: Levy Economics Institute of Bard College.

Hadiz, Vedi. 2010. *Localising Power in Post-Authoritarian Indonesia: A Southeast Asia Perspective*. Stanford: Stanford University Press.

Honna, Jun. 2013. 『民主化のパラドックスーインドネシアにみるアジア政治の深層』 [*Paradox of Democratization: The Deep Structure of Asian Politics from the Indonesian Case*]. Tokyo: Iwanami-Shoten.

Kawamura, Koichi (ed.). 2015. 『新興民主主義大国インドネシアーユドヨノ政権の10年とジョコウィ大統領の誕生』 [*Indonesia as Emerging Democratic Power: A Decade of Yudhoyono's Administration and the Start of Jokowi*]. Chiba: IDE-JETRO.

Kitagawa, Takako. 2002. 「東南アジア史学会 - 最近の活動の紹介を中心に」[The Recent Activities of Japan Society for Southeast Asian History]. アジア経済 [*Asian Economy*] 43 (2): 66–75.

Masuhara, Ayako. 2015. *The End of Personal Rule in Indonesia: Golkar and the Transformation of the Suharto Regime.* Kyoto: Kyoto University Press and Trans Pacific Press.

Mietzner, Marcus and Edward Aspinall. 2010. "Problems of Democratisation in Indonesia: An Overview". In *Problems of Democratisation in Indonesia: Elections, Institutions and Society,* edited by Edward Aspinall and Marcus Mietzner, pp. 1-20. Singapore: ISEAS.

Miichi, Ken. 2014. 『新興大国インドネシアの宗教市場と政治』 [*Religion and Politics in Contemporary Indonesia*]. Tokyo: NTT Press.

Morishita, Akiko. 2015. 『天然資源をめぐる政治と暴力: 現代インドネシアの地方政治』 [*Resources, Politics and Violence: Local Politics in Contemporary Indonesia*]. Kyoto: Kyoto University Press.

Nagazumi, Akira (ed.). 1986. *Indonesia dalam Kajian Sarjana Jepang: Perubahan Sosial-Ekonomi Abad XIX dan XX dan Berbagai Aspek Nasionalisme Indonesia.* Jakarta: Yayasan Obor Indonesia.

Nordholt, Henk Schulte and Gerry van Klinken. 2007. "Introduction". In *Renegotiating Boundaries: Local Politics in Post-Soeharto Indonesia,* edited by Henk Schulte Nordholt and Gerry van Klinken, pp. 1-29. Leiden: KITLV Press.

Okamoto, Masaaki. 2015. 『暴力と適応の政治学: インドネシア民主化と地方政治の安定』 [*The Politics of Violence and Adaptation: Democratization and Local Politics in Indonesia*]. Kyoto: Kyoto University Press.

Priyono, A.E., Stanley Adi Prasetyo and Olle Törnquist (eds.). 2003. *Gerakan Demokrasi di Indonesia Pasca-Soeharto.* Jakarta: Demos.

Purwanto, Bambang. 2015. "Review of Producing Indonesia: The State of the Field of Indonesian Studies". *Pacific Affairs* 88 (2): 366–368.

Reid, Anthony. 2012. "Indonesia's New Prominence in the World". In *Indonesia Rising: The Repositioning of Asia's Third Giant*, edited by Anthony Reid, pp.1-13. Singapore: ISEAS.

Sasagawa, Hideo. 2008. '東南アジア学会、近年の活動' [Recent Activities of Japan Society for Southeast Asian Studies]. アジア経済 [*Asian Economy*] 49 (10): 57–69.

Shiraishi, Takashi (ed.). 1994. *Approaching Suharto's Indonesia from the Margins*. Ithaca: Southeast Asia Program, Cornell University.

———. 2014. "Indonesian Technocracy in Transition: A Preliminary Analysis". *Southeast Asian Studies* 3 (2): 255–281.

Sidel, John. 2015. "Men on Horseback and Their Droppings: Yudhoyono's Presidency and Legacies in Comparative Regional Perspective". In *The Yudhoyono Presidency: Indonesia's Decade of Stability and Stagnation*, edited by Edward Aspinall, Marcus Mietzner and Dirk Tomsa, pp. 55-72. Singapore: ISEAS.

Tagliacozzo, Eric (ed.). 2014. *Producing Indonesia: The State of the Field of Indonesian Studies*. Ithaca: Southeast Asia Program, Cornell University.

Törnquist, Olle. 2013. *Assessing Dynamics of Democratisation: Transformative Politics, New Institutions, and the Case of Indonesia*. New York: Palgrave.

van Bruinessen, Martin (ed.). 2013. *Contemporary Developments in Indonesian Islam: Explaining the "Conservative Turn"*. Singapore: Institute of Southeast Asian Studies.

Warburton, Eva. 2016. "Jokowi and the New Developmentalism". *Bulletin of Indonesian Economic Studies* 52 (3): 297–320.

We are Social. 2020. *Digital 2020 Indonesia*. https://datareportal.com/reports/digital-2020-indonesia (accessed March 1, 2018).

Whittaker, Hugh, Timothy Sturgeon, Toshie Okita and Tianbiao Zhu. 2020. *Compressed Development: Time and Timing in Economic and Social Development*. Oxford: Oxford University Press.

Wilson, Ian. 2015. *The Politics of Protection Rackets in Post-New Order Indonesia: Coercive Capital, Authority and Street Politics*. Oxon: Routledge.

World Bank. 2015. *A Perceived Divid: How Indonesians Perceive Inequality and What They Want Done about It*. Jakarta: The World Bank Office Jakarta. https://documents1.worldbank.org/curated/en/310491467987873894/pdf/101664-WP-PUBLIC-Box394818B-Background-Paper-A-Perceived-Divide.pdf (accessd March 1, 2018)

PART 1
GOVERNANCE AND SOCIAL DYNAMICS

Chapter 1
Managing Multiculturalism in 21st Century Indonesia amid Ethnic and Religious Diversity

Thung Ju Lan

Introduction: Indonesia's Diversity

This chapter argues that it is problematic to adopt multiculturalism as a state policy for managing diversity within Indonesia's democratic framework, particularly given that the dominant discourse focuses on pluralism as the common interpretation of Indonesia's ethnic and religious diversities.

Diversity is part of everyday life for all Indonesian people, but is rarely discussed at the academic level. After the tragic events of May 1998, academics started to talk about plurality, pluralism, and multiculturalism, but few scholars, if any, discussed diversity as a subject matter. I would like to start our discussion with this topic. In Indonesia, diversity is defined as (1) more than one thousand self-identified ethnic groups;[1] and (2) six formally recognized religions (Islam, Catholicism, Protestantism, Hinduism, Buddhism, and Confucianism) as well as the so-called *agama kepercayaan* or local beliefs.

Although the New Order was famous for its prohibition of public discourse on *suku, agama, ras dan antar-golongan* (SARA—ethnicity,

---

1   According to Aris Ananta et al. (2013: 2), "In the 2010 raw coded data set, there are 1,331 categories consisting of ethnic, sub-ethnic, and sub-sub-ethnic groups", but in Ananta's New Classification, there are 375 groups, comprising sub and sub-ethnic groups (Ananta et al., 2013: 13).

religion, race and intergroup) issues, in the *Reformasi* era Indonesians have continued to avoid in-depth discussions of race and intergroup relations. When it comes to race, for example, Chinese, Arabs, Indians, and other nationalities have 'become Indonesian by marriage,' but most often only the Chinese are mentioned. In terms of intergroup relations, categorization of Indonesians is more complicated. For example, traditionally a Javanese community is described as comprising *santri* (pious Muslims), *abangan* (non-pious Muslims), and *priyayi* (Javanese aristocrats).[2] However, one can also find aristocratic groups outside Java; in Kutai, East Kalimantan, one group claims to be the descendants of the Kutai (Islamic) Kingdom. Similarly, in North Maluku, we can still see the influence of the Ternate (Islamic) Kingdom. In each religion we can also find various organizational groupings, such as Nahdlatul Ulama (NU) and Muhammadiyah among Muslims, Gereja Kristen Indonesia (GKI), Huria Kristen Batak Protestan (HKBP), and Gereja Sidang Jemat Allah (GSJA) among Protestants and Pentecostals, and various sect-based groupings, such as Sunni, Syiah, and Salafi or Wahabi in Islam, or Buddhayana and Mahayana in Buddhism.

The New Order's Indonesia also never openly discussed class issues. This began to change as some newspapers started to report on the rise of the Indonesian middle class. *Republika*, Indonesia's main daily newspaper for the Muslim community, has reported on the growing Muslim middle class in Indonesia, with *syariah* insurance premiums reaching more than 30% for the last 5–6 years as an indicator (*Sulistyawati*, 2014).[3] If we include diversity of social environment, the numerous peoples of Indonesia's

---

2 This categorization, formulated by Clifford Geertz, was based on his study between 1952–1954 in a small town of East Java, which he called Modjokuto. The study was first published as a book titled *The Religion of Java* in 1960 by the Free Press, and then by the University of Chicago Press in 1976.

3 The book entitled *A Decade Development for People Prosperity* reported that under Susilo Bambang Yudhoyono's administration, the percentage of Indonesians in the middle class (defined as those spending USD 2–20 daily) increased from 37% in 2004 to nearly 57% in 2013 (Antaranews, 2014). According to a study by the World Bank, the Indonesian middle class (defined as those with incomes of USD 10–20 per month) in 2003 represented just under 38% of the total population, but by 2010 had risen to almost 57%. They consist of 4 groups, namely: (1) with income between USD 2–4 or IDR 1–1.5 million per month (38.5%); (2) with income USD 4–6 or IDR 1.5–2.6 million per month (11.7%); (3) with income USD 6–10 or IDR 2.6–5.2 million per month (5%); and (4) middle class with income USD 10–20 or IDR 5.2–6 million per month (1.3%) (Viva, 2011).

different islands, namely Sumatra, Java, Kalimantan, Sulawesi, Maluku, and Papua, also need to be considered, as the peoples in each of those islands have socially developed distinct characteristics and ways of life.

This variety of perspectives in seeing diversity creates several challenges for implementing multiculturalism in Indonesian society. This chapter will discuss those challenges to clarify the complexities of the relationship between Indonesian diversity and the concept of multiculturalism. According to the *Oxford English Dictionary*,[4] multiculturalism is "[t]he presence of, or support for the presence of, several distinct cultural or ethnic groups within a society." The *Cambridge Dictionary*[5] defines multiculturalism as "the belief that different cultures within a society should all be given importance." Meanwhile, Jennifer L. Eagan, in *Encyclopaedia Britannica*, defined multiculturalism as "the view that cultures, races, and ethnicities, particularly those of minority groups, deserve special acknowledgement of their differences within a dominant political culture" (Eagan, 2015).

The concept of multiculturalism was introduced to Indonesia after the tragic 1998 May riot as a solution to inter-ethnic and inter-religious conflicts. Such conflicts erupted almost continuously in the late 1990s, beginning with the Sambas conflict at the end of 1996 among ethnic groups in Kalimantan (the Dayak, Madurese, and Malay) and reached its peak with the Ambon conflict between Muslims and Christians in 2001, with the armed forces muddying the waters. These violent conflicts indicated the breakup of an Indonesian plural society that was more or less politically integrated under the authoritarian regime of Suharto's New Order. Together with Aceh and Papua's power struggle vis-à-vis the state authority for regional autonomy, the conflicts have inserted a feeling of chaos into the political landscape of Indonesia. Introducing multiculturalism seemed a viable solution, a way to return to the national rhetoric of *Bhinneka Tunggal Ika* (Unity in Diversity) which has long been undermined by Negara

---

4   "multiculturalism." en.oxforddictionaries.com. https://en.oxforddictionaries.com/definition/multiculturalism (accessed October 30, 2017)

5   "multiculturalism." dictionary.cambridge.com. https://dictionary.cambridge.org/dictionary/english/multiculturalism (accessed October 30, 2017)

Kesatuan Republik Indonesia (NKRI—the Unitary State of the Republic of Indonesia), as the dominant discourse of the New Order government. In practice, however, multiculturalism is not simple. Careful consideration of the flaws of multiculturalism, until now avoided by its supporters in Indonesia, is necessary. The following section will discuss these flaws and place them within the context of Indonesia's multifaceted experiences of cultural and religious diversities.

Multiculturalism and Its Limitations

As explained by Radka Neumannova (2007), the idea of a multicultural society has its roots in nation-states, which "recognized the need to react to the cultural diversity" brought about by international immigrants as "a consequence of their immigration and integration policies" (Neumannova, 2007: 2). Countries such as Canada, the United States, and Australia are examples of countries that have tried to accommodate various forms of a multicultural society through public policies. In this specific historical background, multiculturalism has created a variety of problems that originate in the debate between two major stances on multiculturalism, which Neumannova calls "two interconnected issues in contemporary society: cultural diversity and politics of recognition" (Neumannova, 2007: 3). On the one hand, "liberal theories promot[e] multiculturalism as a model of defense of cultural rights having its source in the universal right of an individual", and on the other hand, "cultural relativism demonstrates that the liberal concept of a nation-state ignored for many decades the idea of culture as a system based on multiple relations and meanings, which go beyond nation-states boundaries and where cultural differences are intended as variations existing side by side" (Neumannova, 2007: 1). Therefore, it is not surprising if, as Neumannova has noted, the ethnic clashes in Yugoslavia and Eastern Europe after the fall of communism, and the crisis of the traditional nation-states in Western Europe which have been precipitated by non-European immigration, have placed the problem of multiculturalism as "a challenge to [the] liberal democratic system and to civil society" and can be seen as "the root of possible intra-national ethnic conflicts and discords" (ibid.).

If we pay careful attention to the so-called 'multicultural programs or movements' in Indonesia, it is obvious that supporters of multiculturalism are mostly working to promote the cultural or religious rights of particular groups, such as the customary communities of the Dayaks in Kalimantan, followers of Confucianism within the Chinese community, and the faithful followers of local beliefs, especially by demanding state recognition and protection. Unfortunately, as Neumannova has warned, "the policies designed under the influence of the politics of recognition will lead to divisions among citizens," because their goal is "the formation of 'differentiated citizens', and of a state with sensibility for a difference" (Neumannova, 2007: 4). She argues that the sort of multiculturalism introduced by Will Kymlicka in the 1990s "turns into a non-tolerant policy, denying the mutual recognition and integration, and it leads to the so called 'balkanization' of societies" (ibid.), because the cultural diversities of various groups are "radicalized into political programs, and society is politically and socially increasingly polarized" (ibid.). This pattern is observable in Indonesia: discriminated groups (for example followers of Confucianism and local beliefs) claim the same advantages given to other religious or belief groups, while groups with strong religious-cultural identity—namely, Muslims—claim more privileges "at the expenses of non-supported religious-cultural groups" (for example the Syiah and Ahmadiyah). The situation, for Neumannova, reflects a plural society that has "not specified how to build its social unity, when dealing with different identities." Sustainable integration requires citizens "to will it" (Neumannova, 2007: 5), highlighting the need for citizen responsibility to cooperate to the formation of the expected social unity (ibid.). The danger of this type of multiculturalism according to Neumannova, is that it implies that "we can create differentiated citizenship based on a refusal of a state, which does not recognize cultural or ethnic differences" (ibid.). She terms this "multiculturalism of difference," because it does not refer to "multiculturalism intended as pluralism of cultures" (Neumannova, 2007:

6). I believe, this is the point which indicates why the implementation of multiculturalism in Indonesia becomes socially and culturally problematic. We, or at least the Indonesian government, tend to treat our cultural or ethnic differences as a threat to integration and Indonesian nationalism, such that the state feels obligated to control those differences (e.g. through SARA policy), instead of working on negotiating the cultural and ethnic differences as part of our natural conditions as a nation with a plurality of cultures.

Since "nationalism holds that cultural differences are results of a hierarchy between 'us' and 'them,'" as a consequence, "the existence of cultural differences was interpreted as differences among cultures as closed units" (ibid.). Hence, the plurality promoted by the liberal viewpoint of multiculturalism, which recognizes cultural and ethnic plurality, is "intended as a plurality of cultures as closed units" (ibid.). As such, this perspective has been criticized as "to endorse existing differences and to perpetuate existing cultural stereotypes by using 'culture' as a means to solve the social and political inequalities" (ibid.). Meanwhile, "[t]he risk for multiculturalism to rely on cultural relativism" is that it "can transform multiculturalism into an ideology based on moral appeals to national cultures as majorities." Therefore, it is not surprising that, as in the case of Indonesia after the tragedy of May 1998, "[c]ultural diversity [was] taken for granted by the multiculturalist, in order to give an answer to ethnic conflicts or clashes" (ibid.).

To understand the historical cause of present-day Indonesia's 'problematic' situation of managing diversity, we should turn to J.S. Furnivall's famous theory of "a plural society," created in an "attempt to trace the development of social and economic life in the Netherlands India" known today as Indonesia (Furnivall, 1944).

Furnivall defined a "plural society" as one that comprises "two or more elements or social orders which live side by side, yet without mingling, in one political unit" (Furnivall, 1944: 446). For Furnivall, "in a plural society, there is no common will, except possibly, in matters of supreme importance, such as resistance to aggression from outside," because in "its political aspect a plural society resembles a confederation of allied provinces, united by treaty or within the limits of a formal constitution, merely for certain ends common to constituent units and, in matters outside the terms of union, each living its own life" (Furnivall, 1944: 447). However, he also warned that "a plural society has instability of a confederation," because, unlike a confederation, the constituent elements of a plural society "are not segregated each within its own territorial limits," therefore, while in a confederation, secession is "possible without the total disruption of all the social bonds," in a plural society, "secession is identical with anarchy" (ibid.). In his observation, in the Netherlands India, which is "typical of tropical dependencies where the rulers and the ruled are of different races," "the European, Chinaman, and Native are linked as vitally as Siamese twins, and if rent asunder, every element of the union must dissolve in anarchy." Nevertheless, in his thoughtfulness, Furnivall also suggested that, "[Y]et they are so far from having any common will that among the Natives, the order numerically most powerful, there is pressure for dissolution of the tie even at the risk of anarchy" (ibid.). Clearly, with his theory, Furnivall perceptively foresaw the dissolution of the Netherlands India into the independent [native] Indonesia.

Furthermore, Furnivall discussed a common social demand, which, in his opinion, is also absent in a plural society. He deemed that social demands in a plural society are "disorganized," and that "social wants are sectional" (Furnivall, 1944: 449), therefore, he argued that, "there is [only] one place in which the various sections of a plural society meet on common ground—the market place; and the highest common factor of their wants is the economic factor" (ibid.). He regarded "[t]he fundamental character of the organization of a plural society as a whole is indeed the structure of a factory, organized for production, rather than of a State, organized for the good life of its members" (Furnivall, 1944: 450). As Furnivall explained, one consequence of this emphasis on production rather than on social life is that "although the primary distinction between the groups may be race, creed, or colour, each section comes to have its own functions in production, and there is a tendency towards the grouping of the several elements into distinct economic castes" (ibid.). In Java, he found the distribution of economic functions "coincide[d] largely with racial differences, and certain occupations are reserved, partly of deliberate intention but more by the working of the economic process, for Europeans, others for the Chinese and others again for Natives" (Furnivall, 1944: 451). He described the position of the "Chinaman," who "encroache[d] upon both Native and European spheres," as possible because "he is more apt than either as a medium for the working of economic forces" (ibid.). Perhaps, it is this pluralist perspective of economic relations between the various groups in the Indonesian society that has been missing in our discussion of multiculturalism. As Furnivall observed, "[t]his distribution of production among racial castes aggravates the inherent sectionalism of demand; for a community which is confined to certain economic functions finds it more difficult to apprehend the social needs of the country as a whole" (ibid.).

The independent State of Indonesia, highly focused on political issues, has neglected its most important historical lesson, that, "the conflict between rival economic interests tends to be exacerbated by racial diversity" (ibid.). Furnivall provided the example of sugar estates which reflected the prevalence of rural and agricultural interests over urban and industrial interests. The rural and agricultural interests were largely at one with those of capital, namely European planters, in spite of the sharp clash of interests between the planters and the people (ibid.). This issue is even more problematic, when "within each section the economic side of life is emphasized" (Furnivall, 1944: 452), such as "the single-minded devotion of the Chinese to economic ends," which has been "a favourite theme of European writers from the time of Raffles and earlier" (Furnivall, 1944: 453), or a tendency among Dutch writers on colonial affairs "to stress the lack of economic motive among Natives, and the failure of economic process in the native community by which the cheaper commodity displaces the more costly" (ibid.). In other words, "each lives within a closed compartment and life within each section becomes narrower" (Furnivall, 1944: 458); thus, "within each section of the community the social demand becomes disorganized and ineffective, so that in each section the members are debarred from leading the full life of a citizen in a homogenous community; finally, the reaction against these abnormal conditions, taking in each section the form of Nationalism [for example Chinese or indigenous nationalisms], sets one community against the other so as to emphasize the plural character of the society and aggravate its instability, thereby enhancing the need for it to be held together by some force exerted from outside" (Furnivall, 1944: 459) such as colonial power or the authoritarian power of Soeharto's New Order. However, it should also be noted that, "[t]he principle of Nationalism provides no solution in itself," for, as Furnivall indicated, "in a plural society, nationalism is in effect internationalism," and "Nationalism within a plural society is itself a disruptive force, tending to shatter and not to consolidate the social order" (Furnivall, 1944: 468).

The present picture of Indonesia has largely differed from the one being portrayed by Furnivall, even though the relationship between the Chinese and the so-called natives continues to pull at the strings of Indonesia's social fabric. At the same time, an ethnographic study of the Karo people in the highlands and urban centers such as Medan and Jakarta (Kipp, 1993) illustrates how the interplay of religious pluralism, class differences, ethnic identity, and state power has created "dissociated identities," or the compartmentalization of religious, ethnic, and national identities (Adams, 1994). According to Kipp, this might be related to the New Order "state's assertions that national identities transcend local identities and that religion is a personal affair, irrelevant to citizenship or ethnic affiliation" (ibid). This compartmentalization of identities has resulted in diminishing ethnic cohesiveness (because religious identities foster religious pluralism within ethnic groups), diminishing religious unity (by promoting ethnicity through cultivating ethnic arts to attract tourist revenues), and avoiding class issues (by spotlighting religion and ethnicity) (ibid.). Such an overlooked 'colonial and New Order legacy' is further complicated by the simplification of the interpretation of culture within the context of contemporary Indonesia.

The Interpretation of Culture by the Indonesian State

When examining "pluralism of cultures," it is imperative to discuss culture itself within the Indonesian context, since culture is the main element of multiculturalism. Nevertheless, as indicated in the following examples, the idea of culture is rather vaguely defined in the state's development efforts.

As could be seen within Badan Perencanaan Pembangunan Nasional (Bappenas—National Development Planning Agency), the first task assigned to one of its nine deputies is "human development and the development of community and culture." This demonstrates that culture is considered one of the most important contributors to development. However, it is not clear why the agency was then divided into four sections as follows: (1) public health and nutrition; (2) education and religion; (3) tertiary education, science-technology, and culture; and (4) family development and the development of women, children, youth, and sport.[6]

Koentjaraningrat, a famous Indonesian anthropologist during the 1970s–1980s, classified culture into seven elements, namely: (1) social organization systems, (2) systems of religion and religious ceremonies, (3) livelihood systems, (4) science and knowledge systems, (5) technology and equipment systems, (6) language systems and (7) the arts (Kistanto, n.d.). Within the government bureaucracy, "culture" has been narrowed down to arts that are preserved in museums. This simplistic view focuses on material culture, while ignoring the non-material. Such a perspective not only creates a distortion of the understanding of culture, but also places each element in a separate technical compartment, notably social organization (under the patronage and supervision of the Ministry of Internal Affairs), religion (the Department of Religion), technology (Badan Pengkajian dan Penerapan Teknologi or BPPT—Agency for the Assessment and Application of Technology), language (Badan Pengembangan dan Pembinaan Bahasa— Language Development and Fostering Agency), and arts (Pusat-Pusat Kebudayaan Daerah—Local Cultural Centers). No ministry or institution

---

6   "Struktur organisasi." Bappenas.go.id. https://www.bappenas.go.id/en/profil-bappenas/ struktur-organisasi/ (accessed June 28, 2019)

combines all these functions of culture in the service of the larger idealistic goal of "human development." Of course, we have Bappenas, or the Indonesian Ministry of National Development Planning, for that purpose, but unfortunately, Bappenas itself has been compartmentalized into small technical units (ibid.),[7] without proficient coordination among them.

The misinterpretation of culture has its origins in the 1945 constitution, which refers to the *puncak-puncak kebudayaan daerah*, or the "peaks of local cultures," as the elements that define the national culture. But how does one identify the "peak" of a culture? In Jim Davidson's writing, "Peak Culture" (Davidson 2010), which is about the United States, for example, the term refers only to "the height of their society", that is when in 1969 "they used militarism and socialism to put two guys on the Moon, they trotted out their public private partnership (Concorde) to build exclusive supersonic transport for the rich". It is clear that in that case, Davidson

---

7   Since 2016, there have been nine deputies under the Minister of Planning National Development (Perencanaan Pembangunan Nasional or PPN)/Head of Development Planning Agency (National Development Planning Agency or Bappenas), as follows: (1) the Deputy for human development and the development of community and culture (assisted by directors of public health and nutrition; education and religion; tertiary education, science-technology, and culture; family development and the development of women, children, youth, and sport); (2) the Deputy for political affairs, law, defence and security (assisted by 5 directors: political and communication development; state apparatuses; law and regulations; foreign policy and international development cooperation; defence and security); (3) Deputy for population and man power (assisted bv 4 directors: planning, population and social security; man power and the expansion of employment opportunities; poverty alleviation and the development of social welfare; the development of small and medium scale enterprises and cooperatives); (4) Deputy for economic affairs (assisted by 5 directors: macro-planning and statistical analysis; state finance and monetary analysis; financial services and state-owned enterprises; trade, investment and international economic cooperation; industry, tourism and creative economy); (5) Deputy for maritime affairs and natural resources (assisted by 5 directors: food and agriculture; forestry and the conservation of water resources; marine affairs and fisheries; energy, mineral and mining resources; natural environment); (6) Deputy for infrastructure (assisted by 4 directors: water and irigation development; transportation; energy, telecommunication and informatics; government-private sector partnership and engineering design); (7) Deputy for regional development (assisted by 5 directors: spatial planning and land affairs; regional development and special zones; disadvantaged regions, transmigration and rural development; urban development, housing and settlement areas; regional autonomy); (8) Deputy for development funding (assisted by 5 directors: planning and the advancement of development funding; allocation of development funding; bilateral external funding; multilateral external funding; development funding system and procedures); and (9) Deputy for monitoring, evaluation and control of development (assisted by 3 directors: system and reporting of monitoring, evaluation and control of development; monitoring, evaluation and control of development; monitoring, evaluation and control of regional development).

was discussing technology and material culture. Thus, it is not surprising if Indonesia too perceives the peaks of local cultures through material culture, undermining the existence of non-material culture, or the seven elements mentioned above—as the crux of every culture. Of course, it is not uncommon for societies to focus on material culture as most representative, dismissing the importance of non-material culture, but as a plural society without any dominant culture like in the United States with its White Anglo-Saxon, Indonesia has great difficulty in deciding which material culture should be prioritized.

A new era began when Soeharto stepped down from his position as the President of Republic of Indonesia in May 1998. All Indonesians welcomed the *Reformasi* (Reform) era as one that would usher in political change in every sphere of life. Starting with the general election of 1999, followed by the regional autonomy regulation of 2000, Indonesia began transitioning to a period of democratization, which has continued until today. While regional autonomy is a rational product of democratization, its implementation precipitates the rise of local cultures and identities within Indonesia's 'multicultural' society. In other words, regional autonomy opened the pandora's box of cultural diversity, creating problematic relationships between local and national cultures, as indicated by the emerging identity of *putera daerah*, or native son, together with claims of indigenous rights across the country. Hence "culture" acquires new meanings, catering to identity politics and highlighting the problem of (cultural) representation within Indonesia's democratic system.

How to Manage Indonesia's Diversity?

Returning to the beginning of our discussion about diversity in Indonesia, we find that several perspectives need to be discussed further, namely ethnicity, religion, race, geography, class, and to some extent, gender and sexual orientation. As mentioned, Indonesia has more than 1,000 ethnic groups. It would be difficult to construct a representative institution for all of these groups. Even if we use Aris Ananta et al.'s

New Classification that numbered 375 ethnic groups (see footnote one), it is still a huge number to manage. Since less than 10 groups have a higher percentage of the population compared to others (Javanese 40%, Sundanese 15.5%, Chinese 3.7%,[8] Malay 3.4%, Madurese 3.3%, Batak 3%, Minangkabau 2.7%, Betawi 2.5%, Buginese 2.4%, Arab 2.3%, Banten 2.1%, Banjar 1.7%, and Bali 1.5%),[9] population statistics often combine these groups into one core group and combine the others into another single group. This, however, is highly discriminative because it leaves more than 900 groups with no voice of their own. By combining ethnicity with geographic distinctions, people could be grouped according to each island, but the number of ethnic groups on each island remains large. For example, Papua itself has more than 200 ethnic groups.[10] The best method, therefore, is to construct a picture of representation at the local level, with *kota/kabupaten* (city/regency) as the smallest autonomous unit. However, this does not resolve the issue, either, due to the number of ethnic groups existing in each *kota/kabupaten*. Moreover, this structure would need to be combined with the existing political party structure once it was agreed that ethnicity should be included in the political representation system. Nevertheless, on the issue of ethnicity, we should note the effects of the ethnicization of politics in the case of Ethiopia, which according to Asefa Tola (2007: 2), has "dismantle[d his] country into ethnic enclaves."

West Kalimantan Province is the only area in Indonesia which clearly uses an ethnic approach in building its political structure. As stated by Gusti Suryansyah, the Head of the West Kalimantan Political Studies

---

8   It should be noted that based on their calculation of the 2010 Population Census, Evi Nurvidya Arifin et al. (2017) presented a much smaller (1.2) percentage of the Chinese (or 2.8 million out of 236.7 million), which ranked the Chinese as "the 15th largest group of more than 600 ethnic groups." Unfortunely, Arifin et al. did not specify the exact number or the percentage of the so-called "more than 600 ethnic groups."

9   Those percentages were reported in the so-called Portal Nasional Republik Indonesia, with the title "Jumlah Suku Bangsa Terbesar di Indonesia"; unfortunately no source is included (Portal Nasional Republik Indonesia. n.d).

10   According to forum IDWS, there are 248 ethnic groups in Papua, which is divided into 7 Customary Territories as follows: Territory I—Tabi (87 ethnic groups); Territory II—Saireri (31 ethnic groups); Territory III—Bomberai (19 ethnic groups); Territory IV—Domberai (52 ethnic groups); Territory V—Anim Ha (29 ethnic groups); Territory VI—La Pago (19 ethnic groups); Territory VII—Mee Pago (11 ethnic groups) (Fajratsyah, 2012).

Association, Malay, Dayak and Chinese are "the tripod stand" of West Kalimantan social life. The Malay are usually identified according to the name of their residential area, for example Sambas Malay, Pontianak Malay, and Landak Malay. According to the 2000 Population Census,[11] the Sambas and Pontianak Malay alone comprise about 19% of the population, the three dominant sub-ethnic groups of the West Kalimantan Dayak, namely the Kendayan, Darat, and Pesaguan, make up around 20%, and the percentage of West Kalimantan Chinese, which consists of two dominant sub-ethnic groups, the Hakka (Khek) and Tewciu (Hoklo), is 9.4%.[12] The West Kalimantan Governor and Vice Governor during 2013–2018, Cornelis MH and Christiandy Sanjaya,[13] were a combined ticket of Dayak and Chinese candidates supported by the PDI-P (Partai Demokrasi Indonesia-Perjuangan—Indonesian Democratic Party of Struggle). They received the largest number of votes in Bengkayang, Landak, Sanggau, Sekadau, Sintang, Melawi, and Kapuas Hulu Regencies and Singkawang City (*Kompas*, 2009).

Ethnicity is the least complicated issue compared to others, because as Edward Aspinall (2011) noted, quoting Fenton, "[f]or ethnicity to spring to life it is necessary that real or perceived differences of ancestry, culture and language are mobilized in social transactions" (Aspinall, 2011: 291), which in his opinion, then depends on the political mobilization, state structures, and policies. He describes Indonesia as "a weakly ethnicized polity" by underlining the "institutional design" of the democratization process and the "deep structures" of patronage that have been "underpinning Indonesian politics," which motivate "political actors in plural regions

---

11   The 2000 Population Census is the only ethnic-based statistic which was publicized. As a result of the Dayak's objection, Central Bureau of Statistcs decided not to publicize its ethnic-based information in the 2010 Population Census. In the 2000 Population Census, at the beginning the Dayak numbered less than the Malay. This happened because the Dayak was widely scattered into various sub-ethnic groups.

12   The number of West Kalimantan Chinese presented by Arifin et al. (2007) is much smaller. According to Arifin et al., "[t]he largest percentage of Chinese to the respective province population is 8.2%, seen in two provinces: Bangka Belitung in Island of Sumatra and West Kalimantan in Island of Kalimantan" (2007: 319).

13   It should be noted that even though ethnicity has become the main variable for political mobilization in West Kalimantan, religious issues also play a significant role in political competition, as can be seen in the 2007 *pilkada*. For details, read (Yohanes 2008).

to cooperate across ethnic lines in their pursuit of political power and resources" (Aspinall, 2011: 290–291). As such, Aspinall concludes that "the political salience of ethnicity [in Indonesia] has subsided greatly as a new democratic system has settled into place" (Aspinall, 2011: 289).

Religion, on the other hand, has created a more complex problem because it has long been politicized through a mixed category of Malay, Muslim, and Native. During the New Order administration, religion as a social category was used to divide those recognized by the state (Muslims, Catholics, Protestants, Hindus, Buddhists, and Confucianists) from those who are not (followers of local beliefs). To include representatives of each formal religion is not difficult, but how do we include those from local beliefs? The problem lies not only in the lack of state recognition, but also in defining "local beliefs." As we know, local beliefs are closely connected to ethnic groups, so we may expect followers of hundreds of beliefs asking for the right to be represented. Still, we have to consider the complication of creating a representative structure for religious groups, particularly for the national level.

Another important issue to raise here is that the concept of multiculturalism is rejected by Muslim fundamentalists on the grounds that it is a "Western ideology," similar to liberalism, socialism, and communism, and therefore considered against the religious teachings of Islam. Fundamentalists prefer the term pluralism, because plurality conveys the numeric meaning of different groups, similar to various *aliran* (sects) in Islam itself.[14] This preference ignores that the term "pluralism" refers to J.S. Furnivall's "plural society," which is "in the strictest sense a medley, for they [ethnic groups] mix but do not combine. Each group holds by its own religion, its own culture and language, its own ideas and ways. As individuals they meet, but only in the market-place, [and] … with different sections of the community living side by side, but separately,

---

14 See Zulfikar Hirji (2010: 14) for an explanation of why Islam uses religious plurality and pluralism in discussing diversity and internal differences: "Here, multiple instances of discourses on intra-Muslim difference are presented in order to identify the recurring tropes, strategies and 'overlapping perspectives' on [plurality] held by those who self-identify as Muslim. In short, there is no intent to arrive at a list of features through which we can identify an Islam or a Muslim."

within the same political unit" (Lee, 2009: 33–34). In Muslim communities, as mentioned above, various groups, such as *santri, abangan*, NU, Muhammadiyah, are distinguishable. Although they are bound by Muslim solidarity, each has its own economic and political agenda. For this reason, a single representative entity cannot be constructed by a cohesive religious identity alone, but would also need to include their diverse interests and future orientations.

Religion became an issue in the political representation of Maluku Province, which led to violent conflict in 1999 and 2001. It began with the circulation of an anonymous pamphlet in October 1998 that suggested Maluku's Governor Mohamad Saleh Latuconsina had replaced "all 38" top civil servants in the province with Muslims. For a long time, Maluku had been known as a predominantly Christian society, but since 1992, when Jakarta appointed Akib Latuconsina, Maluku has had a Muslim governor. Nevertheless, it was not until Saleh Latuconsina appointed a non-Protestant deputy governor, and a non-Protestant provincial secretary that the "balance" between Protestant Christians and Muslims was "broken," adding to the growing local feeling against "newcomers" from Sulawesi (Van Klinken, 2007).

In discussing race, the concept of *pribumi-nonpribumi* (indigenous-nonindigenous) is often raised, with the term *nonpribumi* exclusively applied to Chinese Indonesians. The issue of class has also intertwined with this racial category, particularly when, under Soeharto's New Order regime, a number of Chinese conglomerates flourished at the national and international level. It would be difficult for Indonesia to employ racial categories as Malaysia has done since the mid-1960s, for the following reasons: (1) not all *pribumi* Indonesians are Malay; Papuans are part of the Melanesian group; (2) the composition and the distribution of the Indians and the Arabs in Indonesia are much smaller in scale compared to Chinese Indonesians, while the composition of Chinese, Indians, and Malay in Malaysia is much more balanced; (3) Malaysia distinguishes Malay from the native Dayaks, particularly in the Sarawak and Sabah areas, but it would be impossible for the Indonesian government to use the Native categorization, unless it divided the Indonesian population based on each island's original inhabitants, which would be extremely difficult to trace after the hundreds of years of acculturation and assimilation that have shaped the Nusantara people, known as Indonesians today. Considering all these facts, it is obvious that the so-called *pribumi-nonpribumi* categorization is not based on biology or origin, but on a post-colonial political imagination and construction that could not rely on racial categories that worked for Malaysia or Singapore. In other words, the *pribumi-nonpribumi* categorization offered Indonesia a panacea to awaken the colonized natives. The nationalization policy implemented in the 1950s, which took over foreign-controlled companies and plantations, signified the significance of being considered *pribumi*. It seems that the essence of this nationalist reasoning continues today, albeit with some changes to the rhetoric. Today, for example, we hear such things as "to protect national interests, we have to keep foreign capital to a certain limit." How long will it last? The question is not easy to answer, because as we can see, Malaysia too has not yet stopped its Bumiputera Policy, claiming that its use as an affirmative action policy (World Policy, 2016) is still needed even after more than fifty years of implementation. Indeed, some will argue that several decades are not long enough to remedy past discrimination, highlighting the difficulty of putting a time limit on an affirmative policy.

Class is not as straightforward as ethnicity, religion, race, or even geography, because many factors constitute a class. For example, class could be measured by income level, asset ownership, social status, or educational level. All of these markers can be used to measure and thus distinguish members of different classes, making differentiation based on class quite complex, especially when layered with other aspects of identity, such as ethnicity or location, that may influence perceptions or experience of class.

Indonesian society is not only diverse in ethnicity, but also in religion, race, geographic locations, and class, as well as gender and sexual orientation. All these aspects must be considered when managing diversities in Indonesia. Like Soeharto's New Order, which prioritized religion as a social category, we might focus on one category while ignoring others, but in the long term, this single-minded approach will create a larger problem: the threat of national disintegration, such as we are experiencing today.

At the individual and community levels, as Rita Smith Kipp has shown through the example of the Karo people, some important aspects of identities "have pulled apart from each other, becoming conceptually dissociated" (1993: 5) as a result of state policies that aim "to control the disruptive potential of cultural and religious differences." This impacts how people think about other kinds of identities, in particular class interests (ibid.). The Karo way of life, which was once not only culturally and geographically plural, but also religiously plural, has become complicated as some urban Karo Muslims have begun "a movement to de-Batak themselves" (ibid.). For Kipp, this reflects "historical traces of old struggles between Batak and Malay, Karo and Toba Batak, periphery and center" (ibid.), as "repositionings in relation to state power, even states of which Karo were not citizens," namely "surrounding Muslim polities that were themselves nodes in an international trade network" (1993: 6). Kipp's study shows us that some individuals take advantage of and benefit from the compartmentalization of modern life brought forth by the modern Indonesian state, which "capitalizes on the dissociation of people's identities" to exert control for the functional purpose of state stability (1993: 6–7). However, for society as a whole, compartmentalization is dangerous, particularly in the contemporary context of "democratic Indonesia."

The Role of the State

The role of the state is critical in managing Indonesia's diversities. Tony Day's criticism of writings on power and society in modern Southeast Asia, which draw on Geertz and Anderson's works of 1970s, is pertinent here. Day argues that previous studies that use terms like "discrepant histories" (Rafael, 1995), "dissociated identities" (Kipp, 1993), and "fragmented vision" (Kahn and Loh, 1992) have a Furnivallian ring, stressing the role of technologies and Oriental despotism of state rule in causing fragmentation and dislocation of society and culture (Day, 2002: 25–26). They treat culture "largely as the product of the state, rather than as a force that also shapes the powerful inventiveness of authoritarian state formations and their cultural interventions" (ibid.). Culture as the "roles of human agency and culture in the process by which the state itself is formed" (ibid.) has largely been undermined in the academic and public discourse about the relations between the state and society in Indonesia. This has resulted in "the formation of a single, universal moral viewpoint about 'autonomy', not the 'partial, situated' nature of the knowledges that can be posted about 'modern' Indonesian history", similar to the 'modern' Southeast Asian history discussed by Tony Day (2002: 32). In other words, as Day explains, "any interaction between society and state that does occur will take the form of 'resistance', 'rebellion', or 'nationalism', rather than a more ambivalent kind of transcultural localization and hybridization in which human agents involved in relations of power and the formation of states engage in complex acts of domination, submission, and resistance in ways that are shaped by culture" (Day, 2002: 27). Hence, we should consider the Indonesian state as having been formed through "transcultural localization and hybridization" with local (human) agents and cultures at different times and contexts.

Taking Javanese power as an example, Day warned us not to follow Anderson's (1972) suggestion that "concepts of Power from Old Java in modern Indonesia are but temporary 'residues' of a previous cultural mode that exercise a 'continuing cultural hold' of a negative kind on the minds of Sukarno and his successors" (Day, 2002: 11) because, as Laurie Sears' study of Javanese shadow-puppet theatre shows, "the puppeteers themselves are highlighted as agents who react to colonial and postcolonial imperatives in ways that empower them to respond creatively to the colonial inventedness of Javanese culture" (Day, 2001: 26). Moreover, in reference to Jane Drakard, Day argues that "[f]ar from being atavistic residues from 'Old' Minangkabau, concepts about royal authority drawn from Buddhism and Islam were repeatedly activated in the seventeenth and eighteenth centuries by means of the circulation of *surat cap* (seal letters) that stimulated an ongoing process of state formation in the Minangkabau controlled regions of Sumatra and the Malay Peninsula" (Day, 2002: 15), i.e. "a process of transcultural contestation and adaptation" (Day, 2002: 16). Sidel's work clarifies this process even further: "[c]ulture from both the 'old' and the 'new' Philippines, ... when not appropriated by the state in the form of legitimizing myths, expresses popular nationalism and disempowered (rather than culturally empowering) resistance to the state" (Day, 2002: 29). Obviously, in discussing the state, we cannot treat it as the sole agent, because the state only exists in relation to the society and local communities.

By offering "to expand Wolters' notion of localization and think of Southeast Asia history [and, for our purposes, Indonesian history] from early times to the present as overlapping series of localizing transcultural processes, differentially distributed over the whole region and occurring over many centuries at different rates in different places" (Day, 2002: 32), Tony Day has not only opened up a space for locating 'colonialism' but also 'pluralism and/or multiculturalism' in that series. As such, both issues "could ... be located in [that] series in all its heterogeneity, rather than being treated in a reductive way as an unbridgeable watershed that divides the 'traditional' Southeast Asian past from the 'modern' present'" (ibid.), or in our case, the 'traditional' Indonesian past from the 'modern' present. To locate the state in a continuous series of overlapping, cultural localizations "in which 'tradition' and 'modernity' or the varieties of conflicting forces involved in transcultural practices are not mutually exclusive", we need Day's working definition of the state:

> The state is a complex agent that acts through culturally constructed repertoires of potent, rational, authoritative, magical, symbolic, and illusory practices, institutions, and concepts. The state is distinct from yet interactive with societal forces, in ways that vary

according to time and place. The state regulates power and morality and organizes space, time, and identity in the face of resistance to its authority to do so". (Day, 2002: 34)

In this case, as Day also stressed, "[o]f primary importance in practice-theory approaches is the agency of human beings, of their intentions and desires, in forming states" (ibid.). This perspective leads us to question: "[w]here is the exterior that enables one to identify it as an apparatus" of state? because as Day showed, "the processes and conflicts by which potent and authoritative state concepts that regulate power and morality as well as organize space, time, and identity take shape and are represented, purified, and hybridized at all levels of society in cosmological terms that can be found in any period of Southeast Asian history" (Day, 2002: 36), and of course, in Indonesian history. In the terms of our discussion of multiculturalism, I suggest that, as colonialism is central to the long historical process of Indonesian state formation, multiculturalism should also be located in that process. From this perspective, the state, in this case the Indonesian state, is not the 'manager of the society' for implementing multiculturalism, but a product of "multicultural" negotiations between and among the diverse people of Indonesia. Claiming Indonesia as Negara Kesatuan Republik Indonesia or the Unitary State of the Republic of Indonesia is problematic in itself, because it ignores the on-going process of Indonesian state formation which, as the above discussion has shown, involves various social agents at the local and national levels.

Multiculturalism as Political Philosophy and Public Policy

Irene Bloemraad (2011) argues that,

in some arenas multiculturalism has become synonymous with the demographic and social changes that stem from migration, resulting in the conflation of multiculturalism with immigration policy. This is sometimes seen in debates about whether multiculturalism as a demographic fact undermines social capital and social cohesion. When the term multiculturalism is evoked in these debates, it usually refers to population diversity, not a particular philosophy or public policy.

She believes that "multiculturalism means more than demographic pluralism. It can also be a philosophy centered on recognizing, accommodating, and supporting cultural pluralism". As such, she supports the requirement of "governments and institutions to encourage pluralism through public policy", even though she also notices that "the precise way this is done can vary across places and time". Based on "Multiculturalism Policy Index [MCP Index] Scores for Selected Countries, 1980–2010" and her observation in the United States, Canada, Australia, Sweden, the Netherlands, Germany, Denmark, France, Norway, Switzerland, Belgium, New Zealand, U.K., Spain, Portugal, and Italy, she found that "actual policy in many countries is slowly inching toward greater accommodation of pluralism, despite [their] political rhetoric around the perceived problems of diversity". She indicated two real problems that are related to pros and cons toward the adoption of multiculturalist policy, namely (1) "the mechanisms tying multiculturalism to outcomes like employment or educational attainment are not clear" and (2) "[l]abor market policies, educational institutions, and welfare state structures likely influence economic integration much more than policies of multiculturalism". All the studies of multiculturalism, she concludes, "raise difficult questions for academics and policymakers over how to weigh majority preferences against minority interests".

Bloemraad's argument has significant bearing on the Indonesian situation. For example, we must always weigh Javanese majority preferences against non-Javanese minority interests for several reasons: firstly, Java island and its people have been the center of power since the beginning of the Indonesia nation-state; secondly, knowledge production, from educational materials, market strategies, and government policies, are all produced in and controlled from Java, particularly Jakarta. Under these circumstances, how could we adopt multiculturalism, which demands at least an equality of having 'voice'? Perhaps, the first step would be to get out of the trap of (descriptive) demographic multiculturalism as Bloemraad has warned. This would mean discarding the political lenses that rigidly set upon majority-minority divisions, and instead, work toward finding ways to ensure equality of being and becoming diverse Indonesians.

Also, we have to return to Furnivall's criticism of liberalism and utilitarianism which "sought the key to economic welfare in freedom of economic enterprise within the limits of the law" (Furnivall, 1944: 461). As he indicated, however, "with the passage of time, ... it appeared that economic freedom tended to the disintegration of society, and social legislation imposing limits on economic freedom, come to extend over an ever-wider field" (ibid.). Therefore, he argued that, "it went wrong mainly in holding that this principle of the production of wealth could be extended over the whole field of human welfare" (ibid.). The reason western economic theory is of limited application in a tropical dependency [i.e. the Netherlands India], according to Furnivall, "lies in the political constitution of a tropical dependency as a plural society; because in a plural society there is no community as a whole, and problems of political and economic science differ fundamentally from those of homogenous societies" (Furnivall, 1944: 462). As such, in Furnivall's opinion, "in a plural society the basic problem of political science is for more elemental; it is impossible to provide a vehicle for the expression of social will until there is a society capable of will; and the basic problem of political science in such a community is the integration of the society" (Furnivall, 1944: 463). I think, at this point it is quite necessary to re-quote Dr. de Kat Angelino's view that "in normal condition Society is the parent of the State, whereas in Netherlands India, and in the Independent Indonesia, the pressing burden on the State is the creation of Society" (Furnivall, 1944: 463), which is exactly the problem undermining the Indonesian state today.

Although Charles A. Coppel (1997) criticized Furnivall's concept of 'plural society' as misleading because Furnivall overlooked "colonial society in the urban centres of Java" which, according to Coppel, "might in many respects just as well be characterized as a 'mestizo society'"

(Coppel, 1997: 562) when "one considers the phenomenon of the highly acculturated peranakan Chinese of Java" (Coppel, 1997: 569), I believe Furnivall's political economic analysis is still relevant to our discussion of multiculturalism in Indonesia. Coppel himself admitted that, "[t]here were, of course, limitations to the integration of the mestizo society", because of "Government-sponsored segregation by race" (Coppel, 1997: 573). In this case he agreed with Wertheim that, "the multiracial mestizo culture contained the seeds of its own disintegration: [t]hough Indo-Europeans, Indonesian Chinese and modern urban Indonesians were all of them equally imbued with the mestizo culture, they saw themselves as bearers par excellence of European, Chinese and Indonesian cultural values" (Coppel, 1997: 574). As a result, "[p]aradoxically, ... the dwindling cultural differences tended to widen again, insofar as the various groups were the supporters of divergent ideologies." Both Wertheim and Coppel saw that "communal strife worked toward still further disintegration" (ibid.). Apparently, all the above writers are still very concerned about the problem of integrating the Indonesian 'plural' society, rather than accommodating Indonesian 'pluralism' as Bloemraad suggested. I believe this is the main problem that we have to deal with in managing multiculturalism in 21st century Indonesia.

References

Adams, Kathleen M. 1994. "Dissociated Identities: Ethnicity, Religion and Class in an Indonesian Society by Rita Kipp (Review)." https://www. researchgate.net/publication/272785585_Dissociated_Identities_ Ethnicity_Religion_and_Class_in_an_Indonesian_Society_by_Rita_ Kipp_Review (accessed June 27, 2019).

Ananta, Aris, et al. 2013. "Changing Ethnic Composition: Indonesia, 2000–2010." paper prepared for the XXVII IUSSP International Population Conference, August 26–31, 2013, Busan, Korea. https:// www.iussp.org/sites/default/files/event_call_for_papers/IUSSP%20

Ethnicity%20Indonesia%20Poster%20Section%20G%202708%20 2013%20revised.pdf (accessed October 25, 2017).

Anderson, Benedict. 1972. "The Idea of Power in Javanese Culture". IN *Culture and Politics in Indonesia*, edited by Claire Holt, pp.1-69. Ithaca: Cornell University Press. 1-69.

Antaranews. 2014. "Populasi Kelas Menengah Indonesia Meningkat Tajam," April 16, 2014. http://www.antaranews.com/berita/429636/ populasi-kelas-menengah-indonesia-meningkat-tajam (accessed October 23, 2017).

Arifin, Evi Nurvidya. et al. 2017. "Chinese Indonesians: How Many, Who and Where?" *Asian Ethnicity* 18 (3): 310–329.

Aspinall, Edward. 2011. "Democratization and Ethnic Politics in Indonesia: Nine Theses," *Journal of East Asian Studies* 11: 289–319.

Bloemraad, Irene. 2011. "The Debate over Multiculturalism: Philosophy, Politics and Policy." Migration Policy Institute (MPI), September 22, 2011. https://www.migrationpolicy.org/article/debate-over-multiculturalism-philosophy-politics-and-policy (accessed October 31, 2017).

Coppel, Charles A. 1997. "Revisiting Furnivall's 'Plural Society': Colonial Java as a Mestizo Society?". *Ethnic and Racial Studies* 20 (3): 562–579.

Davidson, Jim. "Peak Culture". http://www.ncc-1776. org/tle2010/tle58 4-20100822-03.html (accessed October 30, 2017).

Day, Tony. 2002. *Fluid Iron: State Formation in Southeast Asia*. University of Hawaii Press.

Eagan, Jennifer L. 2015. "multiculturalism". *Encyclopaedia Britannica*. https://www.britannica.com/topic/multiculturalism (accessed October 30, 2017).

Fajratsyah. 2012. "Suku Bangsa di Tanah Papua." *Forum IDWS*, December 24, 2012. http://forum.idws.id/threads/suku-bangsa-di-tanah-papua. 378206/ (accessed October 27, 2017).

Furnivall, J.S. 1944. *Netherlands India—A Study of Plural Economy*. Cambridge: Cambridge University Press.

Hirji, Zulfikar. 2010. "Debating Islam from Within: Muslim Constructions of Internal Other". In *Diversity and Pluralism in Islam: Historical and Contemporary Discourses Amongst Muslims*, pp. 1-30. London: I.B. Tauris Publishers in association with The Institute of Ismaili Studies.

Kahn, Joel and Francis Loh Kok Wah. 1992. *Fragmented Vision: Culture and Politics in Contemporary Malaysia*. Honolulu: University of Hawaii Press.

Kipp, Rita Smith. 1993. *Dissociated Identities: Ethnicity, Religion and Class in an Indonesian Society*. Ann Arbor: The University of Michigan Press.

Kistanto, Nurdien Harry. 2017. "Tentang Konsep Kebudayaan". *Sabda* 10 (2). http://ejournal.undip.ac.id/index.php/sabda/article/view/13248 (accessed October 27, 2017).

Kompas. 2009. "Tiga Tungku di Borneo Barat." February 16, 2009. http://nasional.kompas.com/read/2009/02/16/13463691/tiga.tungku.di.borneo.barat (accessed February 8, 2018).

Lee, Hock Guan. 2009. "Furnivall's Plural Society and Leach's Political Systems of Highland Burma". *Sojourn: Journal of Social Issues in Southeast Asia* 24 (1): 32–46.

Neumannova, Radka. 2007. "Multiculturalism and Cultural Diversity in Modern Nation State." Conference Turin. http://citeseerx.ist.psu.edu/viewdoc/download? doi= 10.1.1.408.7757 &rep=rep1&type=pdf (accessed October 23, 2017).

Portal Nasional Republik Indonesia. n.d. "Jumlah Suku Bangsa Terbesar di Indonesia". http://sejarah-republik-indonesia.blogspot.co.id/p/jumlah-suku-bangsa-terbesar-di.html (accessed October 29, 2017).

Rafael, Vincente. 1995. *Discrepant Histories: Translocal Essays on Filipino Cultures*. Philadelphia: Temple University Press.

Sulistyawati. Rr Laeny. 2014. "Jumlah Kelas Menengah Muslim Meningkat, Ini Buktinya," Republika, October 28, 2014. http://www.republika.co.id/berita/ekonomi/syariah-ekonomi/14/10/28/ne5y2a-jumlah-kelas-menengah-muslim-meningkat-ini-buktinya. (accessed October 23, 2017).

Tola, Asefa. 2007. "The Role of the Diaspora in Ethiopian Politics". https://www.scribd.com/document/204346668/The-Role-of-the-Diaspora-in-Politics (accessed November 1, 2017).

Van Klinken, Gerry. 2007. "What Caused the Ambon Violence?". *Inside Indonesia*, September 11, 2007. http://www.insideindonesia.org/what-caused-the-ambon-violence (accessed February 8, 2018).

Vivanews. 2011. "Kelas Menengah Indonesia Tumbuh Pesat". March 30. http://www.viva.co.id/berita/bisnis/212144-kelas-menengah-indonesia-tumbuh-pesat (accessed October 23, 2017).

World Policy. 2016. "Positive Discrimination: Perspectives on Malaysia". April 12, 2016. https://worldpolicy.org/2016/04/12/positive-discrimination-perspectives-on-malaysia/ (accessed March 25, 2018).

Yohanes Supriyadi. 2008. "Politik Primordial Dalam Pemilihan Kepala Daerah Propinsi Kalimantan Barat 2007". http://yohanessupriyadi.blogspot.co.id/2008/08/politik-primordial-dalam-pemilihan.html (accessed February 18, 2018).

Chapter 2

Post-*Reformasi* Dynamism of the Urban Landscape: A Visual Report of the Street Art of Yogyakarta

Brigitta Isabella

Introduction

What can be learned about post-*Reformasi* changes in Indonesian society from the street art of its urban landscape? The *Reformasi* opened new opportunities for Indonesians to practice and experiment with democracy, and street art is one place way that vernacular democracy is performed. The right to participate in the making of the urban landscape is one of the rights that Indonesians gained after the fall of the New Order's authoritarian regime, which controlled public space through state monument projects and building developments.

What can we learn about urban dynamism when we scratch the surface of the city's walls? In this chapter I will discuss the ongoing transformation of Yogyakarta's urban landscape, a city that is well known for its traditional heritage, yet has witnessed unprecedented changes since 1998. Even a cursory inspection of Yogyakarta's street art reveals a robust art scene. Such dynamism is part of a global cultural trend that emerged in the late 1990s and transformed our ways of seeing and experiencing cities. On the one hand, Yogyakarta's dynamic urban landscape is a specific reference and must be read in terms of its own situatedness. On the other hand, urbanization is a global phenomenon in which neo-liberal market logic continues to limit our access to urban resources and our right to shape the urban landscape where we live. Yogyakarta is no exception.

Yogyakarta has many predicates. Officially, it is Daerah Istimewa Yogyakarta (DIY—Yogyakarta Special Region), a status that enabled the pre-colonial monarchy to govern the region, historically granted because of the late Sultan Hamengkubuwana IX's essential support during the Indonesian struggle for independence (1945–1950). Yogyakarta is often nicknamed the *kota pelajar* (city of students), because it is home to a large number of schools and universities. With its relatively low cost of living compared to other capital cities outside Java Island, Yogyakarta has attracted significant numbers of students from all over Indonesia. It is also one of Indonesia's most famous tourist destinations, known for its cultural heritage of Javanese traditions. Lastly, Yogyakarta is also renowned as Indonesia's "capital of contemporary art" because of its dynamic art scene. With this mix of predicates, Yogyakarta's urban landscape is shaped through harmonies and tensions, between monarchy and democracy; tradition and modernity; cultural heritage and contemporary art.

Nowadays, murals and graffiti are common sights in every corner of the city, and are the most visible visual elements of the formation of the urban landscape of Yogyakarta. Drawing on the thoughts of the French philosopher Jacques Rancière (2004), this chapter comprehends street art as aesthetic actions that reconfigure forms of visibility in urban space by creating new modes of sense perception and political subjectivity. In this chapter, aesthetic practice is seen as a mode of visibility performed by various competing elements in the society: individuals, communities, commercial corporations, and state institutions. By configuring street art as dynamic and competing landscapes, I wish to capture the power relations between those who participate in the making of urban landscapes.

Visual interventions upon the urban landscape of Yogyakarta are not the sole preserve of artists. Individuals—the "non-professional" artists—

such as high school students, kampong gangsters, Muslim youth, and fanatic football fan clubs, are now pointing spray-can nozzles at street walls to communicate their feelings, thoughts, and identities. Doreen Lee argues that, "in the post-*Reformasi* context, where citizens are disenchanted by mass demonstrations and civil society initiatives, street art emerges as new technology of the self" (Lee, 2013: 307). This helps us understand why the landscape of Yogyakarta is never inert. It continuously flows like a river, driven by the forces of the people who are engaging with, appropriating, and contesting it.

Landscape is a reflection of spatiotemporal order controlled and shaped by dominant power order. At the same time, landscape is also a medium in which identities—whether individual, group or, nation-state—are created and disputed (Bender, 1993: 4). Landscape that operates at the juncture of social relations and cultural perceptions is "a concept of high tension" (Inglis, 1977 via Bender, 1993: 4). Landscape, like order, is an ongoing project rather than an accomplished state (Stavrides, 2015: 9). Street art is a significant part of the formation of the urban landscape. Street art is also a practice with a "high tension" of mixed ideas and ideologies, because it may not last long, subject as it is to competition from the overflowing circulation of advertisements, political banners, billboards, and new graffiti or murals made by other street artists in the public space.

This chapter analyzes three sites of street art in order to reveal the texture of the social and spatial struggles of Yogyakarta: the walls of the Lempuyangan flyover, which is the first flyover in the city, where mural artists worked closely with the local government to "beautify" the city; the walls of Kewek Bridge, which is considered part of Yogyakarta's cultural heritage in the area of Kotabaru, where artists have protested against the commercialization of public space; and finally, the walls of an abandoned building at the east corner of Pojok Beteng Wetan near *kraton* (Sultan's palace), where competing visual claims have appeared and spatial politics is monopolized by a violent local patronage network. By examining these three sites, I aim to reveal the dominant power structures that attempt to normalize the politics enabled by the aesthetics of street art.[1] I hope to contribute to a wider discussion on the meaning of street art in post–1998 Indonesia by presenting a visual reading of the development and challenges of urban social dynamism in Yogyakarta during the two decades after *Reformasi*.[2]

Previous studies on street art in Yogyakarta have discussed the patterns of unwritten rules in the street art world, the social-economic harmony and disharmony between artists and other actors in urban space, and its effect on the discourse of street art in Indonesia (Barry, 2008; Indriyati, 2011). This chapter takes a slightly different approach. Rather than focusing on the figure of street artists and their worldviews, it instead emphasizes the spatial nuance of social-aesthetic practices that take place on street walls and looks at the competing power relations in the making and unmaking of public space through an analysis of what is visible on the street walls. I argue that this approach contributes to the discourse of democratization from a visual studies perspective and at the same time serves as a critique of street art, was exclusively done by artists themselves in previous researches.

Street walls are sites of politics, where politics is understood as "an open process through which the dominant forms of living together are questioned and potentially transformed" (Stavrides, 2015: 11). Street walls become sites of politics if they produce an arena for different elements in society to interrupt the established order that controls the city landscape. This chapter focuses on the inexhaustible dynamism of landscapes in different parts of Yogyakarta to reveal the face of the injustice of urban development, the competing claims to the city by various actors in the society, and the struggles of citizens to reclaim their rights to public space.

---

1   David Harvey (1973: 10) argues that a city is always made of geographical and sociological imaginations. In other words, spatial forms contain social processes, in the same manner that social processes are spatial.

2   This chapter acknowledges the need for a gendered perspective in the discussion of Indonesian street art. It is important to provide a critique of the structure of gender hierarchy in street art practice, especially given that street art is a highly masculine practice, and to think about strategic and discursive ways of creating safe common spaces for women and gender non-conforming persons to participate in the making of urban landscapes.

Lempuyangan Flyover: Clash of Identity Politics

The Lempuyangan flyover is just a few steps away from the Lempuyangan railway station. Across the flyover, there is a narrow-paved area next to the railway crossbar; every afternoon this area is full of small children accompanied by their parents excitedly waiting to see the trains pass. Knowing that many kids often spend their free time there, street food sellers and *odong-odong* (kiddie ride) renters flock to the area. It therefore functions as a self-organized, spontaneous public playground in a city with a shortage of accessible public spaces.

The space under the Lempuyangan flyover is now popularly known as *taman mural* (mural park), due to a city mural project called Sama-Sama initiated in 2002 by one of the most important street art collectives in Indonesia, Apotik Komik (Comic Pharmacy).[3] Apotik Komik was founded in 1997 with the mission of encouraging the democratization of public spaces, particularly with enhanced freedom of speech in the *Reformasi* era, and to connect artists' work with wider society. In the Sama-Sama mural project, members of Apotik Komik painted murals on several walls of the city's public infrastructure, including the Lempuyangan flyover. As is evident in the photography archives from the mural project, the south end to the north end of the flyover was filled with murals. Nano Warsono's colorful mural on one of the flyover beams, depicting a man with big muscles above a playground with rollercoasters ridden by two grotesque clowns, is most eye-catching. The mural portrayed a fun yet frightening situation of children running and playing around the railway.

The Sama-Sama mural project was grand, supported by the regency government under the leadership of Herry Zudianto. The murals on the Lempuyangan flyover were untouched by new murals for around six years. Apotik Komik disbanded in 2006, but one of its former members, Samuel Indratma, continued his art activism through the Jogja Mural Forum (JMF). Again with support from the local regency government, Indratma collaborated with traditional artists such as *pelukis kaca* (glass

---

3   *"Sama-sama"* means 'together', although it also means 'you're welcome' to reply when someone says thank you.

painters) and *pelukis kelir* (painters of background screens for *ketoprak* performances) to repaint the murals on the walls of Lempuyangan flyover. With the dominant figures of the Javanese *wayang* story, the overall character of the murals is a visual combination of traditional folk narratives and the ornamentation of urban streets. JMF's initiative is noteworthy for its engagement with traditional artists, who are often marginalized by the dominance of the city's contemporary and cosmopolitan art scene. The involvement of traditional artists in the mural project has lifted the cultural narratives of the *kampung urban* (urban kampong) in Yogyakarta and reflects the conflicting process of modernization with traditional ways of life (Murti, 2001).

The murals on the Lempuyangan flyover bring the cultural history of Yogyakarta to the surface of Yogyakarta's highly urbanized infrastructure. The project also seems to support the agenda of the city's mayor to use murals to communicate the visual identity of Yogyakarta. The eclectic visual outcome has made it quite a popular tourist destination. Tourists and passers-by frequently take selfies in front of the vivid mural background. Many travel magazines have reviewed the Lempuyangan flyover as one of the tourist spots in *"Jogja Kota Mural"* (Yogyakarta, City of Murals). The predicate "City of Murals" is inseparable from the efforts of Apotik Komik and JMF to democratize street art and make it accessible to the public. Since the Sama-Sama project, young street artists have flourished in the city. Apotik Komik also expanded its project by giving workshops to schools and kampongs on how to make murals in their neighborhood. In a reflection on Apotik Komik's projects, anthropologist and member of Apotik Komik Ade Tanesia wrote that she hoped the murals could be "a signifier that stands long enough in order to make them (the society) feel proud of themselves" (Tanesia, 2004: 16).

Pride renders the idea of "personalized urban citizenship," where street art becomes a democratic venue for citizens to claim their belonging to "my city" or "our city" (Lee, 2013: 307). However, the pride of (collective) identity has also become a subject of competing territorial claims to the public space, as illustrated by the August 2017 incident in which one of Lempuyangan flyover's murals was painted over with a logo of the football club Persatuan Sepak Bola Indonesia Mataram (PSIM—Indonesia Football Association of Mataram). Obviously, the football team is a source of pride for its fans, known as "Blue Soldiers." The column was also the location where Nano Warsono painted his mural in 2002. The painted-over mural was made by the senior glass painter Subandi Giyanto (born 1958). It depicts Petruk, Bagong, and Bilung, characters of Panakawan (servant characters in *wayang* stories), in the middle of trading a wad of dollars for a globe that highlights Indonesia. A sentence in the upper part of the Panakawan scene reads *"Aja Adol Negara"* (Don't sell your country), the message conveyed in the mural (see Figure 2.1).

Figure 2.1. Left: *Giyanto's* mural in original condition, Right: Giyanto's mural painted over by PSIM's Blue Soldiers. Credit: Subandi Giyanto.

Giyanto's mural had been left undisturbed for about ten years before the Blue Soldiers painted it over. Giyanto expressed disappointment on his Facebook page, complaining that it was "proof that the youths never respect the elders." He also downheartedly asked, "why didn't they (Blue Soldiers) fix it (his mural) ... knowing how Samuel Indratma and his friends had already worked really hard to ask the department of tourism and culture to make Yogya more beautiful through mural with a sense of traditional art?"[4]

It is important to not reduce the Blue Soldiers' mural to simple vandalism. The definition of vandalism, like beauty, is a matter of perspective. Vandalism can be loosely defined as the deliberate destruction of property without permission from the owner. In the case of murals in public space, the ownership is rather ambiguous. Vandalism is also often regarded as the negative behavior of youth, but it can also be an ideological act to convey a political message.

Competition to paint over murals and graffiti in the public space, or *tumplak tablek* in Javanese, is part of the nature of street art. Informal rules over the ethics of *tumplak tablek* vary in different territories, but temporariness is a primary characteristic of street art. This culture of *tumplak tablek* seems unacceptable from the point of view of Giyanto, who legitimized his "ownership" of the space based on receiving governmental approval to paint it. Giyanto's logic is similar to Tanesia's, which regards Apotik Komik's mural project as a "long-enough signifier" for the city. The majority of people who responded to Giyanto's Facebook post seemed to agree that his mural should be preserved because it has a high aesthetic quality and conveyed an important historical value of the city.

Most people, be they street artists, from the government, or ordinary citizens, seem to agree that everyone has a right to experience beauty in the city (Lee, 2013: 324). But what kind of beauty is it, and who owns it? The construction of beauty is always a subjective matter, but in that construction, we may learn about the dominant power relations at play. Several layers of power relations can be unpacked in the controversy of the mural site of the Lempuyangan flyover.

The first is related to the clash of identity politics that operate in urban spaces. People who defended Giyanto's position that his mural should be preserved treated the piece as an iconic symbol of Yogyakarta's identity,

---

4   Subandi Giyanto's Facebook page on August 22, 2017 (accessed October 30, 2017).

affirming the government's stance. Indeed, the fact that it remained undisturbed for almost ten years means that most people, or "the public," received the reflection of the city's identity conveyed by Giyanto's traditionalist mural. In this regard, Giyanto's mural represents a kind of nationalist urbanism that emerged in the post-*Reformasi* era (Kusno, 2009). It works as a landscape of power, or an aesthetic regime, attempting to represent the city in a unifying image or common value. The street art of the football fans can also be interpreted as the construction of a regional identity, a source of collective pride for the fan club (Fuller, 2014). The discourse of collective and nationalist urban identity in the Giyanto and Blue Soldiers murals operates in the same logic of imagined community. (Indeed, the naming of PSIM as Yogyakarta's football team revives the glorified history of Yogyakarta as the capital of the Mataram Kingdom. The Blue Soldiers logo of PSIM states the year of its establishment as 1929, implying that the existence of the club also has a long history). The mural also marks a territorial claim of the Blue Soldiers in a kampong near the Lempuyangan flyover named Klitren.

Both Giyanto's and the Blue Soldiers' murals stake identity claims over the Lempuyangan flyover. On the one hand, the identity conveyed in Giyanto's Panakawan mural needs to be treated cautiously, as it can reinforce the essentialist view of Yogyakarta's cultural identity. When Giyanto questions why his mural was painted over rather than repaired, he reveals that he is thinking in the problematic logic of cultural heritage preservation, which clashes with the nature of street art in the public space. On the other hand, the Blue Soldiers' mural is also vexing because it is well-known that the fan club often uses violence in expressing their love of their favorite football team. PSIM supporters are often negatively associated as troublemaker youths who like to provoke street battles (Fuller, 2014: 112). The Blue Soldiers' mural is huge, and it certainly took time to create; it is not just spontaneous vandalism, but rather a well-organized act. According to one street artist, it is common knowledge that PSIM supporters will perpetrate violent retribution on anyone who dares to destruct their murals.[5] This widely held belief coupled with the fact that no one stopped the Blue Soldiers from painting over Giyanto's mural could indicate that people were too afraid of them. The Blue Soldiers' mural on the Lempuyangan flyover is one of many by the group spread out across areas of PSIM support, which represent territorial, as much as identity, claims in the city.

While the Blue Soldiers secure their territory with threats and violence, Giyanto was looking for security from a government patron. Both examples reveal the problematic patron-client relationship in Yogyakarta's street art practice. As briefly mentioned above, Apotik Komik and JMF depended on the government's patronage to widen the practice of street art among Yogyakarta citizens. The scale of activity and support from the local government amplified Apotik Komik's art activism such that it had a significant impact on people's enthusiastic support of mural art. Apotik Komik's mural projects of the early 2000s not only attempted to offer art works in public spaces, but also involved people in the creation of the urban landscape. Painting murals became not only a means for a community to communicate to the wider public, but also a meeting place for dialogue and negotiations among the community itself to determine the most representative mural that could articulate their collective identity.

Through analysis of this process, one can expose the dominant norms in the society. For example, Ade Tanesia noted that during Apotik Komik's workshops, participants expressed concern, asking whether the project had permission from the government, although the project took place in what should be considered a "public space." Some also worried about any political connotations in the mural, not wanting to spark conflict with the authorities (Tanesia, 2004: 14). Apotik Komik's successful approach to engaging the kampong communities went relatively smoothly because it had already secured official permission. Nevertheless, as Tanesia reflected, people's anxiety about participating in the creation of the urban landscape attests to the difficulties of overcoming conformity to the dominant and centralized norms of the New Order regime.

---

5   Interview with Anti-Tank, October 13, 2017.

The close cooperation between street artists and the government has been criticized by some researchers who argue that the partnership can lead to the normalization and de-politicization of street art. Barry (2008) and Indriyati (2011) make use of Benedict Anderson's concept (2000) of *kramanisasi*[6] or *penghalusan* (euphemism) to assert that the development of street art in Yogyakarta is losing its criticality because street artists are merely serving the interests of the government to "beautify" and decorate the city. Nowadays many murals are painted on kampong street walls by kampong inhabitants. Yet, the claim that murals have created a democratic venue needs to be interrogated, because most of the murals convey normative and moralist messages, such as "Keep your kampong clean" or "beware of drugs." As an example, in 2009 the Yogyakarta City government cooperated with the military to organize a mural competition titled Jogja Wall Nation with the theme "Spirit of the Great Commander Sudirman." The sponsor and the theme of the event are obviously rendering the process of *kramanisasi* in street art.

Under the patronage of government officials there is less space for street art projects to deliver sharp criticism about social and political conditions, and particularly to criticize the government. At best, they might only convey normative public service messages affirmed by the government. The socio-political content of Giyanto's mural is quite normative. Creating street art with the permission and financial backing of the government is problematic because official power is used to dominate a space, which carries the real danger of reinforcing existing power dynamics, thus stabilizing an otherwise unhindered dynamism of the urban landscape in favor of supporting state narratives. Within the context of urban spatial ordering, it is "attempts to establish spatial relations that encourage social relations and forms of behaviour, which are meant to be repeatable, predictable and compatible with taxonomy of the necessary social roles" (Stavrides, 2015: 9). *Kramanisasi* therefore does not work through any act of censorship, but rather by subtly normalizing the politics of street art in

---

6   *Krama* in "*kramanisasi*" is a Javanese term for a fine language, hierarchically, in contrast to *ngoko* (a low language, often connoted as a rude language).

support of the status quo. In the case of Giyanto and other mural artists of the Lempuyangan flyover project, the *kramanisasi* of street art is revealed through the glorification of the romanticized heroic and archaic past to decorate the city in line with the government's agenda to boost the city's tourism industry. The project was an aesthetic regime for almost a decade before PSIM supporters shifted the power balance. While the murals of PSIM might not be a better form of aesthetic practice, their existence is useful to unpack the hidden power relations at the Lempuyangan flyover site.

In the next site, we will see how the government uses street art to seemingly promote its supposed agenda of cleanliness, order, and beauty while selling the street walls to capitalist corporations.

Kewek Bridge: Clash of Purple and White

Kewek Bridge functions as a railway bridge close to Yogyakarta's main train station as well as a highway bridge that connects the area of Malioboro and Kotabaru. Malioboro is the most popular tourist destination of the city and Malioboro Street is always crowded on the weekend. Kotabaru is known for its many colonial buildings and has been registered as a cultural heritage area since 2011.[7] The traffic in this area increases during holiday seasons due to a flood of visitors.

The mural by the famous Indonesian poet Chairil Anwar, made by Sanggar Bambu in 2011, is still etched in the memories of the many people who often pass under the Kewek Bridge, including me. The mural carried a quotation from Anwar's poem *Sia-Sia* (Wasted, 1943), that reads "*Mampus kau dikoyak-koyak sepi*" (Loneliness would kill you mercilessly). Driving under the bridge at night, the mural created a poetic experience—the city lights felt dimmer, as if time was frozen for a moment.

The mural lasted for around two years, until Kewek Bridge became a site of political contestation in 2013. First, AXIS, a provider of cellular

---

7   Keputusan Gubernur DIY (Decree of Yogyakarta Governor) No 186/KEP/2011 on August 15, 2011.

service, painted over the existing mural with an advertisement with official permission from the regency government. AXIS covered the entire wall of Kewek Bridge purple, its corporate color. The advertisement depicted four figures of the Panakawan on a tandem bike (Figure 2.2.). The rear rider held a mobile phone in his hand; certainly, he used AXIS as his provider. On the left corner of the wall, the slogan *Sego Segawe* (Sepeda Kanggo Sekolah lan Nyambut Gawe—Bicycling to School and Work) referenced a program initiated by Mayor Herry Zudianto. When Zudianto's successor, Haryadi Suyuti, took the leadership in 2011, he suddenly stopped Zudianto's car-free day program, which was a setback to the spirit of bicycling promoted by the previous government.[8] It was ironic, then, to see AXIS appropriating Sego Segawe for their advertisement, knowing that Suyuti's government, which gave the corporation permission to use the Kewek Bridge, was implementing policies against the environment-friendly spirit of Sego Segawe.

Figure 2.2. The AXIS mural on the Kewek Bridge wall. Credit: Elanto Wijoyono, from his personal blog https://elantowow.wordpress.com/2013/03/01/serangan-oemoem-1-maret-rebut-kembali-jembatan-kewek/kewek-1/.

---

8   Surat Edaran (Form Letter) No. 645/57/SE/2012 on September 7, 2012. According to Suyuti (then the Mayor of Yogyakarta City), he issued the new policy because the car-free day program had caused many cars to park in front of the city hall (*Tribun Jogja*, 2012).

The co-optation of street art by commercial companies to promote their products has been going on for some time. Since the second half of 2000, many cigarette companies and cellular service providers have been sponsoring subculture music and arts festivals to promote their products to urban youth. Street art is one of the most featured elements of this youth marketing strategy. The AXIS mural was painted by a popular street artist in the city and stirred a debate among the local street artists about the ethics of street art practice. Indeed, the interaction between capitalism and subculture in urban settings is a global phenomenon (Florida, 2002; Arvidsson, 2007). When co-opted by a profit-driven actor, street art that perhaps sought to challenge a specific system, authority, or way of thinking is reduced to an instrument of money-making. While *kramanisasi* tames street art politics into repeatable and predictable social forms, capitalist commodification turns the ideology of street art rebellion into merely a cool lifestyle. The alliance between the creativity imagined by capitalism and the "ideology" of underground culture, is what Thomas Frank (1997) called "the conquest of the cool." In the realm of urban spatial ordering, the state and capital are conquering the public space through dominant and repressive modes of art for their own political and commercial interests. However, Kewek Bridge did not remain uncontested as a site of politics.

One month after AXIS's mural appeared on the Kewek Bridge, hundreds of people from biker and street art networks gathered at the underpass to protest against the vulgar purple advertisement. They insisted that Kewek's wall be returned to the public. The protest was a notable performative action in that together they painted over the AXIS mural with white paint, resetting the bridge wall as a blank canvas (Figure 2.3.). The event occurred on the anniversary of the Serangan Umum 1 Maret 1949 (the General Offensive of March 1, 1949). The date was deliberately chosen by the protesters to invigorate the revolutionary spirit of their actions. The press release from the protest stated, *"Putihkan Kewek* (Make Kewek white again), preserve our cultural heritage for the society, free Yogyakarta from the commercialization and privatization of public space." Two spokespersons of the protest, urban activists Yoan Vallone and Elanto

Wijoyono, argued that Kewek Bridge is a national cultural heritage site that needs to be protected from destructive commercial agendas. Wijono affirmed that Kewek Bridge, which was built during the Dutch occupation, had already been listed on the register of Potential Heritage issued by Yogyakarta's Government Tourism and Culture Office in 2011.

Figure 2.3. Street artists and bikers painting the Kewek Bridge walls white. Credit: Anti-Tank.

Although the actions of the protesters could be considered politically radical and aesthetically salient, the rhetoric they employed—of the need to conserve Kewek Bridge because of its cultural heritage background—risked replicating the logic of colonial conquest. This logic regards cultural sites or objects as static artefacts that need to be preserved. The sites become a means of glorifying a particular narrative of the past while neglecting and marginalizing the narratives of daily life that happen around them. It is a colonial epistemic mode that disconnects the past from the present. The philosopher of post-colonialism Gayatri Spivak (1988: 291) warned of the romantic tendency of post-colonial society to preserve its "heritage" because, "a nostalgia for lost origins can be detrimental to the exploration of social realities within the critique of imperialism". We need to expand our understanding of imperialism not only as a colonial history, but also as a present-day system imposed by those who wield dominant power in policing and ordering the urban landscape.

It is important to note that the identification of Kotabaru as a heritage area aligns with the government's attempt to promote the area as a tourist attraction. The spatial classification of Kotabaru as a historical area will most likely act as a pretext to guarantee that the site will continue to produce social and spatial relations that serve to reproduce the interests of the state and capital. In the view of the government, the tourism industry contributes to the growth of the local economy, which is indeed true to a certain extent. However, the fundamental problem with this view is that it defines, indeed reduces, social-spatial bonds between humans and the city to economic transactions alone, limiting participation in politics to only those that are considered profitable in economic terms.

At the Kewek Bridge, purple represents "the private" and white represents "the public." In order to dismantle these two competing "colors", it is useful to draw on Stavrides's critical notion of private and public space. According to Stavrides, a public space is owned by a particular authority (local, regional, or state), which controls the order of that space by applying some rules for people who want to access it. Meanwhile, a private space is owned and controlled by an individual or economic entity with rights to establish the conditions under which people can use it (Stavrides, 2015: 11). In this analysis, the order of both public and private spaces is controlled by a dominant authority, not through equal and dynamic power relations. On the one hand, the action taken by the protesters to "make Kewek white again" is an apt intervention to AXIS's aesthetic regime. On the other hand, the cultural heritage argument used by the protestors to justify the action is troublesome, because it asks to return the ownership of Kewek to the state, not the public. The protest is a call to control commercial power, but it does not question state power, and therefore fails to fundamentally reconfigure the relationships that determine the order of the space.

Instead of considering the Kewek Bridge walls as a public space, we should value them as a common space. Common space, as defined by

Harvey (2012: 73), is constructed by "an unstable and malleable social relation between a particular self-defined social group and those aspects of its actually existing or yet-to-be-created social and/or physical environment deemed crucial to its life and livelihood." Hence, common space is defined through self-organized rules and dynamic power relations among those who are attached to the space. In this way, we may redraw the line between "the purple," or the private, and "the white," or the public, to transform the dominant power relations.

To establish a balanced critique of the protest action, I would argue that the biker and street artist community involved in the protest failed to acknowledge the socio-spatial relationship between Kewek Bridge and people who live around it. Beyond that, their action should be appreciated because the Putihkan Kewek protesters were successful in deflecting the commercialization of Kewek Bridge walls. Since the protest, street artists have mainly used the Kewek Bridge wall to voice social and political problems in the city. This pattern is new and attests to the success of the Putihkan Kewek movement to raise political awareness among street artists to use public spaces as the sites of politics that they are.

In October 2014, Kewek Bridge's white walls were "dirtied" by Warga Berdaya (Empowered Citizens) street artists with murals conveying message from "*Jogja Asat*" (Dried Jogja) movement.[9] The mural expressed their critique of the massive development of hotels in Yogyakarta since the Suyuti administration came to power. Indeed, Yogyakarta is facing rapid urban development, with the number of hotels and apartments increasing at a rapid pace. Skyscrapers are now a common sight in Yogyakarta, not to mention the seven new mega malls built during the last five years. The massive infrastructure development in Yogyakarta aligns with a larger

---

9   Jogja Asat began as a movement in August 2014. It was initiated by residents of the Miliran area who live in the neighborhood near Fave Hotel on Kusumanegara Street. The hotel development has caused many wells in that area to run dry. A Miliran resident, Dodok Putra Bangsa, took a shower with sand in front of the hotel to symbolize his protest of the environmental problems that the hotel development had caused. After this event, Jogja Asat came to refer to the common struggle organized by residents in other parts of the city who share similar problems. For more detailed narratives on the problem of hotel development in Yogyakarta as well as the struggle of Yogyakarta residents, see the comprehensive report by online media, *Tirto* (2017).

national agenda, which aims to push ten big cities in Indonesia towards the standard of "global city" in order to facilitate the "event industry" or MICE-based tourism (Meeting, Incentives, Conferences, and Events). Yogyakarta, like many other large cities in the world,[10] has become an engine of capital accumulation.

The visual and textual textures of the Jogja Asat mural which filled Kewek Bridge's walls were heterogeneous. The dominant color of white was maintained as a backdrop for the monochromatic mural, which was accentuated here and there with touches of red and orange. A realist mural depicts farmers protecting their land, accompanied by a poetic yet radical message that reads, *"Tanahmu adalah nyanyian kering tentang keabadian. Hotelmu adalah misteri kebisuan semesta!"* (Your land is a dry song about immortality. Your hotel is the mystery of the universe's silence!). The visual character of other murals aligns with the vocabulary of global street art and is accompanied by sharp and witty remarks such as, *"Ojo nyembah duit!"* (Don't worship money!), *"Rungokno, Har!*[11]*"* (Listen, Har!) and *"Miliran Sumure Asat Dicolong Hotel Fave*[12]*"* (Wells in Miliran run out of water because Hotel Fave robs it). Less than 24 hours after the murals were completed, the local state apparatus immediately censored some parts of them, specifically painting over criticisms of Haryadi with grey paint.

Here, we need to distinguish censorship by the state apparatus and the *tumplak tablek* culture practiced among street artists. Censorship is the suppression of speech or public communication. It is an abuse of power driven by fear and anger because a dominant authority is being challenged. At the same time, *tumplak tablek* is also a practice based on the exercise of power; but, it is based on the aspiration to share and redistribute the ownership of a common space. Indeed, the censorship of the Kewek Bridge was a threat to freedom of speech; however, the community of street artists in Yogyakarta remains resilient and proves that they are not afraid. Until now, Kewek Bridge still functions as a site of politics, in which different circuits of power intersect dynamically to express their voices.

---

10 See Harvey (2012) for a thorough analysis of the city as the center of capital accumulation, as well as utopian thinking about the revolutionary struggles of urban movements.

11 Har, is the short nick name for Haryadi Suyuti.

12 The name of the hotel they protested.

An Abandoned Building: A Collage of Power Relations

The last site of politics discussed in this chapter exposes a collage of power relations among different actors in Yogyakarta and reflects the competing "high tension" visualities of their aesthetic modes of existence. The site was the location of a censored mural, a year before the Jogja Asat movement became widespread. The mural was on an abandoned building at the corner of Pojok Beteng (Jokteng) Wetan, near the *kraton* area. In October 2013, on the night of the anniversary of Yogyakarta city, the local state apparatus, Satuan Polisi Pamong Praja (Satpol PP—Civil Service Police Unit) arrested a 17-year-old biker and street artist, Muhammad Arif Buwono, while he was highlighting the mural on the upper side of the building that read "*Jogja Ora Didol*" (Yogyakarta is not for sale, see Figure 2.4.). The mural had been painted by a group of street artists a few hours before, and Arif thought that the writing did not look very clear, so he decided to repaint it to make the message more visible. The Satpol PP team arrived and threatened to shoot him.

Figure 2.4. The Jogja Ora Didol mural on the abandoned building in Jokteng Wetan.
Credit: Selamatkan Bumi.

The criminal law against street art is rarely enforced in Yogyakarta, especially since the government gave an official permit to the Sama-Sama mural project in 2002. In many cases, street artists escape the law by bribing policemen with a relatively small amount of money (Indriyati, 2011:73). Arif's trial was the first time a street artist was tried in a court of law. He was charged with violating the *Peraturan Daerah tentang Pengelolaan Kebersihan* (Local Regulation about Hygienic Management),[13] although it is obvious that his arrest was an attempt to shut down the explicit political message of the mural. After Arif was arrested, the state apparatus immediately covered the Jogja Ora Didol mural with black paint. They allowed other murals and graffiti on the abandoned building to remain as they were, signaling that they only worried about the Jogja Ora Didol message. In the following months, despite more raids by Satpol PP, the message of Jogja Ora Didol continued to spread throughout the corners of the city.[14]

Government censorship of street art is one thing, but sporadic, unorganized censorship by unknown parties is quite another. Such is the case of a poster that read *"Ketuhanan yang Maha Ormas"* (Belief in the One and Only Ormas, a wordplay on the first principle of Pancasila) made by the street artist Anti-Tank. Since early 2017, Anti-Tank has put this poster on many walls in the city. The poster was his response to the growing intolerance and violent actions of Islamists based on *organisasi masyarakat* (*ormas*—mass organization), which rose sharply in Indonesia after the *Reformasi* era. Evidently this poster was made not so long after the controversial 212 protest in Jakarta. The words of Anti-Tank's poster were painted over with green on the abandoned building that we are currently discussing. In other places, the posters were painted over with black or destroyed with sharp objects (see Figure 2.5.). In my interview, Anti-Tank mentioned that one of his friends had witnessed a sewer cleaner trying to peel off the poster when he was sweeping the street early in the morning.

---

13 After the trial, Arif Buwono was sentenced to seven days in prison and a probationary period of 14 days. He also had to pay a penalty amounting to IDR 100,000, which is the equivalent of what one pays to park their motorbike in Yogyakarta (Kompas, 2013).

14 Interview with Anti-Tank, October 13, 2017.

It was possibly a spontaneous act by an individual who disagreed with the poster's message. On another occasion, another friend saw a group of four people painting over the poster with black paint at noon on a busy road, equipped with a ladder to reach the posters, which were placed high on an advertisement pole.[15] The different types of "censorship" against this politically sensitive poster make it difficult to conclude who took such actions and what their motivations or ideologies were.

Figure 2.5. Censorship of Anti-Tank's poster in several locations. Credit left to right: Brigitta Isabella (left) and Anti-Tank (center and right).

Over the past seven years, I have passed the abandoned building in Jokteng Wetan almost three times a week because it is on the route to my office. The traffic in that area is increasingly frustrating for people who use the road, but the traffic congestion, at the same time, slows us down and provides a chance to carefully observe that grungy building. According to a street artist friend, the abandoned building has been used as a street art wall since early 2000.[16] This site has the "messiest" landscape of the sites explored in this chapter, and conveys the most dynamic street art compared to other locations in the city. By street art, I mean murals and graffiti—be they political or entertaining, a commercial advertisement or part of

---

15   Ibid.
16   Personal correspondence with Prihatmoko Moki, October 12, 2017

a political party's campaign, *organisasi kemasyarakatan* (ormas—societal organization) banners or other. Some would regard it as *sampah visual* (visual garbage), but for me these various modes of being deserve close scrutiny.

Traces of the visual competition among different actors cover the abandoned building. It looks dirty and alluring at the same time. A short fence, approximately one meter high, encloses the building, so it is easy to jump on to its terrace. Occasionally banners were installed on the fence. Reading the messages on the banners, one could get updates on the most current issues that fundamentalist groups were dealing with. Banners that I have documented include anti-LGBT messages, a claim of blasphemy for saying Merry Christmas, and a condemnation of communism; all made and installed by anonymous parties (see Figure 2.6.). In front of the building, a flag of Gerakan Pemuda Ka'bah (GPK—Kabah Youth Movement), the Partai Persatuan Pembangunan (PPP—United Development Party)'s youth wing, hangs on a pole. The GPK is known for its aggressive and intolerant violent acts and its members occasionally install banners on the building's fence. The messages of the banners are visual manifestations of the current state of freedom of religion or belief, which is threatened by non-state actors. Indeed, according to research published by the Setara Institute for Democracy and Peace in 2017, Yogyakarta had a high number of intolerance cases during 2013–2016. They include the forced termination of a transgender *pesantren* (Islamic boarding school), the forced termination of the screening of films on the 1965 tragedy, a lawsuit against the construction of a Christian religious site, and the cancellation of a Wiji Thukul-themed art exhibition.

Figure 2.6. Banners with intolerant messages in front of the abandoned building.
Credit: Brigitta Isabella.

While murals and graffiti made by street artists on the abandoned building are constantly changed at a rapid pace, the banners with intolerant messages, as far as I have observed, have never been contested. Two visual authorities that street artists have not dared to challenge are football supporters and intolerant Islamic *ormas*. There is indeed a close yet complex organizational link between football fan clubs and *ormas* in Yogyakarta. The PSIM supporters' club, Brajamusti, has a strong bond with the GPK and the PPP. However, as football researcher Andy Fuller observed, the connection is rather curious, because Brajamusti members, who are largely urban poor youth often involved in street battles, rarely show overt displays of piety (Fuller, 2014: 107). Another link that can be made between Brajamusti and the GPK is that both groups use violence and suppression to claim their space on the walls of Yogyakarta. Anti-Tank recounts several cases in which Brajamusti members intimidated anyone who dared to paint over their murals. This violent aesthetic mode of existence in public space illustrates the emergence of mass leaders, violent groups, and local bosses that become new centers of power following the loosening power of the central government's authority in the post-*Reformasi* era (Okamoto and Rozaki, 2006). These new patronage networks monopolize public space with violence, and their abuse of power is detected when the landscape becomes stagnant.

Nevertheless, the voices of political Islam in Yogyakarta, as everywhere else, is not singular. The *Reformasi* era enabled the emergence of a multi-dimensional politics of Islam. Its complex existence can be sensed through popular culture, as Ariel Heryanto (2015) asserts. We can also witness this in the heterogenous visual materials in the city that present narratives of Islam. For example, since 2011 the Jogokaryan Mosque, located in the southern area of Yogyakarta not far from the abandoned building in Jokteng Wetan, has organized an annual Islamic mural competition during the month of Ramadhan. The Jogokaryan Mosque is known as the base of Muhammadiyah followers. The organizer of this competition said he wanted to demonstrate to the youth that "mural(s) can be used for a good cause, including dakwah (Islamic preaching)" (*Harian Jogja*, 2011). None of the winners' murals convey conservative or intolerant messages (see Figure 2.7.). Most of the content celebrates the feast of Ramadhan in Jogokaryan kampong, and although the murals might look insipid, the competition encourages the kampong dwellers' participation in the making of their neighborhood landscape and in countering the narratives of Islamic militant *ormas* that have dominated the area. The street art posters of Gus Dur wearing a hipster shirt and a "Turn Back Peace" cap made by Anti-Tank must also be mentioned, as they have also enriched the multiple images of Islam in the Yogyakarta urban landscape (Figure 2.8.). These posters still appear in many places and no one seems to dare to damage them. Further research on the relationship between Islam and street art is necessary, but beyond the scope of this chapter.

Figure 2.7. The first winner of Jogokaryan Mosque's mural competition in 2012. Credit: Brigitta Isabella.

Figure 2.8. Anti-Tank's poster of Gus Dur in several locations in Yogyakarta. Credit: Anti-Tank.

The visual order and chaos of the abandoned building near Jokteng Wetan can be regarded as a collage of complex power relations among different actors in the city. The building accommodates a dynamic, high tensioned landscape and is a site of politics that marks the on-going formation of the public sphere, which thrives on conflict and negotiation.

Practices of spatial classification and hierarchy are always imposed by those with dominant power, but at least the building remains a common space for collective aesthetic experiments and creates a self-regulatory system that interacts with urban reality. However, since September 2017—when this chapter was written—a mid-size yellow banner appeared announcing that the building is for rent. The banner signals that the fate of the abandoned building will soon be transformed. I contacted the phone number on the banner and pretended to be a prospective tenant. The woman who answered my call said that the rent price of the building is IDR 750 million per year (~USD 52,000), with a minimum tenancy of ten years. The price is of course beyond my working-class imagination, but attests to the quickly rising property values in Yogyakarta. I also asked the owner about the building's history. Interestingly, she said the building was once a Dutch hospital and later, for a long time, functioned as a storage warehouse of an asbestos factory. The building has been empty for at least four years and the owner said that she is upset, but could not bother with the chaotic street art on the façade of the building because "it is too expensive to clean it."[17]

While we have no clue of the building's future, certainly the next tenant will be someone with a large amount of capital. We do not know the new function of the abandoned building or its effect on the lively social processes that have been unfolding at the site. This may create anxiety, but also optimism, because, after all, street art is always a matter of survival and endurance in the situated urban context. It is important to ensure that street art does not only re-appropriate small pieces of available spaces just to exist. Street art practice as a social movement needs to reclaim as well as redistribute power in the ownership of common space, and give form to a de-centering and re-centering dialectic that keeps the urban landscape moving.

---

17 Personal correspondence with the owner, October 14, 2017.

Spatial Politics in Yogyakarta's Urban Landscape

The spatial memories of the three sites of politics discussed in this chapter show the most visible signs of how the loosening power of the state-centered authority in the post-*Reformasi* era has enabled a new politics of aesthetics to emerge that expands the participation of society in a democratic public space. Power relations in the formation of urban landscape encompass not only street artists, but also various modes of existence practiced by different actors. Acknowledging this is useful to capture the mood of the masses in post-*Reformasi* democracy. In the case of Lempuyangan's street walls, I show that the *kramanisasi* of street art, where mural projects were only able to maintain dominant social norms in society, tamed the potential of visual-political intervention through the medium of street art. In the case of Kewek Bridge, where social opposition arose to the commercialization of the city's landscape, I argue for rethinking the notion of public space and advocate for distributing power through the concept of common space. Finally, in the case of the abandoned building in Jokteng Wetan, I identify the precariousness of claiming visibility in common space, and the violent censorship practiced by a new network of patronage that has monopolized the spatial politics of street walls.

City street walls constitute a space and a screen for different technologies of the self to exist. The *tumplak tablek* culture and the self-regulatory systems of distributing common space in street art practice have the potential to serve as an experimental medium for practicing democracy. Perusing the street culture two decades after *Reformasi*, we see that censorship of public space is not exercised only by the State, but also by large capitalist companies and local thugs and bosses. More often than not, these actors work together to commodify and monopolize the public space, stifling the dynamics of the urban landscape. At the same time, this chapter has also highlighted cases of meaningful and forceful demands by citizens to reclaim their right to common spaces in the city.

The city is like a collective work of art in the making. The definitions of beauty, cleanliness, and order are part of the on-going project of urbanity.

In the context of the formation of landscape, one of the challenges of urban social movement in Yogyakarta is to ensure that common space should not only be made by secluded communities of street artists in isolated pockets. The activism of Apotik Komik in early 2000 demonstrates the possibility of bringing street art closer to wider swathes of society. However, the relationship of street artists with the government has proven to be problematic because it eventually normalizes the politics of street art. The challenge of today's urban spatial politics is not for government reforms to preserve public spaces for us, but to configure democratic self-regulatory principles and procedures in determining the co-ownership of common spaces.

References

Arvidsson, Adam. 2007. "Creative Class or Administrative Class? On Advertising and the 'Underground'" *Ephemera* 7 (1): 8–23.

Barry, Syamsul. 2008. *Jalan Seni Jalanan Yogyakarta*. Yogyakarta: Penerbit Studium.

Bender, Barbara (ed.). 1993. *Landscape, Politics and Perspectives*. Oxford: Berg.

Florida, Richard. 2002. *The Rise of the Creative Class*. New York: Basic Books.

Frank, Thomas. 1997. *The Conquest of Cool*. Chicago: University of Chicago Press.

Fuller, Andy. 2014. *The Struggle for Soccer in Indonesia, Fandom, Archives and Urban Identity*. Yogyakarta: Tan Kinira Books and Bawah Skor Press.

Harian Jogja. 2011. "Masjid Jogokariyan Gelar Lomba Mural Religi." July 11, 2011. http://www.harianjogja.com/baca/2011/07/11/masjid-jogokariyan-gelar-lomba-mural-religi-147595 (accessed October 30, 2017).

Harvey, David. 1973. *Social Justice and the City*. Maryland: The John Hopkins University Press.

_____. 2012. *Rebel Cities*. London: Verso.

Heryanto, Ariel. 2015. *Identitas dan Kenikmatan*. Gramedia: Jakarta.

Indriyati, Rias Fitriana. 2011. *Politik dan Graffiti*. Yogyakarta: PolGov.

Kompas. 2013. "Tebalkan Tulisan "Jogja Ora Didol", Arif Divonis 7 Hari". October 10, 2010. http://regional.kompas.com/read/2013/10/10/2038286/Tebalkan.Tulisan.Jogja.Ora.Didol.Arif.Divonis.7.Hari (accessed October 30, 2017).

Kusno, Abidin. 2009. *Ruang Publik, Identitas dan Memori Kolektif: Jakarta Pasca-Suharto*. Yogyakarta: Penerbit Ombak.

Lee, Doreen. 2013. "'Anybody Can Do It': Aesthetic Empowerment, Urban Citizenship, and the Naturalization of Indonesian Graffiti and Street Art". *City and Society* 23 (3): 304–327.

Murti, Yoshi Fajar Kresno. 2011. "'Babad Kampung' from Yogyakarta: Unfinished Story of Contesting Identities and Creating Negotiation Space on the History of Urban Development". In *Kampung Perkotaan Indonesia: Kajian Historis-Antropologis atas Kesenjangan Sosial dan Ruang Kota*, edited by La Ode Rabani. Yogyakarta: Penerbit New Elmatera.

Okamoto Masaaki and Abdur Rozaki (eds). 2006. *Kelompok Kekerasan dan Bos Lokal di Era Reformasi*. Yogyakarta: Center for Southeast Asian Studies (CSEAS), Kyoto University and IRE Press.

Rancière, Jacques. 2004. *The Politics of Aesthetics: The Distribution of the Sensible*. London: Bloomsbury.

Spivak, Gayatri Chakravorty. 1988. "Can the Subaltern Speak?" In *Marxism and the Interpretation of Culture*, edited by C. Nelson and L. Grossberg, pp. 271-313. Basingstoke: Macmillan Education.

Stavrides, Stavros. 2015. "Common Space as Threshold: Urban Commoning in Struggles to Re-appropriate Public Space." *Footprint* 9 (16):9–20.

Tanesia, Ade. 2004. "Proses Sosial dalam Praktek Seni di Ruang Publik". *Jurnal Karbon* 6 (4): 10–23.

Tirto. 2017. "Risiko dan Nasib Buruk Pembangunan Hotel di Yogyakarta." July 10, 2017. https://tirto.id/risiko-dan-nasib-buruk-pembangunan-hotel-di-yogyakarta-bkWg (accessed October 30, 2017).

Tribun Jogja. 2012. "Tanggapan Haryadi Suyuti tentang Video "Ora Masalah Har!". October 16, 2012. http://jogja.tribunnews.com/2012/10/16/tanggapan-haryadi-suyuti-tentang-video-ora-masalah-har (accessed October 30, 2017).

Chapter 3

Religious Intolerance after *Reformasi*: Violence against the Shia Community in Sampang Regency, Madura

Kayane Yuka

Introduction

Recent electoral events in Indonesia have shown that religion increasingly plays a role in political contestation. While there have been numerous reports and studies on the persecution of religious minorities in Indonesia (see Setara Institute, 2009–2018; Lindsey, 2012; Crouch, 2014; Human Rights Watch, 2017),[1] probably the most remarkable case since the fall of Suharto in 1998 is that of Christian and ethnic Chinese Jakarta

---

1   On the involvement of judicial institutions, Lindsey (2012), Crouch (2014), and Human Rights Watch (2017) elaborate how intolerant actors use legal institutions and legal disputes to further their agenda. As the Indonesian courts are generally weak in the face of external pressures in the form of threats, intimidation, and bribery, intolerant actors are adept at using Article 156 and 156 (a) of the *Kitab Undang-Undang Hukum Pidana* (KUHP—Criminal Code) to legitimize attacks against minorities. The blasphemy law, as set in Article 156 (a) of the Criminal Code, has become a particularly useful tool for such actors. Article 156 prohibits expression of feelings of *permusuhan* (hostility), *kebencian* (hatred), or *penghinaan* (contempt) toward one or more *golongan* (groups) of Indonesian people, sentencing violators to a maximum imprisonment of four years. The provision more frequently used to convict members of religious minority groups and "*aliran sesat*" (deviant sects) is Article 156 (a) (Lindsey, 2012: 53). It provides that a person who deliberately and publicly expresses feeling or acts in a manner that: (a) involves *permusuhan* (hatred), *penyalahgunaan* (misuse), or *penodaan* (insulting) of a religion believed in Indonesia, or; b) has the intention that a person should not practice any religion at all that is based on Belief in Almighty God, shall be sentenced to a maximum of five years in jail.

Governor Basuki Tjahaja Purnama (Ahok) from late 2016 to early 2017. Massive rallies organized by Islamist leaders calling for the arrest of Ahok for his "blasphemy" against Islam drew support from tens of thousands of Muslim citizens all over the country. What was striking about the case is not only that the rallies affected the result of the gubernatorial election, but also the legal disputes around his alleged blasphemies. Protestors urged prosecutors to file religious blasphemy charges against Ahok; Jakarta's district court found him guilty and the sentence was quickly handed down.

While such large-scale rallies in the capital had been unprecedented since 1998, Ahok's case is not new in that similar legal cases have used Articles 156 and 156 (a) of the Criminal Law (KUHP) on blasphemy in prosecutions against minorities (Lindsey, 2012; Crouch, 2014). Indeed, more than 200 religious intolerance cases have been recorded each year from 2008 to 2016, with the exception of two temporary periods in the run-up to the presidential elections of 2009 and 2014, when the central government tightened security control (Setara Institute, 2017: 34–35).[2] Since 1998, the Shia[3] have been one of the most attacked religious minorities.[4] The Sampang incidents in Madura, in which two people were killed and more than 300 Shia villagers were expelled from the island, drew significant attention from Indonesia's media and human rights groups. The case was one of the worst persecutions against a religious minority after 1998 in terms of the number of victims. Like the case of Ahok, the Shia leader in Sampang was also prosecuted for religious blasphemy based on Article 156 (a) of KUHP, during a local election. How and why did the

---

2   It should be noted, however, that according to a report by the Setara Institute (2018), the number of incidents in 2017 remarkably decreased to 155 shortly after the protests against Ahok took place in Jakarta.

3   Although the exact number of the Shia population in Indonesia is unavailable, according to a report by the Institute for Policy Analysis of Conflict (IPAC), it is estimated to be roughly 2.5 million (IPAC, 2016: 2; Zulkifli, 2009: 15). Ikatan Jamaah Ahlulbait Indonesia (IJABI), a Shia organization in Indonesia, estimates the number to be between one and five million (interview with Miftah Rakhmat, February 15, 2016).

4   The Ahmadiyya are one of the religious minorities that have endured numerous intolerant attacks. Severe cases include the attack against Ahmadiyya in Lombok, Nusa Tenggara Barat, and the expulsion of the Ahmadiyya by the Bangka regency in 2011. In these cases, although there was no conviction for blasphemy, many Ahmadiyya residents faced expulsion from their homes. See Setara Institute 2017 for details of the cases.

intolerant actors succeed in legitimizing the persecution? What accounts for this pattern?

Many have pointed out that accusations of "blasphemy" and protests in the name of Islam are often relevant to political gains before elections. For instance, Ahnaf et al. (2013) examines the local elections in three provinces (Sampang in East Java, Bekasi in West Java, and Kupang in East Nusa Tenggara) where violence against religious minorities occurred.[5] According to the authors, the direct elections for local heads, instituted in 2005, provide ample opportunities for intolerant actors to seek patronage of candidates by exploiting anti-religious minority sentiments (Ahnaf, 2012: 7–10). Afdillah (2013, 2016) closely examines the Sampang case in relation to the local elections and provides extensive analysis of the process by which Shia villagers were violently attacked. Several reports by human rights organizations also point to the direct election for local heads as a trigger for a spike in intolerant acts (Setara Institute, 2017: 37; IPAC, 2016: 11).[6] Thus, the implementation of the direct election without accompanying safeguards has structurally facilitated the persecution of minorities, as access to state elites, especially before elections, is opened to intolerant actors.

However, not all intolerant provocations before local elections succeeded in legitimizing violence against minorities. Rather, many attempts ended in failure. In seeking to identify what determines success in the legitimization of violence, Pangabaean (2016) notes the importance of alliance making with mainstream elites. He argues that when intolerant groups can forge broad alliances with other Sunni elites, the violence escalates, because the local government—including the police—as a part

---

5   East Java ranks second highest in Indonesia for the number of violent incidents against minorities. Attacks against the Shia have also been prevalent in this area, as there are several prominent local Shia clerics and schools, including Indonesia's largest Shia school, the Foundation for Islamic Education (Yayasan Pesantren Islam or YAPI) in Bangil, Pasuruan regency.

6   The case of Sampang is well documented. For instance, Kontras (Komisi untuk Orang Hilang dan Korban Tindak Kekerasan—Commission for Missing People and Victims of Violence) Surabaya published several detailed reports on the case (Kontras Surabaya, 2012). Like Kontras, the Setara Institute publishes an annual report on human rights issues in Indonesia (Setara Institute, 2012, 2017) that included information on the incidents in Sampang.

of the Sunni community, cannot be impartial (284–285). However, he does not identify under what conditions such alliances are made.

To further develop an understanding of how intolerant groups in Sampang were able to influence state actors, this chapter focuses on the distinct features of the political power structure of the regency. It argues that the political power structure in Sampang was fragmented and uncompetitive, with virtually no powerful groups to compete for influence. This fragmentation provided space for vocal political entrepreneurs calling for the persecution of Shia to gain influence over state actors, more so than in places where many organizations and preeminent figures constantly compete for state access and grassroots support.

The following section provides a general background and highlights several features of the power structure in the regions of Madura Island. It focuses on the religious authorities to establish an analytical framework of the case. Recognizing the importance of the religious authorities in politics, it examines the political process of the persecution of the Shia community in Sampang Regency in Madura Island to uncover how and why the religious authorities legitimize violence.

The Religious Authorities and Political Power in Madura Island

This section elucidates the role of religious authorities in politics in Madura and some of the key elements of the case of religious violence in Sampang. The role of the *kiai* (religious leader and the head of the *pesantren* or religious boarding schools) in society is critical to understanding political power in Sampang and Madura.[7] In East Java, a predominant number of *kiai* identify themselves as members of Nahdlatul Ulama (NU). While NU has local branches all over the country, its presence is particularly dominant in East and Central Java Provinces, where the NU's founders' renowned

---

7 See Pribadi (2013) for the role of *kiai* in Madura. *Blater* (thug or strongman) are, like *kiai*, also known as powerful actors in Madura; both often exercise hegemonic influence in Madurese society (Rozaki, 2009). The role of prominent *blater* in the Sampang incidents, however, was rather limited, as the conflict was largely stoked by the religious authorities.

pesantren are located. Prominent *kiai* have often held the highest positions on the *syuriyah* (religious councils) in NU's local branches and headquarters in Jakarta. Although NU is known for its loose and "decentralized" organizational structure, in terms of political mobilization, it is at least as equal as and sometimes more powerful than political parties in both provinces. As long as NU can continue to consolidate support among a small number of prominent *kiai* whose positions are by and large well integrated into the NU's structure, the NU's leadership of the provinces is relatively stable in East and Central Java Provinces. In fact, when Partai Kebangkitan Bangsa (PKB—National Awakening Party) was established in 1998 by Abdurrahman Wahid, NU's former chair, it greatly benefited from NU's well-established infrastructure, connections, and network, as the party was essentially formed by the huge demand from NU's *kiai* who sought to represent the organization's interests (Bush, 2009: 118–122). Today, NU members run PKB's local branches in both East and Central Java, and the party's executives at the local level mostly include influential *kiai* and other NU notables (Hamayotsu, 2011: 142–143; Feillard, 2013: 561). The PKB has secured the highest votes in 11 to 19 of the 38 cities and regencies in East Java in every election since 1999, largely due to support from prominent *kiai*[8] (Miichi, 2015). The NU's network has often been viewed as a rich source of political support, and candidates usually rely on it to win elections.

Madura Island, part of East Java Province, consists of four regencies known for their unique behavior, particularly toward the NU's leadership. Although *kiai* in Madura identify as NU members, they are not necessarily well integrated into the NU's organizational hierarchy. Rather, *kiai* in Madura who do not institutionally belong to the NU often act independently for their own interests rather than following the NU's leadership and dictates. Without the benefits of an institutionalized hierarchy of NU, candidates who seek political support from religious authorities in Madura have to rely on the networks of many individual *kiai* to win votes. In turn, individual

---

8   Due to the internal conflict over the PKB's leadership that divided the NU, the PKB garnered significantly fewer votes in the 2009 election. However, the PKB reconsolidated support from NU and regained votes in 2014 and 2019.

kiai often shift their support for candidates and political parties depending on the conditions of the deals offered. Particularly in places where the dominant leadership of prominent *kiai* is absent, the political constellation shaped by the religious authorities tends to be fragmented and ad-hoc. In fact, except for Sumenap Regency, since 2004 the ruling parties of the local parliaments in three regencies in Madura have changed in every election due to the inconsistent support from individual *kiai*. Furthermore, among the regions in Madura, the power structure of the religious authorities in Sampang Regency is the most fragmented. As such, it is the only electorate of the 38 cities and regencies in East Java where the incumbent head has lost every election since the direct election system for local heads was instituted in 2005. This distinct power structure in Sampang, marked by an absence of dominant leadership and tight competition, provides numerous opportunities for an ambitious political entrepreneur to dominate influence over state actors, even to legitimize violence.

Among those who led the persecution of the Shia in Sampang, the most vocal was Kiai Ahmad (pseudonym), who lives in Pamekasan, the regency next to Sampang. He is neither from one of the most powerful families nor is he a leader of any of the largest Islamic schools in Madura, but he is well connected with many powerful *kiai* in other regions. Due to the absence of outstanding leaders who dominate political influence in Sampang, he could easily access the state elites by mobilizing his religious resources outside the regency. His initial motivation was to curb the emerging influence of his rival, Tajul Muluk, who attracted many villagers in Sampang through his Shia teachings. Although Tajul was Ahmad's relative, his growing popularity annoyed, and threatened, many Sunni *kiai*, including Ahmad. He exploited feelings of threat among the *kiai* and attacked Tajul by mobilizing state power via the incumbent local head, who desperately needed support from religious authorities. The following sections will examine the way in which the conflict between Ahmad and Tajul became a trigger for violence, which developed into widespread persecution of Shia villagers.

Prelude to the Sampang Incidents

For the past several decades, most of the small Shia enclaves in Madura have been engaged in establishing good communications and networks with local religious authorities, who overwhelmingly come from the Sunni majority. First and foremost, they are careful to avoid any trouble or noticeable problems with their Sunni neighbors. Unlike other Shia in Madura, the emerging Shia group in Sampang was disconnected from local authorities and faced persecution in 2000s.[9]

In the early 1980s, a respected local *kiai*, Kiai Ma'mum, was attracted by the idea of the Iranian revolution and started to learn Shi'ism on his own. In 1983 he sent his children, including Ali Murtadha, known as Tajul Muluk (born 1973), to Indonesia's largest Shia school, Yayasan Pesantren Islam (YAPI—Foundation for Islamic Education). Ahmad, Tajul's relative and a former teacher of his in Madura, opposed the move. Even after they left for YAPI, Ahmad persistently insisted that the children be sent instead to his alma mater, a school owned by Sayyid Muhammad Al-Maliki in Saudi Arabia. Tajul was one of the children persuaded to study in Saudi Arabia in 1993. However, not satisfied with the Sunni teachings, Tajul dropped out of school and worked in Saudi Arabia until he returned to his village in 1999 (Afdillah, 2013: 54, 60, 169).

In early 2004, Tajul and his brother built the religious school Misbahul Huda in their village. Unlike his father, Tajul openly proclaimed his inclination to Shi'ism and propagated its teachings (Kontras Surabaya, 2012: 3). His egalitarianism had a reformist impact and attracted so many followers that the local Sunni *kiai* could not ignore it. Aside from teaching Shi'ism, Tajul also publicly criticized the other kiai for exploiting the poor by taking their money in exchange for blessings during Maulid, the Prophet's birthday celebration. For the Sunni *kiai*, including Ahmad, Tajul's

---

9   Anti-Shia sentiment was heightened during the Iranian revolution (1978–79), when the Indonesian government became concerned about the spread of revolutionary forces as many Indonesian students were inspired by the event and converted to Shia, especially among campus activists in Makassar and Bandung. For a detailed history of the development of anti-Shia discourse and violence since the Suharto regime, see Formichi (2014) and IPAC (2016: 6–11).

teachings threatened to undermine their traditional social and economic standing as the religious authorities in the surrounding area.

The anti-Shia offensive began shortly after Tajul's respected father, Ma'mun, died in June 2004. Ma'mun was the only religious authority who could prevent the vicious attacks against Tajul. Shortly after the death of the respected *kiai*, Ahmad began attacking Tajul. Ahmad lives in nearby Pamekasan Regency, and has many followers in Sampang, where his former disciples live and run schools. Although he came from a modest family in the area, he is particularly vocal compared to other *kiai*. In addition, he is well connected to prominent *kiai* in other regions, and is adept at mobilizing religious resources as a means to attract the attention of state elites and mass voters.

Through his four wives, whose families lead the largest *pesantren* in Madura and the Saudi alumni association of Al-Malikiyyah (Hai'ah Ash-Shofwah Al-Malikiyyah), Ahmad has developed a vast network beyond Madura Island. In 2009, he took the chairmanship of Badan Silaturahmi Ulama Pesantren Madura (BASSRA—Association of *Pesantren*-Based Ulama's Friendship in Madura), which was founded by several influential *kiai* in Madura in 1991 to mobilize local resistance to the government's industrial policy at that time (Pribadi, 2013: 73, 171–183).[10] Neither the alumni association of Al-Malikiyyah nor BASSRA are NU organizations, but some of the members are also high-ranking *kiai* in NU's formal organizations. Through these personal networks, Ahmad can utilize broad support from religious authorities in other regions without using the NU's institutions.

Ahmad was aggravated by Tajul's teachings and started to circulate a pamphlet entitled "29 Deviations in Tajul's Teaching." He spread anti-Shia rumors that Tajul was preaching deviant teachings that were blasphemous toward Sunni traditions; for instance that Tajul promoted prostitution in the name of *nikah mut'ah* (temporal marriage contract), insulted wives and companions of the Prophet Muhammad, and used a false Quran. By

---

10   In October 2014, Ahmad established the Aliansi Ulama Madura (AUMA—Alliance of Madurese Ulama) to replace BASSRA.

circulating the pamphlets among Sunni villagers, other *kiai,* and local officials, he fostered the image of Shia as a threat to the purity of Islam and to the harmony of the Muslim community (Ahnaf et al., 2015: 23; IPAC, 2016: 16).

In February 2006, Tajul began a new form of Maulid, where everyone came together at the village mosque so that they no longer needed to pay *kiai* for blessings. This attempt threatened many *kiai,* whose incomes depended on Maulid (Afdillah, 2013: 63–70)[11]. Ahmad did not miss this chance to attack Tajul, and mobilized his followers and mobs carrying weapons such as hatchets and clubs, to attack Shia. Other *kiai* remained silent and no one came to stop the mobs.

Fadhilah Budiono,[12] the local head at the time, was preparing to run for re-election in December 2007. For Fadhilah, the support of the *kiai* was indispensable to secure his win; therefore, he did not dare to take any action to halt the violence.[13] On February 24, Ahmad organized a meeting with 40 *kiai* in Madura and Fadhilah to condemn Tajul for his teachings and religious activities, including his "alternative" Maulid (Hilmy, 2015: 37). The *kiai* tried to persuade Tajul to return to the Sunni by pressing upon him that he would otherwise face legal consequences. Although Tajul bowed to the *kiai* that month, he has never stopped his teachings.

The Involvement of Political Elites and the Bureaucracy

Noer Tjahja, the local head of Sampang during 2008–2013, desperately sought support for his re-election to a second term. A former bureaucrat who had worked for the Central Bank, he lacked social and political capital in Sampang society. The *kiai*'s support was therefore invaluable for him to win the election, and he tried to appeal to them by demonstrating his efforts to deal with the Shia issue. Noer Tjahja initiated a local intelligence

---

11   Interview with a NGO member working on reconciliation, August 11, 2017.
12   Fadhilah Budiono, a former policeman, was the last regional head during the New Order regime, but was appointed as the head again by the local parliament in 2001. Although he lost in the 2007 election, he was re-elected as a vice regional head with Fannan Hasib as the head in 2012. After Fannan passed away, he became the regional head again for fourth time.
13   The *kiai* themselves often participate in Sampang's regional head election and partner with bureaucrats.

community meeting called Komunitas Intelijen Daerah (Kominda—Local Intelligence Community)[14] and pressured the members to expel Tajul and his family (Kontras Surabaya, 2012: 6–7) from Madura. After several Kominda meetings held in April, the regional police joined in deciding to expel Tajul (Kontras Surabaya, 2012: 7–8).

The local bureaucracy also played a crucial role in exacerbating the conflict. One of the key institutions is the Badan Kesatuan Bangsa dan Politik (Bakesbangpol—the National Unity and Political Institution).[15] Bakesbangpol's function is to monitor political, religious, ethnic, and ideological organizations in the regency in coordination with other law enforcement institutions.[16] The head of Bakesbangpol is an influential figure whom every local head must have support from, due to his powerful leverage over the bureaucracy and intelligence agency, as well as his wide range of networks among the religious authorities of Sampang Regency. He was well connected to Ahmad and other *kiai* in Sampang, and his relatives were the heads of several villages in Karang Gayam and surrounding areas. It was said that while he was well aware of *kiai* influence that infiltrated into local government and was afraid of being persecuted by ignoring them, he also coveted a career promotion before retirement. Therefore, he provided powerful brokerage between the bureaucracy and the *kiai*[17].

On October 26, 2009, the Sampang Regency police demanded that Tajul stop teaching. The police, assured by the powerful bureaucracy of Bakesbangpol and backed by Noer Tjahja, warned Tajul that he would face legal consequences if he did not stop teaching. A statement of the 'agreement' was signed by Bakesbangpol, the head of the Dewan Perwakilan Rakyat Daerah (DPRD—local People's Assembly), the local branch head of the Ministry of Religion, the head of the Sampang's

---

14 The Kominda consists of intelligence elements including the military, the police, prosecutors, members of the judiciary, the Badan Intelijen Negara (BIN—National Intelligence Bureau), and local government representatives (Muradi, 2014: 111).

15 Bakesbangpol was a former military intelligence body, referred to as the Kantor Sosial-Politik (Kantor Sospol—Office of Social and Political Activities) under the Suharto regime (Muradi, 2014: 114).

16 See: Decree of the Minister of Internal Affairs No.43/2015 Articles 144 and 145.

17 Interview with researcher Y, August 18, 2017

Majelis Ulama Indonesia (MUI—Indonesian Ulama Council), and NU *kiai* (Kontras Surabaya, 2012: 5).

In February 2011, BASSRA again mobilized thousands of people to demand the expulsion of Tajul and his followers (IPAC, 2016: 16). On April 16, Tajul escaped to Malang, where his wife's family lived. Still, Ahmad was not satisfied, as Tajul's followers and other Shia leaders continued to operate in the village. Severe violence broke out at in late-2011 for the first time. An anti-Shia mob set fire to the house of one of Tajul's followers on December 20 (IPAC, 2016: 16). On December 29, a mob of roughly 500 people burned down Tajul's house, destroyed the Shia madrasah, and robbed goods and livestock from Shia villagers. Nearly 300 people fled to the Sampang Sports Stadium (IPAC, 2016: 16–17). The regional police, pressured by Bakesbangpol and Noer, did not intervene to stop the violence and looting that took place in the village.

Aiming to legitimize the violence against Tajul and his followers, Ahmad and his fellow *kiai* took a second measure: they urged the regional MUI in Sampang to issue a *fatwa* (legal opinion). Hardline groups often make use of *fatwa* issued by the MUI to condemn minorities for blasphemy (Crouch, 2014).[18] As members of local MUI branches are often closely linked to the local religious authorities, the latter are able to pressure MUI to issue *fatwa*.[19] Although MUI fatwa are not legally binding, prosecutors and judges have come to accept them as evidence in trials.[20]

The head of the local MUI at the time was, like Ahmad, a graduate of Al-Malikiyyah, and shared the same ideas regarding the Shia persecution. On January 1, 2012, the regional MUI issued a *fatwa* contending that Tajul's

---

18　MUI is a quasi-government organization that became independent from the Ministry of Religion in 1999, but still receives an annual budget from the Ministry of Religion (Lindsey, 2012: 132). The central board of the MUI has issued a number of controversial *fatwa* constraining and undermining the civil rights of minorities. For instance, the MUI issued *fatwa* to condemn religious pluralism, liberalism, secularism, and so-called deviant beliefs, including of the Ahmadiyya, in 2005 (Ichwan, 2013: 70).

19　As the MUI's central organization in Jakarta does not have clear hierarchical authority over its regional branches, local branches can produce a *fatwa* even if it contradicts a *fatwa* issued by the central organization (Lindsey, 2012: 131).

20　MUI's *fatwa* are barely recognized within the legal system, with the exception of the Islamic banking and finance sectors and Halal certification (Lindsey, 2012: 117–118).

teachings were deviant and promoted *sesat dan menyesatkan* (deviancy), were a *penistaan* (defamation) and *penodaan* (disgrace) against Islam, and that those who spread the teachings would have to face the court in accordance with current regulations and laws (MUI Sampang, 2012). The NU branches in Madura issued a similar statement the next day. Ahmad's personal networks had been mobilized among Sunni religious authorities beyond the region.

On January 3, Tajul's brother reported Tajul to the police for blasphemy, using the *fatwa* as evidence.[21] To prosecute Tajul, the head of Bakesbangpol again played a key role, this time in mobilizing prosecutors of Badan Koordinasi Pengawas Aliran Kepercayaan Masyarakat (Bakorpakem—Coordinating Board for Monitoring Mystical Beliefs in Society).[22] Bakorpakem is a government body that prosecutes organizations, individuals, or sects that are considered to be heretical, under the Public Prosecutors Office. Bakorpakem in Sampang is virtually under the control of the head of Bakesbangpol. Members include police intelligence, military intelligence, the office of the Ministry of Religion, the Ministry of Culture, Tourism and Sport, and the BIN (Sihombing, 2008: 85; Setara Institute, 2012: 9).

---

21   Tajul's brother Robi (pseudonym) converted to Sunni in 2011 due to the personal issues with Tajul. Robi, together with Ahmad, actively spread anti-Shia rhetoric that aggravated feelings of anxiety and hatred among the neighbors toward both Tajul and his followers.

22   Bakorpakem (officially referred to as "Tim Pakem" in the related statutes) was originally set up under the Ministry of Religion in 1953 to collect information regarding traditional mystical beliefs and sects and to monitor them. In 1961, it was transferred under the Public Prosecutors Office by the Law Number 15 Year 1961 Article 2 (3), about the principal of Public Prosecution. Then, the Surat Keputusan Jaksa Agung (Decision of the Chief Public Prosecutor) No.004/JA/01/1994 ordered the establishment of the current form of Bakorpakem (Sihombing, 2008: 26–27, 85; Amnesty, 2014: 14). Tim Pakem in the central government is composed of a Chief Prosecutor as the head, deputy Jaksa Agung Muda Intelijen (Chief Prosecutor of Intelligence), and representatives from the Ministry of Internal Affairs and Education; the Ministry of Religion; the Ministry of Education and Culture; the military; police; and BIN; the Forum Kerukunan Umat Beragama (Forum of Religious Harmony). For membership of the provincial and regional Pakem, see Peraturan Jaksa Agung (Regulation of Chief Prosecutors Office) No. 019/A/JA/09/2015, Articles 4 and 5. This institution almost ceased operations under the presidency of Abdurrahman Wahid, who stressed religious diversity. In 2004, however, Yusril Ihza Mahendra, then state secretary, drafted a new Law Number 16 Article 30 (3) and (4) to re-operationalize Bakorpakem under the Yudhoyono presidency (Interview with a former regional leader of Bakorpakem on August 26, 2017; ICG, 2008: 3–4).

On January 4, Bakorpakem issued a report that concluded that Shi'ism was deviant (Kontras Surabaya, 2012: 14). The East Java provincial MUI also issued a *fatwa* that found Shi'ism heretical on January 21. *Kiai* in high ranks of NU in East Java Province expressed concerns over the threat of Shia and shared anti-Shia sentiments (*NU.online*, 2010). Noer Tjahja, expecting the coming election to be a tough competition, did not miss the chance to appeal to the *kiai*. Noer Tjahja had managed to win the 2007 election with support that his vice-local head, Fannan Hasib (who was a NU *kiai*) had helped to garner from fellow *kiai* of Sampang, with whom he was well connected. But in the 2012 election, Tjahja had to seek support from *kiai* on his own, as Fannan Hasib did not partner with him. He started condemning Tajul for his "deviant" teachings and declared during his campaign that Shia followers should be driven out of Sampang (Ahnaf et al., 2015: 24–26; IPAC, 2016: 17–18).

The Regency Police, however, could not find sufficient evidence to prove Tajul guilty of blasphemy. They handed the case to the police of East Java on January 24. They also found it difficult to prove Tajul guilty. However, Noer Tjahja frequently visited the police office in Surabaya to urge them to continue the investigation. Ahmad and fellow *kiai* also pressured the police. After consulting with prosecutors in East Java, the police arrested Tajul on April 10, 2012. Noer Tjahja knew that prosecutors would convict Tajul based on Article 156 (a) before it was released to the media, and proudly announced it to the public on the same day (*Tribunnews*, 2012).

Initially, lawyers on Tajul's side were concerned that pressure from the *kiai* and their mob would be an obstacle to a fair trial, and demanded that the case be tried in Surabaya, rather than Sampang[23] but to no avail. As the trial began, the prosecutors referred to many non-legally binding documents, such as the Sampang MUI *fatwa*, the Sampang NU branch statement, and the Bakorpakem report (Setara Institute, 2012: 27–29). The

---

23   Interview with Asfinawati on August 31, 2017. Asfinawati is a lawyer from the Yayasan Lembaga Bantuan Hukum (Legal Aid Foundation) and he was Tajul's leading defence lawyer.

prosecutors demanded a four-year sentence based on Article 156 (a) of KUHP (Mahkamah Agung, 2012: 3–9).

The trial was conducted as if the decision had already been made. Some witnesses from the prosecution's side could not even tell the difference between Sunnism and Shiism, and some said they had never heard Tajul's teachings directly. In addition, although many witnesses spoke only Madurese, not Indonesian, there was no translator present[24] (Setara Institute, 2012: 24). The chief judge, who was Madurese, repeatedly asked the witnesses leading questions to elicit favorable testimony for the prosecutors (Ahnaf et al., 2015: 29; *Berita Satu*, 2012).[25] As Tajul's lawyers could not speak Madurese, the judge had significant leeway in to arbitrarily interpret the testimonies (interview with Asfinawati on August 31, 2017). During the trial, Achmad Zain Alkaf, a sayyid preacher from an anti-Shia foundation called Al-Bayyinat,[26] was also invited to testify as an expert witness.[27] The prosecutors were not well prepared for the trial, even referencing the wrong criminal code (Berita Satu, 2012). However, the judges refused to accept testimonies from the defence witnesses, as they were family members and followers of Tajul, who, the judges believed, would lie because of the "taqiyya" teaching (Pengadilan Negeri Sampang, 2012: 90, 92–97). The practice of "taqiyya" in Shi'ism allows someone to hide the truth when necessary. Accusing Shia of being liars based on the taqiyya practice is common among *kiai* in East and Central Java, as anti-Shia activists and organizations, often supported by Saudi Arabia, have vigorously engaged in spreading this discourse since the Iranian revolution

---

24 Interview with Asfinawati on August 31, 2017.

25 The Madurese judge was Purnomo Amin Tjahjo (from Bangkalan Regency). He became a Chief Judge of Court in Banyuwangi soon after the trial.

26 Al-Bayyinat launched a book on Shia in 2010 and gained support from the head of East Java branch of NU (NU.online, January 10, 2010). According to an IPAC report, Thohir Alkaf, a former student of Habib Husein, the founder of YAPI, became a vigorous opponent of Shi'ism after returning from Saudi Arabia. He helped to establish the anti-Shia organization Al-Bayyinat in 1986 to "defend" Sunnism (Mahkamah Agung, 2012: 33; IPAC, 2016: 15).

27 Other expert witnesses included Buchori Ma'shum, who initiated issuing the *fatwa* on the Shia in January 2012, Abd Halim Soebahar, the Head of Jember MUI, Abdus Somad Buhari, the Head of East Java MUI, Ali Daud Bey, a former bureaucrat of Sampang Regency. Prosecution witnesses included bureaucrats from Bakesbangpol and the regional office of the Ministry of Religion (Pengadilan Negeri Sampang, 2012: 25–30, 30–38).

in 1979 (Zulkifli, 2009; Formichi, 2014). In spite of the travesty of the trial, the judges sentenced Tajul to two years in prison (Pengadilan Negeri Sampang, 2012: 95–97).[28] Tajul immediately appealed to the high court in Surabaya. To counter this move, Ahmad and his fellow *kiai* quickly began pressuring the high court in Surabaya.

Meanwhile, the East Java Governor Soekarwo and Vice Governor Saifullah Yusuf were seeking re-election and had been looking for support in the 2013 gubernatorial election. The timing of the approaching local election worked in favor of Ahmad and his supporters. In March 2012, 50 *kiai* representing MUI, NU, and Muhammadiyah met Soekarwo to ask him to ban the propagation of Shi'ism in East Java, as he had done with Ahmadiyya teachings in 2011. Soekarwo issued a decree on the "Guidance of Religious Activities and Monitoring of Deviant Sects in East Java" (East Java Governor Regulation Number 55 Year 2012), which officially banned religious activities categorized as heretical sects, in accordance with the criteria and consideration of the MUI (Article 5). The regulation further endorsed discrimination of and offenses against the Shia.

The central government did not stop or interfere in the violence, either: indeed, one cabinet member virtually endorsed the violence. The Minister of Religious Affairs, Suryadharma Ali, repeatedly condemned the Shia (*Berita Satu*, 2012). The president of the Islamic political party Partai Persatuan Pembangunan (PPP—United Development Party), Suryadharma Ali was motivated to retain *kiai* support in Madura, as the island is one of the largest bases of PPP support in the country (Ahnaf et al., 2015: 18). Although President Susilo Bambang Yudhoyono criticized the police at the onset of the violence and called a meeting to issue stern warnings to prevent further violence, he did not stop the minister from condemning the Shia and endorsing BASSRA's views (Bush, 2015: 244). With the support

---

28　Based on the testimonies of the prosecution witnesses, the *fatwa* issued by the Sampang MUI, several letters from the Board Branch of NU and Bakorpakem in Sampang, as well as Shia books and CDs submitted as evidence, the judges stated, in essence that Tajul "committed a criminal act which are…blasphemous against Islam" and has "disturbed the community, especially the Islamic community in Kecamatan Omben dan Kecamatan Karang Penang" (Pengadilan Negeri Sampang, 2012: 94–96). The judges reduced the sentence because Tajul behaved well and was responsible for his family.

of the state elites, BASSRA mobilized a mob again. On August 26, 2012, a mob of 500 people attacked two Shia communities (*Suara Pembaruan*, August 27, 2012). The incident took place one month after Tajul appealed his conviction to the high court. When Shia followers were taking their children to YAPI by car after a school break, an armed mob chased after them and forced them to stop on the road. Two of Tajul's followers were slashed to death, five people were seriously injured, and almost 50 houses in the village were destroyed by the mob (*Tempo*, 2012). On August 29, the Regency Police named Tajul's brother, Robi (see footnote 20), as a suspect. However, the Surabaya Court acquitted him of all charges, as the judges deemed the evidence against him insufficient (Mahkamah Agung, 2014: 1–9).

In the end, more than three hundred people were expelled from their villages and had to evacuate to the Surabaya sports stadium. The judges of the high court in Surabaya doubled Tajul's sentence to four years. They pointed to the burning of houses as proof that Tajul's teachings had caused disharmony in the Islamic community (Mahkamah Agung, 2012: 12, 25, 26). The *kiai* persistently pressured judges in the Supreme Court in Jakarta to uphold the verdict (Afdillah, 2013: 133, 198, 199; Mahkamah Agung, 2012: 27). In July 2013, 10 months after fleeing to the sports stadium, 354 refugees were relocated to the Puspa Agro blocks in Sidoarjo Regency more than 100 km from their homes, without prior consultation or notification. Most of them have been unable to return to their villages in Sampang and still live in Sidoarjo at the time of writing. Although Joko Widodo's government has strived to pave a way for them to return home to Sampang and to seek reconciliation (Miichi and Kayane forthcoming), as long as hostile anti-Shia *kiai* hold significant influence on the state actors in the local government, the risk of provocation remains.

Expanding Anti-Shia Network

Anti-minority discourse has connected nodes of local conservative figures who have ambitions of influencing the established order. After the persecution of Shia in Sampang, the anti-Shia network has significantly expanded beyond Madura Island. In September 2013, Ahmad reached out to Athian Ali, the founder of Forum Ulama Ummat Indonesia (FUUI—Indonesia's Ulama Community Forum), a hardline Sunni advocacy organization.[29] FUUI itself has close ties to Persatuan Islam (Persis—Unity of Islam), an established reformist organization, whose members include local politicians, particularly in West Java. Ahmad, together with a dozen *kiai* from East Java, paid a visit to FUUI in Bandung on February 28, 2012. Two months after the meeting, the FUUI issued a *fatwa* during a congress attended by the West Java governor, declaring Shi'ism to be "deviant and promoting deviancy" (IPAC, 2016: 21). In April 2014, Ahmad, as head of BASSRA, and the other *kiai* took part in the declaration of Aliansi Nasional Anti-Syiah (ANNAS—National Alliance of Anti-Shia) in Bandung, with Athian Ali as a head. Supporting speeches were delivered by Abdul Hamid Baidlowi as a NU *kiai* in Rembang, Central Java[30] as well as Islamist preachers and activists from Persis and MUI[31] (IPAC, 2016: 22). Luthfi Bashori, another NU *kiai* and a member of FUUI from Malang, East Java, liaised between NU *kiai* and other Islamist activists in West Java. Anti-Shia *kiai* have been using the network of Indonesian alumni of Al-Malikiyyah and vocal critics against Said Aqil Siraj, NU's current national chair, and have occasionally allied with Islamists.

Since its declaration, ANNAS has attempted to increase its number of local branches, arousing controversy in many areas. Although ANNAS

---

29 FUUI was founded by Athian Ali, a Bandung-based reformist *kiai* in 2001. The organization aims to counter liberalism, Christianization, apostasy and deviant sects (IPAC, 2016: 20).

30 Baidlowi (1945–2014) was a senior figure of NU, known as a vocal critic of Shia and Ahmadiyya. He publicly criticized NU moderate leadership such as Gus Dur and Said Aqil Siradj.

31 Other participants in the ANNAS meeting included Maman Abdurrahman, a former leader of Persis (2010–2015) and now a Head of the Adviser Council of the organization, and Muhammad Al-Khaththath, a Chairman of Forum Umat Islam (FUI—Islamic Community Forum). Al-Khaththath is a graduate of Institut Pertanian Bogor (IPB—Bogor Agricultural University) and a former member of Hizbut Tahrir Indonesia. He is one of the leading organizers of the protests against Ahok during 2016–2017. Ahmad Cholil Ridwan (born 1947), one of the chairmen of MUI (2005–2015) also participated. He was a former leader of Dewan Da'wah Islamiyah Indonesia (DDII) (2005–2011), and an alumni of the Islamic boarding school (*pesantren*) of Gontor and Islamic University of Madinah in Saudi Arabia. Another participant was Lailurrahman, a former chairman of MUI Pamekasan, a head of the *kiai* association Harkat Pondok Pesantren Madura, and an active member of AUMA.

has branches in several regencies in West Java Province and elsewhere, its establishment of branches in Cirebon and Bogor was strongly opposed by civil society, including the youth wings of NU, namely Gerakan Pemuda Ansor (GP Ansor—Ansor Youth Wing) and Barisan Ansor Serbaguna (Banser—Multipurpose Ansor Front), Muslim student organizations, and various human rights NGOs. The power structures in these places are significantly different from Sampang. In Cirebon, NU, which has been represented by four large *pesantren*, has dominated local politics. One of the *pesantren* has particularly strong political influence, as it is an original base of support for the current NU chairman in the central leadership. In Bogor, the religious authorities are significantly fragmented like Sampang, but much more competitive due to the various organizations constantly striving to win support from both state actors and the grassroots. It is therefore extremely difficult for a newcomer such as Ahmad or Athian Ali to compete and influence the state actors.

Ahmad also strengthened ties with the Jakarta-based Front Pembela Islam (FPI—Islamic Defenders' Front), as some heads of the local FPI in East Java were also Al-Malikiyyah graduates.[32] However, the FPI headquarters in Jakarta had difficulties in explicitly using anti-Shia rhetoric because the organization's leadership had been consolidated by the *sayyid* (descendants of the Prophet) community in Jakarta, which has members who studied in YAPI, a prominent Shia school in Bangil, as well as Shia converts. The leader of FPI, Rizieq Shihab, has strived to avoid provoking the Shia issue due to the affinity with Shia leaders among the sayyid community in Jakarta. Even during the anti-Ahok rallies in Jakarta of 2016–2017, the FPI leadership carefully restrained anti-Shia rhetoric long-utilized by some Islamist groups[33]. Similar to Bogor, the power structure in Jakarta is much more competitive, leaving little room for anti-Shia provocateurs to rise. At the same time, religious minorities can count on the informal network with various competitive religious organizations as an indispensable social capital for their own protection.

---

32   His nephew was also appointed as a Head of Sampang FPI shortly after the incident.

33   Interview with Shia activists in Jakarta, December 22, 2018.

As we have seen, while the intolerant *kiai* have increasingly extended their network through anti-Shia rhetoric across the regions, their attempts to attack Shia have hardly been successful beyond Sampang due to the differing power structures outside Sampang Regency. In other words, the legitimization of religious intolerance requires particular conditions within the political power structure that enable violent provocateurs to influence state actors.

Conclusion

This chapter explores the political process behind a series of attacks against the Shia in Sampang, Madura in the 2000s. Violent provocateurs cultivated feelings of anxiety and hatred among villagers against a local Shia leader (Tajul) and his followers through anti-Shia rhetoric. Through the networks of individual *kiai,* namely the alumni association of Al-Malikiyah and BASSRA, they utilized the *fatwa* to legitimize the attacks. Local politicians who sought re-election gave in to the anti-Shia rhetoric due to the fragmented and uncompetitive nature of the political power structure in Sampang. As the intolerant actors managed to silence and incorporate a wide range of state elites, they were able carry out violent attacks against the Shia without being accused of criminal acts. More specifically, support from incumbent local heads enabled them to utilize the bureaucracy to ultimately legitimize the entire process of the violence against the minorities. Ever since the incidents, the anti-Shia rhetoric has expanded beyond Madura Island by reaching out to other Islamists.

Legitimatization of violence, however, is contingent upon the local political power structure. In regions where many powerful organizations and preeminent figures have competed for political support and access, and where minorities can count on one of those competitors, the chances of anti-Shia provocateurs influencing the state is significantly reduced because such provocateurs do not have a mass base of support compared to the other powerful competitors. Therefore, the probability of legitimization of religious violence is highly dependent on the power structure, which is becoming increasingly competitive as electoral democracy evolves in Indonesia.

References

Afdillah, M. 2013. "Dari Masjid ke Panggung Politik: Melacak Akar-akar Kekerasan Agama antara Komunitas Sunni dan Syiah di Sampang, Jawa Timur". Thesis. Gadjah Mada University (unpublished).

_____. 2016. *Dari Masjid ke Panggung Politik: Melacak Akar-akar Kekerasan Agama antara Komunitas Sunni dan Syiah di Sampang, Jawa Timur*. Yogyakarta: CRCS, UGM.

Ahnaf, M. I. et al. 2015. *Politik Lokal dan Konflik Keagamaan: Pilkada dan Struktur Kesempatan Politik dalam Konflik Keagamaan di Sampang, Bekasi, dan Kupang*. Yogyakarta: CRCS, UGM.

Amnesty International. 2014. *Prosecuting Beliefs: Indonesia's Blasphemy Laws*. https://www.amnestyusa.org/files/_index-_asa_210182014.pdf (accessed April 1, 2018).

Badan Pusat Statistik. *Indeks Pembangunan Manusia Jawa Timur 1999, 2002, 2004-2015*. https://jatim.bps.go.id/linkTabelStatis/view/id/235 (accessed April 1, 2018).

Beritasatu. 2012. "Babak Akhir Peradilan Sesat Tajul Muluk". *Berita Satu*, July 7 2012. https://www.beritasatu.com/nasional/58947/babak-akhir-peradilan-sesat-tajul-muluk (accessed April 3, 2018).

Bush, R. 2009. *Nahdlatul Ulama and the Struggle for Power within Islam and Politics in Indonesia*. Singapore: ISEAS.

_____. 2015. "Religious Politics and Minority Rights during the Yudhoyono Presidency". In *The Yudhoyono Presidency: Indonesia's Decade of Stability and Stagnation*, edited by Edward Aspinall, Marcus Mietzner and Dirk Tomsa, pp. 239-257. Singapore: Institute of Southeast Asian Studies.

Crouch, M. 2014. *Law and Religion in Indonesia Conflict and the Courts in West Java*. London and New York: Routledge.

Feillard, A. 2013. "Nahdlatul Ulama in Indonesia". In *The Oxford Handbook of Islam and Politics*, edited by John L. Esposito and Emad El-Din Shahin, pp. 558-573. Oxford: Oxford University Press.

Formichi, C. 2014. "Violence, Sectarianism, and the Politics of Religion: Articulations of Anti-Shia Discourse". *Indonesia* 98 (October): 1–27.

Hamayotsu, K. 2011. "The End of Political Islam? A Comparative Analysis of Religious Parties in the Muslim Democracy of Indonesia". *Journal of Current Southeast Asian Affairs* 3: 133–159.

Hefner, R. W. 2000. *Civil Islam: Muslims and Democratization in Indonesia*. Princeton and Oxford: Princeton University Press.

Hilmy, M. 2015. "The Political Economy of Sunni-Shi'ah Conflict in Sampang Madura". *Al-Jami'ah: Journal of Islamic Studies* 53 (1): 27–51.

Human Rights Watch. 2013. *Religion's name Abuses against Religious Minorities in Indonesia.* https://www.hrw.org/report/2013/02/28/religions-name/abuses-against-religious-minorities-indonesia (accessed April 5, 2018).

Ichwan, M. N. 2013. "Towards A Puritanical Moderate Islam: The Majelis Ulama Indonesia and the Politics of Religious Orthodoxy". In *Contemporary Developments in Indonesian Islam: Explaining the Conservative Turn,* edited by Martin van Bruinessen, pp. 60-104. Singapore: Institute of Southeast Asian Studies.

Institute for Policy Analysis of Conflict (IPAC). 2016. *The Anti Shi'a Movement in Indonesia.* IPAC Report no. 27. Jakarta: IPAC.

International Crisis Group (ICG). 2008. *Indonesia Implications of the Ahmadiyah Decree Asia Briefing 78.* https://www.crisisgroup.org/asia/south-east-asia/indonesia/indonesia-implications-ahmadiyah-decree (accessed April 2, 2018).

Kontras Surabaya. 2012. *Laporan Investigasi Syiah di Sampang.* Surabaya: Kontras.

Lindsey, T. 2012. *Islam, Law and the State in Southeast Asia. Volume 1: Indonesia.* London/ New York: I.B.Tauris.

Mahkamah Agung. 2012. *Putusan No. 1787 K/Pid/2012*

_____. 2014. *Putusan No. 1331 K/Pid/2014*

_____. 2018. *Profil Ketua Pengadilan Negeri Banyuwangi.* http://pn-banyuwangi.go.id/profil-ketua (accessed April 25, 2018)

Mathari, R. 2012. *Mereka Sibuk Menghitung Langkah Ayam: Reportase Kasus Syiah Sampang.* https://rusdimathari.com/2012/08/27/mereka-sibuk-menghitung-langkah-ayam-reportase-kasus-syiah-sampang/ (accessed April 3, 2018).

Menchik, J. 2016. *Islam and Democracy in Indonesia: Tolerance without Liberalism.* Cambridge: Cambridge University Press.

Miichi, K. 2015. *Quantitative Research for Islamic Parties in Indonesia.* Jakarta: Lembaga Ilmu Pengetahuan Indonesia (unpublished).

Miichi, K. and Y. Kayane. (forthcoming). "The Politics of Religious Pluralism in Indonesia: The Shi'a Response to the Sampang Incidents in 2011–2012". *TRaNS: Trans-Regional and -National Studies of Southeast Asia.*

MUI Sampang. 2012. *Keputusan Fatwa No. A. 035/MUI/Spg/I/2012.*

Muradi. 2014. *Politics and Governance in Indonesia: The Police in the Era of Reformasi.* New York: Routledge.

NU Online. 2010. "Buku Kupas Bahaya Syiah Diluncurkan". *NU.Online,* January 10, 2010. https://www.nu.or.id/post/read/21030/buku-kupas-bahaya-syiah-diluncurkan-nu-jatim-dukung (accessed April 4, 2018).

Pangabaean, S. R. 2016. "Policing Sectarian Conflict in Indonesia. The Case of Shi'ism". In *Religion, Law and Intolerance in Indonesia,* edited by Helen Pausacker and Tim Lindsey, pp. 271-288. London, New York: Routledge Curzon.

Pengadilan Negeri Sampang. 2012. *Putusan No. 69/Pid.B/2012/PN.Spg.*

Peraturan Gubernur Jawa Timur No. 55/2012

Pribadi, Y. 2013. "Islam and Politics in Madura: Ulama and Other Local Leaders in Search of Influence". Dissertation, Leiden University (unpublished).

Rozaki, A. 2009. "The Social Origins and Political Power of Blaters (Thugs) in Madura". *Kyoto Review of Southeast Asia* no. 11. http://kyotoreview.org/issue-11/the-social-origins-and-political-power-of-blaters-thugs-in-madura/ (accessed April 3, 2018).

Setara Institute. 2011. *Negara Menyangkal: Kondisi Kebebasan Beragama/ Berkeyakinan di Indonesia 2010*. Jakarta: Pustaka Masyarakat Setara.

_____. 2012. *The Condition of Freedom of Religion/ Belief in Indonesia 2011*. Jakarta: Pustaka Masyarakat Setara.

_____. 2013. *Kepemimpinan Tanpa Prakarsa: Kondisi Kebebasan Beragama/ Berkeyakinan di Indonesia 2012*. Jakarta: Pustaka Masyarakat Setara.

_____. 2014. *Stagnasi Kebebasan Agama: Kondisi Kebebasan Beragama/ Berkeyakinan di Indonesia 2013*. Jakarta: Pustaka Masyarakat Setara.

_____. 2015. *Dari Stagnasi Menjemput Harapan Baru: Kondisi Kebebasan Beragama/ Berkeyakinan di Indonesia 2014*. Jakarta: Pustaka Masyarakat Setara.

_____. 2016. *Politik Harapan Minim Pembuktian: Kondisi Kebebasan Beragama/ Berkeyakinan di Indonesia 2015*. Jakarta: Pustaka Masyarakat Setara.

_____. 2017. *Supremasi Intoleransi: Laporan Kondisi Kebebasan. Beragama/ Berkeyakinan di Indonesia 2016*. Jakarta: Pustaka Masyarakat Setara.

Sihombing, U. P. 2008. *Menggugat Bakor Pekem Kajian Hukum Terhadap Pengawasan Agama dan Kepercayaan di Indonesia*. Jakarta: The Indonesian Legal Resource Center.

Suara Pembaharuan. 2012. "Inilah Kronologis Kekerasan Warga Syiah di Sampang". *Suara Pembaruan*, August 27, 2012. http://

sp.beritasatu.com/home/inilah-kronologis-kekerasan-warga-syiah-di-sampang/23865. (accessed April 4, 2018).

Tempo. 2012. "Kronologi Penyerangan Warga Syiah di Sampang". August 27, 2012. https://nasional.tempo.co/read/425697/kronologi-penyerangan-warga-syiah-di-sampang. (accessed April 2, 2018).

Tribunnews. 2012. "Keadilan Atas Nama Syahwat Mayoritas". *Tribunnews.com,* April 13, 2012. https://www.tribunnews.com/tribunners/2012/04/13/keadilan-atas-nama-syahwat-mayoritas. (accessed April 3, 2018).

Zulkifli. 2009. "The Struggle of The Shi'is in Indonesia". Dissertation, Leiden University (unpublished).

Chapter 4
The Uneasy Road to Peace:
Papuanization and the Politics of Recognition

Rosita Dewi

Introduction

The fall of the Suharto authoritarian regime in 1998 and the subsequent *Reformasi* have created political democratization, demilitarization, and decentralization. In that context, Papua,[1] after experiencing prolonged conflict and violence, gained momentum to voice political and social demands similar to Aceh, but with a different political outcome.

Daerah Operasi Militer (DOM—military operation areas) were common during the Suharto regime in Papua to combat the separatist movement that arose after the 1962 New York agreement, which marked the end of Dutch control over Papua. With *Reformasi*, a campaign for independence through a peace dialogue grew in Papua. In July 1998,

---

1   During the Dutch occupation (1828–1962), the western part of the island was known as Netherlands New Guinea. Sukarno changed its name to West Irian (1963) to assert Indonesia's sovereignty over it. Suharto changed the name to Irian Jaya in 1973. Abdurrahman Wahid (Gus Dur) returned the island's original name, Papua, in 2000. Until 2002, it was administered as one province. In 2003, Megawati Sukarnoputri signed an order that divided it into three provinces: Papua, Irian Jaya Barat (West Papua), and Irian Jaya Tengah (Central Irian Jaya) but the order was declared unconstitutional. In this chapter Papua means both Papua and West Papua provinces.

Papuan intellectuals established a loose group known as Forum Rekonsiliasi Masyarakat Irian (FORERI—Irian Reconciliation Forum), and Habibie agreed to meet with its representatives to discuss a resolution to the conflict in Papua. Unexpectedly, FORERI demanded independence and the central government ended the dialogue. Nevertheless, in the context of democratization, the central government realized it could not maintain its military operations in Papua due to the international spotlight on human rights abuses.

Under Abdurrahman Wahid, the central government recognized the Morning Star flag and the song *Hai Tanahku Papua* (Oh My Land Papua) as cultural symbols of the Papuans (Widjojo et al., 2009: 46–48). It was during his presidency (1999–2001), often called the era of *"Kebangkitan Papua"* (Papuan Spring), that a bill on Papuan Special Autonomy was initially discussed.

Subsequently, the central government enacted Law Number 21 Year 2001 on special autonomy for Papua. The law clearly states that the indigenous people of Papua are of the Melanesian race and have their own culture, history, and languages. Papuans' limited political access was expanded with the enactment of the law and gradually they have become an important part of the local politics and administration in Papua. This process is widely perceived as a form of papuanization.

Papuanization is seen as a mechanism for respecting and standing for Papuans, as it emphasizes economic redistribution and broadens Papuans' political access (Widjojo et al., 2009). It ostensibly provides greater opportunities for Papuans as indigenous people to hold local political and administrative positions as decision makers in their provincial and local governments. Through some affirmative actions, it is viewed as a remedy for Papuan problems. The 2001 special autonomy law grants the provincial government the power to regulate community interests autonomously of the central government, based on Papuan aspirations and rights.

Papuanization is neither a new term nor concept. The Dutch colonial government began *papoeanisering* (papuanization) after World War II by selecting a number of Papuans as junior and senior bureaucrats to govern Papua. Under the administration of Indonesia, many of these bureaucrats were replaced, mostly by Javanese migrants, through the government's *transmigrasi* (transmigration) program. The domination of Javanese bureaucrats continued until the fall of Suharto's regime in 1998. Many hoped that Special Autonomy would not only rectify this imbalance but bring about structural changes in Papua.

This chapter studies on Papuan recognition through papuanization after the implementation of Papua special autonomy. Studies on Papua have either dealt with Papua independence and self-determination issues (Mote and Rutherford 2001; Chauvel 2005; King 2004; Gibbon 2004b) or failed implementation of Papua autonomy (McGibbon 2004b; Sumule 2003; Sullivan 2003; Anderson 2015). Studies on Papuan recognition have focused more on the unfulfilled Papuan *adat* land rights (Hadiprayitno 2015; Dewi 2016; Savitri and Price 2016; Alhamid, Ballard and Kanowski 2009; Zakaria, Kleden, and Frangky 2011; Ito, Rachman, and Savitri 2014). This paper is also on Papuan recoginition, but the major focus is on the papuanization, which has not been studied well before but the analysis on papuanization will vividly reveal the ambivalent situations faced by Papuans during the two decades of Papuan special autonomy.

This chapter discusses how papuanization has been implemented in Papua during the past 20 years (2001–2021) to accommodate the political and social demands of the Papuans. It describes how papuanization, despite its stated intentions, has created a new set of problems for Papuans. It highlights the importance of the definition of *Orang Asli Papua* (OAP— native or indigenous Papuans) in the political lexicon and the related competition among *adat*[2] organizations to represent Papuans. Increasing Papuan ethnocentrism resulting from papuanization and fragmentation at the provincial and regency levels is threatening Papuan horizontal relations

---

2   Adat describes as a way of life that links the history of a particular community. It refers to the accepted norms, values and beliefs of the community (Davidson and Henley, 2007).

and solidarity. Left unmitigated, such social cultural tensions could trigger further internal conflict in Papua.

Governing Papua: Seven Decades of Shifting Power

After Indonesia's declaration of independence in 1945, Papua remained under Dutch occupation. In 1946, the Dutch established Papua as a residency separate from Molucca, and appointed Jan van Eechoud as its first resident governor. Negotiations between Indonesia and the Netherlands at the Roundtable Conference in 1949 failed to reach agreement on the status of Papua, which remained under Dutch administrative control for 12 more years (Chauvel, 2004: 9).

After the Roundtable Conference, Dutch efforts to win the trust of Papuans became more fervent (Mansoben, 1995: 296). The abundant mining and agriculture resources and its importance as a hub of trade were strong reasons to retain Papua as a Dutch colony. Van Eechoud promoted education to produce a *pamong pradja* (civil service) made up of Papuan elites who would help the Dutch administer Papua. Only indigenous Papuans could enter the *pamong pradja* training school and generally, students were selected from the sons of *adat* leaders, tribal leaders, and village heads. After graduation, they were expected to work in the Dutch administration to influence *adat* communities, thus acting as the bulwark of Dutch colonialism against rising Indonesian nationalism (Visser, 2012: 6). The Dutch referred to this strategy as *papoeanisering* or papuanization (Renwarin and Pattiara, 1984: 132).

Papuanization had intensified by the end of the 1950s as many young Papuans were promoted from junior to senior officials in Papua's government (Visser, 2012: 13). By 1957, the Dutch administration had placed Papuans in 30% of government posts, with the target of filling 90% of government posts with Papuans by 1970 (Osborne, 1985: 20). Papuan officers, called *tuan bestir*, became mediators between the community and the state under Dutch domination.[3] The Dutch administration also

---

3   In 1961, it was reported that 4,950 of the 8,800 government officers in Papua were Papuans. This papuanization was used to enhance the Papuan identity (Kroef, 1968: 693–694).

began establishing regional councils called *Streekraden*. All of this was in preparation for Papuan self-rule should the negotiations for Papua to be part of the Dutch commonwealth fail (Rutherford, 2012: 69).

In 1959, the Dutch government successfully formed *Streekraden* in Biak-Numfor, Yapen-Waropen, Fakfak, Merauke, and Sorong. Village representatives elected the council members, and the councils were assigned to engage Papuans, especially those who graduated from the Dutch *pamong pradja* school, in a new democracy. These regional councils were to comprise Nieuw Guinea Raad (NGR—New Guinea Council) that was mandated in the 1949 roundtable negotiation (Visser, 2012: 204–206).

The NGR was formed in April 1961 following a general election held during February 18–25, 1961. The council functioned as a legislative body and became the first parliament of Papua. It had 28 members (16 elected and 12 appointed), of which 23 were Papuans and the remaining 5 were Dutch (3 elected and 2 appointed) (*The Sydney Morning Herald,* 1961).[4] By creating the Regional Councils and the NGR, the Dutch government expected to retain its grip over Papua.

Dutch control over Papua officially ended on August 15, 1962, when the Netherlands and Indonesia signed the New York agreement. The United Nations Temporary Executive Authority (UNTEA) prepared a transition, and on May 1, 1963, administration of Papua was transferred from the UNTEA to the Indonesian government under UN supervision. Three days later, Sukarno visited Papua as a part of Indonesia for the first time. During his visit, he appointed Eliezer Bonay[5] as its first governor, marking a restructuring of the governing administration. On this short visit, Sukarno

---

4   Delegations from Australia, Papua New Guinea, New Zealand, Britain, and France attended the inauguration of the council members in Holland. However, the United States did not send a delegation, to the disappointment of Nicholaas Jouwe, who became vice chairman of the council. There was speculation among council members that the Indonesian government had influenced the United States decision not to recognize the NGR (*The Sydney Morning Herald*, April 6, 1961).

5   Eliezer Bonay was a student of Opleidings School voor Inheemse Bestuursambtenaren (OSIBA). He became a *pamong pradja* after graduation. Eliezer was the Head of Partai Nasional (Parna—National Party) in Papua, whose mission was to integrate Papua with Indonesia. Eliezer was appointed as a member of Nieuw Guinea Raad (NGR) in 1961.

114

banned all existing Papuan political parties and thereafter began limiting political activity in Papua (Saltford, 2003: 74).

Sukarno quickly formed a temporary provincial parliament to replace the NGR. He appointed all members of the new Dewan Perwakilan Rakyat Daerah-Gotong Royong (DPRD-GR—Regional People's Assembly-Mutual Cooperation), many of whom were non-Papuan (Brookfield, 1972: 117). As NGR members lost their position in the new Papua government, several formed or joined resistance movements against Indonesian presence in Papua and were subsequently exiled to the Netherlands due to their activities (Visser, 2012).

In addition to hand-picking the members of parliament, the Indonesian government began replacing Papuan officers that had been hired by the Dutch government with relocated non-Papuan officers. By April 1963, the number of non-Papuans working as administrators in Papua had reached 1,564 (Gruss, 2005: 111). This restructuring disappointed many Papuans who had become senior civil servants during the Dutch colonization, but who were viewed by the Indonesian government as a threat to Indonesian sovereignty (Visser and Marey, 2008: 75).

The transfer of power from Sukarno to Suharto saw further policy changes in Papua that cemented Indonesian dominance. Suharto delegated Adam Malik to oversee Indonesia's return as a UN member and conduct the Act of Free Choice, an "election on the determination of opinion of the people" in Papua in 1969. The two projects were inseparable, as Indonesia wished to join the United Nations with Papua firmly as a part of the country. In the "election," the Indonesia government chose 1,026 representatives from all areas of Papua to vote in the Act of Free Choice conducted in Merauke, Jayawijaya, Paniai, Fak Fak, Sorong, Manokwari, Cenderawasih Bay, and Jayapura from July 14 to August 2, 1969. The results showed that all the selected representatives voted for integration.

Through this vote, Papua officially became a part of Indonesia, and the Indonesian government officially began ruling the Papua Province.[6] Several new administrative institutions were established to support this new provincial administration. During Suharto's regime, the majority of government officers in Papua were non-Papuans.[7]

To fill local government positions in Papua during the 1960s, many Javanese were encouraged to move to Papua through transmigration programs. These migrants not only replaced the Dutch or Indo-European officers, but also the Papuan officers. This triggered jealousy and resentment among Papuan elites, who had experienced a long history of being treated as the lowest class in society, beneath the Dutch/Europeans, the "foreign Orientals" (Chinese and Arabs), and the Indonesians. The replacements during the transfer of power sharpened the competition between the Papuans and the Indonesians (Kroef, 1986: 691–707).

The massive transmigration spurred competition not only for government positions in Papua, but also over resources and land between migrants and Papuan communities who claimed traditional ownership. This competition intensified with the ebb and flow of migration during the 1970s–1990s. Figure 4.1. shows the number of families that migrated from Java (mainly, Central Java) to Papua during 1967–1997 under the government's program. The transmigration policy in Papua was implemented not only to support national development by bringing in skilled labor from Java, but also to hasten national integration (McGibbon, 2004a: 28–29).

---

6   Based on Law Number 12 Year 1969, this province consisted of nine regencies: Jayapura, Biak Numfor, Manokwari, Sorong, Fakfak, Merauke, Jayawijaya, Paniai, and Japen Waropen. The provincial government structure followed the structure that had been formed by Sukarno. The provincial government was led by a governor. The regency government was led by the *bupati* (head of the regency). Usually, each regency contained around four heads of *kepala pemerintahan setempat* (KPS—local government). Each KPS consisted of three or four regencies and administered around thirty villages (Garnaut and Manning, 1974: 23).

7   According to statistics from each regency in Papua in 1970, 1980, and 1993, more than 50% of *bupati* in Papua were non-Papuan.

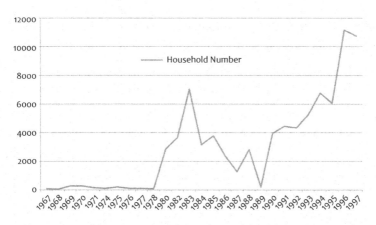

Figure 4.1. Number of families migrating from Java to Papua through the government transmigration program in 1967–1997. Note: this figure only shows the number of migrant families from the government transmigration program and does not include military or spontaneous migration. Source: the data were collected from statistics Papua from 1967 until 1980; and third, fourth, fifth and sixth of *rencana pembangunan lima tahun* (repelita—five-year development plan).

In addition to the civilian transmigration program, a policy of military transmigration relocated military personnel to Papua, which was categorized as a frontier region for the purposes of "national security and defense". Active and retired military personnel were also peppered through the ranks of the civil administration, reporting through a hierarchical chain linking the villages to the army commander. About 550 military families were settled through this program between April 1984 and February 1986 (Fearnside, 1997: 557–558). Many people also migrated to Papua from Sulawesi Island, but this was not well recorded.

Papuans became more marginalized in the governing of Papua after the enactment of the Law Number 5 Year 1979 on Village or the Village Law, which aimed to unify all village governments across Indonesia, including Papua. This directly impacted the role and duties of *adat* leaders, who had once held important functions in the administration of their villages, but after the Village Law consequently only held authority in customary rituals (Bakker, 2009: 122–123). Under the new law, the head of the village no longer had to be an *adat* member with a strong position in the community, but could instead be any official appointed by the government. Although the village head was determined through an election mechanism, the election result had to be approved by the Ministry of Home Affairs. If the ministry disagreed with the result, an acceptable village head would be appointed according to the central government's will. The central government also appointed village secretaries to assist the village heads. The village secretary was appointed as a civil servant in a permanent position until his retirement. This policy was used to control the activities that took place at the village level. According to several interviews I conducted during my research, many village secretaries were Javanese.

Table 4.1. Policy approach to Papua 1942–2004.

Government	Policy	Notes
Dutch (1942–1962)	Papuanization	Established a civil service of elite Papuans to support Dutch administration.
Sukarno (1963–1965)	Transition from papuanization to Indonesianization	Formed non-Papuan parliament; began replacing Papuans in government positions.
Suharto (1966–1998)	Cementing Indonesianization	Integration, transmigration, and *koteka* operation.[83]
Habibie (1999)	Transition	Held national dialogue between *tim seratus* (100 Papuans) and the government. Tried to divide Papua into three provinces, but Papuans rejected this plan.
Abdurrahman Wahid (2000–2001)	Recognition of Papuan identity and the "Papuan Spring"	Recognized the existence of Papuan independence movement and allowed the Papua Second Congress.
Megawati Sukarnoputri (2001–2004)	Dualistic	Enacted Special Autonomy Law for Papua as a form of papuanization, but also tried dividing Papua into three provinces as a strategy for Indonesianization.

Source: author's compilation.

---

8   *Koteka* is the penis gourd, traditionally worn by Papuans, especially in the highland area. In 1970, Suharto's government launched the military operation called *Operasi Koteka* (*Koteka* Operation) made efforts to persuade the Papuans, especially in highland areas, to wear clothes and discard the *koteka*. Some experts interpreted this operation as an Indonesian government effort to eliminate the resistance of highlanders towards the Indonesian government after the integration. Further information about *Operasi Koteka* can be read in Glazebrook (2008: 51–52).

After Suharto's fall, the demand for independence grew in Papua. In July 1998, Papuan intellectuals established FORERI, which actively organized for a national dialogue between Papua and Jakarta. In February 1999, 100 Papuans (*tim seratus* or one-hundred team, led by Tom Beanal, met with President Habibie to settle the problem of Papua. Unexpectedly, the FORERI representatives directly asked for Papuan independence and the government ended the dialogue.

In response to this meeting, the central government issued Law Number 45 Year 1999 to divide Papua into two provinces (Central Irian Jaya and West Irian Jaya) and to create three new regencies and one city. This was expected to accelerate development in Papua and at the same time reduce the demand for independence. However, a series of large demonstrations against the law took place over three consecutive days (October 14–16, 1999), forcing the government to scrap the plan. Despite this, two important Papuan leaders, Theys Hiyo Eluay and Tom Beanal, expressed their appreciation of Habibie, who had respected the dignity of Papua. During his government, granting special autonomy to Papua and Aceh was specifically mentioned in a special section on local government of the People's Consultative Assembly Decree Number IV Year 1999.[9]

Habibie's successor, President Abdurrahman Wahid, also known as Gus Dur, demonstrated the central government's commitment to solving the conflict in Papua. He began by changing the name Irian Jaya—which was believed to be an acronym of "Ikut Indonesia anti Nederland" (Follow Indonesia anti-Netherlands) and perpetuated negative stereotypes—to Papua.[10] He also allowed Papuans to express their identity by recognizing the Morning Star flag and the Oh My Land Papua song as cultural symbols of Papua. Respecting their efforts to gain recognition, he allowed the

---

9   The special section on local government of People's Consultative Assembly Decree Number IV Year 1999 mentions that "(a) to defend national integrity and Indonesian unity by respecting the equality, and social and cultural diversity of the Irian Jaya communities through the establishment of special autonomous region regulated by law; (b) to solve human right violations in Irian Jaya through a fair and dignified trial process.

10   The meaning is synonymous with Indonesia and anti-Netherlands. In the Dutch period, the name of Papua was used to distinguish between Indonesia and Papua. Therefore, after integration, Indonesia's government changed the name to Irian Barat in Sukarno's era, then Irian Jaya in Suharto's period.

Presidium Dewan Papua (PDP—Presidium of the Papua Council) to hold the Papuan Second Congress.[11] Gus Dur gained the respect of Papuans through this approach (Komunike Politik Papua, 2000; Suhanda, 2010).

This approach, however, changed after the Gus Dur impeachment. The new president, Megawati Sukarnoputri, opposed granting special autonomy to Papua, but increasing demands for independence left the central government out of options after three months of discussion and lobbying. Granting special autonomy became a new form of papuanization under President Megawati, who proceeded with dividing Papua into two provinces despite Papuan concerns.

Obtaining Special Autonomy as a Means of Papuan Recognition

After the Papuan Second Congress, an uncertain situation arose with the rise of a moderate group led by J.P. Solossa, who was elected as Papua's governor on November 23, 2000. Solossa initiated preparation of a draft of the Papua Special Autonomy Law, following the mandate of the People's Consultative Assembly Decree Number 4 Year 1999. At the end of December 2000, Solossa asked Cenderawasih University to promote the idea of special autonomy and gather input from Papuans on the ideal form it should take. Frans Wospakrik, rector of Cenderawasih University, led an independent team consisting of Papuan intellectuals to prepare the concept of special autonomy through public consultation. This effort faced challenges from Papuan groups who supported independence of Papua, such as the PDP, Papuan youth groups, and *adat* leaders (Solossa, 2005: 19–29).

---

11   The Second Papuan People's Congress was held May 29 – June 4, 2000. The name Second Papuan Congress refers to the First Papuan Congress, which was held by the NGR on December 1, 1961. This event was successful in mobilizing Papuans to support the independence declaration of the Presidium Dewan Papua and appointed Theys Hiyo Eluay to be the Papuan great leader. It gave momentum to the independence movement in Papua under the international spotlight. The DAP became an important pillar in mobilizing Papuans to join this event, which was attended by 2,700 participants who represented all Papuan regions and Papuan exiles from PNG, Australia, and the Netherlands (Malley, 2001).

Following public consultations and a revision of the draft, a proposed Special Autonomy Law was brought to the parliament on April 16, 2001 to be approved. The law included provision for a referendum to be held after three years of special autonomy. However, fearing that the proposed law created by the Papuans would lead to Papuan independence, the central government created its own version of a Special Autonomy Law, drafted by the Ministry of Home Affairs (Elisabeth et al., 2005: 19). During discussions of the Special Autonomy Bill for Papua, Gus Dur was impeached by the parliament and replaced by the then vice president Megawati Sukarnoputri in July 2001.[12]

The team from Papua did not abandon lobbying the central government to pass its version of the Special Autonomy Law. In the parliament, Megawati's Partai Demokrasi Indonesia-Perjuangan (PDI-P—Indonesian Democratic Party of Struggle), opposed the Papuans' bill (Elisabeth et al., 2005 : 20). However, a campaign by activists and backed by the Partai Kebangkitan Bangsa (PKB—National Awakening Party)[13] and the Partai Golongan Karya (Golkar) pushed for the Papuan bill to become law (Suhanda, 2010). The team from Papua finally forced the central government to withdraw its version of the bill by giving it the ultimatum of either withdrawing its draft or granting independence to Papua. To avoid increasing independence demands, the Minister of Home Affairs withdrew its bill from the Parliament. Therefore, the Papuan version was the one discussed in the legislature. On July 19, 2001, Parliament formed *panitia khusus* (pansus—special committee), chaired by Sabam Sirait from PDI-P, to discuss the draft Special Autonomy Law for Papua. The committee was comprised of 40 parliamentarians, including all members of parliament

---

12 Gus Dur was impeached over charges of corruption (in the Bulogate and Bruneigate case) and incompetence due to his eye blindness. On July 23, 2001, Majelis Permusyawaratan Rakyat (MPR—People's Consultative Assembly) unanimously voted to impeach Wahid and replace him with Megawati as president. Wahid continued to insist that he was the president and stayed for some days in the Presidential Palace, but eventually left the residence on July 25, 2001 for a trip overseas to the United States for health treatment.

13 Abdurrahman Wahid, popularly known as Gus Dur, was an Indonesian Muslim religious political leader who served as the President of Republic Indonesia from 1999–2001. His grandfather was the founder of Nahdlatul Ulama (NU), one of the biggest Islamic organizations in Indonesia. Gus Dur was the leader of NU and the founder of Partai Kebangkitan Bangsa (PKB) in 1999.

from Papua. After three months of discussion and lobbying, the draft was finalized on October 20, 2001 (Elisabeth et al., 2005: 20).

Theys and other PDP members rejected the new Special Autonomy Law, demanding full Papuan independence. It was believed that his resistance toward implementation of the Law was the reason for his kidnapping and murder by the Komando Pasukan Khusus (Kopassus—Special Forces Command) on November 10, 2001 (Ramandey, 2004). His death strengthened demands for Papuan independence and intensified international monitoring over human rights violations in Papua. Several incidents were categorized as severe human right violations during this time, including those in Wamena on October 6, 2000, in Abepura on December 7, 2000, and in Wasior on June 13, 2001 (Team Papua LIPI, n.d). This situation put pressure on the central government to enact the Special Autonomy Law for Papua on November 21, 2001, just one month after its finalization. The enacted version, however, had several significant omissions, including the provision for a referendum that was requested in the draft from Papua. Hari Sabarno, then minister of home affairs, said that, "the special autonomy is the comprehensive solution for resolving conflicts in Papua" (Elisabeth et al., 2005: 20). Special autonomy for Papua came to be widely viewed as a win-win solution for Jakarta and Papua. For Papuans, it provided a path to "cooperate" with the central government to solve the problems of marginalization and human rights abuses, and also to enshrine the rights of Papuans. For Jakarta, it became a means of tampering further conflict and calls for independence.

The special autonomy law required the central government to recognize the existence and basic rights of Papuans. One of the main aims of the Law was to enshrine basic *adat* rights. It specifically defines *Orang Asli Papua* (OAP) as Melanesian people, consisting of indigenous tribes in Papua and/or people who have been accepted or recognized as indigenous Papua by Papuans. The status of special autonomy became a new form of papuanization (Widjojo et al., 2009) that was defined as *mem-Papua-kan Papua* (making Papua into Papua). The law thus became a stepping-stone for Papuans to *menjadi tuan di tanahnya sendiri* (become the masters of their land). In 2000, the vice governor of Papua, R.G. Djopari, spoke about the need for papuanization to ensure wider opportunity for Papuans to be decision makers in Papua, saying, "the Papuan people are capable of handling their own affairs and have the freedom to control and develop their territory" (Elisabeth et al., 2004). The affirmative action policies in the law also strive to give Papuans greater opportunities to participate in Papuan politics and economics, which were dominated by non-Papuans during Suharto's regime. The Law's papuanization thus had the capacity to unseat long-held power dynamics in which important and strategic positions as decision makers were occupied by non-Papuans or Papuans with military backgrounds.

The Role of *Adat* Organizations in Papuan Recognition

Adat became a renewed source of political and economic power after the Special Autonomy Law formally recognized the *adat* right of indigenous Papuans and obligated the *adat* community's involvement in the decision-making process. Recognition was legally given by the central government to Papuan communities, which formally cemented *adat* values and customs as central to the Papuan way of life. The Special Autonomy Law mandated the establishment of the Majelis Rakyat Papua (MRP— Papuan People's Assembly), a formal government body charged with protecting and promoting Papuan values and interests. The formation of the MRP became an important element of institutionalizing the recognition of Papuans. Based on the Papua Special Autonomy Law, the MRP has the authority to recommend and approve *peraturan daerah khusus* (perdasus—special local regulations) proposed by the Dewan Perwakilan Rakyat Papua (DPRP—People's Representative Council of Papua) and the governor. Cooperation with a third party also requires approval from the MRP if it relates to the protection of Papuan rights. The role of the MRP is to voice the aspirations of Papuans and to facilitate resolution of problems. Based on the Special Autonomy Law, the MRP has the right to ask and even review *peraturan daerah provinsi* (perdasi—provincial government bylaw) if a regulation might harm the rights of Papuans. These broad powers of the MRP became a concern of the central government which was therefore careful in drafting the government regulation to limit the authority and rights of the MRP. It took more than three years to establish the MRP, even though the Special Autonomy Law regulated that the central government should establish it within a year after the enactment of the law.

The implementation of the Special Autonomy Law for Papua opened opportunities for the creation of *adat* organizations. Besides the MRP as a formal *adat* representative, the law also influenced the growth of the non-government *adat* organization called the Dewan Adat Papua (DAP—Papua Customary Council). The DAP claims to represent more than 300 tribes in Papua and was established by Theys Eluay during the Suharto regime. Its name was changed from the Lembaga Musyawarah Adat (LMA—Customary Deliberative Assembly) to DAP after Theys was murdered, to reflect the change in the organization's direction from supporting the central government to opposing it. After the second Papua Congress, the DAP became an important *adat* organization in Papua. It aimed to incorporate grassroots Papuan aspirations and concerns in a revitalization of *adat* institutions, which were legitimized by the Second Papuan People's Congress.

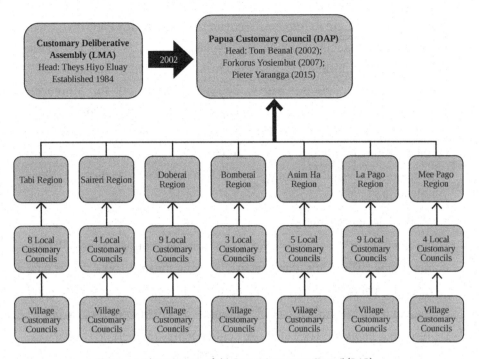

Figure 4.2. The structure of the Papua Customary Council (DAP).

The organizational structure of the DAP followed *adat* regional divisions. Dewan Adat Wilayah (DAW—Regional Customary Council) consisted of the seven *adat* regions: (1) Tabi, (2) Saireri, (3) Domberai, (4) Bomberai, (5) Anim Ha, (6) La Pago, and (7) Mee Pago. The Regional Customary Council is divided into Dewan Adat Daerah (Local Customary Councils) and Dewan Adat Kampung (DAK—Village Customary Councils). Although the village councils are the lowest level of the customary council, they maintain an important role in articulating the aspirations of the DAP at the local level. Conversely, the village councils often introduce topics to be discussed at higher levels of the council and as such, the concerns and aspirations of the Papuans are channeled to the government through the village councils.

These bottom-up characteristics are the source of the DAP's legitimacy as a representative *adat* institution. However, because the DAP frequently criticizes the central government, the government does not recognize it, resulting in its failure to implement concrete programs for Papuans, which has bred dissatisfaction among the Papuan elite. This *adat* institution only became the principal dialogue partner during Abdurrahman Wahid's presidential term in 2000 (Chauvel, 2005; McGibbon, 2004b). Moreover, the central government was suspicious of the DAP and feared that it would mobilize Papuans against the Indonesian Government because key DAP members also supported the Papua independence movement (Focus group discussion with several members of MRP in Jakarta on August 25, 2005; Elisabeth et al., 2005).

The Special Autonomy Law ensured that the central government could not ignore the role of *adat* institutions as representatives of *adat* communities. The Unit Percepatan Pembangungan Papua dan Papua Barat (Papua and West Papua Development Acceleration Agency), a hand of the central government, could no longer be effectively recognized as representing Papuans. The MRP also could not play this role due to Papuan, as well as central government, distrust.[14] Therefore, eight years after the enactment of the Special Autonomy Law, the central government created the Lembaga Masyarakat Adat (LMA—Customary Community Council)[15] as an ostensibly reliable and representative *adat* institution.

This LMA is supported by the central government to deligitimize DAP. Different from DAP, LMA has delivered concrete programs to Papua and, therefore, has begun to receive support from some of the Papuan elite. The LMA was formed to garner Papuan support to counter DAP's influence

---

14   The central government was suspicious that the MRP would become a "super body" of Papuans against the central government because several elected members of the MRP were perceived to be separatist supporters. Conversely, Papuans distrusted the MRP because its membership selection did not accord with the Government Regulation Number 54 Year 2004. Several MRP members elected by Papuans and considered pro-Papuan were not even inducted. The central government divided the MRP, which from 2005–2010 covered all of Papua, into two bodies (MRP Papua and MRP West Papua) in 2011 with the intention of reducing the MRP's power and authority and making the MRP just an 'ornament' of special autonomy (Focus group discussion with several member of MRP in Jakarta on July 19, 2006).

15   This Lembaga Masyarakat Adat led by Lenis Kogoya is different from the LMA (Lembaga Musyawarah Adat) led by Theys Eluay. The LMA led by Theys changed into the DAP. The same abbreviation of the new council under Kogoya—LMA—was used deliberately to confuse the *adat* communities.

and bring *adat* institutions further under the influence of the central government. When the DAP was the only *adat* organization, its support by the Papuan peoples was assumed to be unequivocal. With the emergence of the LMA, DAP was no longer the sole body of *adat* representation. The policy to form the LMA and make Kogoya its leader successfully gnawed at the DAP's support base[16].

Lenis Kogoya comes from a tribe in Jayawijaya, in the Papuan highlands. He has a close relationship with Joko Suyanto, the Coordinating Minister of Political, Legal and Security Affairs under President Yudhoyono[17]. The close ties between Kogoya and Joko Suyanto are apparent when considering Kogoya's previous positions within the government. Furthermore, under President Jokowi (2014–2019), Kogoya was appointed as one of the President Special Staff. His appointment was the strategy of the central government to use LMA, purported to represent the Papuan people, as an instrument to justify and implement central government policies. In addition, Kogoya's placement as the LMA leader may form part of a strategy on the part of the central government to balance political power in Papua, as the highlands are seen as a center of the Papuan separatist movement (interview with SM, October 22, 2015), and people from the highlands had been filling key Papuan political positions. These included the Provincial Governor (2013–2018), Lukas Enembe, who comes from Tolikara, the first and second Head of the Papuan People's Assembly (MRP), and the DAP leader Forkorus Yaboisembut (2007–2015) from Sentani, who replaced Tom Beanal (2002–2007) from the Amungme tribes in the Timika Regency.

As an *adat* organization recognized by the government, the LMA plays a significant role in coordinating Papuan policies with the central government. The Special Autonomy Law requires that Papuan *adat* communities must be consulted before any policy is implemented in Papua. Consulting the LMA may suffice to legitimize government policies implemented in Papua, even if the organization clearly aligns with the

---

16 Interview with JW, October 23, 2015.

17 Interview with JW, October 23, 2015

motives of the central government. To strengthen its position, the new LMA has intensified its presence at the regency, district, and village levels. The LMA was formed in several regions of Papua that are strategically important from the central government's point of view. The central government promotes the LMA as representative of Papuan society and a legitimate *adat* organization, and it in turn functions as a pawn of the central government through which specific policies may be implemented in Papua without violating human rights.

Claiming to be Papuan and Granting the Status of *Anak Adat*

Article 1 (t) of the Papua Special Autonomy Law defines OAP as Melanesian people consisting of indigenous tribes in Papua and/or people whom Papuans have accepted or recognized as indigenous Papuans. This definition of OAP has since been debated. The definition has become significant because it relates to which Papuans can avail of greater opportunities for economic and political access (in the political realm, for example, the Law states that the governor and the vice governor of Papua must be OAP).

As the first-ever Papuan cultural representative institution, the MRP provided a detailed definition of OAP. It first developed criteria of what constitutes an OAP for the Papua governor and vice governor candidacy in 2005, as follows: someone born of a person whose parents are both native Papuans (Melanesian race), a person whose father is a native Papuan (Melanesian race), a person who has a cultural base (in Papua). These criteria were determined with the assumption that the Papuan inheritance system was patrilineal (Musa'ad, 2013: 194), thus closing the door to Papuans born of Papuan mothers and non-Papuan fathers and non-Papuans to occupy important positions in Papua. Papuans born of only Papuan mothers, non-Papuans from transmigrant families who had lived in Papua for decades, and non-Papuans who married Papuan women challenged these criteria. Members of this group accused the MRP of violating their rights as Papuans, guaranteed in the Papua Special Autonomy Law. The law only states that the OAP comprises people who belong to the Melanesian race, consisting of native tribes in Papua Province and/or people who are accepted and recognized as OAP by Papua's *adat* community. Therefore, the law does not limit OAP status based on patrilineal descent. The law also accommodates non-Papuans as OAP, as long as they are acknowledged by the Papuan community[18].

To respond to the protests, the MRP used the analogy that Papuans who had lived for decades in Java or Sulawesi would be called Papuans in those places, but would not be counted as *Orang Asli Jawa* (Java Natives) or *Orang Asli Sulawesi* (Sulawesi Natives). Therefore, the MRP argued that the transmigrants and non-Papuans who had lived in Papua could not claim to be OAP. Regarding patrilineality, the MRP contended that as the cultural representative, it should respect and uphold the Papuan culture on which it based its decision, and claimed that the majority of Papuans practice patrilineal inheritance. Moreover, the MRP stated that it made this decision in order to return Papuan supremacy to Papua.

Although the MRP decision was non-binding and only a recommendation, it was used to determine the qualified candidates for governor and vice governor in the first direct election in Papua. On November 16, 2005, the DPRP submitted the names of five pairs of proposed gubernatorial and vice gubernatorial candidates to the MRP for approval as OAP. On November 18, the MRP announced that two vice gubernatorial candidates, Komaruddin Watubun and Mohammad Musa'ad, were ineligible for candidacy because they were not OAP. Watubun's case was uncontroversial because neither of his parents were Papuan. However, the decision on Musa'ad sparked hours of heated debate within the MRP. Musa'ad's mother was a Papuan from Fakfak, while his father was of Arab descent. According to the MRP, since he was not born of a Papuan father, he did not meet the MRP's first criterion for being OAP. The issue became a controversy because Musa'ad was only evaluated based on the first criterion; he was not assessed on the criterion that says someone who

---

18   Interview with MM, August 15, 2008.

is acknowledged and accepted by the *adat* community can be classified as OAP, as also mentioned in MRP Decree Number 6 Year 2005. If he was assessed based on this criterion, he would have been qualified for the vice governor candidacy. One MRP member, who was an *adat* leader from the Bomberay tribe, declared that he supported Musa'ad and rejected the MRP decision during its meeting. This decision was marred by a violent protest outside the MRP office, which injured 27 people, including 11 police officers (ICG, March 23, 2006).

Since the MRP is a formal cultural institution in Papua, whose function is to protect the *adat* and Papuan rights, its definition of OAP presents a dilemma. On the one hand, it is expected to restore and protect Papuan supremacy; on the other hand, the MRP criterion emphasizing patrilineality alone marginalizes Papuans born of Papuan mothers and non-Papuan fathers. It should be remembered that during the military operations (called DOM) in Papua, many Papuan women were victims of rape by military personnel. Not a few Papuans were born from these women (unpublished document on LIPI research, 2006). The MRP criterion of OAP marginalizes this group. Looking back, the reason for enacting the Papua Special Autonomy Law was the human rights violations, which galvanized international support for the independence movement in Papua. It could be said that the victims mentioned above were another reason why the central government enacted this law. Yet ironically, those victims who expected to gain from the law remained marginalized. The MRP and other *adat* organizations in Papua should consider this irony regarding the question of how to define the OAP without harming any Papuan. Beny Giay (2000) argues that the victims of the government's military operations in Papua should be called OAP. Others argue that Papuans cannot automatically be called OAP simply because they have black skin and curly hair; Papuans who like to "sell" Papuan dignity cannot be called OAP; and that non-Papuans who always work for Papua should be called OAP. From the long debate on defining OAP, even going as far as to question Papuan authenticity among the Papuan tribes, the status of being a "native Papuan" has become a political commodity. Therefore, the definition of OAP is an ongoing process and one that is especially accentuated during the general or local election period.

After the gubernatorial election of 2005, the debate on the OAP definition seemed to diminish, but it was back in the news when the MRP issued Decree Number 14 Year 2009, stating that all heads and vice heads of regencies, mayors, and vice mayors in Papua had to be OAP. The MRP expected that the DPRP and the provincial governor would use the decree to determine the qualified candidates in the direct local i heard elections of 2009. The issuance of this decree was based on the MRP's function to protect the rights of OAP regulated in Article 20 (1) of the Papua Special Autonomy Law. The MRP's function is clarified in the explanation section of this law, specifying that this function includes considering the DPRD of cities and regencies in the determination of eligible candidates for regency heads/vice heads and mayors/vice mayors running for the local election. Therefore, with the approaching local i heard elections, the MRP released a new decree recommending that the candidates must be OAP. The OAP criteria referred to MRP Decree Number 6 Year 2005.

Similar to the 2005 decree, this new decree also attracted its proponents and protesters. The group that supported the decree viewed it as a form of affirmative action. It would offer greater opportunities for OAP to occupy significant positions in Papua as mandated in the Papua Special Autonomy Law. The decree would reduce competition from non-Papuans and non-Papuan domination in Papua's political and economic sectors. It aimed to make OAP masters of their own land. The decree was not fully supported, however. Transmigrants argued that they had been part of the Papuan community for over 20 years. Political parties with non-Papuan candidates also contested this decree. They accused the MRP of abuse of authority on this matter, arguing that its scope was limited to the provincial level under the Papua Special Autonomy Law and did not include the regency or city levels. Authority over those levels, they argued, should follow the Law Number 32 Year 2004 on local government, and therefore the MRP had no authority to be involved in the process of local elections at the regency or city level.

Similar to the gubernatorial candidacy process in 2005, the 2009 MRP decree was non-binding and had to be implemented by the DPRD. Several regencies and cities in Papua did not follow the MRP recommendation. Nonetheless, gaining OAP status had become important, whether or not the MRP's recommendation was implemented. This can be observed in the eagerness of non-Papuans to become Papuans by becoming *anak adat* (custom bearers). Bestowing the *anak adat* status to non-Papuans is not new in the Papuan tradition. Non-Papuans are initiated as *anak adat* of a certain tribe because they are meritorious for that tribe. Currently, induction as *anak adat* is flourishing, especially when local i heard elections approach. The induction of non-Papuans is not only based on merit for a tribe, but also a transaction process through the *adat* leader. Today, this transaction is seen as more prevalent even among non-Papuans who have not previously worked or stayed with Papuans. During the past few years, it can be observed that suddenly, some Javanese become *anak adat* of the Biak tribe, or some North Sumatrans become *anak adat* of the Sarmi[19].

Granting *anak adat* status is not only for election purposes; non-Papuan induction as *anak adat* is also used to gain access to *adat* land in Papua. Such was the case in the establishment of the Merauke Integrated Food and Energy Estate (MIFEE) in Merauke regency. Arifin Panigoro, the CEO of the Medco Group, which initiated the project, was appointed to be a member of the Marind tribe, the largest in Merauke Regency[20]. The close relationship between Panigoro and John Gluba Gebze, the head of Merauke Regency that also claimed as *adat* leader, was solidified when the latter granted the former the title "Arifin Dipanigoro Warku Gebze" as a member of the Gebze clan. Panigoro's induction as *anak adat* of the Marind tribe thus enabled him to become an *adat* landowner (*Tabloid Jubi*, 2009). All of these examples illustrate how OAP status has been commodified in Papua.

---

19   Interview with SM October 22, 2015.
20   Interview with JGG, August 29, 2014.

The process of granting the status of *anak adat* is quite interesting. From a positive point of view, the transaction illustrates how the roles of *adat* leaders and *adat* organizations have been revitalized. The *adat* leader's authority, which was shifted to the village leader during the Suharto regime through Village Law Number 5 Year 1975, was restored after the special autonomy. On the negative side, however, a current *adat* leader in Papua can grant the *anak adat* status to anyone without consideration of the *adat* values or welfare of his tribe. *Adat* leaders of several tribes have granted the status of *anak adat* without the consent of the *adat* community, to the benefit of the leader alone. This is particularly true when political advantage is to be gained. This practice has become a concern of elders from several tribes. They are afraid that if the status of *anak adat* is given to non-tribe members or non-Papuans, it will destroy the *adat* values of their tribes. Moreover, it can create conflicts among the *adat* members between groups that support and reject offering *anak adat* to outsiders.

The phenomenon of granting non-Papuans *anak adat* status for local election purposes changed with the gubernatorial election of 2018. While previously it was mainly non-Papuans who pursued *anak adat* induction, during the 2018 election, two OAP candidates sought the status. Two gubernatorial candidates were from the highlands. The first, Lukas Enembe, was the incumbent governor who comes from Tolikara. He is *anak adat* in Kembu Valley (Wonda, 2015). The second candidate, John Wempi Wetipo, had been the head of Jayawijaya Regency for two periods (2010–2015 and 2016–2021). Famously called JWW, he was *anak adat* of the Dani tribe from Baliem Valley, Wamena.

Pater Neles Tebay, the leader of Jaringan Damai Papua (Papua Peace Network), calls the 2018 gubernatorial election an *anak koteka* battle. The fact that both candidates were highlanders was a first in the history of Papua. Unlike a regency head, the governorship includes all the highland and coastal areas. The candidates for governor therefore must garner votes from the coastal areas, a potentially difficult thing to do for candidates from the highlands. The form of support from the tribes in this area is shown through the induction of the gubernatorial candidates as *anak adat*. The highland areas are parts of Me Pago and La Pago *adat* regions where both candidates came from. There are still other three *adat* regions in the coastal area, Mampta-Tabi, Saereri and Animha. Therefore, these two candidates need to gain the sympathy form these three *adat* regions in Papua Province. The Mampta-Tabi adat region's DAP regarded Lukas Enembe as one of the best *anak adat* and inducted him as (*Bapak Pembangunan Sejati Papua*) the Sincere Father of Papua's Development (*Papua Today*, 2018). Similar to Enembe's induction, *onodoafi* (*adat* leaders) from five tribes in the Mampta-Tabi adat region inducted John Wempi as *anak adat*, suggesting their support to Wempi in the next gubernatorial election (*Tabloid Jubi*, 2017).

The question arises as to why candidates still need to be inducted as *anak adat* of tribes other than their own. This situation shows that currently, it is not enough to have the OAP status, even though the criteria only mentions that the candidate must be OAP. Papuanization has unexpectedly risin ethnocentrism among the Papuans. The term OAP can be more debatable due to this new phenomenon occurring during the gubernatorial election. The debate is not limited to distinguishing between non-Papuans and Papuans, but extends to the *keaslian* (authenticity) of Papuans. It does not only involve the matter of patrilineality or matrilineality; it expands to the tribe of origin of each Papuan. This kind of debate can exacerbate ethnocentrism among Papuans.

Expanding Political Opportunity for Papuan through New Papuanization, and Its Impact

Limited political access for Papuans was opened after the enactment of Papua Special Autonomy Law Number 21 Year 2001. Several institutions were formed to open the political access for Papuans as mandated by the law, such as the MRP as the cultural representative organization and the DPRP as legislative body. All members of MRP must be Papuan. Meanwhile, DPRP consists of elected and appointed members. The appointed members must be Papuan. The appointed DPRP members are elected by *adat* communities in seven *adat* regions.[21] The formation of these formal bodies aims to recognize and protect Papuan rights based on the Papuan *adat* and culture. Moreover, Papuans are gradually becoming an important part of the local politics and administration in Papua. Although there is no obligation that the regency head or mayors in Papua have to be Papuan as explained in the previous discussion, papuanization has influenced this, illustrating how Papuan elites are coming to dominate the local politics.

The number of Papuans who have a seat in the DPRP showed the significant number for period 2004–2009 and 2009–2014; 60% (Widjojo et al., 2008: 42) and 46% (Musa'ad, 2013: 192). The domination of Papuans can also be seen in the regency level DPRD. Figure 4.3. shows the percentage of Papuans who were members of DPRD during 2009–2014 in several regencies in Papua Province. Since 2004, many political parties nominated *adat* leaders or elders to increase the popularity of their political party.

After the election of 2014, the MRP, the DPRP, and *adat* elements in Papua forced the government to require an *adat* share of the DPRP through *adat* appointment as mandated in the Papua Special Autonomy Law (Article 6 of the law states that DPRP members consist of both elected and appointed members). Therefore, Papuan elites asked the central government to comply with the law's mandate. After waiting for years, the central government inducted 14 appointed members in Papua Province and 11 appointed members in West Papua to the DPRP at the end 2017.

---

21   DPRP is a provincial legislative body in Papua and West Papua. DPRP consists of elected members and appointed members who represent the Papuan communities. The appointed members comprise a quarter of the DPRD for Papua Province. There are 68 DPRP members for Papua Province. Meanwhile, there are 56 DPRP members for West Papua Province. There are 14 appointed members of DPRP of Papua Province and 11 appointed members of DPRP of West Papua Province.

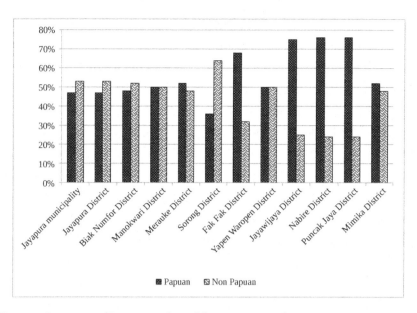

Figure 4.3. Percentage of Papuan members of the DPRD in several regencies in Papua Province in 2009–2014 (Musa'ad, 2013: 185–226).

In addition to the DPRP and the MRP, papuanization has also led to Papuan domination of local government positions. The MRP regulated that the governorship and vice governorship must be held by OAP. Following the patrilineal culture in Papua, the MRP defines OAP as persons who have a Papuan father. This regulation allows Papuan to sit in the highest positions in Papua's government. Papuan domination is not only seen at the provincial level, but also at the regency and city levels of government (see Figure 4.4.). Since 2001, nearly all (98%) the heads of local government in Papua—including Papua and West Papua Provinces—have been Papuan. Usually, non-Papuans who sit as the head of a regency are temporary appointees of the Ministry of Home Affairs. The background of the local government head is not dominated by the military anymore; the number of local government heads with a bureaucrat background has continuously increased since 2001.

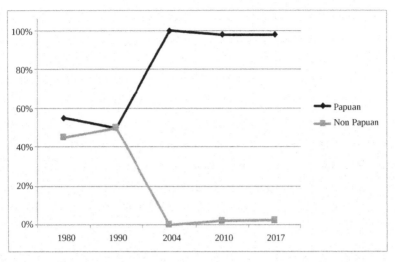

Figure 4.4. Local government heads in Papua and West Papua Provinces (Papuan and non-Papuan). Source: data were collected by the author from various statistics data of each regency in Papua 1970, 1980 and 1993, result of direct elections of local government in Papua and West Papua Provinces published by KPUD, and from various newspaper clippings from 2000–2017.

It seems that the papuanization brought about by the 2001 Special Autonomy Law has marked "the return" of Papuan political supremacy in Papua. On the numbers alone, it appears to be a positive story. The negative impact must also be considered, however. The narrow understanding of papuanization can trigger horizontal conflict in Papua. We can see in the early process of MRP's formation in 2005, the unreliable election of MRP members from *adat* representatives triggered conflict among several tribes in Papua. Many tribe leaders were not satisfied with the selection of fourteen *adat* representatives from more than 300 tribes. Dissatisfaction with the election of MRP members repeated every five years often reduced Papuan social cohesion and solidarity.

The problem of identity continued after the *pemekaran* (division) of Papua into the two provinces of Papua and West Papua. The *adat* representative from West Papua Province wanted to form its own MRP of West Papua (MRP-PB), arguing that only that way could proper representation be guaranteed. This triggered a rift in identity and the *pemekaran* of Papua Province succeeded to disunite Papuan solidarity, as there was no longer a single identity as "Papuan" (Focus group discussion with several members of MRP on July 19, 2006). This sparked ethno-nationalism—no longer Papuan nationalism—among the tribes in Papua. This condition was worsened by the official request from the local government of Merauke Regency to divide Papua Province further into Papua Province and South Papua Province. Several regencies in the south identified as coastal Papuans and did not feel adequately represented by the Papuan Provincial government, which was primarily composed of Papuan highlanders. They argued that the Papuan highland could not represent the Papuan coast[22]. The fragmentation of Papuan identity will get worse if the government grants the division of South Papua Province.

Pemekaran occurred not only at the province level, but also at the regency level. After *Reformasi*, the first *pemekaran* was initiated by President Habibie through Law Number 45 Year 1999. This law mandated the creation of two new provinces (West Irian Jaya and Central Irian Jaya), separated from the mother province of Papua (Irian Jaya) and the creation of three new regencies (Paniai, Mimika, and Puncak Jaya) and one city (Sorong). Unlike the *pemekaran* of Papua Province, there was no resistance to the creation of three regencies and one city, because these had been prepared since 1996 through the appointment of provisional regency heads and mayors in charge of the creation of new autonomous governments. The *pemekaran* of regencies accelerated with the implementation of the 2001 Special Autonomy Law.[23] The number of requests from Papuans for regency *pemekaran* rose sharply in the proceeding years; in 2013 alone, the DPR discussed 33 candidates for new regencies in Papua. The DPR agreed on a plan to create these new regencies in October 2013, but it was eventually cancelled due to the objection of the Governor of Papua (*Tabloid Jubi*, 2013).

---

22 Interview with SL, November 11, 2015.

23 After the *pemekaran* of three regencies and one city mandated in the Law Number 45 Year 1999, there were other *pemekaran* of regencies under the Law Number 26 Year 2002. This law regulated the formation of the regencies of Sarmi, Keerom, Sorong Selatan, Raja Ampat, Pegunungan Bintang, Yahukimo, Tolikara, Waropen, Kaimana, Boven Digoel, Mappi, Asmat, Teluk Bintuni, and Teluk Wondama.

The *pemekaran* awakened ethnic politics in Papua. The phenomena of ethnocentrism gained momentum after the implementation of direct elections for local government heads and vice heads in 2005. Direct local elections increased ethnocentrism among the tribes in Papua, fragmenting Papuan identity.

This fragmentation continued during the *pemilihan kepala daerah* (*pilkada*—local head election) and the *pilkada serentak* (concurrent local head election) in 11 regencies in 2017. Issues such as the *keaslian* (authenticity) of Papuan identity and tribe superiority in Papua not only sharpened the fragmentation, but also triggered horizontal conflict. During 2010–2014, the local elections in Papua caused 71 deaths. The local election in Tolikara in 2012 sparked inter-tribal conflict that caused six deaths and dozens of injuries (*Kompas,* 2012). The conflict was repeated again in the 2017 local head election, causing 19 deaths and dozens of injuries. Conflict among Papuans also occurred during the local i heard election in 2017 in Puncak Jaya and Intan Jaya Regencies (Juliawati, 2018). Furthermore, the battle between two *anak koteka* in the Papua governorship election together with local i heard elections in seven regencies in highland areas— Jayawijaya, Puncak, Paniai, Deiyai, Memberamo Tengah, Biak Numfor and Mimika—has entrenched internal Papuan conflict.

Conclusion

This chapter has discussed how papuanization – the implementation of an affirmative policy to support Papuans in the political sphere – is problematic. From the Papuan elite point of view, the papuanization policy implemented during Dutch colonization respected Papuans and provided them with wider political access, allowing Papuans to occupy strategic positions in Papua's bureaucracy and parliament. Papuanization was renewed with the 2001 Papua Special Autonomy Law, which ostensibly allows Papuans to be the "masters of their land." In exchange for allowing Papuans to occupy important positions in the local politics and bureaucracy, the central government expects to gain back Papuan trust and reduce the threat of a separatist movement. While on the surface this policy may seem to have good intentions, its underlying assumption is patriarchal because Papuan "fate was being decided by others without them being consulted." (Chauvel, n.d.).

Since enactment of the Special Autonomy Law in 2001, Papuans are facing several problems. The definition of OAP, still contested among the central and local government, the local parliament, and *adat* institutions, has become hotly contested due to papuanization. The definition of OAP has broad implications for the distribution and commodification of power, particularly in terms of the marginalization of certain Papuan groups, including those born of Papuan mothers and non-Papuan fathers. This is ironic given that the origins of the passage of the law lie in seeking justice for victims of human rights abuses such as those born from the raped Papuan women.

Contestation over the OAP definition increased after the implementation of direct local head elections in 2005, which fueled a rise in ethnocentrism among the tribes in Papua, further fragmenting Papuan identity. This presents another paradox: championing the OAP and seeking criteria for who deserves to be called a Papuan native is weakening a unified Papuan identity.

This chapter has also described the increasing trend of non-Papuans and Papuans alike seeking the *anak adat* status of particular tribes in order to be considered a "true Papuan" and gain supporters in local elections. All of these situations raise concern about the implementation of papuanization. While it seemingly might strengthen and unify the Papuan identity, in fact it has eroded a unified Papuan identity and reinforced tribal identity instead.

The central government has cultivated divisions among Papuans through the establishment of the LMA, led by Lenis Kogoya. The LMA succeeded in reducing the DAP's role as a Papuan representative, and as an *adat* organization at the village level, LMA can challenge the definition of OAP if it does not align with the central government's interest. The central government further eroded the solidarity of Papuans through the division of

Papua Province into Papua and West Papua Provinces. The fragmentation could continue to divide Papuans, decreasing their bargaining position *vis-a-vis* the central government. Amid this dynamic, it is easy to conclude that an excess of papuanization is actually used as an instrument of the central government to spur internal conflicts to divide and rule Papuans.

The papuanization brought about by the Special Autonomy Law has also provided the central government with a convenient means to avoid any blame for the slow progress of development, continuing poverty, and other problems in Papua. According to the central government, local governments and Papuans are responsible for dealing with the problems in Papua, particularly as local governments have access to huge amounts of special autonomy funds to manage their affairs.

Approaching two decades of Special Autonomy implementation, the political, economic, and social structures in Papua have changed through affirmative action policy. Indeed, the nature of papuanization itself has also changed. This special autonomy will be evaluated after 20 years, especially regarding the special autonomy fund and affirmative policy. Continuance of special autonomy with the same or different approaches will depend on how it is evaluated. After 2021, will there be special funds or affirmative policy for Papuans? What will the future hold? Papuans definitely need to think about them seriously to prevent further horizontal conflicts due to increasing ethnocentrism. If they do not, Special Autonomy may be considered a successful central government strategy to reduce the power of *adat*. The central government realized how strong the *adat* system is in Papua for political legitimation and mobilization. Therefore, the control goverment's political agenda is to reduce its role in order to co-opt Papua.

References

Alhamid, Hidayat, Chris Ballard, and Peter Kanowski. 2009. "Forest for the people? Special Autonomy, Community Forestry Cooperatives and the Apparent Return of Customary Rights in Papua," In *Community, Environment and Local Governance in Indonesia: Locating in the Commonweal,* edited by Carol Warren and John F McCarthy, pp. 145-163. New York: Routledge.

Anderson, Bobby. 2015. *Papua's Insecurity: State Failure in the Indonesian Periphery.* Honolulu: East West Center.

Badan Pusat Statistik. *Penduduk Indonesia menurut Provinsi 2010.* Jakarta: BPS.

Brookfield, H. C. 1972. *Colonialism, Development, and Independence: The Case of Melanesian Islands in South Pacific.* New York: Cambridge.

Chauvel, Richard. 2005. *Constructing Papua Nationalism: History, Ethnicity and Adaptation.* Washington D.C.: East-West Center.

_____, Richard. n.d. *Decolonising without the Colonised: The Liberation of Irian Jaya* (unpublished).

Chauvel, Richard and Ikrar Nusa Bhakti. 2004. *The Papua Conflict: Jakarta's Perceptions and Policies.* Hawaii: East-West Center.

Davidson, Jamie S. and David Henley. 2007. *The Revival of Tradition in Indonesian Politics: The Deployment of Adat from Colonialism to Indigenism.* Routledge: New York.

Departemen Dalam Negeri. 1969. *Capita Selekta Propinsi Irian Barat.*

Elisabeth, Adriana et al. 2004. *Pemetaan Peran dan Kepentingan.* Jakarta: LIPI Press.

Elisabeth, Adriana et al. 2005. *Agenda dan Potensi Damai di Papua.* Jakarta: LIPI Press.

Elmslie. Jim and Camellia Webb-Gannon. 2013. "A Slow-Motion Genocide: Indonesia Rule in West Papua." *Griffith Journal of Law & Human Dignity* 1: 142–166.

Fearnside, Philip M. 1997. *Transmigration in Indonesia: Lessons from its Environmental and Social Impacts.* http://philip.inpa.gov.br/publ_

livres/Preprints/1997/TRANSMEM-EM.pdf (accessed March 28, 2015).

Garnaut, Ross and Chris Manning. 1974. *Irian Jaya: The Transformation of Melanesian Economy*. Canberra: ANU Press.

Glazebrook, Diana. 2008. *Permissive Residents: West Papua Refugees Living in Papua New Guinea*. Canberra: ANU Press.

Griapon, Alexander Leonard. 2010. *Lembaga Musyawarah Adat: 10 Tahun Terakhir dari 30 Tahun Pemerintahan Propinsi di Tanah Papua*. Jayapura: Penerbit Arika-Pemerintah Kabupaten Jayapura.

Gruss, Daniel. 2005. "UNTEA and West Guinea." In *Max Planck Yearbook of United Nations Law*, edited by Armin Von Bogdandy and Rudiger Wolfrum, pp. 97-126. Leiden: Martinus Nijhoff Publishers.

Hadiprayitno, Irene. 2015. Behind Transformation: the Right to Food, Agricultural Modernisation and Indigenous Peoples in Papua, Indonesia. *Human Right Review* 16: 97-126.

International Crisis Group (ICG). 2006. "Papua: the Dangers of Shutting Down Dialogue." *Asia Briefing* 14. Jakarta/Brussels. https://www.crisisgroup.org/asia/south-east-asia/indonesia/papua-dangers-shutting-down-dialogue (accessd March 1, 2017).

Ito, Takeshi, Noer Fauzi Rachman and Laksmi Savitri. 2014. "Power to Make the Land Dispossession Acceptable: A Policy Discourse Analysis of Merauke Integrated Food and Energy Estate (MIFEE), Papua, Indonesia." *Journal of Peasant Studies* 41: 29-50.

Juliawati, Linda. 2018. "Pilkada di Papua Rawan Konflik, Ini Penyebabnya". *IDN Times*. January 31, 2018. https://news.idntimes.com/indonesia/linda/pilkada-di-papua-rawan-konflik-ini-penyebabnya-1/full (accessed April 24, 2018).

King, Peter. 2004. *West Papua and Indonesia since Suharto: Independence, Autonomy or Chaos?*. Sydney: UNSW Press.

Koentjaraningrat and Harsja W. Bachtiar. 1963. *Penduduk Irian Barat*. Jakarta: PT Penerbit Universitas.

Kompas. 2012. "Situasi Tolikara Masih Mencekam". February 19, 2012. https://nasional.kompas.com/read/2012/02/19/06134143/Situasi. Tolikara.Masih.Mencekam?page=all (accessd March 1, 2016).

Kroef, Justus Maria van der. 1968. "West New Guinea: The Uncertain Future." *Asian Survey* 8: 691–707.

Lundry, Chris. 2009. "Separatism and State Cohesion in Eastern Indonesia". Dissertation. Arizona State University (unpublished).

Malley, Michael. 2001. "Indonesia: Violence and Reform beyond Jakarta". *Southeast Asian Affairs* 2001, pp. 159-174.

Mansoben, J.R. 1995. *Sistem Politik Tradisional di Irian Jaya.* Jakarta: LIPI-RUL.

McGibbon, Rodd. 2004a. *Plural Society in Peril: Migration, Economic Change, and the Papua Conflict.* Washington D.C.: East West Center.

_____. 2004b. *Secessionist Challenges in Aceh and Papua: Is Special Autonomy the Solution?* Washington D.C.: East-West Center.

Mollet, Julius Ary. 2007. "Educational Investment in Conflict Areas of Indonesia: The Case of West Papua Province". *International Education Journal* 8: 155–166.

Mote, Octovianus and Danilyn Rutherford. 2001. From Irian Jaya to Papua: The Limits of Primordialism in Indonesia's Troubled East. *Indonesia*, 72: 115–140.

Musa'ad, Muhamad A. 2013. "Implementasi Otonomi Khusus Papua dalam Perspektif Politik dan Pemerintahan". In *Implementasi Otonomi Khusus Papua dan Papua Barat dalam Pandangan Cendekiawan Orang Asli Papua*, pp. 185-226. Jayapura: Majelis Rakyat Papua.

Osborne, Robin. 1985. *Indonesia`s Secret War: The Guerilla Struggle in Irian Jaya.* Boston: Allen & Unwin.

Papua Today. 2018. "Gubernur Lukas Enembe Dinobatkan Bapak Pembangunan Sejati Papua". February 7, 2018. https://www. papuatoday.com/2018/02/07/gubernur-lukas-enembe-dinobatkan-bapak-pembangunan-sejati-papua/ (accessed March 18, 2018).

Ramandey, Frits. 2004. *Selamat Jalan Sang Pemimpin: Menguak Tabir Kematian Tokoh Papua Theys Hiyo Eluay.* Jakarta: Pusham UI.

Renwarin, Herman and John Pattiara. 1984. *Sejarah Sosial Daerah Irian Jaya dari Hollandia ke Kotabaru (1910–1963)*. Jakarta: Departemen Pendidikan dan Kebudayaan RI.

Rollings, Leslie B. 2010. "The West Papua Dilemma". Thesis. University of Wollongong (unpublished).

Rutherford, Danilyn. 2012. *Laughing at Leviathan: Sovereignty and Audience in West Papua*. Chicago: University of Chicago Press.

Saltford, John. 2003. *The United Nations and the Indonesian Takeover of West Papua, 1962–1969: The Anatomy of Betrayal*. London: Routledge.

Savitri, Laksmi, and Susanna Price. 2016. "Beyond Special Autonomy and Customary Land Rights Recognition: Examining Land Negotiations and the Production Vulnerabilities in Papua." In *Land and Development in Indonesia: Searching for the People's Sovereignty*, edited by John F. McCarthy and Kathryn Robinson, pp. 343-362. Singapore: ISEAS Publishing.

Solossa, Jaap Perviddya. 2005. *Otonomi Khusus Papua: Mengangkat Martabat Rakyat Papua di dalam NKRI*. Jakarta: PT Pustaka Sinar Harapan.

Suhanda, Irwan. 2010. *Perjalanan politik Gus Dur*. Jakarta: Kompas.

Sumule, Agus. 2003. *Satu Setengah Tahun Otsus Papua, Refleksi dan Prospek*. Manokwari: Penerbit Yayasan Topang.

Tabloid Jubi. 2009. "Ada Apa di Balik Pemberian Gelar Adat?". August 27, 2009. http://arsip.tabloidjubi.com/?p=588 (accessed March 3, 2014).

_____. 2013. "Gubernur Papua Tolak Usulan DOB". October 3, 2013. https://jubi.co.id/gubernur-papua-tolak-usulan-dob/ (accessed March 10, 2015).

_____. 2017. "JWW Diangkat Jadi Anak Adat Skouw". January 24, 2017. https://jubi.co.id/jww-diangkat-jadi-anak-adat-skouw/ (accessed October 19, 2017).

Team Papua – LIPI. n.d. *Repression and Human Right Violation (Kekerasan dan Pelanggaran HAM di Papua 1969–2006)* (unpublished).

The Sidney Morning Herald. 1961. "New Council for West N.G. Begins Session". April 6, 1961. https://wpik.org/Src/SMH/19610406p6.pdf (accessed September 5, 2015).

Visser, Leontine (ed.). 2012. *Governing New Guinea: An oral history of Papuan administrators, 1950–1990.* Leiden: KITLV.

Visser, Leontine, and Amapon Josh Marey. 2008. *Bakti Pamong Praja di Papua di era transisi kekuasaan Belanda ke Indonesia.* Jakarta: Kompas.

Widjojo, Muridan S. et al. 2009. *Papua Roadmap: Negotiating the Past, Improving the Present and Securing the Future.* Jakarta: Yayasan Obor.

Wonda, Sendius. 2015. *Lukas Enembe, Gubernur Papua: Tokoh pluralis, moderat, dan modern.* Yogyakarta: ETM Press.

Yuniarti, Fandri (ed). 2008. *Ekspedisi Tanah Papua: Laporan Jurnalistik Kompas.* Jakarta: Kompas.

Zakaria, R. Y., Emilianus Ola Kleden, and Yafet Leonard Frangky. 2011. *MIFEE*

PART 2
PATHS TO EQUALITY

Chapter 5

The Dynamic of Education Outcome in Decentralized Indonesia (2000–2014)

Abdul Wahid Fajar Amin

Introduction

During the past three decades (1988-2018), Indonesia has shown remarkable progress in improving its educational outcomes. The national primary school enrolment rate increased from below 70% in 1970 to above 90% in the mid-1990s. Interestingly, Tobias et al. (2014) find that these improvements were mainly due to the central government's policies, including expanding coverage and restructuring school buildings, the reform-oriented institutional environment, and a constitutional commitment to allocating national budget funding to the education sector. These performances continued after 1998 under decentralization, and by 2013, the primary, lower, and upper-secondary enrolment rates had steadily risen to 96, 77, and 59% respectively.

However, Indonesia still faces several challenges in enhancing its educational outcomes. First, compared to other developing countries in Asia and Latin America, Indonesia has a high rate of between-cycle dropouts, or a large proportion of students who complete primary school, but do not enter lower secondary school and/or complete lower secondary school, but do not enter upper secondary school (Di Gropello, 2006). Second, regional disparities remain considerable at both the provincial and regency levels (see Lanjouw et al., 2001; Tobias et al., 2014; OECD/Asian Development Bank, 2015; Jones and Pratomo, 2016).

Studies on the factors affecting educational outcomes in Indonesia point to different determinants of outcomes from different perspectives. Studies by van de Walle (1992), Ramesh (2009), and Saraswati (2012) point to the prominent role of the Indonesian government in enhancing educational attainment, especially through education policies and budget allocation. Similar results were reported by World Bank studies (2013, 2014), which highlight the crucial role of the central and local governments' budget allocations in achieving successful educational outcome during decentralization. Meanwhile, Suryadarma, et al. (2006a) point to household welfare as the foremost factor affecting Indonesia's low secondary enrolment rates, and Jones (2003), Parker (2009), Rammohan and Robertson (2012), and Jones and Pratomo (2016) discuss the importance of social factors in educational attainment.

However, studies on the effect of decentralization on education show different results. Kristiansen and Pratikno (2006) show that decentralization has hampered educational outcomes by increasing household spending on education which led to regional disparities. In contrast, Gallego (2010), Falch and Fischer (2012), and Jeong et al. (2017) use the advanced levels of schooling and increased student outcomes to argue that decentralization has a positive effect on education.

While decentralization has shifted the authority to manage and deliver education services to local government, especially at the regency level, it is important to note that most of the studies on education outcomes utilize either household (see Lanjouw et al., 2001; Suryadarma et al., 2006a), national (World Bank, 2013, 2014; Tobias et al., 2014), or province level data (see Suryadarma et al., 2006b; Azzizah, 2015; Jones and Pratomo, 2016). Although Tobias et al. (2014) and Jones and Pratomo (2016) mention several regencies in their papers, their discussions are quite limited. Most studies have not offered a deeper analysis at the regency level.

Previous studies of educational outcomes have tended to focus narrowly, analyzing either primary or lower-secondary level education. They have not analyzed educational outcomes at the upper-secondary level. Moreover, despite regional disparities and gender disparities in Indonesia, few studies have discussed these issues at the regency level.

This chapter discusses educational outcomes in three dimensions. First, it applies regency level data from 2002–2014 covering 497 regencies. Second, it focuses on secondary education (both lower- and upper-secondary schooling). Third, it discusses the regional and gender disparities in education that have arisen during the last decade. To do so, we utilize econometric, statistical, and spatial analysis to identify the determinants of regional educational outcomes and assess factors affecting regional and gender disparities. Further, related to the implementation of decentralization, we examine how local government policies, including education budget provision and school expansion, may affect and improve educational outcomes. Finally, we discuss the policy implications for enhancing and improving educational outcomes in Indonesia's regions.

This chapter starts with a literature review on the determinants of education outcome. After that, it discusses the education system in decentralized Indonesia. It then presents empirical results based on school enrolment data during decentralization, and a statistical description. Next, it discusses empirical results from a regression analysis and the dynamic of regional educational outcomes. Finally, it provides some concluding remarks and policy recommendations.

Literature Review

Many factors contribute to a household's enrolment decisions, including both supply-side and demand-side determinants. From the supply-side, Duflo (2001) and the World Bank (2004) show that school expansion increases enrolment rates. Meanwhile van de Walle (1992) and Saraswati (2012) stress the role of government policy in affecting the success of educational attainment, especially through government budget allocations and subsidies that reduce the cost of attending school. From the demand-side, household welfare is a prominent factor affecting enrolment rates (see Glewwe and Jacoby, 2004; Suryadarma et al., 2006a; Sabates et al., 2010). Numerous studies demonstrated that social factors affect educational outcomes (see Jones, 2003; Gnezzy et al., 2009; Machimu and Minde, 2010).

Van de Walle (1992) argues that public spending on primary education increases enrolment rates and suggests that an increase in household standard-of-living and a pro-poor public spending approach will have positive impacts on the enrolment rate. Similarly, Saraswati (2012) argues that increasing in public spending has a positive effect on the poor by improving their welfare through enrolment rate improvement. Interestingly, she shows that the effect of government spending on education for the poor varies across Indonesia's regions, with developing regions demonstrating more efficiency in spending their budget to improve the welfare of the poor compared to more developed regions. Moreover, Ramesh (2009) shows that during crises, government education and health care programs are needed to maintain the population's education and health needs.

Previous studies on the effects of decentralization have produced different results. Kristiansen and Pratikno (2006) observed negative consequences of decentralization in the education sector. They warn that decentralization may lack transparency and accountability in government spending on education, increase household spending on education, and lead to geographical disparities. Gallego (2010), however, found that political decentralization has a positive and significant impact on more advanced levels of schooling. Similarly, using local education government level (LEA) data from Korean education statistical yearbooks, Jeong et al. (2017) show that fiscal decentralization is positively related to student outcomes.

Studies on household characteristics identify different educational outcomes. Using Vietnam's living standard survey from 1980–1998, Glewwe and Jacoby (2004) show a positive correlation between change in wealth and change in demand for education. Sabates et al. (2010) show that there is no single cause of school dropout and among salient factors, poverty appeared to be the dominant factor since it left households unable to pay school fees and is associated with the high opportunity cost to attend school.

Meanwhile, using a longitudinal household survey dataset, Suryadarma, et al. (2006a) show that household welfare has a significant impact on the low secondary enrolment rate in Indonesia. They also show the impact of other socio-economic factors such as religion, employment opportunities, and gender on educational outcomes. In addition, Utomo, et al. (2014) argue that a household income's impact on child employment also affects educational attainment. While a household may view early school-leavers as potential workers, its decision to send children to school is also affected by the opportunity cost of attending the school.

While previous studies on the determinants of educational attainment might come with a general assumption that male and female pupils have equal opportunity to attend school, some studies note the relative impact of ethnic background and gender on educational outcomes. Based on a comparison between one tribe in India and another in Tanzania, Gnezzy, et al. (2009) show that the matrilineal family system gives women better opportunities for education and jobs. Similarly, Machimu and Minde (2010) show that women from a matrilineal family attain higher education levels since they have a more influential position in deciding property rights.

In the case of Indonesia, Rammohan and Robertson (2012) discuss the role of kinship norms on gender differences in educational outcomes.

They argue that ethnic groups with strong patrilineal norms, such as the Bataks in North Sumatera and the Balinese, prioritize sons, therefore girls from these regions have lower educational outcomes. Further, they show an opposite result among the Minangnese in West Sumatra, one of the world's largest matrilineal ethnic groups, who have higher educational access and attainment levels for women than for men (also see Parker, 2009). Interestingly, Jones (2003) shows that the Madurese community traditionally arrange their daughters to marry as soon as they finish primary school, leaving female members to drop out of school without further formal education.

Aside from those socio-cultural factors, Gylfason (2001) discusses the impact of natural resources on education. He argues that nations or regions with abundant natural resources tend to neglect the development of their human resources. These regions are mostly confident that their natural resources are their most important asset, and they may inadvertently and perhaps even deliberately underrate the need for good economic policies as well as for good education. Further research by Alvares and Vergara (2016) indicate a lower educational attainment in higher natural resource export regions. They show that high labor demand in natural resource-rich areas discourages young people from continuing their study in favor of joining the labor market.

It is also important to note that Indonesia's regions still face educational disparities. Suryadarma et al. (2006) and Azzizah (2015) mention educational outcome disparities between Western and Eastern Indonesia. Suryadarma, et al. (2006) discuss ethnicity disparities and the difference in educational outcomes between urban and rural areas (also see Jones, 2003; Parker, 2009; Rammohan and Robertson, 2012). Related to that, Kristiansen and Pratikno (2006) and Jones and Pratomo (2016) show the presence of regional inequality between and within Indonesia's provinces.

All these studies demonstrate how different factors affect educational outcomes and point to the presence of educational disparities among

Indonesia's regions. From here we will discuss the education system in Indonesia and the structural changes to it following the implementation of decentralization.

The Education System in Decentralized Indonesia

Unlike education systems in other countries that are commonly administered by one ministry, Indonesia's education system has two managing ministries, Kementerian Pendidikan dan Kebudayaan (Kemdikbud—Ministry of Education and Culture and Kementerian Agama (Kemenag—Ministry of Religious Affairs). As the authority, both ministries not only set the policies, national curriculum, and standards, but also manage the education system. While Kemdikbud manages public (or secular) schools and Kemenag supervises Islamic-based schools, known as *madrasah*, both ministries establish similar compulsory curriculum that is applied to both types of schools. The main difference between these schools is that the madrasah emphasizes religious content for its pupils (Suryadarma et al., 2006a; World Bank, 2013).

The implementation of decentralization policies, by the establishment of local government laws in 1999 (Law Number 22 Year 1999 and Law Number 25 Year 1999), shifted the authority for managing local affairs and delivery of services away from the central government to local governments. This includes the authority to deliver education services, both at the primary and secondary levels of public/secular schools. However, the law preserves authority over religious affairs at the national level, therefore the authority to manage madrasah is still centralized and managed under Kemenag.

Age	School year	Education Level	Education Delivery		
			Decentralized	Centralized	
23 or above	19			Master and Doctoral	
22	18	Higher Education		Undergraduate (both general and Islamic and vocational and academic)	
21	17				
20	16				
19	15				
18	14	Secondary Education	Upper-secondary school both general and vocational (SMA & SMK)	Islamic upper-secondary School both general and vocational (MA & MAK)	
17	13				
16	12				
15	11		Lower-secondary school (SMP)	Islamic lower-secondary school (SMP)	
14	10				
13	9				
12	8	Basic Education	Elementary school (SD)	Islamic elementary School (SD)	Public and Private Institution
11	7				
10	6				
9	5				
8	4				
7	3				
6	2	Early Childhood Education	Kindergarten (TK)	Islamic kindergarten (TK)	
5	1				

Figure 5.1. Indonesia's education system in the decentralization period. Source: extrapolated from the Ministry of Education and Culture (2013); overview of the education sector in Indonesia 2012—Achievement and challenges, as cited in OECD/Asian Development Bank (2015) and World Bank (2013).

Figure 5.1. shows that the curriculum system has not changed much since decentralization; it continues to be managed by Kemdikbud and Kemenag. The role of central government remains significant in supporting education programs especially on providing huge transfers to local governments for education programs. These transfers include the *Dana Alokasi Khusus Bidang Pendidikan* (Allocations of Specific Grants for Education), *Bantuan Operasional Sekolah* (BOS—School Operating Grants), and other financial supports. The allocation of *Dana Alokasi Umum* (DAU—Block Grants) as the main source of local government revenue, is primarily based on the number of local civil servants (with the number of teachers making up a big proportion of local civil servants).

Figure 5.1. also shows that the management and delivery of education services became more complicated by the existence of two different governmental tiers. However, we may highlight that the authority of local government focuses on delivering education services, while the central government focuses on setting the curriculum and educational standards. Local government has an immense authority, especially through its budget provision and other technical policies. We find that the decision on school restructuring and expansion, school facilities provision, and teachers/ education staff recruitment and payment are managed fully by local governments.

As a result, local governments bear most of the education expenditures for provision of both primary and secondary level education (see Table 5.1.). According to annual local government financial reports, we find that most local budgets on education are spent on teacher salaries. Moreover, teacher salaries represent a major share of overall expenditures of local governments in Indonesia.

Table 5.1. Share of education expenditures by level of government and level of education in 2009.

	Central	**Province**	**Regency**
Primary	26*	3	71
Secondary	41	6	53
Higher	100	-	-

Note: *Including BOS of around 16%. Source: World Bank (2013).

Interestingly, although more than 85% of Indonesia's population is registered as Muslim, an OECD/ Asian Development Bank report (2015) shows that by the end of the 1990s less than 15% of pupils attended religious schools under Kemenag. In 2014, this trend had continued, with more than 90% of pupils (Susenas, 2014), more than 85% of schools (Podes, 2014), and more than 80% of teachers managed under secular schools (Tobias et al., 2014).

Private schools are also numerous in Indonesia. Regardless of the type of school, private schools also need to follow the national curriculum. In 2007, about 48% of all schools were private institutions, providing services for at least 31% of the total number of pupils and employing 38% of the country's total teachers for both primary and secondary level education (World Bank, 2010). However, a huge school expansion by local governments in the last decade had reduced the share of private school to 34% of total schools by 2014 (Podes, 2014).

Table 5.2. Distribution of population, pupils, education institutions and average distance between schools by level of education and age in 2002–2014.

School level	Age	Population (millions)	Students (millions)	Number of institutions	Average distance (km)
Year 2000*					
Primary	7–12	24.50	22.72	166,633	
Lower secondary	13–15	11.20	6.91	31,462	
Upper secondary	16–18	11.82	4.51	17,139	
Higher	19–22	14.15	1.32	2,472	
TOTAL		61.67	35.46		
Year 2011					
Primary	7–12	27.93	25.40	162,102	8.71
Lower secondary	13–15	12.38	8.43	48,286	7.98
Upper secondary	16–18	11.50	5.51	29,498	12.47
Higher	19–22	14.37	2.07	3,945	
TOTAL		66.18	41.40		
Year 2014					
Primary	7–12	28.11	27.09	162,102	8.68
Lower secondary	13–15	13.16	10.19	48,286	7.42
Upper secondary	16–18	11.53	6.82	29,498	11.83
Higher	19–22	14.65	3.43	3,945	36.45
TOTAL		67.45	47.54		

Note: *Used Podes (2003) to calculate number of institutions in 2002.
Source: Author's calculation from Susenas (2002, 2011, and 2014) and Podes (2003, 2011, and 2014).

Although the composition of Indonesia's school age population has not changed much since 2000, we find that with decentralization, local governments have expanded the number of schools, especially at the secondary level, since 2002 (see Table 5.2.). We also find that the number of students enrolled in secondary schools has increased rapidly over the same period. Similar to Duflo (2001), we may associate this improvement with expansion of both public and private schools in both urban and rural areas. The expansions reduce the average distance between schools of the same level, thus increasing the opportunity for children, especially the poor, to access education.

School Enrolment Rates in Indonesia

Indonesia has made strong progress in improving educational outcomes since 1970 (World Bank, 2013, 2014; Tobias et al., 2014). A 6-year compulsory education policy, followed by the expansion and restructuring of school-building and infrastructure during the Suharto administration was acknowledged as the world's largest documented school-building initiative (Duflo, 2001; Tobias et al., 2014). As a result, the national primary school enrolment rate increased significantly and has remained above 90% since the 1990s. However, success at the primary level has not been replicated at the secondary level. The enrolment rate in both lower- and upper-secondary levels dropped between one-third and one-half of the student-age population during the same observation periods.

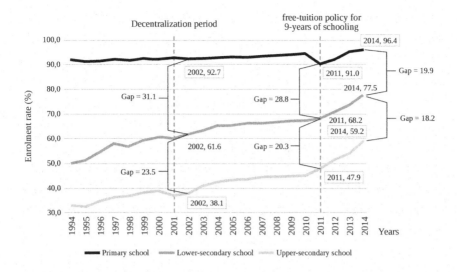

Figure 5.2. Indonesia's net enrolment rate —primary and secondary education.
Source: BPS (2017) https://www.bps.go.id/linkTabelStatis/view/id/1525.

A policy of 9-year compulsory education was initiated in 1994 by the Suharto administration, but there has not been a full commitment from the central government to support the policy through budget allocations and law enforcement. Although children are mandated to attend school until age fifteen, there are no penalties faced by parents for failing to enrol their children in school (Hsin, 2007). We find only a small improvement in the enrolment rate at the lower-secondary level since the policy was announced in 1994. A decade after its campaign, educational attainment grew less than 1% annually. Figure 5.2. shows that gap in enrolment between each education level has remained stagnant over time, confirming that the phenomenon of between-cycle dropouts has remained similar to the early decentralization period.

Di Gropello (2006) shows Indonesia's between-cycle dropout rate is one of the highest among developing countries. He cites the lack of access to the next education cycle (particularly in rural areas) as one possible reason for this phenomenon. According to Susenas (2009), a lack of education access is not only limited to physical accessibility (such as being children living in a rural or remote area), but also includes cost constraints that prevent pupils from entering secondary school. We find that more than 58% of between-cycle dropouts at both the lower- and upper secondary school levels positively correlate with cost constraints, while working and education sufficiency are mentioned as the second and third largest reasons respectively (see Table 5.3.). Our findings confirm Suryadarma et al., (2006a), who demonstrate that cost constraints and working are the main cause of lower enrolment rates in secondary schools in Indonesia. In addition, we find that other factors, such as marital status, distance between home and school, and economic conditions, also contribute to the decision not to attend school.

Table 5.3. Reasons for not continuing to secondary school.

Reasons	2009		2014	
	Lower	Upper	Lower	Upper
	All	all	all	all
Cannot afford the cost	58.75	58.83	41.34	43.54
Working	6.36	11.88	7.17	14.97
Married	0.58	4.09	1.37	7.93
Education sufficiency	3.12	6.59	4.16	8.03
Ashamed (economic factor)	2.06	1.08	1.55	0.81
Too far (distance)	3.20	1.95	3.83	1.58
Disabled	1.46	0.63	2.08	0.65
Waiting for enrolment	0.68	1.61	-	2.27
Not accepted	0.52	0.62	0.13	0.28
Others	23.25	12.72	38.37	19.94
TOTAL	100.00	100.00	100.00	100.00

Source: Author's calculation from Susenas (2009 and 2014).

At the national level, it is plausible to claim that success in increasing secondary level enrolment rates was achieved after the introduction of free-tuition for 9-years of compulsory education in 2011. We find that the enrolment rates in both levels of secondary school increased significantly, although the between-cycle dropout pattern only changed slightly (see Figure 5.2.). However, analysis using regency data shows results vary across Indonesian regions, and hence we assume that the program does not automatically enhance school enrolment, but rather depends on specific conditions.

The free-tuition program seems to gradually reduce the number of between-cycle dropouts citing costs as the main constraint for not continuing school at the secondary level (see Table 5.3.). Nonetheless, we find that in Susenas (2014), costs are still considered the main cause of between-cycle dropouts, representing more than 40% of all cases. Unfortunately, Susenas 2014 does not ask in detail about cost burdens on the households sending the children to secondary school, although given the free-tuition program, it can be surmised that the cost constraint is more or less related to other expenditures, such as transportation and school materials. As the program leaves households, especially the poor, to settle other cost burdens, it may be inadequate in addressing the between-cycle dropout phenomenon (Al-Samarrai et al., 2014).

Interestingly, Susenas (2014) also exposes other factors contributing to high between-cycle dropouts, such as marital and employment status. Although the general data only considers marriage as the fourth cause for dropout, analysis on a gender basis shows a significant difference between males and females. While only 1% of male students consider marriage a cause for a between-cycle dropout, 16% of females cite it as a cause of dropout (see Appendix A.3.).

With those facts, we suggest that improvement in educational outcomes is not solely affected by the free-tuition policy. It may be related to local government budget allocation and school expansion, which increases opportunities for children to attend school. Educational outcomes are also

Empirical Results and Discussion

Based on our regression result, we find that in both levels of secondary education, enrolment rates in the prior education level show positive and statistically significant correlation to enrolment rates at the secondary level. With all other variables being equal, our estimation value may indicate the turnover rate between school grades are more than 77 and 43% for lower- and upper-secondary school respectively. Moreover, we associate the small estimation with the existence of higher between-cycle dropout rates in the Indonesia regions (see columns 1 and in table 5.4).

Table 5.4. Determinants of school enrolment for lower- and upper-secondary level education.

| Dependent variable | Lower secondary enrolment | | | Upper secondary enrolment | | |
| | With regional FE | Without regional FE | | With regional FE | Without regional FE | |
	1	2	3	4	5	6
Primary enrolment rate	.22614982**	.93099031***	.97037852***			
	0.0910831	0.1135345	0.1181406			
Lower secondary enrolment rate				.55835814***	1.0209342***	1.0156707***
				9.0679453	0.0450703	0.0448028
Special fund on education	0.0049246	0.00284236	0.00105604	.01706701***	0.00644549	0.00329454
	0.0064878	0.0044438	0.0043565	0.0060114	0.0054071	0.0055574
Local expenditure on education	-0.01339036	0.00635503	0.00775865	0.00414861	.04993923***	.05312943***
	0.0085851	0.006694	0.006711	0.0091727	0.0091596	0.0095596
Household expenditure on education	.05847127***	.07153053***	.0682708***	.07385679***	.10043919***	.09645606***
	0.0196894	0.0066899	0.0066932	0.0150015	0.0082837	0.0082454

Indonesia at the Crossroads: Transformation and Challenges

Table 5.4. Determinants of school enrolment for lower- and upper-secondary level education. (continued)

Number of schools	.05234333** 0.0264809	.02954503*** 0.0056156	.03208777*** 0.0054538	.05490763** 0.0222207	-.02328748*** 0.0074056	-.01875831*** 0.0072087
Average distance (km)	-.02644855*** 0.0097834	-.06084072*** 0.0049655	-.06097897*** 0.0047544	-0.03600845 0.0224764	-.07989131*** 0.005461	-.08531798*** 0.0054536
Free tuition policy	.03077581*** 0.011519			.05614074*** 0.0092565		
Java-Bali regencies		-.04742686*** 0.0094151			-.11039808*** 0.0103476	
Western regencies		.07856309*** 0.0084257			-.03958989*** 0.0099965	
Mining regencies		-.01646213** 0.0079677			-0.01687521 0.0102696	
Sumatera islands			.06748784*** 0.00816			.13275946** 0.0097804
Kalimantan islands			-0.00772765 0.0130095			.06782671*** 0.0157417
Nusa Tenggara islands			-.10444841*** 0.0144338			.11754955** 0.021163
Sulawesi islands			-0.01261666 0.0105734			.13916947*** 0.0124174
Molucca-Papua islands			0.00896183 0.0165455			.2262578*** 0.0189529
Constanta	2.4138878*** 0.472113	-1.0782345** 0.5057091	-1.2125807** 0.5291542	0.33319049 0.2837235	-2.0469139*** 0.1768301	-2.1703544*** 0.1806693
Year fixed effect	Yes	-	-	Yes	-	-
Regional fixed effect	Yes	-	-	Yes	-	-
Clustered standard error	Yes	-	-	Yes	-	-
R^2	0.7048	0.4693	0.4841	0.7628	0.6253	0.6313
Number of obs	3,815	3,815	3,815	3,812	3,812	3,812

Notes: * $p<.1$; ** $p<.05$; *** $p<.01$. Robust standard error

Source: Stata output.

165

The variable of free-tuition policy shows a positive effect on the enrolment rate, but the value is relatively small compared to other independent variables. We may infer that the policy per se does not successfully change regional educational outcome as the government may think, even for the lower-secondary level. Since the program was designed to support students by providing an equal amount of grant to each student in Indonesia, regardless of his/her residency, we suspect that the effect of this program may be diminished by regional price differences and regional variations in initial endowments for education and infrastructure. Moreover, while the grant amount may be unfair to certain regions, it may not cover the total student needs, especially in rural or remote areas such as Eastern Indonesia. The program may leave what Al-Samarrai et al. (2014) describes as another cost burden for households. The central government provides a huge budget for its 9-year free-tuition program, yet our empirical results show that it has a small effect on secondary enrolment rates. Hence, we would like to suggest the central government to re-examine the scheme of the program, especially by considering regional differences in its design.

Surprisingly, the variable of local expenditures on education (Educexp) is not statistically significant in affecting the enrolment rate at both secondary levels. We suspect two possible reasons, first the budget may include the payment for government officers that is not directly connected to the delivery of education services. Second, our statistical descriptive shows that the value of this variable is dispersed between regions with lower and higher education outcomes, in other words, higher education expenditures per capita region may expose both lower and higher enrolment rates and vice versa (see Appendix A.6. and A.7.). These facts correspond to the variable of specific transfer on education (Dakeduc), which only shows positive impact on the upper secondary enrolment rate.

Similar to previous studies (see Glewwe and Jacoby, 2004; Suryadarma et al., 2006a; Sabates et al., 2010), our regression results confirm the prominent role of household expenditure on education in affecting educational attainment, having a positive and statistically significant estimation for both lower- and upper–secondary levels of education. Although the central and local governments may already provide huge subsidies for education (especially by removing tuition fees for primary and lower-secondary students), many households still need to pay other education expenditures, such as transportation and other costs to attend the school. Our regression results emphasize the role of demand-side factors in educational outcomes, since they represent household welfare in the decision to send children to school. Moreover, comparing the estimation result of each independent variable, we find that household expenditure on education is more elastic compared to other variables.

In line with our expectation, upper-secondary enrolment demonstrates a higher elasticity compared to lower-secondary enrolment. This result is in line with the fact that, unlike lower-secondary level, school operational costs at the upper-secondary level are not fully covered by the central and local governments. Moreover, the decision to attend an upper-secondary school may not only be related to the ability of household to afford additional costs, but also to bear the opportunity cost of the student not entering the unskilled labor market.

Moreover, our regression analysis confirms the positive effect of both the school and distance variables on the enrolment rate. The number of schools exposes a positive and statistically significant estimation in both levels of education (see columns 1 and in table 5.4). Although variable distance shows a negative value in both estimations, indicating that reducing the distance will increase the enrolment rate, yet it is only statistically significant at the lower-secondary level. Since the decision to support school operations, restructure and expand (public) schools, and even the decision on school location and capacity have been shifted to local governments, we may associate the results with decentralization. Further analysis shows that impact of the combination of those two variables is higher compared to other supply-side and demand-side variables, highlighting the role of local government in school enrolments, especially by increasing opportunity and accessibility for pupils to attend school that result in improving regional educational outcomes.

To fully understand the dynamic of educational outcomes in Indonesian regions, this chapter utilizes several dummy variables (see columns 2 and 5). For both secondary levels of education, the variable Java-Bali shows a negative and statistically significant estimation, indicating that Java-Bali has a lower elasticity in enrolment rate compared to outside Java-Bali. This result corresponds to Oey-Gardiner (1991), which showed that children living in Java are not necessarily better off than those elsewhere in Indonesia's regions. This chapter associates this fact with several reasons. First, it is related to the higher dispersion of educational outcome in Java-Bali—some regencies have high enrolment rates while others have extremely low rates (see Figure 5.4.). Second, Java-Bali demonstrates a larger turnover, either from primary to lower-secondary or from lower-secondary to upper-secondary, resulting in higher between-cycle dropouts in both lower- and upper-secondary schools. Finally, areas outside Java-Bali demonstrate higher achievement in improving educational outcomes, especially regencies in Sumatera, East Kalimantan, Sulawesi, and West Nusa Tenggara.

When comparing the Western and Eastern regions of Indonesia, our regression results exhibit different patterns for lower- and upper-secondary levels. Despite lower enrolment rates in Java-Bali, Western Indonesia demonstrates higher educational outcomes compared to Eastern Indonesia at the lower secondary level. The main contributor to the higher enrolment rate comes from Sumatera's regencies and East Kalimantan's regencies. Meanwhile, regencies in Papua and East Nusa Tenggara had the lowest enrolment rates in Eastern Indonesia.

Interestingly, we find the opposite result at the upper-secondary level, with western regions demonstrating lower outcomes. We argue that this is related to the high level of between-cycle dropouts in Java and Sumatera's regencies. With a large concentration of industrial agglomeration in these regions, the high demand for unskilled labor creates a higher opportunity cost to attend school.

Moreover, we expand our regional analysis by grouping Indonesia into six main islands with Java-Bali as a control variable (see columns 3 and 6). We find that, due to its higher initial enrolment rate, Sumatera regencies consistently show higher educational outcomes at both lower- and upper-secondary schools compared to Java-Bali's. Meanwhile Nusa Tenggara regions show lower educational outcomes at the lower-secondary level. Thus, we confirm that due to the higher between-cycle dropout rate in Java-Bali regions, other groups may show higher outcomes at the upper-secondary level.

Further analysis using the variable natural resource shows that, in general, natural resource-based regencies tend to have lower outcomes at both the lower- and upper-secondary levels. The expansion of natural resource extraction may decrease the enrolment rate by increasing demand for unskilled labor, raising the opportunity cost of attending school. Our regression results corroborate Gylfason (2001) and Alvares and Vergara (2016), which show the negative impact of natural resources on educational outcomes.

Regardless of the negative estimation of the variable natural resource, we find some exceptional cases in East Kalimantan, Riau, and Aceh regencies. Although these regencies possess abundant natural resources, they successfully maintain educational outcomes above the national average. We argue that there are two main reasons. First, those regions already had higher attainment rates in the early stages of decentralization. Second, these regions demonstrate higher public spending on education by expanding and restructuring schools at the secondary level and hence, we find the number of schools in these regions has risen to the national level or even higher.

Regional Disparities

In addition to econometric analysis that provides empirical results on the determinants of school enrolment, this chapter also examines regional disparities and gender disparities in enrolment rates. As some regions have already achieved certain levels of educational attainment, the Indonesian government should focus on dispersing the achievement acceleration by promoting equal educational outcomes across Indonesia's regions. Although our main analysis utilizes regional data at the regency level, it is also important to expand our discussion to the provincial level. Provincial level analysis may elucidate whether or not regional disparities are randomly scattered across Indonesian regencies or occur in certain provinces.

Lower-Secondary Level

Provincial Level

We find that in the early stages of decentralization, regional enrolment rates for lower-secondary schools vary from 78.7% in Aceh to 38.6% in East Nusa Tenggara, with lower rates in the Papua islands (see Figure 5.3.). Further, we find that only 13 of 33 Indonesia provinces have enrolment rates higher than the national rate. With the exception of North Sulawesi, all higher enrolment rate provinces are located in Western Indonesia.

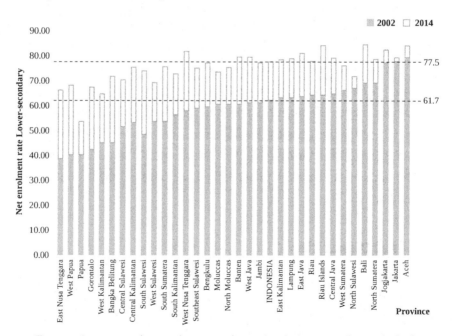

Figure 5.3. Lower-secondary enrolment rates by province in 2002–2014. Source: Author's

calculation from Susenas 2002–2014

Despite the focus of Indonesian development efforts in Java-Bali provinces during Suharto's rule (Booth, 1998; Hill, 2000) and during early decentralization, lower enrolment rates are also found in Java islands, supporting Oey-Gardiner's (1991) concern that children living in Java are not necessarily better off than those elsewhere. We find that West Java and Banten Provinces (Banten was previously part of West Java) have lower educational outcomes than the national level.

Although the introduction of BOS has successfully maintained the primary school attainment rate above 93%, since 2002 the secondary level enrolment rate has only grown slightly, at a pace of around 1% annually. The implementation of the free tuition for 9-year compulsory education program since 2011 may be seen as a big achievement in improving educational outcomes at the national level: the enrolment rate increased from 68.2% in 2011 to 77.5% in 2014. However, regional level data reveal that the program has not been equally successful across the nation, with many regions (province and regency) still struggling to improve educational attainment. Moreover, the difference in enrolment rates between the highest and the lowest provinces has only decreased slightly, remaiing at more than 32%, between Aceh (85.2%) and Papua (53.4%) (see Figure 5.3.). These facts corroborate our previous regression results, which indicate that, empirically, the free-tuition program has only a small effect on school enrolment rates.

Our results confirm general knowledge that western regions record higher outcomes than eastern regions, although we find that variations also arise within groups (see Figure 5.4.). Having a scattered performance in 2002, Java's provinces have since converged outcomes, especially through an acceleration of results in West Java and Banten Provinces. A similar phenomenon has occurred in Sumatera's provinces. In contrast, eastern regions consistently show lower performance, with the exception of West

Nusa Tenggara, which had a massive improvement at 2% annually during 2002–2014.

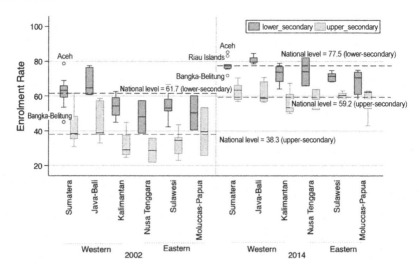

Figure 5.4. Disparities in regional enrolment rates in 2002–2014 (provincial data).
Source: Author's calculation from Susenas (2002–2014).

Regency Level

At the regency level, our spatial distribution shows that, similar to province level data, regencies with higher enrolment rates are more concentrated in Western Indonesia (see Figure 5.6.). These regencies are mainly located in the Aceh, North Sumatera, West Sumatera, some in Java, Bali, and Central and East Kalimantan. Meanwhile, higher enrolment rates are only found in cities in West Nusa Tenggara, Sulawesi, Moluccas, and Papua, and some regencies close to a provincial capital city.[1]

1   Due to the large data sample, numerical regency data are available by request.

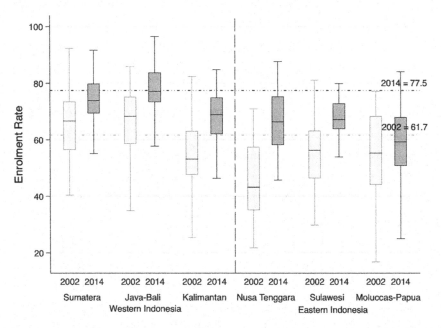

Figure 5.5. Regional disparities in lower-secondary enrolment rates in 2002–2014 (regency level data). Source: Author's calculation from Susenas (2002–2014).

Moreover, our data also confirms Lanjouw et al. (2001), Tobias et al. (2014) and Jones and Pratomo (2016) on the presence of regional disparities that emerged not only between western and eastern regions, but also within group observations. As can be seen from Figure 5.5., there is a different trend in the educational outcome over observation periods. Despite having a higher median value above the average national level, Sumatera and Java show a wide dispersion of educational attainment in 2002. The range between the lowest and the highest outcome for Sumatera and Java spreads from 40.4% to 92.4% and 19.2% to 85.8% respectively. It represents the highest variation within regions in Indonesia. Kalimantan also exhibits a similar pattern, with outcomes varying between 25.3% and 82.3%. Although the average enrolment rates in Eastern Indonesia regions seem to be lower, they also possess wide variations. Sulawesi's rates range from 29.8% to 81.1%, while Nusa Tenggara's range from 21.8%–71.0%, and Moluccas-Papua regions from 16.8% to 77.1%.

Although Western Indonesia shows some convergence, the general pattern of disparity among regencies still holds in 2014, with a gap of more than 40% between the highest and the lowest. Sumatera's gap is even larger, at 60%. In contrast, the dispersion among Sulawesi and Nusa Tenggara regencies becomes smaller, converging over time. Sulawesi shows the lowest standard deviation among group observation in all of Indonesia's regions. Unlike other regions, which show progress in reducing variation, Moluccas and Papua remain stagnant from 2002 to 2014, with the gap among regencies ranging from 25% to 84%.

Exploring Java's regencies, the data reveals that lower performance regencies in Banten and West Java Provinces are mainly located in the southern part of both provinces. These areas are well known for being mountainous and lacking infrastructure (mainly in transportation), making student accessibility to schools a challenge. Moreover, Banten and West Java are notable for higher rates of child-marriage (Jones, 2001) causing students, especially girls, to leave school at a younger age. During the last decade these provinces have shown a significant improvement in educational outcomes through school expansion and restructuring, but due to their lower initial condition, their enrolment rates remain below the national level.

Meanwhile, regencies with lower educational outcomes in East Java are located mainly in the Madura Island or regencies with high concentration of Madurese, such as Bondowoso, Probolinggo, and Pasuruan. Also known for their practice of early marriage (Jones, 2001; Jones, 2003; Nooteboom, 2015), Madurese tend to perceive education as consumption rather than investment, creating a reluctance to send their children to school (Nooteboom, 2015).

Indonesia at the Crossroads: Transformation and Challenges

Lower-secondary enrolment

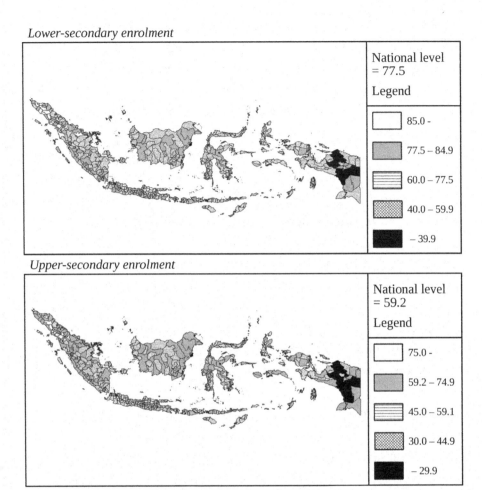

Figure 5.6. Regional patterns in secondary enrolment in 2014.
Source: Author's calculation Susenas (2014).

According to Figure 5.6., we find regencies with higher enrolment rates located mainly in Aceh, Riau, Riau Island Provinces, and regencies in the west coastal area. Meanwhile, most of Sumatera's east coast regencies have lower enrolment rates. Although most regencies in Aceh, Riau, and Riau Islands possess abundant natural resources, they have managed to maintain enrolment rates through school expansion programs and increasing education provision budgets, preventing the negative impact of natural resources on educational outcomes.

Similar cases are found in East Kalimantan's regencies which possess plentiful natural resources, yet demonstrate higher local spending on education. However, most regencies in the Kalimantan islands have low enrolment rates. These regencies, such as in West Kalimantan, are mainly associated with higher poverty rates, modest economic development, and poor infrastructure.

We may draw on the success story of West Nusa Tenggara Province and its regencies in increasing enrolment rates. Despite its lower initial condition during early decentralization, West Nusa Tenggara has successfully promoted educational attainment, resulting in a growth rate of two percentage points annually from 2002 to 2014. The performance comes from a high commitment of local government to allocate budget to the education sector and expand the number of schools, which rose from 734 in 2003 to 1,473 in 2014. The expansion is not only concentrated in urban areas, but also covers rural and remote areas in West Nusa Tenggara. Our data from Podes confirms that by 2014, the average distance between the nearest school and the village without a school had been reduced by half.

Still, most Eastern Indonesia regencies suffer from lower enrolment rates, with only 26 of 164 regencies showing enrolment rates higher than the national rate in 2014. Aside from regencies in West Nusa Tenggara, we find only the following regencies with enrolment rates higher than the national rate: Bolaang Mongondow and Tomohon in North Sulawesi; Morowali and Poso in Central Sulawesi; Barru, Bone, Tana Toraja, North Toraja, Palopo, and Pare-pare in South Sulawesi; Konawe, North Buton, and Bau-bau in Southeast Sulawesi; Southwest Moluccas and South Buru in Moluccas; and North Halmahera and Ternate in North Moluccas. Meanwhile, regencies in Papua, West Papua, and East Nusa Tenggara consistently have lower enrolment rates.

As the lower enrolment rate regencies are typically found in the Eastern Indonesia, especially in Papua and East Nusa Tenggara, we may associate this condition with several factors (see Appendix A.6.). First,

Eastern Indonesia has fewer schools and faces geographical disadvantages such as poor infrastructure and lack of accessibility that result in lengthy distances between a village and the nearest school. Some regencies in Papua and East Nusa Tenggara record distances of more than 100 km (Podes, 2014). Second, the average budget allocation for education per pupil in Eastern Indonesia, except for Papua, is relatively lower compared to Western Indonesia. Third, we find that most of the regencies have high poverty rates, causing a burden for households to the bear additional costs of education and higher opportunity costs of schooling (Table 5.3. shows that in 2014 more than 40% of dropout cases were due to cost constraints). The combination of local government budget shortages, the limited number and coverage of schools, the long distances to the nearest school, and the higher poverty incidence has contributed to reducing opportunities for pupils in Eastern Indonesia to access education.

Although perhaps not as severe as in Eastern Indonesia regencies, we also find an association between lower enrolment rates and the poor economic and/or infrastructure conditions in Western Indonesia. For example, higher poverty rates in Madura regencies, lack of school availability and accessibility in Banten regencies, and the combination of those factors in some regencies scattered in each island of Indonesia result in lower enrolment rates. All these facts remind us that there remains a lot of work to do for both central and local governments to solve the problems.

Upper-Secondary Level

Provincial Level

Analysis of the upper-secondary level produces results coherent with lower-secondary level. In 2002, we find that provinces with lower enrolment rates at the lower-secondary level tend to have lower performance at the upper-secondary level and vice versa (see Figures 5.3. and 5.7.). Although 18 out of 33 provinces in 2014 demonstrated higher educational outcomes compared to the average national level (previously only 13 out of 33 provinces in 2002), we cannot directly infer that Indonesia has made huge gains at the upper-secondary level. The rise in the number of provinces is mainly the result of the slower pace of school enrolment and the larger between-cycle dropout level that causes a lower national average level, rather than an acceleration of educational outcomes in the provinces.

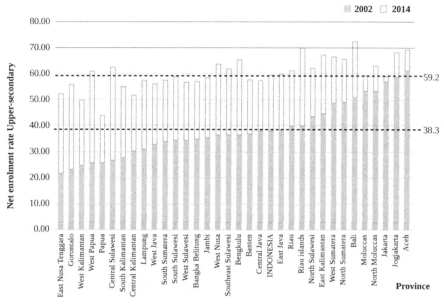

Figure 5.7. Upper-secondary enrolment rates by province in 2002–2014. Source: Author's calculation from Susenas (2002–2014).

Among western regions, only Aceh, Riau, Riau Islands, North Sumatera, West Sumatera, Bali, Yogyakarta, East Java, Jakarta, and East Kalimantan show consistent outcomes at both secondary levels. Meanwhile, due to higher between-cycle dropouts that reduce the number of students attending upper-secondary school, Central Java and Lampung Provinces perform lower than the national level.

On the other hand, in eastern regions, namely West Nusa Tenggara, North Sulawesi, Central Sulawesi, Southeast Sulawesi, Moluccas, North Moluccas, and Papua surprisingly perform higher than the average national level. In line with our previous argument, this result comes from two factors: the higher level of between-cycle dropouts in Western Indonesia and the capacity of Eastern regions to maintain a lower level of between-cycle dropout.

Regency Level

We find simultaneous results between provincial and regency level data at the upper-secondary level. Although our econometric analysis indicates that Eastern Indonesia performs better compared to Western Indonesia, spatial data shows that some regencies in Western Indonesia also present higher educational attainment.

As the free-tuition policy only support students for the 9 years of compulsory education and does not cover all school costs for upper-secondary education, households need to bear more costs to let their children attend upper-secondary school. Therefore, corresponding to the regression results, we may expect that the policy does not largely affect upper-secondary attainment; indeed, many regencies show lower enrolment rates at the upper-secondary level. Moreover, other than cost constraints, the decision to continue or quit secondary school is also related to other factors, such as the decision to work or marry, and education sufficiency (see Table 5.3.).

We find that in western regions, the gap between the regencies with the lowest and the highest enrolment rates remains large, at 75% and 50% in 2002 and 2014 respectively. However, regional dispersion has decreased during the past decade, with the exception of Moluccas and Papua, which consistently show a broad dispersion, and Kalimantan islands, which show an increasing dispersion (see Figure 5.8.).

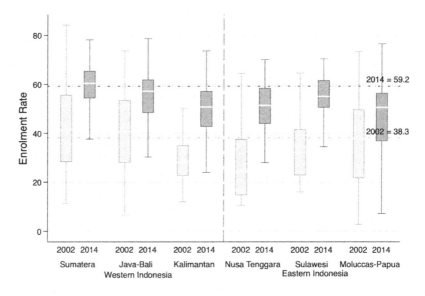

Figure 5.8. Regional disparities in upper-secondary enrolment rates by regency in 2002–2014.
Source: Author's calculation from Susenas (2002–2014).

Moreover, our spatial data shows that regencies with lower upper-secondary attainment in Java are scattered in the southern part of West Java and Banten Provinces, the northern part of Central Java, and northeast part of East Java, including regencies in Madura (see Figure 5.6.). Aside from socio-economic factors that affect educational outcome, we may associate the result with the presence of industrial agglomeration scattered in Java islands, in regions mainly located in urban areas close to Jadebotabek (the greater Jakarta area) and the Sidoarjo area of East Java.

The agglomeration of industry places high demands for unskilled labor, which may create higher opportunity costs for attending school, since pupil may generate revenue for themselves and their families by entering the labor market. Aside from the unskilled labor market, we still associate regencies with lower educational performance in East Java with the higher concentration of Madurese. Meanwhile, West Java and Banten regencies also record similar reasons for their lower education performance, in addition to the practice of early marriage and limited school accessibility in the southern part of region.

In Sumatera, regencies with lower education outcomes at the upper-secondary level are still found in the east-coast area, especially in southeast part of the islands. Although these areas do not have as many industrial areas as Java regions, they are well known for having large palm oil plantations, which provide large numbers of employment opportunities for unskilled labor. We find a similar pattern in Kalimantan's regencies, which also have large palm oil plantations.

West Nusa Tenggara demonstrates the most exceptional improvement in educational outcomes, even at the upper-secondary level. As discussed in the previous section, the commitment of the local government to allocate budgets and expand schools has been successful in increasing the opportunities and accessibility to attend school.

It is important to note that the higher enrolment rates shown in some regencies in Eastern Indonesia (such as Nusa Tenggara, Sulawesi, Moluccas, and Papua) do not necessarily mean that these provinces have better education policies compared to those in Western Indonesia. With the higher between-cycle dropout rate in Western Indonesia, the average national enrolment rate for upper-secondary school also decreases significantly. Hence, regencies in Eastern Indonesia with lower between-cycle dropout rates may exhibit higher enrolment rates at the upper-secondary level.

Because regions with poor performance at the lower-secondary level tend to show similar performance at the upper-secondary level, we may associate a similar conclusion for the presence of regional disparities. Lower education performance regencies are linked to a lack of infrastructure and facilities and poor economic development (see Appendix A.6.). Aside from those factors, other socio-economic conditions, such as the practice of early marriage and the demand for unskilled labor, also affect the education outcomes at the upper secondary level.

The Longevity Achievement of Aceh's Regencies: A Commitment of Local Government

Aside from the Indonesian success story in improving educational attainment at both the provincial and regency levels, this chapter discusses the case study of Aceh for two reasons. First, political conflict and armed struggles that occurred between the central government and separatist movements colored the local situation in Aceh from 1976–2005. Second, in spite of those conflicts, Aceh is the only province whose regencies have successfully maintained high educational outcomes over decades.

In spite of a nearly 30-year conflict that destroyed or damaged more than 600 schools and left more than 55,000 children with reduced educational opportunities (Shah and Cardozo, 2014), Susenas data reveals that Aceh enrolment rates at the lower-secondary level are second only to Jakarta Province, and the highest nationally at the upper-secondary level. The Eurotrends report (2009) shows that the higher education attainment in Aceh is a result of the strong commitment of school principals and committees to keep schools open and the willingness of parents, students, and teachers to keep attending school under adverse circumstances. Moreover, education has been supported by community and donor mobilization of funds to restore school infrastructure. In addition, Parker (2009) argues that the implementation of fervently Islamic cultures in Aceh encouraged a higher level of female educational access and attainment, undeniably affecting the general enrolment rate level.

Despite the massive earthquake and tsunami that hit Aceh in 2005, killing hundreds of thousands of people and students (including an estimated of 2,500 teachers), displacing families, and destroying over 2,500 schools (Eurotrends, 2009), Aceh remains the only province with consistently higher performance at both provincial and regency levels after 2005. In 2006, almost all of Aceh's regencies recorded enrolment rates higher than the national level for both lower- and upper-secondary schools, with the exception of Nagan Raya Regency which had a slightly lower enrolment rate for lower-secondary schools. This pattern holds in 2014, with Nagan

Raya and Aceh Tamiang having slightly lower performance compared to the national rate at the lower-secondary level (see Figure 5.9.).

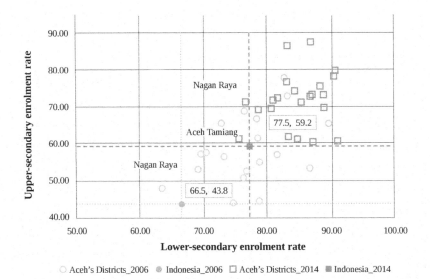

Figure 5.9. Aceh's enrolment rates compared to Indonesia by regency in 2006–2014. Source: Author's calculation from Susenas 2006 and 2014.

With its challenges, it is worth understanding how Aceh preserved its accomplishments. We find that aside from a high commitment of the Acehnese society to education, local institutions, especially in the post-tsunami and post-conflict period, contribute to the sustained success of its education outcomes.

After the tsunami, the influx of international funds for Aceh's reconstruction bolstered the education system's resilience (Eurotrends, 2009). Moreover, the establishment of Law Number 11 Year 2006 on the Government of Aceh grants sweeping powers to Aceh's government to manage and govern its own affairs, more than other regions in Indonesia. The law bestows Aceh with additional natural resource revenues, providing Aceh with huge reserves to finance its programs. This confirms what Manor (1997) describes as the most important success factor in decentralization.

Moreover, the law mandates that the Aceh government allocates at least 30% of its additional revenues to education expenditures. Finally, the Aceh government established local law (Qanun Number 5 Year 2008) that mandates all children aged 7 to 18 to attend school without exception. This program includes a 12-year free education program that covers all school costs from primary until upper-secondary school.

The commitment of the local government together with the availability of sufficient resources to accomplish important tasks and services has allowed Aceh to successfully maintain its educational outcomes. Moreover, the commitment is not only limited to school expansion and restructuring to cover rural and remote areas, but also includes supporting teachers to deliver education services in rural areas. The Aceh government offers special incentives for teachers who serve in rural and/or remote areas. As a result, we find that Aceh records the second highest education expenditure per capita in Indonesia, more than twice the national average (World Bank, 2008).

Gender Disparities

Unlike regional disparities that have been discussed in many studies as an issue of decentralization (see Lanjouw et al., 2001; Tobias et al., 2014; OECD/Asian Development Bank, 2015; Jones and Pratomo, 2016), we find that studies on gender disparities at the regency level are quite limited.

Studies on this issue mainly argue that Indonesia demonstrates a nearly universal gender neutrality (see Hsin, 2007; Grant and Behrman, 2010; and Jones and Pratomo, 2016). Those studies seem to correspond with the fact that since 2001 the enrolment gap between male and female students at both the lower- and upper-secondary level narrowed, with girls showing a slightly higher enrolment rate compared to male students at both levels. However, regency level analysis shows disparate results. The difference between boys and girls ranges from 10 to 20 percentage points, with the positive value indicating higher educational attainment for boys than for girls.

According to Appendix A.4., we find that in 2002 Indonesian provinces, namely Aceh, West Sumatera, East Kalimantan, Bangka Belitung, and Southeast Sulawesi recorded higher female enrolment rates in lower-secondary schools than other provinces. However, during the last decade, Indonesian provinces have performed unevenly: some provinces have reduced gender disparities in enrolment rates while others have increased. In 2014, we find that Riau, Lampung, Jambi, Central Kalimantan, South Kalimantan, West Kalimantan, and East Nusa Tenggara show gender disparities that favor girls over boys. An exception is West Sumatera, which consistently demonstrates higher disparity that favors girls over boys. Our data corroborates Parker (2009), who argues that among Indonesia's regions, West Sumatera has demonstrated a high level of female educational access and attainment for decades.

At the upper-secondary level, Susenas (2002) shows that West Sumatera, East Kalimantan, and Southeast Sulawesi consistently record enrolment rates that favors females. Although other provinces, such as Bengkulu, Gorontalo, and North Sulawesi show similar levels of inequality, we suspect that this is mainly attributed to the higher between-cycle dropout rate of boys who do not enter upper-secondary school, rather than solely a matter of higher rates of female enrolment. In other words, despite lower enrolment rates at the lower-secondary level in these regions, girls achieve higher secondary attainment since boys drop out of school.

Bali and Jakarta were the only provinces demonstrating the opposite trend, having higher enrolment rates for boys. In 2002 the gaps in the enrolment rate between males and females in these regions were more than 9 and 14% respectively. Both provinces continuously showed a similar pattern in 2014. We suspect the female unskilled labor markets are the primary explanation for the higher dropout rate for girls in both provinces. Unlike other provinces that demonstrate high male between-cycle dropout for working, we find similar results for female in Jakarta and Bali. Aside from labor-intensive manufacturing industries such as foods, textiles, garments, and apparel which often employ young women, the growth of the service sector in Jakarta area also provides jobs for girls, such as waitress, maid, or servant. Meanwhile, the development of the tourism sector in Bali provides girls with the opportunity to enter the labor market and quit school.

Although, gender disparities seem to be limited to several provinces, further analysis using regency level data shows that less than one quarter of Indonesian regencies preserve gender parity in education at the lower or upper-secondary levels (see Figure 5.10.). Moreover, our Susenas data confirms Grant and Behrman's (2010) finding of higher educational attainment for girls. Unlike the presence of regional disparities that can be easily associated with regional economic or geographical conditions, we find that gender disparity is randomly distributed among Indonesia's regencies.

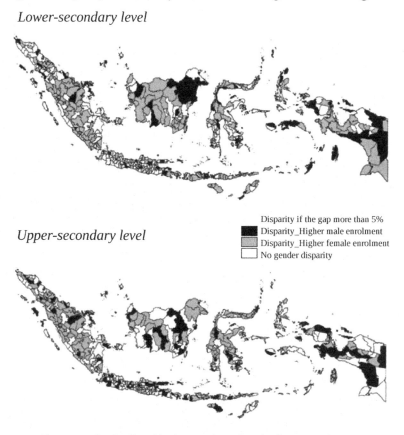

Figure 5.10. Gender disparities in secondary education by regency in 2014.
Source: Author's calculation from Susenas 2014

However, we may link gender disparities with social conditions such as kinship or norms that are specific to each region. For example, we may associate the matrilineal family system with gender disparity in education, since it favors girls over boys. We find that regencies with a high concentration of Minangkabaus, one of the world's largest matrilineal ethnic groups, show a higher gender disparity that favors girls (also see Parker, 2009; Rammohan and Robertson, 2012). These regencies are mostly located in West Sumatera and some regencies in Riau, Jambi, North Sumatera, and Bengkulu. On the other hand, the use of the patrilineal system does not necessarily manifest similar results in the opposite direction. Even when we investigate regencies with higher concentrations of Bataks in North Sumatera, we find few regencies that show a gender disparity that favors boys over girls. The regions with strong patrilineal kinship that expose a strong gender disparity that favors boys over girls are regencies in Bali. Yet this disparity is only prevalent at the upper-secondary level.

Aside from the presence of matrilineal kinship, gender disparity that favors girls over boys in West Sumatera also may be the result of the highly Islamic cultures in this region (Parker, 2009), similar to Aceh and Gorontalo (Kimura, 2007; Sakai and Fauzia, 2013).

Although Madurese apply a bilateral kinship system, neither lower nor upper-secondary enrolment rates in Madurese areas record parity between boys and girls. As discussed in the previous analysis, Madura is well-known for its lower performance in education. Analysis on a gender basis reveals the staggering fact that enrolment of girls in Madura was less than half that of boys in 2002. We will discuss the Madura case as one example of severe gender disparity in educational outcomes.

Finally, to support our argument of the existence of gender disparity in Indonesia, we conducted further analysis using a T-test. We divided enrolment data based on gender and grouped it into two periods, 2002 and 2014. As can be seen in Table 5.5., in 2002 we found no significant difference between the mean male enrolment rate and the mean female enrolment rate at both lower- and upper-secondary schools at the regency level, meaning that in general, regency gender disparity was not significant in the early stages of decentralization. However, Susenas shows a different result for 2014. Even with the coefficient confidence of 1%, we found a significant difference between the mean enrolment rates of the male and female groups in both lower- and upper-secondary schools, meaning that in the later decentralization period, gender disparity increased at the regency level.

Table 5.5. T-test for gender disparity at the regency level in 2002 and 2014.

Year/Level of Education	Mean		T-test
	Male	Female	
2002			
Lower secondary school	0.6017	0.6220	-1.7633
Upper secondary school	0.3815	0.3890	-0.5520
2014			
Lower secondary school	0.7326	0.7696	-5.1146***
Upper secondary school	0.5907	0.6160	-3.1057***

*** significant at level 1%

Source: Author's calculation from Susenas (2002 and 2014).

Improving educational attainment is not limited to increasing the number of pupils, but includes providing equal opportunity for boys and girls to attend school. The free-tuition program may increase the opportunity for girls to go to school. However, a higher between-cycle dropout rate caused by work, especially for boys, may exacerbate gender disparities. This fact may indicate disparity in the availability of unskilled labor demand that favors boys rather than girls. However, we argue that the central and local governments should consider gender issues when designing education systems and programs; they should not limit the discussion to gender issues in education alone, but broaden it to include corresponding areas. Solving gender inequality in education may require appropriate labor policies as well.

Poor Education for Girls in Regencies in Madura

With a slightly higher outcome than Papua islands and East Nusa Tenggara for both secondary levels, regencies in Madura have shown a consistently lower educational performance vis-a-vis the national average during the past decades (Susenas, 2002; Nooteboom, 2015). Despite primary enrolment rates reaching 92% in 2002 (slightly below the national level), the enrolment rate at the secondary level fell drastically and is less than half the national average, confirming a severe problem of between-cycle dropouts in these regions. Moreover, among regencies in Madura, we find Sampang has the lowest performance, with rates less than one-third and one-sixth of the national level for lower- and upper-secondary schools, respectively.

Table 5.6. School enrolment, school institution, average distance of school, and poverty rate in Madura Island in 2002–2014.

Regions	Lower secondary					Upper secondary					Poverty rate
	Enrolment rate			# of school	Average distance (km)	Enrolment rate			# of school	Average distance (km)	
	Total	Male	Female			Total	Male	Female			
2002											
Bangkalan	37.54	35.02	40.05	81	4.04	14.27	12.74	16.07	25	9.14	34.69
Sampang	19.21	24.65	13.53	52	4.95	6.58	6.57	6.60	15	13.41	41.78
Pamekasan	40.69	51.70	29.28	134	2.65	28.18	36.85	19.99	61	6.44	34.87
Sumenep	47.39	46.38	48.45	182	3.42	19.54	25.71	13.63	63	12.31	31.08
Indonesia	61.68	60.91	62.49			38.21	38.76	37.63			18.20
2014											
Bangkalan	61.48	59.89	63.35	209	3.96	45.51	50.03	41.70	97	5.92	22.38
Sampang	67.71	74.12	62.32	309	2.41	38.99	51.14	24.17	139	5.12	25.80
Pamekasan	76.98	83.30	69.56	340	2.02	51.04	60.56	39.01	205	4.21	17.74
Sumenep	87.33	89.29	85.17	417	5.21	55.32	66.71	45.66	244	7.58	20.49
Indonesia	77.45	75.75	79.24			59.18	58.69	59.71			11.30

Source: Author's calculation based on Susenas (2002, 2014) and Podes (2003, 2014).

Using the same dataset, we find that this phenomenon is not limited to regencies in Madura. Other regencies with a higher proportion of Madurese community, mainly found in the northern part of East Java Province, such as Bondowoso, Probolinggo, Pasuruan, Jember, and Tuban, also record lower educational attainment rates at both the lower- and upper-secondary levels.

Despite increasing enrolment rates by more than double (in lower secondary) and by more than six times (in upper secondary) during last decade (Susenas, 2002 and 2014), regencies in Madura continue to have rates below the national level. The only exception is Sumenep, with a higher enrolment rate for lower-secondary schools. We may associate the lower enrolment rate in Madura with the higher poverty rate, the lower regional per capita income, and poor school accessibility (see Table 5.6.).

While educational outcomes for both genders is low for both levels of school, indeed, regencies in Madura fall far short in educational attainment for girls, exposing that Madurese girls are denied equal education opportunity. In the early decentralization period, the gap between girls and boys stood between 11 and 22% at the lower-secondary level and more than around 15% at the upper-secondary level. Even after the introduction of the 9-year free tuition program, Madura's gender disparity remained at 11% and 20% at the lower- and upper-secondary levels respectively, leaving Madurese regencies with the highest gender disparity restricting girls from opportunities to attend school.

Although our data in Table 5.6. shows that during the last decade the number of schools has increased dramatically and the average distance to the nearest school has reduced, which increased the opportunity for girls to attend school, it does not clearly explain the large gap between female Madurese students and their male counterparts.

This section investigate how these phenomena have arisen in regencies in Madura. Nooteboom (2015) argues that Madurese performance in education is affected by a perception of education that views it as consumption rather than investment, causing a reluctance to send children to school. While in general children in Madura already meet some constraints to access higher education, Nooteboom shows another obstacle facing girls there, noting that Madurese girls are expected to marry as soon as they finish primary school, leaving them with no further education. Jones (2001, 2003) asserts a similar argument, correlating lower education attainment and early female marriage patterns in Madurese.

Although most studies associate average early marriage as the main cause of between-cycle dropout for girls, only a few provide empirical evidence of this phenomena. Utilizing the same dataset from Susenas, this study investigates the reasons for leaving school. According to Table 5.7, we confirm the existence of early marriage for girls, which causes higher between-cycle dropouts in Madura, yet we surprise with the result that this issue affects more than 40% of dropout cases in upper-secondary education. In addition, we find a similar pattern in several regencies in northern East Java Province with a higher Madurese population. Therefore, solving the gender disparities in education in Madura is related with what Jones (2001) cites as the unsettled problem of marriages below the legal minimum age.

Table 5.7. Reasons for not continuing school in regencies in Madura in 2014.

| Regions | Three main reasons for not continuing the school in 2014 | | | | | |
| | Lower secondary | | | Upper secondary | | |
	Both sexes	Male	Female	Both sexes	Male	Female
Bangkalan	Cannot afford the cost (39%), education sufficiency (10%)	Cannot afford the cost (49%) and distance (7%)	Cannot afford the cost (28%), education sufficiency (21%)	Cannot afford the cost (45%), married (14%), and working (10%)	Cannot afford the cost (45%), married (7%), and working (16%)	Cannot afford the cost (45%), married (18%)
Sampang	Cannot afford the cost (20%), education sufficiency (6%), and working (5%)	Cannot afford the cost (20%)	Cannot afford the cost (20%), education sufficiency (9%), and working (8%)	Married (27%), cannot afford the cost (19%), and working (9%)	Working (16%), cannot afford the cost (14%), and education sufficiency (6%)	Married (44%), cannot afford the cost (22%), and working (5%)
Pamekasan	Cannot afford the cost (100%)	Cannot afford the cost (100%)	Cannot afford the cost (100%)	Cannot afford the cost (40%), education sufficiency (22%), and married (21%)	Cannot afford the cost (40%), education sufficiency (31%), and working (6%)	Cannot afford the cost (40%), education sufficiency (14%), and married (36%)
Sumenep	-	-	-	Married (40%), cannot afford the cost (29%)	Cannot afford the cost (49%), education sufficiency (13%)	Married (53%), cannot afford the cost (22%)

Source: Author's calculation from Susenas (2014).

Conclusion

During decentralization, Indonesia achieved remarkable improvements in its national education participation both at the lower- and upper-secondary levels. However, Indonesia still faces a high between-cycle dropout rate that emerges at the national and regional level. In addition, regional and gender disparities remain as unsettled problems.

This study shows that household expenditure on education, numbers of schools, and the average distance to the nearest school, as well as the free-tuition policy are statistically significant in affecting school enrolment in Indonesia's regions. Although we find that the free-tuition policy seemed to increase educational attainment, its impact is smaller compared to other factors. On the other hand, the local government policies of school expansion and restructuring are more prominent factors impacting enrolment rates.

Further, this study also emphasizes the role of households, not only related to their capability to bear education costs, but also connected to factors affecting their decision to allow their children to attend or quit school. We find that household's socio-economic and cultural perceptions are also highly related to educational outcomes, for example how they comprehend the opportunity costs of attending school, how they discern gender bias in education, and how their ethnic background impacts their views of education.

In general, this study corroborated previous studies that found higher educational outcomes in Western Indonesia compared to Eastern regions, with Sumatera's regencies demonstrating prominent outcomes in lower- and upper-secondary enrolment rates and Java not necessarily better off than elsewhere. Meanwhile, Papua and East Nusa Tenggara regencies fall behind the rest of the country, and regencies in other islands show various patterns of educational outcomes. Aside from geographical distribution, we may associate the outcomes with regional economic performance and infrastructure. Regions with lower regional income per capita and/or higher poverty incidence tend to show lower educational outcomes.

193

This chapter has highlighted the gender disparities in Indonesia's regencies. Unlike regional disparities that can be understood in terms of geographical and economic bases, gender disparity is more scattered and randomly distributed. Although the free-tuition policy and school expansion during the past decade increased the opportunity and accessibility for girls to attend school, some regions, such as Madura, are falling behind in providing girls with equal education opportunity. At the same time, other regions demonstrate gender disparity as higher between-cycle dropout rates of boys because they enter the labor force. This fact may be used as the first signal of gender bias in labor force, as it may indicate a higher demand for unskilled male over female labor.

This study has found that budget support and other administrative policies, although necessary, may not be sufficient for improving regional educational outcomes. I argue that the free-tuition policy should be combined with efforts to improve school accessibility through school expansion, restructuring, and reducing school distances. Additionally, both central and local governments should consider socio-economic and cultural factors when designing education policies. Therefore, education policy should be region-specific rather than proposing a panacea for all regions.

All in all, this chapter considers only household expenditure as a control variable that represents a demand factor and left other socio-economic indicators unobserved. We also did not consider how household income/ expenditure was affected by decentralization. To design more appropriate regional policies, future research may consider those concerns as well as other socio-cultural factors such as kinship, norms, and gender in its empirical models. Finally, future research that considers more detailed regency level data on regional socio-economic conditions and policies may shed more light on the impacts of decentralization on regional educational outcomes.

References

Al-Samarrai, Samer. 2013. *Local Governance and Education Performance: A Survey of the Quality of Local Governance in 50 Indonesian Districts. Human Development.* Jakarta: World Bank.

Al-Samarrai, S. et al. 2014. *Assessing the Role of the School Operational Grant Program (BOS) in Improving Education Outcomes in Indonesia.* Jakarta: World Bank Group. http://documents.worldbank.org/curated/en/779451468253241136/Assessing-the-role-of-the-school-operational-grant-program-BOS-in-improving-education-outcomes-in-Indonesia (accessed May 29, 2018).

Alvarez, Roberto and Damián Vergara. 2016. *Natural Resources and Education: Evidence from Chile.* University of Chile. http://www.econ.uchile.cl/uploads/publicacion/1182443d544ae867ccc144a0b6b64c42b1fd921f.pdf (accessed April 7, 2019).

Azzizah, Yuni. 2015. "Socio-economic Factors on Indonesia Education Disparity." *International Education Studies* 8: 218–230.

Badan Pusat Statistik (BPS). 2000–2014. *Potensi Desa (Podes)* [Village Potential Statistics].

_____. 2002–2014. *Survei Sosial Ekonomi Nasional (Susenas)* [National Socio-Economic Survey].

Booth, Anne. 1998. *The Indonesian economy in the Nineteenth and Twentieth Centuries: A History of Missed Opportunities.* London: Macmillan Press Ltd.

Di Gropello, Emanuella (ed.). 2006. *Meeting the Challenges of Secondary Education in Latin America and East Asia.* Washington, DC: The World Bank.

Duflo, Ester. 2001. "Schooling and Labor Market Consequences of School Construction in Indonesia: Evidence from an Unusual Policy Experiment." *The American Economic Review* 91 (4): 795–813.

Eurotrends. 2009. *Study on Governance Challenges for Education in Fragile Situation: Aceh Indonesia Country Report*. Brussels: European Comission.

Falch, Torberg and J.A.V Fischer. 2012. "Public Sector Decentralization and School Performance: International Evidence." *Economics Letters* 114: 276–279.

Gallego, Francisco A. 2010. "Historical Origins of Schooling: The Role of Democracy and Political Decentralization." *The Review of Economics and Statistics* 92 (2): 228–243.

Glewwe, Paul and Hanan G. Jacoby. 2004. "Economic Growth and the Demand for Education: Is There a Wealth Effect." *Journal of Development Economics* 74 (1): 33–51.

Gnezzy, U. et al. 2009. "Gender Differences in Competition: Evidence from a Matrilineal and a Patriarchal Society." *Econometrica* 77 (5): 1637–1664.

Grant, M. J. and J. R. Behrman. 2010. "Gender Gap in Educational Attainment in Less Developed Countries." *Population and Development Review* 36 (1): 71–89.

Gylfason, Thorvaldur. 2001. "Natural Resource, Education, and Economic Development." *European Economic Review* 45: 847–859.

Hill, Hal. 2000. *The Indonesian Economy*. Cambridge: Cambridge University Press.

Hsin, Amy. 2007. "Children's Time Use: Labor Divisions and Schooling in Indonesia." *Journal of Marriage and Family* 69: 1297–1306.

Igeo, Kengo and Takako Yuki. 2015. Determinants of School Enrolment of Girls in Rural Yemen: Parental Aspirations and Attitudes toward Girls' Education. JICA-RI Working Paper No. 107. Tokyo: JICA Research Institute.

Jeong, D.W. et al. 2017. "Education Decentralization, School Resources, and Student Outcomes in Korea." *International Journal of Educational Development* 53: 12–27.

Jones, Gavin W. 2001. "Which Indonesian Women Marry Youngest, and Why?". *Journal of Southeast Asian Studies* 32: 67–78.

_____. 2003. *Pengamatan Cepat SMERU tentang Permasalahan Pendidikan dan Program JPS, Beasiswa, dan DBO di Empat Provinsi* [SMERU Rapid Assessment on Education Problems and Social Safety Net, Scholarship, and Operational Subsidy Programs in Four Provinces]. Jakarta: SMERU Research Institute. http://www.smeru. or.id/sites/default/files/publication/education-ina.pdf (accessed May 7, 2018).

Jones, G.W. and D. Pratomo. 2016. Education in Indonesia: Trends, Differential, and Implication for Development. In *Contemporary demographic transition in China, India, and Indonesia*, edited by C. Guilmoto and G. W. Jones, pp. 195-214. London: Springer.

Joshi, Arun R. and Isis Gaddis (eds.). 2015. *Preparing the Next Generation in Tanzania: Challenges and Opportunities in Education*. Washington, DC: The World Bank.

Kimura, Ehito. 2007. "Marginality and Opportunity in the Periphery: The Emergence of Gorontalo Province in North Sulawesi". *Indonesia* 84: 71–95.

Kristiansen, Stein and Pratikno. 2006. "Decentralising Education in Indonesian". *International Journal of Educational Development* 26: 513–531.

Lanjouw, P. et al. 2001. *Poverty, Education, and Health in Indonesia: Who Benefits from Public Spending?*. Jakarta: World Bank

Machimu, Gervas and Josephine Joseph Minde. 2010. "Rural Girls' Educational Challenges in Tanzania: A Case Study of Matrilineal Society". *The Social Sciences* 5: 10–15.

Male, Chata and Quentin Wodon. 2016. *Basic Profile of Child Marriage in Indonesia*. http://documents.worldbank.org/curated/ en/476891467833356935/pdf/105928-BRI-ADD-SERIES-PUBLIC-HNP-Brief-Indonesia-Profile-CM.pdf (accessed November 5, 2017).

Manor, James. 1997. *The Political Economy of Democratic Decentralization.* Washington D.C: The World Bank.

Nooteboom, Gerben. 2015. Forgotten People: Poverty, Risk, and Social Security in Indonesia: The case of the Madurese. Leiden: Brill.

OECD/Asian Development Bank. 2015. *Education in Indonesia: Rising to the Challenge.* Paris: OECD Publishing.

Oey-Gardiner, M. 1991. "Gender Differences in Schooling in Indonesia". *Bulletin of Indonesia Economic Studies* 27 (1): 57–79.

Parker, Lyn. 2009. "Religion, Class and Schooled Sexuality among Minangkabau Teenage Girls". *Bijdragen tot de Taal-, Land- en Volkenkunde* 165 (1): 62–94.

Plank, David. 2005. *Understanding the Demand for Schooling.* A report to OECD. https://www.oecd.org/edu/ceri/35393937.pdf (accessed November 5, 2017).

Ramesh, M. 2009. "Economic Crisis and its Social Impacts Lessons from the 1997 Asian Economic Crisis". *Global Social Policy* 9: 79–99.

Rammohan, Anu and Peter Robertson. 2012. "Do Kinship Norms Influence Female Education? Evidence from Indonesia". *Oxford Development Studies* 40 (3): 283–304.

Sabates, R. et al. 2010. "School Dropout: Patterns, Causes, Changes, and Policies". Background paper prepared for the Education for All Global Monitoring Report 2011. http://unesdoc.unesco.org/images/0019/001907/190771e.pdf. (accessed March 14, 2018).

Sakai, Minako and Amelia Fauzia. 2014. "Islamic Orientations in Contemporary Indonesia: Islamism on the Rise?". *Asian Ethnicity* 15 (1): 41–61.

Saraswati, Erwin. 2012. "Public Spending Education and Inequality: A Case Study in Indonesia". *International Journal of Social Science and Humanity* 2: 427–431.

Shah, Rites and Mieke Lopez Cardozo. 2014. "Education and Social Change in Post-Conflict and Post-Disaster Aceh". *International Journal of Education Development* 38: 2–12.

Sundaram, Aparna. 2005. *Life Course and Marriage Timing in Indonesia*. http://paa2006.princeton.edu/papers/61709 (accessed November 5, 2017).

Suryadarma, D. et al. 2006a. Cause of Low Secondary School Enrolment in Indonesia. Labor Economics Working Papers 22546. East Asian Bureau of Economic Research.

Suryadarma, D. et al. 2006b. From Access to Income: Regional and Ethnic Inequality in Indonesia. SMERU Working Paper. Jakarta: SMERU Research Institute.

Tobias, J. et al. 2014. *Toward Better Education Quality: Indonesia's Promising Path*. London: Overseas Development Institute. https://www.odi.org/sites/odi.org.uk/files/odi-assets/publications-opinion-files/9065.pdf (accessed May 7, 2018).

Utomo, A. et al. 2014. "What Happens after You Drop Out? Transition to Adulthood among Early School-dropout Leavers in Urban Indonesia". *Demographic Research* 30: 1189–1218.

Van de Walle, Dominique. 1992. The Distribution of the Benefits from Social Services in Indonesia, 1978-87. Policy Research Working Paper 871. World Bank.

World Bank. 2004. *Poverty in Guatemala*. Washington, DC: The World Bank.

————. 2008. "The Impact of the Conflict, the Tsunami and Reconstruction on Poverty in Aceh". *Aceh Poverty Assessment 2008*. Jakarta/Washington, DC: World Bank Group.

————. 2010. Transforming Indonesia's Teaching Force. Report No. 53732. Jakarta: World Bank.

————. 2013. *Spending More or Spending Better: Improving Education Financing in Indonesia. East Asia and Pacific Region*. Jakarta: World Bank.

Appendix A.1. Data and Methodology

Data and Sample

In general, our data covers 497 regencies for the years 2002–2014. However, due to availability of some independent variables and some restrictions at the regency level, our econometric analysis only covers data for 2004–2013. Moreover, we exclude several regencies in the following regions: (1) Jakarta's regencies, since these regions are not decentralized and managed by a provincial government, (2) around 20 regions in Eastern Indonesia, due to missing data.

Our dataset covers macro level socio-economic indicators that are recorded by the Badan Pusat Statistik (BPS—Central Statistics Bureau), the World Bank's Indonesia Database for Policy and Economic Research, and the Ministry of Finance. We also utilize micro level data from core Susenas and Podes. Core Susenas is annual cross-section micro level data that represents household and individual conditions in Indonesia, while Podes records the availability and accessibility of village infrastructure.

No.	Variable	Sources
1.	Enrolment rate (Total)	BPS and INDODAPOER
2.	Enrolment rate (Gender basis)	Susenas
3.	Reasons for leaving school	Susenas
4.	Households expenditure on education	Susenas and INDODAPOER
5.	The number of schools per regency	Podes
6.	The average distance between a village without a school and the nearest school	Podes
7.	Central government transfers for education expenditure	Ministry of Finance
8.	Local government expenditures on education	Ministry of Finance

Methodology

We build our econometric model from both supply-side and demand-side factors. Based on our literature review, we develop our model as follows:

$$\text{Lower (upper)-secondary}_{it} = \alpha + \beta_1 \, Primary_{it} \, (Lower\text{-}secondary_{it}) + \beta_2 \, Dakeduc_{it} + \beta_3 \, Educexp_{it} + \beta_4 \, Householdexp_{it} + \beta_5 \, school_{it}$$

$$+ \beta_6 \, distance_{it} + \beta_7 \, free\text{-}tuition_{it} + \beta_8 \, region_{it} + \varepsilon$$

Where

Upper-secondary : Net enrolment in upper-secondary level (Ln)

Lower-secondary : Net enrolment in lower-secondary level (Ln)

Primary : Net enrolment in primary level (Ln)

Dakeduc : Central government transfer in education sector (Ln)

Educexp : Local government expenditure in education sector (Ln)

Householdexp : Households expenditure in education sector (Ln)

School : Number of either Lower- or Upper-secondary schools (Ln)

Distance : The average distance of the school from the village-km (Ln)

Free-tuition : Dummy variable of free-tuition policy. It shows 1 for each year after 2011 and 0 otherwise

Region : Control variable regions

In addition to the econometric model, this chapter applies statistical and spatial analysis in examining the patterns of regional and gender disparities in Indonesia regions and assessing factors that affect the disparities. In addition, regarding measurement of regional gender disparity, this study adopts the basic concept of a gender parity index (GPI), calculated by dividing the female value of an indicator with the male value of the same indicator.[2]

Since most of the research on this topic defines gender disparity as the different level of outcome between males and females without clearly expressing and quantifying at which level gender disparity may arise, it should be treated carefully. Therefore, this study proposes a simple calculation using the average standard deviation to address the existence of gender disparity in Indonesia. We define gender disparity as a difference between male and female enrolment rates that exceeds 5% in either direction for both levels of education.[3]

---

2   GPI_i =Female$_i$ / Male$_i$ where i = measured indicator. We interpret GPI equal to 1 as an indicator of parity between females and males, while a value less/greater than 1 shows a signal for disparity that favor boys or girls respectively. In addition, we should infer the other way around to interpret an indicator that should ideally approach 0.

3   We use the average standard deviation of the enrolment between gender in both lower- and upper secondary education for year 2002 and 2004.

Appendix A.2. Statistic Descriptive

Variable	obs	Mean	Max	Min	St.dev
Enrolment rate - Upper-secondary	4,900	46.674	87.85	1.35	14.556
Enrolment rate - Lower-secondary	4,911	65.701	95.71	3.76	12.507
Enrolment rate - Primary	5,351	93.197	100.00	6.60	6.902
Number of schools - Lower-secondary	5,434	83.589	688	2	76.891
Average distance (km) - Lower-secondary	5,431	7.460	86.75	0	10.599
Number of schools - Upper-secondary	5,434	46.828	406	1	46.961
Average distance (km) - Upper-secondary	5,434	13.870	99.00	0	15.667
Specific transfers for education (Ln)	3,952	10.609	14.21	5.50	1.154
Local expenditure on education (Ln)	4,785	13.080	17.24	6.81	0.820
Household expenditure on education (Ln)	4,886	11.960	14.59	8.98	0.778
Free-tuition policy	5,434	0.182	1	0	0.386
Java-Bali regencies	5,434	0.257	1	0	0.437
Western regencies	5,434	0.672	1	0	0.470
Mining regencies	5,434	0.158	1	0	0.365
Sumatera regencies	5,434	0.304	1	0	0.460
Kalimantan regencies	5,434	0.111	1	0	0.315
Sulawesi regencies	5,434	0.146	1	0	0.353
Nusa Tenggara regencies	5,434	0.061	1	0	0.239
Moluccas-Papua regencies	5,434	0.121	1	0	0.327

Source: Stata output

Appendix A.3. Reasons for not continuing study

Reasons	2009						2014					
	Lower			Upper			Lower			Upper		
	all	male	female	all	male	female	all	male	female	all	male	female
Cannot afford the cost	58.75	56.09	62.14	58.83	58.67	41.34	41.34	36.62	48.41	43.54	42.53	44.63
Working	6.36	7.10	5.43	11.88	13.36	7.17	7.17	8.39	5.34	14.97	17.52	12.22
Married	0.58	0.08	1.21	4.09	0.19	1.37	1.37	0.04	3.35	7.93	0.43	16.04
Education sufficiency	3.12	2.16	4.36	6.59	6.58	4.16	4.16	3.58	5.04	8.03	8.07	7.98
Ashamed (economic factor)	2.06	2.21	1.87	1.08	1.08	1.55	1.55	1.84	1.11	0.81	1.03	0.58
Too far (distance)	3.20	2.71	3.82	1.95	1.98	3.83	3.83	2.57	5.56	1.58	1.36	1.81
Difable	1.46	1.60	1.28	0.63	0.65	2.08	2.08	2.06	2.11	0.65	0.64	0.65
Waiting for enrolment	0.68	0.79	0.54	1.61	1.44					2.27	2.13	2.43
Not accepted	0.52	0.46	0.61	0.62	0.64	0.13	0.13	0.15	0.10	0.28	0.26	0.31
Others	23.25	26.81	18.74	12.72	15.41	38.37	38.37	44.65	28.98	19.94	26.02	13.37
TOTAL	100.00	100.00	100.00	100.00	100.00	100.00	100.00	100.00	100.00	100.00	100.00	100.00

Source: Author's calculation based on Susenas 2002 and 2014

Appendix A.4. Net enrolment rate based on gender, province, and level of education in 2002–2014

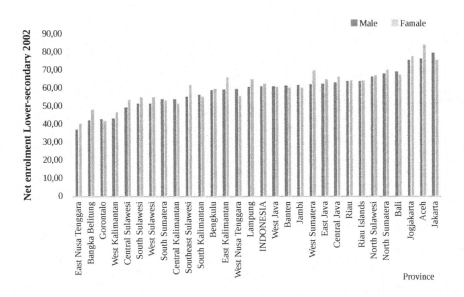

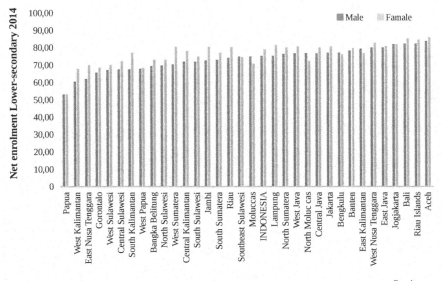

Indonesia at the Crossroads: Transformation and Challenges

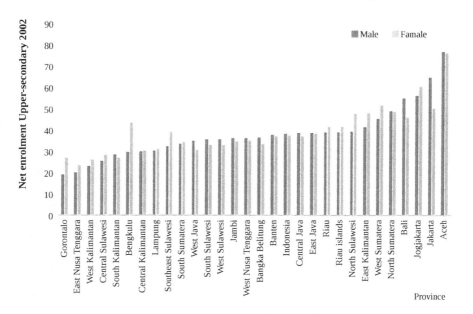

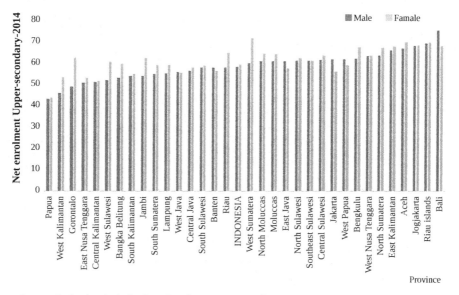

Source: Author's calculation based on Susenas 2002 and 2014.

Appendix A.5. Number of schools and average distance to the nearest school by province in 2003–2014)

No	Province	2003				2014			
		Lower second		Upper second		Lower second		Upper second	
		# of school	dist (km)	# of school	dist (km)	# of school	dist (km)	# of school	dist (km)
Western Indonesia									
1	Aceh	1,056	4.23	405	7.68	1,233	2.74	806	4.64
2	North Sumatera	1,560	5.61	1,487	10.73	2,987	4.82	2,114	8.08
3	West Sumatera	932	3.66	433	7.05	1,004	4.02	603	7.19
4	Riau	970	7.51	533	16.35	1,470	5.55	840	10.52
5	Riau Islands*					325	6.27	210	11.43
6	Jambi	596	5.29	270	14.75	881	3.68	495	8.85
7	South Sumatera	934	7.66	537	19.07	1,497	4.66	883	8.42
8	Bengkulu	394	4.77	148	10.97	452	2.87	241	7.04
9	Lampung	808	3.68	700	9.02	1,783	3.45	1,044	6.30
10	Bangka Belitung Islands	934	7.66	537	19.07	217	5.30	123	10.82
11	Jakarta**	640	0.07	951	0.72	1,163	8.72	1,080	4.94
12	West Java	2,934	2.21	2,141	5.98	6,657	2.65	4,477	5.17
13	Banten*					2,010	2.90	1,340	5.09
14	Central Java	3,186	2.14	1,997	5.53	4,569	2.67	2,755	5,21
15	Yogyakarta	478	0.86	356	3.39	491	2,24	378	4.67
16	East Java	3,080	2.20	2,530	5.65	6,894	2.85	4,174	5.01
17	Bali	390	2.43	245	5.64	384	3.21	314	5.96

Appendix A.5. Number of schools and average distance to the nearest school by province in 2003–2014) (continued)

18	West Kalimantan	656	11.89	363	23.84	1,349	13.04	650	21.32
19	Central Kalimantan	528	21.02	200	37.08	837	11.62	377	22.11
20	South Kalimantan	694	5.27	285	13.07	877	4.15	419	8.02
21	East Kalimantan	582	18.04	316	32.37	676	13.21	463	20.92
22	North Kalimantan*					155	16.19	88	28.11
Eastern Indonesia									
23	West Nusa Tenggara	566	2..51	378	7.88	1.473	2.13	951	6.07
24	East Nusa Tenggara	604	7.58	259	21.99	1,514	4.73	691	12.76
25	North Sulawesi	536	3.19	251	9.36	706	2.86	378	8.60
26	Gorontalo*	536	3.19	251	9.36	372	2.08	137	6.31
27	Central Sulawesi	584	7.25	229	21.77	983	5.05	463	11.85
28	South Sulawesi	1,500	4.76	725	12.28	2,033	3.32	1,145	7.75
29	West Sulawesi*	1,500	4.76	725	12.28	419	4.39	231	12.27
30	Southeast Sulawesi	580	4.70	210	16.71	849	3.12	449	6.86
3	Moluccas	344	13.11	170	35.06	642	13.88	369	20.66
32	North Moluccas*	344	13.11	170	35.06	534	5.40	332	10.73
33	West Papua*	524	31.84	193	57.16	264	17.45	159	37.02
34	Papua	524	31.84	193	57.16	586	34.08	310	49.71

* proliferated region (we assume that the data for 2003 is similar to its parent data)

** an increase in the average distance is related with the new establishment of Seribu Islands Regency from North Jakarta City.

Source: Author's calculation from Podes (2003 and 2014).

Appendix A.6. Determinants of lower-secondary enrolment by regency

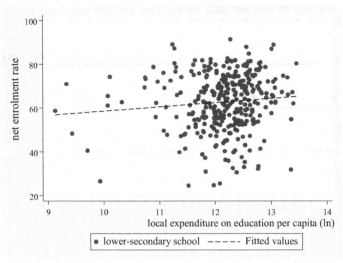

Source: Stata output

Appendix A.7. Determinants of upper-secondary enrolment by regency

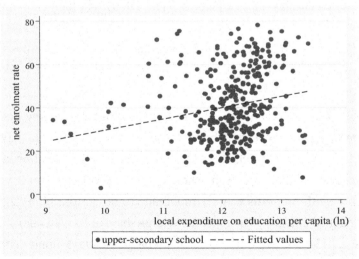

Source: Stata output

Chapter 6
Understanding Metropolitan Poverty:
The Profile of Poverty in Jabodetabek

Asep Suryahadi and Cecilia Marlina[1]

Introduction

The growth of cities and their surrounding areas is closely linked to changes in the economy, especially since such growth creates opportunity for more productive jobs, which can contribute to attracting foreign trade and investment (World Bank, 2009). Through economies of scale and the process of agglomeration, economic growth is expected to be exponential (Christiaensen and Yasuyuki, 2014). Hence, cities play a central role as engines of national economic development (UN Habitat, 2011).

With careful planning, urbanization can become a key tool for accelerating development and the engine of growth through higher levels of productivity (Becker, 2008; Duranton and Puga, 2004). In addition, a well-managed metropolitan area can encourage the growth of secondary cities through a spill-over effect. A metropolitan region is, to a high degree, a self-contained universe that generates a large share of its own demand (UN Habitat, 2011). Although it has become cheaper to travel long distances, more and more people are clustering closer and closer together in large metropolitan areas (Glaeser, 2011).

---

1 We would like to thank Ridho Al Izzati for research assistance and Bambang Hadi for providing the poverty map of Jabodetabek area.

However, the positive results outlined above only materialize when the work generated in cities also accounts for marginalized people, in particular maximizing employment generation for the unskilled poor. Empirical studies have found that mega city agglomeration resulted not only in faster income growth, but also higher income inequality (Christiaensen and Yasuyuki, 2014). Addressing poverty in metropolitan areas is therefore critical to maximizing the benefits of urban development.

In addition, as more of the urban population earns higher incomes, they demand more living space and entertainment (Almeida et al., 2005). Therefore, growth in the core of the city needs support from the regions nearby. Those supports include, but are not limited to, cheaper housing options and new employment opportunities. In addition to non-demographic factors, population variables of size and growth are critical components affecting wellbeing in cities of developing countries (Brockerhoff and Brennan, 1998).

To prevent the negative effects of the agglomeration process, a better understanding of poverty conditions in metropolitan areas is necessary. Developing countries often institute programs to tackle poverty problems uniformly across the country and based on the national poverty profile. If the poverty profile in a metropolitan area is significantly different from the national profile, alleviation programs based on the national profile may not be suitable or effective in addressing poverty problems. For example, one major poverty reduction initiative in Indonesia is the village fund, which is a block grant of around IDR 1 billion (around USD 70,000) per year for each of the approximately 70,000 rural villages in the country (Suryahadi and Izzati, 2018). Since the grant is provided only for rural villages, the majority of regions within metropolitan areas are not eligible to receive it.

This paper aims to contribute to a better understanding of poverty conditions in metropolitan areas, focusing on the Greater Jakarta metropolitan area of Indonesia, commonly known as Jabodetabek. Jabodetabek refers to the inner part of the metropolitan region, Jakarta, the capital of Indonesia, and the outer part of the region, Bodetabek, which consists of five municipalities (Bogor, Depok, Tangerang, South Tangerang, and Bekasi) and three regencies (Bogor, Tangerang, and Bekasi). Hence, Jabodetabek covers areas in three provinces: Jakarta, West Java, and Banten. The total area of Jabodetabek is around 7,000 km^2. Figure 6.1. shows the map of the Jabodetabek metropolitan area.

Figure 6.1. Map of Jabodetabek metropolitan area (Rustiandi et al., 2015).

The remainder of this chapter is organized as follows. Section two reviews the literature on poverty in metropolitan areas. Section three discusses the trends and distribution of poverty in Jabodetabek. Section four describes the method and data used in the analysis. Section five presents and discusses the results of the analysis. Finally, section six concludes and offers some policy implications.

Poverty in Metropolitan Areas

Poverty in metropolitan areas is expected to continue to be a challenge in developing countries as the number of poor people seeking opportunities in cities is expected to grow. The growing number of migrants, when not accommodated by land, infrastructure, and jobs, results in increased poverty rates. Poverty in metropolitan areas presents a particular set of characteristics and challenges which are distinct from rural areas, including for example the health and sanitation problems of slums, the nature of unemployment, and violent crime (Ferré et al., 2012). Dealing with these specific challenges impacts the costs of providing basic services, such as the improvement of roads, water systems, and sanitation (Joassart-Marcelli et al., 2005).

For example, the metropolitan city of Manila, which consists of 17 cities and municipalities, faces constant traffic congestion which costs an estimated USD 70 million a day. Around 11% of Manila's population lives in slum areas due to a lack of affordable housing. Economic growth, which is led by the manufacturing sector in the city, has been stagnant in recent years, adding pressure on people with low skilled jobs (World Bank, 2017).

Bangkok has an issue with segregation of the middle class and the poor. Lack of urban planning and regulation in the city, coupled with the influx of rural people, has made the problem worse. Apparent boundaries across parts of Bangkok mark inequalities. Outer Bangkok is well known for its production sector, while the commercial and financial sector is more concentrated in inner Bangkok. Rattanakosin (also known as the early settlement of Bangkok), located in the inner area, is considered the most congested area of Bangkok where many slum dwellers live. Many slums are also found in the Central Business District (CBD) area of Bangkok where many offices and governments operate (World Bank, 2017).

Like other metropolitan areas in developing countries, most slum dwellers in Bangkok have a primary level of education and low skills. Hence, most work in the informal sector, living near their worksite to avoid travel costs. Bangkok is expected to have a population surpassing 10 million people by 2030. Consequently, the slums in the metropolitan area will become a more pressing problem (Choiejit and Teungfung, 2005).

A study found that one third of Hanoi residents live in very crowded slums (Minnery et al., 2013). The Vietnamese government strictly regulates urban property ownership. Despite the high migration of people from rural areas to the city, the government only provides the right to own urban property to people with urban residency status. This exacerbates the situation as poor people settle on illegal premises in the city (Word Bank, 2017).

People in rural Vietnam perceive rural-urban migration as a support strategy in the face of agricultural and economic shocks in their village, such as floods or failing crops (Nguyen et al., 2013). For better-off households, migration is deemed important in order to obtain higher education, which is not easily accessible in the village.

The poverty rate in New Delhi, the capital and second largest metropolitan area in India, was 14.2% in 2009/10, which is about half the national rate. However, while the poverty rate is decreasing for India as a whole, it is slightly increasing in New Delhi. A significant proportion of the poor in New Delhi work as rickshaw pullers. About half of them are natives, while the other half are migrants from rural areas. They work for about 12 hours per day and the majority have occupational health issues such as body aches, joint issues, and respiratory problems. They live in rented one-room houses with no toilet facilities or drinking water connections; some sleep on the pavement and footpaths or under flyovers and bridges. Many of them are illiterate, as are their family members. They own very few assets, and some are indebted. Almost none of them receive benefits from government programs (Risbud, 2016).

Rio de Janeiro is the largest metropolitan region in Brazil. It is famous for its squatter settlements, the favelas. They are highly consolidated concentrations of poor people on public or private land, equipped with little but self-built shelters and lacking any kind of design plan. They exist in large numbers and are spread across the city, frequently occupying hilly sites (Xavier and Magalhaes, 2003). In 2010, 1.4 million people, or 22% of Rio's population, lived in favelas. This proportion is set to grow as the population growth in favelas during 2000–2010 reached 27.5% compared to just 7.4% for the whole of Rio. The favelas exist not far from affluent neighborhoods, making Rio a divided city and reflecting the stark inequality, segregation, and exclusion that exist in the city. For example, in 2008 the poverty rate for Rio as a whole was approximately 10%, while in the favelas the rate was 15%. In addition, the favela population has higher rates of early death by homicide, low income, illiteracy, teenage pregnancy, and under-five mortality (Jovchelovitch and Priego-Hernandez, 2013).

One of few metropolitan areas in Africa is Lagos in Nigeria. Similar to Rio de Janeiro, there is a stark contrast between affluence and poverty in Lagos. However, there has been a general deterioration in the quality of life in Lagos during the last two decades due to the high level of poverty, a proliferation of slums, environmental degradation, a dilapidated and congested road system, massive flooding, a disrupted sewerage network, and increasing crime rates. Largely, the communities that live in urban slums belong to the class of low-income households who migrate to the city seeking a better future. Lagos is estimated to have more than 100 slums, with 2 out of 3 Lagosians living in slums (Akanle and Adejare, 2017).

To summarize, metropolitan areas in developing countries are generally characterized as divided regions, where affluent neighborhoods and slums occupy different areas and the borders are visually apparent. The slums, where most of the poor live, are informal settlements, developed without plans, and often illegally occupying public or private land, hence providing residents with no property security. Many of the poor are migrants from rural areas, or their descendants, who come to cities in search of a better life. They have low levels of formal education and employable skills, work in the informal sector, and earn low incomes. They often cannot access public services, such as clean water and electricity, education, and health services.

Poverty in Jabodetabek

The term 'urban sprawl' is commonly used to refer to a peripheral area that supports the growth of a city (Struyk et al., 1990; Aksoro, 1994 as cited in Henderson and Kuncoro, 1996). In this context, Bodetabek is an example of 'urban sprawl' because it acts as the support system of the main capital, Jakarta. It provides more residential and commercial space than Jakarta. Hence, it is common in Jabodetabek to find land for residential and commercial use side by side. Furthermore, some low or middle income housing occupies small areas within higher income residential areas (Henderson and Kuncoro, 1996).

The population of Jakarta rose 17%, from 8.2 to 9.6 million, between the population censuses of 1990 and 2010. Meanwhile, the population of Bodetabek doubled in the same period, from 8.9 million to 18.3 million. Thus, the population of Jabodetabek as a whole increased by 63%, from 17.1 million to 27.9 million (Jones et al., 2016), making Jabodetabek one of the largest metropolitan areas in the world.

Jabodetabek has one of the lowest, but stagnant, poverty rates in Indonesia. Figure 6.2. shows poverty rates during 2004–2014 in Jabodetabek metropolitan area, all urban areas, and Indonesia as a whole. During the period, the Indonesian poverty rate significantly declined from 16.7% in 2004 to 11% in 2014. Similarly, the poverty rate in urban areas declined from 12.1% to 8.3% over the same period. Meanwhile, in Jabodetabek the poverty rate declined only slightly from 6% in 2004 to 5.3% in 2014. In particular, from 2012 to 2014, the poverty rate in Jabodetabek did not change at all. This shows that despite the high economic growth in Jabodetabek, poverty remains stagnant in this area.

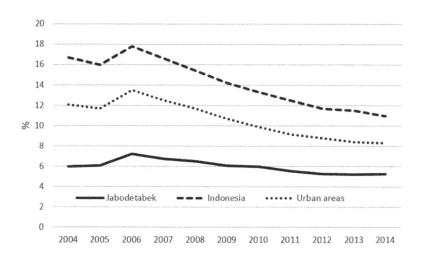

Figure 6.2. Poverty rates in Jabodetabek, all urban areas, and Indonesia, 2004–2014. Source: BPS

The 2014 poverty rates in the cities and regencies within Jabodetabek are shown in Table 6.1. The table shows that, in general, the poverty rates in Jakarta are lower than in the Bodetabek areas. However, the lowest poverty rate (1.7%) is found in South Tangerang City, which is located in Bodetabek. At the same time, the highest poverty rate (11.6%) is in Seribu Islands Regency, which is located in Jakarta.

Table 6.1. Poverty rates in the cities and regencies of Jabodetabek in 2014.

City/ Regency	Poverty rate (%)
Jakarta	
- South Jakarta City	3.72
- East Jakarta City	3.43
- Central Jakarta City	4.12
- West Jakarta City	3.72
- North Jakarta City	6.00
- Seribu Islands Regency	11.56
West Java	
- Bogor City	7.74
- Bekasi City	5.25
- Depok City	2.32
- Bogor Regency	8.91
- Bekasi Regency	4.97
Banten	
- Tengerang City	4.91
- South Tangerang City	1.68
- Tangerang Regency	5.26

Source: BPS (2015).

Figure 6.3. shows the poverty rates of Jabodetabek at the village level in 2015. In this map, darker areas indicate higher poverty rates. The map confirms that Bodetabek areas generally have higher poverty rates than Jakarta areas. However, poverty pockets are found in the northern parts of West Jakarta and North Jakarta areas.

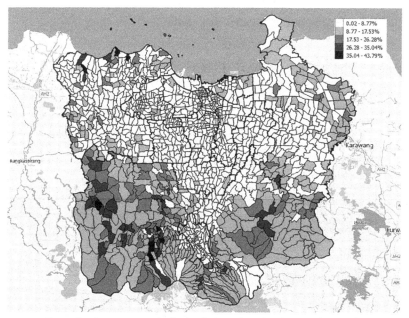

Figure 6.3. Poverty map of Jabodetabek at village level in 2015 (percent).
Source: Poverty and Livelihood Map Indonesia (povertymap.smeru.or.id)

Poverty Profile: Method and Data

The Model

The analysis of the poverty profile in this chapter uses a binomial logistic (logit) regression model of household poverty status and its correlates. The correlates included in the model are based on findings from previous studies on correlates or determinants of poverty.

An assessment using the Malawi Integrated Household Survey in 1998 found that increasing educational attainment, especially for women, and reallocating labor from the agricultural sector to trade and services sectors proved to be significant in reducing poverty rates (Mukherjee and Benson,

2003). Meanwhile, a broader assessment on metropolitan cities across Asia cites access to land for housing, and access to basic infrastructure like water, sanitation, and solid waste management as the key features for measuring the inclusiveness of cities (Dahiya, 2012). One study focusing on the urban poor in Malaysia looks at the link between housing conditions (types of dwellings, surrounding environments, and house tenure) and quality of life (health, safety and social support). It found that the housing condition is significant in determining the quality of life and therefore should be taken into consideration when assessing the determinants of urban poverty (Zainal et al., 2012).

Furthermore, poverty is often attributable to the demographic characteristics of the household, which include family size, education level of the household head, gender of the household head, and the age composition. A larger family size, particularly one with many young children, is positively linked to chronic poverty as it burdens the limited resources available to a poor family (Bayudan-Dacuycuy and Lim, 2013).

Based on these findings, the correlates included in the model are household size, house size per capita, household head education, age of the household head, gender of the household head, household head employment sector and employment status, and household access to infrastructure such as safe drinking water, the internet, and toilets.

Data

This study uses data from the 2014 Survei Sosial Ekonomi Nasional (Susenas—National Socio-Economic Survey) from Badan Pusat Statistik (BPS—Central Statistics Bureau), which uses a sample of around 300,000 households across Indonesia. This household survey contains information on basic demographic and socio-economic conditions of households, including access to basic facilities, education attainment, household expenditure, and types of employment. To determine household poverty status, the 2014 national poverty lines at the *kabupaten* (regency) level are used as the threshold.

Results and Discussion

Results

The model is estimated using data from Jabodetabek metropolitan area as well as Indonesia nationally. Comparing the results of both estimations shows whether the poverty profile of Jabodetabek metropolitan area is significantly different from the national poverty profile. The estimation results for both Jabodetabek metropolitan area and Indonesia as a whole are shown in Table 6.2.

Discussion

Household size

The correlation of household size with household poverty status appears to be similar both in Jabodetabek metropolitan area and Indonesia as a whole. The correlation is positive with a decreasing rate, indicated by the positive coefficient of the household size variable and the negative coefficient of the household size squared variable, which are all statistically significant. This means that as household size increases, the probability of that household being poor also increases. However, this correlation gets smaller as household size increases further. The magnitude of the coefficients also indicates that the correlation between household size and poverty in metropolitan area is much smaller, only around one half, than that of the national figure.

This finding aligns with a study in the Philippines that examined the relation between household size, poverty, and vulnerability (Orbeta, 2005). It found that a greater number of family members has a negative impact on household savings, increases the probability of children dropping out of school, and discourages the mother in the household from taking paid employment.

Table 6.2. The correlates of poverty in Jabodetabek and Indonesia (in marginal effects after logit).

Variable	Jabodetabek		Indonesia	
	dy/dx	p-value	dy/dx	p-value
Household size	0.0191**	0.00	0.0357**	0.00
Household size square	-0.0010**	0.00	-0.0015**	0.00
House size per capita	-0.0011**	0.00	-0.0031**	0.00
Education level: (base: unfinished primary)				
- Primary education	-0.0016	0.12	-0.0176**	0.00
- Junior secondary education	-0.0086**	0.00	-0.0330**	0.00
- Senior secondary education	-0.0173**	0.00	-0.0495**	0.00
- Tertiary education	-0.0278**	0.00	-0.0671**	0.00
Access to clean drinking water	0.0020	0.47	-0.0128**	0.00
Access to the internet	-0.0149**	0.00	-0.0485**	0.00
Access to improved sanitation	-0.0044**	0.00	-0.0321**	0.00
Age of household head	-0.0015**	0.00	-0.0037**	0.00
Age of household head square	0.0000**	0.00	0.0000**	0.00
Gender of household head	0.0034*	0.05	0.0184**	0.00
Urban	0.0068**	0.00	0.0042**	0.00
Job sector: (base: agriculture/unemployed)				
- Services	-0.0071**	0.00	-0.0229**	0.00
- Trade	-0.0060**	0.00	-0.0310**	0.00
- Manufacturing	-0.0132**	0.00	-0.0152**	0.00
- Other sectors	-0.0060**	0.00	-0.0175**	0.00
Status of employment: (base: labor/unemployed)				
- Own a business	0.0013	0.24	-0.0009	0.13
- Own a business with the help of laborer	-0.0089**	0.00	-0.0001	0.90
- Work in a family business/unpaid worker	-0.0158**	0.00	0.0256**	0.00

Note: ** significant at 1% level, * significant at 5% levels

House size per capita

The correlation of house size per capita to household poverty status is similar in Jabodetabek and Indonesia nationally. The coefficient is negative and statistically significant, indicating that the smaller the size per capita of a house, the higher the probability that its inhabitants are poor. The magnitudes of the coefficients again indicate that the correlation in the metropolitan area is much smaller, only one third, than that of the national level.

Education level

The correlations between education level of household head and household poverty status indicate that in general, a higher formal education level is associated with a lower probability of being poor. This is indicated by the negative and statistically significant coefficients with larger magnitude as education level increases. However, there are important differences in the correlation between education and poverty in Jabodetabek and Indonesia as a whole.

First, in Jabodetabek, there is no added value in having only a primary education compared to those who did not complete primary school in terms of one's probability of being poor. At the national level, however, the coefficient is statistically significant, indicating that the effect of a primary education on lowering the probability of being poor is still significant. Second, the magnitude of the coefficients in Jabodetabek is much smaller, only around one half, than that of those for Indonesia nationally. For example, nationally a university graduate has a 6.7% lower probability of being poor compared to those who did not finish primary education. In Jabodetabek, however, the probability is lowered by only 2.8%.

To look at this issue further, Table 6.3. compares the educational attainment of the poor in Jabodetabek and in Indonesia. As expected, the poor have relatively low education levels. Only around 1% attain tertiary education, both in Jabodetabek and across Indonesia. However, the table clearly indicates that, in general, the poor in Jabodetabek have higher education levels than their counterparts in the country. While around one quarter of the poor in Indonesia did not complete primary education, only around 19% of the poor in Jabodetabek did not complete primary education. However, around 16% of the poor in Indonesia have completed senior secondary education, while in Jabodetabek around 24% of the poor completed senior secondary education. This shows that the impact of each education level in helping people to escape from poverty is lower in Jabodetabek than nationally.

Table 6.3. Education level of the poor population in Jabodetabek and Indonesia in 2014 (percent).

Education Level	Jabodetabek	Indonesia
Unfinished primary education	18.63	24.66
Primary education	34.91	38.66
Junior secondary education	21.62	19.46
Senior secondary education	23.91	16.14
Tertiary education	0.93	1.08

Source: Authors' calculation using Susenas (2014).

Access to clean drinking water

Nationally, access to clean drinking water is significantly associated with poverty, indicated by a negative and statistically significant coefficient. In Jabodetabek, however, drinking water appears to have an insignificant correlation with household poverty status as indicated by the insignificant coefficient. This implies that while nationally the poor still face problems in accessing clean drinking water, in Jabodetabek even the poor already have sufficient access to clean drinking water. This finding is further supported by an earlier study by the World Health Organization and Unicef (2006), which postulates that urban areas have significantly better access to drinking water from an improved source than rural areas.

223

This seems to be related to the phenomenon of the mushrooming of refillable water kiosks in urban areas, which are convenient and affordable. With these kiosks selling drinkable water, now people living in the slums do not have to rely solely on access to the Perusahaan Daerah Air Minum (PDAM—Regional Drinking Water Company) for clean water. However, it should be noted that Susenas only provides data about access to clean water, without further assessment of the water's quality. There is an argument that peri-urban poor are more frequently exposed to harmful water compared to their peers in urban or rural areas, because surface and household drainage systems are often located close to each other (Allen et al., 2006). Therefore, there is a need for local governments to conduct regular inspections of the quality of the drinking water commonly sold at kiosks to ensure that it is suitable for consumption.

Access to the internet

Access to the internet appears to have a significant correlation with poverty in both Jabodetabek and Indonesia nationally. The negative and statistically significant coefficients indicate that lack of access to the internet is a good indicator of poverty. The magnitude of the coefficient in Jabodetabek is much smaller, only around one quarter of the coefficient at the national level, indicating much worse access to the internet for the poor in areas outside Jabodetabek.

The vast development of communication technology has the ability to reach marginalized people who are otherwise left behind, provided there is reliable infrastructure like good connectivity and electricity (Prahalad and Hammond, 2002). In addition, providing skills to understand the information gathered from the internet is deemed necessary to improve individual productivity. Thus, it is hoped that the poor can utilize knowledge gained from the internet to find a better paying job and subsequently move out of poverty.

Access to sanitation

Another basic service analyzed in this study is access to proper sanitation. It turns out that both in Jabodetabek and at the national level, this variable has a significant correlation with poverty. The coefficients are negative and statistically significant, indicating that people who do not have access to proper sanitation are more likely to be in poverty. However, the magnitude of the coefficient for the national level is almost eight times the coefficient for Jabodetabek, indicating a much worse sanitation problem for the poor outside the metropolitan area.

Building proper sanitation infrastructure often ranks second in priority to access to drinking water. It is found that poor people who reside in the slums of the city are reluctant to invest in sanitation in their individual houses out of fear that they will lose their investment due to the land and housing tenure insecurity (Allen et al., 2006). One study conducted in Jakarta about solid waste management systems concluded that a barrier to improving sanitation conditions in Jakarta is the limited availability of land (Aprilia et al.en, 2012). Since many poor people in the metropolitan area live in the compact or slum area of the city, there is urgent need to build communal sanitation infrastructure to accommodate the needs of the poor.

Age

Household head age is significantly correlated with poverty both in Jabodetabek and at the national level. The coefficients of household head age are negative, and the coefficients of household head age squared are positive, all are statistically significant. This indicates that as people age, the probability of being poor decreases, but at a decreasing rate. However, the correlation between age and poverty is much smaller in Jabodetabek than nationally, indicated by the magnitude of the coefficient in Jabodetabek, which is only around one half of the coefficient at the national level.

Gender

Gender of the household head is also significantly correlated with household poverty status. The coefficients are positive and statistically significant, indicating that households headed by women have a higher probability of being in poverty compared to households headed by men. However, the magnitude of the coefficient at the national level is much higher, around six times, of the coefficient in Jabodetabek. This indicates that women-headed households outside Jabodetabek face higher difficulties in earning a living compared to women-headed households in Jabodetabek.

The majority of households, both in Jabodetabek and at the national level, are headed by a man. In households headed by a woman, the breadwinner of the family is a woman. There are at least two reasons why households headed by women have a higher probability of being poor. First, women have a higher chance of facing discrimination in the labor market both in terms of employment opportunities and wages. Second, because a woman household head is often a single parent, they face the double burden of having to work and take care of the family at the same time (Peters, 2016).

Urban area

Although Jabodetabek is a metropolitan area, it includes four regencies, which contain areas still classified as rural. This is a specific feature within Asian megacities, where extending urbanization has penetrated the dense agricultural area and caused chaotic urban-rural land use as well as mixed urban-rural livelihoods (Rustiandi et al., 2015). Therefore, it is still possible to examine the correlation between urban status and household poverty. The estimation results indicate that the correlation is positive and significant, indicating that living in urban areas is associated with a higher probability of being poor. The coefficient is greater for Jabodetabek compared to the national level. It means that the probability of being poor is even higher for those residing in the urban area of Jabodetabek as opposed to other urban areas.

Where a person is born has a significant impact in determining whether they live in poverty or not. Being born in an urban area with all the public facilities available might give an advantage starting point for living a better life compared to those born in a rural area. However, living in an urban area also comes with the heavy price tag of being more prone to fall into poverty (Dahiya, 2012). The price of goods in urban areas are more prone to fluctuation, putting vulnerable people at risk of falling into poverty if their wages are not sufficient to cover the cost of living. Moreover, urban areas are more complex compared to living in rural areas in terms of the goods and services needed to survive, such as transportation costs. People in rural areas have the ability to grow their own crops to survive during times of rising food prices, while in urban areas, limited land availability prevents this.

Employment sector

Services, trade, manufacturing, and other employment sectors are all significant in both Jabodetabek and at the national level. People working in these sectors have a lower probability of being poor compared to those working in the agricultural sector or who are unemployed. Table 6.4. shows that while most of the poor people in Indonesia earn their livelihood in the agricultural sector, most of the poor in Jabodetabek work in the services sector.

Table 6.4. Employment sector of the poor population in Jabodetabek and Indonesia in 2014 (percent of total population).

Jabodetabek		Indonesia	
Employment Sector	Percent	Employment Sector	Percent
Public services	24.34	Food crop agriculture	29.16
Trade	22.99	Trade	12.43
Manufacturing	17.96	Plantation	11.17
Construction	8.35	Manufacturing	10.85
Food crop agriculture	6.56	Public services	8.51
Others	19.80	Others	27.88

Source: Authors' calculation using Susenas 2014.

In Jabodetabek, the job sector with the highest correlation to a lower poverty rate is the manufacturing sector. This is followed by the services and trade sectors. Meanwhile at the national level, the sector with the greatest coefficient is the trade sector, followed by the services sector. The importance of manufacturing sector in Jabodetabek can be traced to the 1980s, a period marked by the growth in manufacturing industries in Jakarta and the surrounding regions. In the mid-1980s, due to the rising cost of land in Jakarta and the toll road extension to Bekasi and Tangerang, many manufacturing firms began building factories in the peripheral areas of Jakarta to reduce their production costs (Henderson and Kuncoro, 1996). Hence, Jabodetabek today has many well-known industrial zones, such as Jababeka and Pulogadung. The ability of the manufacturing sector to absorb large numbers of workers contributes to its high significance in lowering the probability of people falling into poverty.

Status of employment

Both in Jabodetabek and Indonesia, the variable owning a business appears to be insignificant. This means that compared to people who are unemployed or working as a laborer, people who own a business do not show any significant difference in terms of the probability of being poor. Two types of employment status are correlated with poverty in Jabodetabek: operating a business with the help of a laborer(s) and working for family, commonly known as an "unpaid family worker". People with either of these employment statuses have a lower probability of being poor. In contrast, nationally, unpaid family workers have a higher probability of being poor.

People who work for their family as unpaid family workers have a significant correlation with poverty both in Jabodetabek and at the national level. However, it is interesting that the coefficient is negative in Jabodetabek, while it is positive nationally. This indicates that in Jabodetabek, people who work for their family are more financially secure than people who work as a laborer. The opposite is true at the national level: compared to a laborer, people who work as an unpaid laborer for their family are more vulnerable to poverty. One underlying difference can be explained by the characteristics of the job sector in which people work in different areas. Table 6.5. shows that in Jabodetabek, around 78% of those who work for their family are working in the trade or hotel/restaurant sector. Meanwhile, in Indonesia as a whole, 35% of people who work as an unpaid family worker are working in the trade sector and 32% are working in the agriculture sector.

Table 6.5. Job sector of people who work in a family business without pay.

Job sector	Indonesia		Living outside Jabodetabek		Living in Jabodetabek	
	Freq	%	Freq	%	Freq	%
Agriculture (Paddy and Palawija)	120,299	22.37	118,352	23.36	1,947	6.27
Horticulture	21,644	4.02	21,011	4.15	633	2.04
Plantation	37,743	7.02	37,743	7.45		
Fisheries	4,963	0.92	4,963	0.98		
Farm	30,149	5.61	30,149	5.95		
Forestry and other agriculture	4,680	0.87	4,225	0.83	455	1.46
Mining and quarrying	1,222	0.23	1,222	0.24		
Processing industry	39,510	7.35	37,417	7.38	2,093	6.74
Construction	15,545	2.89	15,545	3.07		
Trade	199,332	37.07	180,131	35.55	19,201	61.81
Restaurant and accommodation services	32,486	6.04	27,162	5.36	5,324	17.14
Transportation, warehousing	2,058	0.38	2,058	0.41		
Information and communication	528	0.1	528	0.1		
Financial agency, insurance	102	0.02	102	0.02		
Education services	1,186	0.22	382	0.08	804	2.59
Health services	1,612	0.3	1,612	0.32		
Public, social and individual services	16,477	3.06	15,870	3.13	607	1.95
Other	8,225	1.53	8,225	1.62		
Total	537,761	100	506,697	100	31,064	100

Source: Authors' calculation using Susenas (2014).

Conclusion and policy implications

Despite rapid economic development, the poverty rate in Jabodetabek metropolitan area has been relatively stagnant at around 6% since the early 2000s. There is a possibility that poverty reduction programs are not effective in Jabodetabek because these programs were developed based on the national poverty profile. If the poverty profile in metropolitan areas is significantly different from the national profile, these programs may not be suitable or effective in addressing the poverty problems of metropolitan areas. This study finds that the poverty profile in Jabodetabek is significantly different from the national profile, especially in terms of education attainment, access to drinking water, employment sector, and status of employment. Therefore, tackling poverty in the Jabodetabek metropolitan area requires policy that is distinct from the national poverty reduction policy.

Basic necessities such as water show no correlation with poverty in Jabodetabek, while they remain significant at the national level. In terms of education attainment, it is found that the completion of only up to elementary school is no longer sufficient to support a decent living in Jabodetabek, even though it still appears significant at the national level. Tertiary education has the highest impact in lowering the chance that one lives in poverty both nationally and in Jabodetabek, but its impact in Jabodetabek is much smaller than at the national level. Employment sector also correlates highly with poverty status. The manufacturing sector, with its capabilities to absorb a great number of laborers, appears to make a significant contribution to minimizing the poverty rate in Jabodetabek. Meanwhile, at the national level, the impact of the trade sector is more prevalent than the manufacturing sector. In addition, this study finds that people who work for their family without pay have a lower probability of being poor in Jabodetabek, while at the national level that type of work seems to increase the probability of being poor. This is related to the difference in employment sectors in which most unpaid family workers work in Jabodetabek and nationally.

This study has important implications as the number of metropolitan areas in Indonesia and the world continues to grow. In Indonesia, for example, the cities of Surabaya and Makassar have grown into metropolitan areas just in the last 20 years. The findings of this study indicate that social and economic policies in metropolitan areas should be tailored to achieve higher education attainment levels for their residents, while at the same time fostering the growth of the manufacturing sector. Improvement in basic infrastructure such as sanitation is also found to be relevant. Additionally, scaling up internet access for all is deemed necessary to broaden the scope of knowledge and information for poor people. Designing and implementing these policies in Jabodetabek is challenging, as they involve the governments of 3 provinces, 10 cities, and 4 regencies. Hence, developing a mechanism for policy coordination among these governments should be a priority.

References

Akanle, O. and G.S. Adejare. 2017. "Conceptualising Megacities and Megaslums in Lagos, Nigeria". *Africa's Public Service Delivery and Performance Review* 5 (1): 1–9.

Allen, A. et al. 2006. "The Peri-urban Water Poor: Citizens or Consumers?". *Environment and Urbanization* 18 (2): 333–351.

Almeida, C. et al. 2005. "GIS and Remote Sensing as Tools for the Simulation of Urban Land-use Change". *International Journal of Remote Sensing* 26 (4): 759–774.

Aprilia, A. et al. 2012. "Household Solid Waste Management in Jakarta, Indonesia: A Socio-economic Evaluation". In *Waste Management – An Integrated Vision*, edited by Luis Fernando Marmolejo Rebellon. http://doi.org/10.5772/51464 (accessed May 24, 2017).

Badan Pusat Statistik (BPS). 2015. *Data dan Informasi Kemiskinan Kabupaten/Kota Tahun 2014* [Data and Information on Poverty at Regency/City Level in 2014]. Jakarta: Badan Pusat Statistik.

Bayudan-Dacuycuy, C. and J.A Lim. 2013. "Family Size, Household Shocks and Chronic and Transient Poverty in the Philippines". *Journal of Asian Economics* 29: 101–112.

Becker, C. M. 2008. *Urbanization and Rural–Urban Migration*. Edward Elgar Publishing.

Brockerhoff, M. and E. Brennan. 1998. "The Poverty of Cities in Developing Regions". *Population and Development Review* 24 (1): 75–114.

Choiejit, R. and R. Teungfung. 2005. "Urban Growth and Commuting Patterns of the Poor in Bangkok". In *World Bank Institute of Applied Economic Research*. Third Urban Research Symposium on Land Development, Urban Policy and Poverty Reduction. Brazil.

Christiaensen, L. and Todo Y. 2014. *Poverty Reduction during the Rural-urban Transformation: The Role of the Missing*. http://ac.els-cdn. com.ezproxy.lib.monash.edu.au/S0305750X13002143/1-s2.0-S0305750X13002143-main.pdf?_tid=728e377e-17ea-11e6-92b0-00000aab0f26&acdnat=1463020819_85cddb7243c4ef0a41e3bc3efa 7d2379 (accessed May 12, 2016).

Dahiya, B. 2012. "Cities in Asia, 2012: Demographics, Economics, Poverty, Environment and Governance". *Cities* 29 (SUPPL.2): S44–S61.

Ferré, C. et al. 2012. "Is There a Metropolitan Bias? The Relationship between Poverty and City Size in a Selection of Developing Countries". *World Bank Economic Review* 26 (3): 351–382.

Glaeser, E. 2011. *Triumph of the City*. London: Macmillan.

Henderson, J.V. and A. Kuncoro. 1996. "The Dynamics of Jabotabek Development". *Bulletin of Indonesian Economic Studies* 32 (1): 71–95.

Joassart-Marcelli, P.M. et al. 2005. "Fiscal Consequences of Concentrated Poverty in a Metropolitan Region". *Annals of the Association of American Geographers* 95 (2): 336–356.

Jones, G. 2016. "Migration, Ethnicity, and the Education Gradient in the Jakarta Mega Urban Region: A Spatial Analysis". *Bulletin of Indonesian Economic Studies* 49 (2): 1–36.

Jovchelovitch, S. and J. Priego-Hernandez. 2013. *Underground Sociabilities: Identity, Culture, and Resistance in Rio de Janeiro's Favelas*. Paris: United Nations Educational, Scientific and Cultural Organization.

Minnery, J. 2013. "Slum Upgrading and Urban Governance: Case Studies in Three South East Asian Cities". *Habitat International* 39: 162–169.

Mukherjee, S. and T. Benson. 2003. "The Determinants of Poverty in Malawi, 1998". *World Development* 31 (2): 339–358.

Nguyen, L.D. et al. 2015. "Rural-urban Migration, Household Vulnerability, and Welfare in Vietnam". *World Development* 71: 79–93.

Orbeta, A. C. 2005. *ADB Institute Discussion Paper No. 29 Poverty, Vulnerability and Family Size: Evidence from the Philippines*. Tokyo: Asian Development Bank Institute.

Peters, R. 2016. "Single Working-class Women and the City in Java and Vietnam". *Asian Studies Review* 40 (1): 36–52.

Prahalad, C. K. and A. Hammond. 2002. "Serving the World's Poor, Profitably". *Harvard Business Review* 80 (9): 48-57. http://doi.org/10.1108/02756660710732611 (accessed May 24, 2017).

Risbud, N. 2016. *Delhi: City Profile. Poverty, Inequality and Violence in Urban India*. New Delhi: Institute for Human Development.

Rustiandi, E. et al. 2015. "Jabodetabek Megacity: From City Development toward Urban Complex Management System". In *Urban Development Challenges, Risks and Challenges in Asian Mega Cities*, edited by R. B. Singh, pp. 421-445. Springer Japan. http://doi.org/10.1007/978-4-431-55043-3_22 (accessed June 29, 2017).

Suryahadi, A. and R.A. Izzati. 2018. "Cards for the Poor and Funds for Villages: Jokowi's Initiatives to Reduce Poverty and Inequality". *Journal of Southeast Asian Economies* 35 (2): 200–222.

UN Habitat. 2011. *The Economic Role of Cities*. Nairobi: United Nations Human Settlements Programme.

WHO and UNICEF. 2006. *Meeting the MDG Drinking Water and Sanitation Target: The Urban and Rural Challenge of the Decade*. World Health Organization and United Nations Children Fund.

World Bank. 2009. *World Development Report 2009*. Washington, D.C.: The World Bank. http://www-wds.worldbank.org/external/default/WDSContentServer/WDSP/IB/2008/12/03/000333038_20081203234958/Rendered/PDF/437380REVISED01BLIC1097808213760720.pdf (accessed May 12, 2016).

———. 2017. *Unlocking the Philippines' Urbanization Potential.* http://blogs.worldbank.org/eastasiapacific/unlocking-the-philippines-urbanization-potential (accessed September 20, 2017).

Xavier, H.N. and F. Magalhaes. 2003. "Urban Slums Report: The Case of Rio de Janeiro, Brazil". In *Understanding Slums: Case Studies for the Global Report on Human Settlements 2003*.

Zainal, N.R. et al. 2012. "Housing Conditions and Quality of Life of the Urban Poor in Malaysia". *Procedia—Social and Behavioral Sciences* 50 (July): 827–838.

Chapter 7

Between Land Tenure Security and Agricultural Production:

Problems of Farmland Liquidation in Rural Java

Ernoiz Antriyandarti and Susi Wuri Ani

Introduction

Indonesia's agricultural sector played an important role in the economic recovery following the economic reforms implemented since the *Reformasi* era. However, as the country's economy has shifted decidedly toward industrialization, the contribution of the agricultural sector to the gross domestic product (GDP) has declined, from 56% in 1970 to 13% today.[1] Nonetheless, the agriculture sector remains a major source of employment (29.7% nationally in 2017). Additionally, at times when the industrial and other non-agricultural sectors have not been able to fully absorb the labor force, agriculture often provides employment.

Figure 7.1. shows that while the industrial sector's 24% contribution to GDP is the largest, the agricultural sector still holds an important and strategic role in the national economy, contributing 14% of GDP. This is dominated by food crops, with rice, maize, and soybean the primary

---

1   Pearson et al. (1991: 12) notes that, "Although the output of rice, corn and soybeans more than doubled, the share of agriculture in national income fell from over one-half in 1968 to one-fourth in 1987. Within the agricultural sector, the contribution of rice to total GDP decreased from almost 20% to about 8%."

235

contributors to GDP. Approximately 60% of these major crops are produced in Java, which has fertile soil more suitable for rice farming than the outer islands.[2] The rice sector plays a prominent role in providing job opportunities, especially in Java. The National Farmers' Household Panel Survey (PATANAS), conducted by the Indonesia Center for Agriculture and Socio-Economic Policy Studies, found that 75% of rural households in Java engaged in rice farming in 2012, indicating the importance of rice farming to the economy of rural households in Java, where more than half of Indonesians live (Antriyandarti, 2016; Prayitno and Arsyad, 1987; Aulia, 2008).

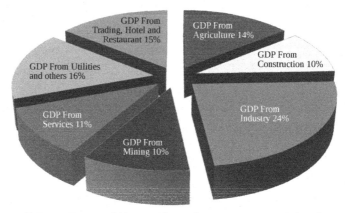

Figure 7.1. Percent of GDP contribution by sector. Source: BPS (2018).

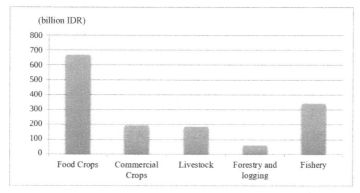

Figure 7.2. GDP contribution by agricultural sector. Source: BPS (2018).

---

2   To simplify the description about rice production, hectare, and productivity, we divide the many provinces of Indonesia into two areas: Java and outside Java.

The fact that the agricultural share of GDP is lower relative to its share of the labor force (see Pearson et al., 1991; Godoy and Dewbre, 2010) implies that the agricultural sector's labor productivity is on average lower relative to other sectors of the economy. It is also important to note that the income gap between the agricultural and non-agricultural sectors has widened (Figure 7.3.) since the early 2000s, suggesting that the relative income from agricultural labor has declined. According to the Ministry of Agriculture (2015), most agricultural activities in Indonesia since the 1980s, particularly food crop farming, are small scale, low efficiency, and low productivity, resulting in low incomes in the agricultural sector.

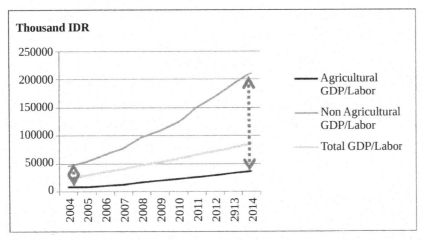

Figure 7.3. Income gap between the agricultural and non-agricultural sectors.
Source: Author's calculation from BPS (2016b).

One of the main causes of the decline in the agricultural sector's contribution to the GDP in the two decades after *Reformasi* was the decrease in the amount of agricultural land under cultivation and the small farm size, especially for food crops such as rice. Farm income has declined relative to other sectors since 2000. Small farm size limits the potential of Indonesian agriculture, especially rice farming, in terms of global competitiveness. The main cause of small farm size in Indonesia is the undeveloped market for farmland (Antriyandari, 2015: 2018). The issue of farmland liquidation—

or the release of owned land to the market—in Indonesia is very new and has not been well explored. Farmers in Indonesia usually are not willing to sell their farmland. Therefore, farmland liquidation in Indonesia is typically through leasing, not purchasing. The increasing supply of farmland in the market will raise the farmers' possibility to enlarge their farmland.

Rice production during the decade 2005–2015 continued to rise, except for a slight decline in 2014 (see Figure 7.4.). Java was the dominant producer of rice, exceeding the combined production in all areas outside Java. Consumption also rose, following population growth. Indonesian rice has not performed significantly well in the international market, exporting only small quantities. Export of Indonesian rice increased only slightly in 2013. On the contrary, Indonesia is a net importer of rice, with imports increasing until 2012, when they began to slowly decline (BPS, FAO).

Despite being the major national producer of rice, Java's land area under rice cultivation has declined since 2003, from 3.3 million ha to 3.2 million ha in 2015 (Figure 7.5.). There are two possible reasons for this decrease. The first is the conversion of paddy fields to non-agricultural land. The second is the reluctance of farmers to enlarge their farm size.

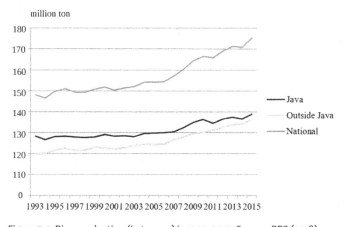

Figure 7.4. Rice production (in tonnes) in 1993–2015. Source: BPS (2018).

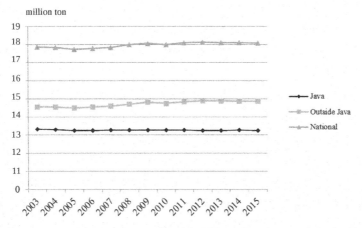

Figure 7.5. Area under paddy cultivation (in hectares) in 2003–2015. Source: BPS (2018).

The rice sectors in Central and East Java Provinces do not have a comparative or competitive advantage due to the small farm size in those provinces (Antriyandarti, 2015, 2016). This indicates that farm size is an issue in maintaining rice production.

Rice production in rural Java is important due to its high yields relative to other areas. The high productivity of Java's rice sector has the potential to increase national rice production. Although the rice sector in both provinces has already achieved economies of scale (Antriyandarti and Fukui, 2016), farm sizes have remained small (less than 0.5 ha). Therefore, optimizing farmland usage and size is critical to achieving rice self-sufficiency in Indonesia. Farmland liquidation plays an important role in transferring farmland to more efficient farmers and allowing farmers to increase their farm size. However, farm liquidation in rural Java has been very slow.

This chapter attempts to examine farmland liquidation, specifically the process of making farmland available through lease arrangements, in rural Java. Land liquidation is generally defined as supplying land to the market through rent (lease) or sale.[3] In rural Java, maintaining ownership of land is important to social status and inheritance. Sale of farmland is

---

3   Farmland liquidation is the release of owned land to the market. In this study we determine the farmland liquidation through leasing not purchasing. We promote farmland liquidation through transferring farmland from households with less productivity to those with high productivity.

therefore very rare and, in many cases, when a sale does happen, it is a difficult process. Lease arrangements are more common and offer more opportunities to transfer and amplify the use of land for agricultural production in Java.

This chapter focuses on farmland liquidation in four areas: Cilacap and Grobongan in Central Java, and Jember and Lamongan in East Java.[4] In this study we investigate the current scope and process of farmland liquidation using data from our own field survey in both provinces. Although Indonesian rice-growing farmers have already met the necessary conditions to produce on larger farms, most of them continue to cultivate small farms and rent agricultural machines. Based on this analysis, we suggest that farmland liquidation is an important issue for Indonesia's agricultural sector which needs to be addressed to ensure the country's food security.

Farmland Liquidation in Other Countries

It is important to note that the farmland utilization problem in Indonesia is not exceptional. Many high-and middle-income countries face similar problems regarding farm size. In Japan, for example, average farm size in the rice sector has not increased significantly since the 1990s, even after some constraints were addressed (Deininger et al., 2007; Arimoto and Nakajima, 2010; Takahashi, 2012; Kusakari and Nakagawa, 2013). Farmland liquidation has been slow to develop in Japan's agricultural sector due to significant increases in land prices in anticipation of future conversion for non-agricultural use. The promotion of liquidation through leasing, such as through amendment of the Agricultural Land Law and the introduction of the farmland utilization program by the Agricultural Land Utilization Promotion Project, has been an important response. Takahashi (2012) and Kusakari and Nakagawa (2013) highlight three important constraints to farmland liquidation in Japan. They are: transaction costs,

---

4   We selected two main rice producing regencies for each province which had the largest rice production. About 200 rice farm households were selected for interviews through a random sampling method. Descriptive and farming analyses were applied to investigate the farmland liquidation in the study areas.

uncertainty of returns on land lease investments, and the impact of farmland leases on the activities of local communities and the characteristics of farmland.

Likewise, China, which has witnessed tremendous changes in its agrarian sector, faces similar challenges. The Rural Shareholding Cooperatives (RSCs) in China promote farmland liquidation to achieve efficient and sustainable agricultural land use. The RSCs facilitated farm size enlargement in some regions, but with limited results. Previous studies have demonstrated that there are two important preconditions for encouraging land lease in agriculture: out-migration and the enhancement of security and transferability of land rights. RSCs can pave the way for the extension of property rights to farmland and promote more efficient land use patterns. According to Ito (2016), RSCs can facilitate to reduce transaction costs and encourage land lease/consolidation activities. This accords with Wang et al. (2015) and Ma et al. (2015), who find that land documents, tenure security, and institutional innovation contribute significantly to the development of land rental markets. Although recent land tenure reforms have significantly improved legal tenure security, farm households continue to experience substantial insecurity of actual and perceived land tenure in China.

The Chinese Government promotes the formation of large-scale and mechanized farms. In the Chinese Central Document Number 1 Year 1984, the central government encouraged large-scale farming by promoting the development of farmland lease markets. Farmland lease markets and large-scale farming were further emphasized in the Chinese Central Document Number 1 Year 2012 to 2017. Furthermore, to promote farmland lease and large-scale farming, the government launched a series of agricultural policies, including farmland certification schemes, subsidies for leased land, and provision of agricultural insurance. Off-farm jobs also contribute to the development of farmland lease markets. Households who have off-farm employment and imigrated family members are typically more willing to lease out their farmland. The challenges facing farmland liquidation in

China have received special attention by economists and policy makers, with many studies focusing on understanding the determinants of farmland rentals (Liu et al., 2017).

In Indonesia, farm size is still considered a new policy area. The Basic Agrarian Law of 1960 limits the size of agricultural land holdings to a minimum of 2 ha and a maximum of 20 ha. In general, the number of farmers producing food crops in Indonesia since the late 1960s has increased, while the size of household land holdings has remained small (less than 1 ha), particularly in Java. Enlargement of farm size without radical institutional changes is only possible on the outer islands, where the land is not as fertile as Java. Average farm size in Java in the 1990s was much smaller (0.66 ha) than in the outer islands (>1.22 ha). After colonization and the transmigration programs of the late 1940s, farmers in Java continued to farm intensively. Since the 1990s, the growth of the industrial sector and urban centers in Java has increased the demand for land (see Tjondronegoro and Wiradi, 2008).

Industrialization has also brought about demographic changes and changes in the labor market. The percentage of the labor force working in the agricultural sector decreased from 55.1% of the population in 1990 to 29.7% in 2017. The percentage of the labor force working in the non-agricultural sector has increased by an average annual growth of 4.4% since 1970 (BPS, 2018). In 1960, 14.6% of the population lived in urban areas; this increased to 30.6% in 1990, and was 54.5% in 2016 (World Bank, 2018). The accelerated conversion of paddy fields to non-agricultural uses has far-reaching implications for the future performance of the agricultural sector in Indonesia This situation implies that the transaction costs of any land transfer in Java are very high (Anwar and Pakpahan, 1990). Thus, as in Japan and China, this situation poses a serious challenge to farmland liquidation. During two decades of *Reformasi*, the Indonesian government has yet to implement policies relating to the liquidation of land, focusing instead on tightening regulations on the conversion of agricultural land, land protection programs, and opening new rice fields.

Four Case Studies in Java

Agriculture Conditions

Although the four areas in this study (Cilacap and Grobongan in Central Java and Jember and Lamongan in East Java) have roughly similar conditions, the particular local situation regarding land use, crop rotation, and the availability of off-farm jobs contributes to the status of farmland liquidation. We will see how these elements impact the overall agricultural condition in each area.

Both Cilacap and Grobongan Regencies are important rice producing areas in Central Java due to their geographical advantages. Nearby mountains provide a good supply of natural water, while uninhibited lowland areas provide ideal conditions for paddy production. The agricultural sector in Cilacap Regency employs about 32% of its population, and contributes about 17% of its GDP. Food crops, particularly rice, corn, sweet potatoes, and soybeans, are the dominant products of the area. In 2014, the regency contributed about 19% of Indonesia's total agricultural commodities. In 2016, rice production in Cilacap Regency amounted to 872,168 tons with a harvested area of 138,089 ha (BPS Cilacap, 2018).

Surrounded by two limestone mountains (Mountain Kendeng to the south and Montain Kapur Utara to the north), Grobongan Regency has lowland areas between the two in a valley that stretches from west to east and provides productive agricultural land, supported in part by irrigation infrastructure. In addition to the natural river tributaries, irrigation water is drawn from the reservoirs of four major dams in the area (Sedadi, Kali Lanang, Klambu, and Kedung Ombo). Rice farming is dominant in Grobogan. Production of rice in 2013 amounted to 622,575 tons with a harvested area of 4,222 ha and yields of 6.42 tons/ha. The contribution of the agricultural sector to the regional GDP in 2015 reached 43%, with 38.6% of the population working in the agricultural sector. (BPS Grobogan, 2018).

Lamongan Regency is located on the northern coast of Java. It is cleaved by the Bengawan Solo River and has three types of land: (1) a fertile lowland in the center and south, (2) a rocky limestone mountain with medium fertility in the south, and (3) a flood-prone area in the north central part of the regency. More than half of the regency is lowland and swampy. Surface water is predominant, with frequent flooding disasters during the rainy season. At the same time, this abundant water makes the irrigation of farmland secure. There is still a lot of water in swamps, reservoirs, retention basins, and rivers in the dry season.

The economy of Lamongan is dominated by the agricultural sector, which contributed 38.6% of the regional GDP in 2016. The agriculture sector employs 49.6% of the regency's population. Food crops are the main commodity, dominated by rice farming, which produced 1,053,796 tons of paddy on 151,439 ha of harvested area with yields of 6.6 tons/ ha in 2017 (BPS Lamongan, 2018).

In contrast to Lamongan, most of Jember is located at an altitude of 500–2,000 m above sea level. Two thirds of land use in Jember Regency is agriculture and forest area. It is a mountainous area with a fertile canyon in the center and south surrounded by mountains that extend to the western and eastern borders. The southwest region has an altitude of 0–25 meters above sea level. It has several major rivers that are useful for agricultural activities. The abundant water resources in Jember ensure that the paddy fields are never short of water. With these conditions, Jember has become the food barn of East Java province. Its agricultural sector plays an important role in local economic development. Approximately 31.9% of its population works in the sector. Before 2010, the agricultural sector contributed to more than 40% of the total regional GDP, but this proportion continues to decline (it was 28.9% in 2014). Like other areas in this study, agriculture in Jember is dominated by food crops, especially rice, with a production of 986,653 tons on a harvested area of 166,179 ha and yields of 5.9 tons/ha in 2017 (BPS Jember, 2018).

Farmland Conditions

Farmers in these four regencies enjoy technical irrigation throughout the year. Rice farming and double cropping during the year is common. Figures 7.6. to 7.9. depict the farmland in these regencies. The main crop in Cilacap, Grobogan, Lamongan and Jember is paddy. In Cilacap, all farmers plant paddy only. However, in Grobogan, some farmers plant corn, green beans, and soybeans, making crop rotation there more complicated. There are five cropping patterns in Grobogan, the dominant one being paddy to paddy to corn.

Table 7.1. Crop rotation in the study areas.

Regency	Season 1	Season 2	Season 3	Number of Plots
Cilacap	Paddy (Jan–Apr)	Paddy (Jun–Sep)	---- (Oct–Dec)	80
Grobogan	Paddy (Jan–Apr)	Paddy (May–Aug)	Corn (Sep–Dec)	54
	Paddy (Jan–Apr)	Paddy (May–Aug)	Green bean (Sep–Dec)	16
	Paddy (Jan–Apr)	Paddy (May–Aug)	Soy bean (Sep–Dec)	8
	Paddy (Jan–Apr)	Paddy (May–Aug)	----	2
	Paddy (Mar–Jun)	Corn (Jul–Oct)	Paddy (Nov–Feb)	13
Lamongan	Paddy (Feb–Apr)	Paddy (May–Aug)	Green bean (Nov–Jan)	14
	Paddy (Feb–Apr)	Paddy (May–Aug)	Soy bean (Nov–Jan)	1
	Shrimp (Feb–Apr)	Paddy (Jun–Sept)	Shrimp (Nov–Jan)	53
	Shrimp (Jan–Mar)	Shrimp (Apr–Jun)	Paddy (Aug–Nov)	2
Jember	Paddy (Jan–Apr)	Paddy (May–Aug)	Corn (Sep–Dec)	22
	Paddy (Jan–Apr)	Paddy (May–Aug)	Soy bean (Sep–Dec)	20
	Paddy (Mar–Jun)	Soy bean (Jul–Oct)	Paddy (Nov–Feb)	33

Note: --- = no crops. Source: Farm Household Survey (2017)

Crop rotation in Lamongan is combined with shrimp cultivation, as the water supply is abundant throughout the year and it is located near the sea. There are four crop rotation patterns in Lamongan. The dominant pattern is shrimp to paddy to shrimp. There are 53 plots implementing this pattern. In Jember, the farmers plant food crops three times per year. They cultivate paddy two times per year. In other seasons they plant corn or soybean. Table 7.1. describes the different crop rotation patterns in the study areas. Cropping patterns affect farmland liquidation, as farmers who only plant in two seasons are able to lease out their land in the third season.

Figure 7.6. Farmland in Cilacap. Source: photographed by authors with Credit: Ernoiz Antriyandarti and Susi Wuri Ani.

Figure 7.7. Farmland in Grobogan. Source: photographed by authors with Credit: Ernoiz Antriyandarti and Susi Wuri Ani.

Figure 7.8. Farmland in Lamongan. Source: photographed by authors with Credit: Ernoiz Antriyandarti and Susi Wuri Ani.

Figure 7.9. Farmland in Jember. Source: photographed by authors with Credit: Ernoiz Antriyandarti and Susi Wuri Ani.

Household Economic Conditions

The majority of the household heads that participated in this study work as farmers (Table 7.2.) However, the majority of the household heads are also engaged in off-farm jobs, such as traders, salaried workers, daily unskilled wage laborers. Traders are engaged in miscellaneous trade in their houses or in a local market. Most trade livestock, food, snacks, vegetables, seasonings, and rice. A few farmers in East Java work in the roof tile industry. The permanent off-farm worker category includes factory workers who work in various kinds of factories, for instance, food factories, or shoe and cement factories in city, while the unskilled daily labor category includes construction laborers, servants, agricultural hired laborers for transplanting, weeding, harvesting, and tractor operations. Some households raise livestock like chickens, goats, and cattle, and sell them to increase household income. In Cilacap, many farmers earn supplementary income as pine tappers. Farmers who live on the slopes usually work as pine tappers in the morning from 6:00 to 10:00 am. and then work in the rice fields from the late morning. Farmers working as pine tappers live on the plateau in the middle of a pine forest, far from the city with poor transportation access. In Grobogan and in Jember, many farmers earn supplementary income as construction workers, mobile food traders, and bricklayers, while in Lamongan, some farmers become laborers at the port.

Off-farm income plays an important role in total household income. The households that have high off-farm income have higher total incomes. The fact that farmers try to earn off-farm income suggests that they cannot earn sufficient income from agriculture. About 30% of the households engaged in farming also have supplementary off-farm jobs.

Table 7.2. Occupations of farm household heads in study areas.

No	Occupation	Major Occupation (person)				Supplementary Occupation (person)			
		Cilacap	Grobogan	Lamongan	Jember	Cilacap	Grobogan	Lamongan	Jember
1	Farmer	45	48	41	48	6	2	9	1
2	Non-farm self employed	3	1	2	-	16	9	18	13
3	Daily unskilled labor	-	-	1	-	15	14	8	2
4	Permanent off-farm job	3	1	6	1	2	23	6	22

Source: Farm Household Survey (2017).

The status of farmland liquidation in the four regencies of the study is presented in Table 7.3. Farmland liquidation in the study areas is not well developed; only a small percentage of farmers lease out their land. The two main reasons farmers cite for why they lease out their farmland were (1) due to old age or (2) they do not have time to cultivate their land. Older farmers with no formal education or those who have completed only primary school have no options for securing off-farm jobs. They work full-time farming in their villages as a subsistence farmer on small-scale farms. Farmers keep their land, and many find it difficult to find good job opportunity (Hirasawa, 2014). This is common in Cilacap Regency, while farmers in Grobogan tend to expand the scale of their activities through leasing additional farmland from other farmers. These borrowing and lending activities have contributed to the development of farmland liquidation in rural areas.

Table 7.3. Farmland liquidation in the study areas.

Regency	Owned		Lease in		Lease Out		Off-farm jobs (%)	Farm size	Production (kg)	Productivity (kg/ha)
	plot	ha	plot	ha	plot	ha				
Cilacap	68	11.0177	9	1.9416	3	0.271	66	0.2594	2440	9406
Grobogan	55	18.34	37	8.9075	8	1.37	92	0.5524	6473	11719
Lamongan	59	24.9265	9	4.11	2	1.475	78	0.6102	3979	6521
Jember	71	27.26	3	0.53	1	0.5	65	0.5773	5432	11142

Source: Farm Household Survey (2017).

Grobogan Regency has the most developed market for farmland (the highest rate of farmland liquidation). It is also the regency with the highest percentage of the population engaging in off-farm jobs (92%). Many farmers in Grobogan lease in and lease out their land. The development of farmland liquidation has delivered the highest production and productivity of the other four regencies studied. In Cilacap Regency, off-farm work engagement is only around 66%, and the number of farmers who lease out their land is very small. As a result, farm size in Cilacap Regency is very small, only 0.259 ha, and production is the lowest of the four regencies. Likewise in Lamongan and Jember Regencies, farmland liquidation has not been well developed, and off-farm engagement in those regencies is much lower than Grobogan.

Engagement in the off-farm labor market is known to play an important role in farmland liquidation. Off-farm jobs can overcome the problem of surplus labor in rural areas, which restrains farm size enlargement (see Deininger et al., 2007). As Li (2013) notes in the case of China, engaging in off-farms jobs increases participation in the rental market by rural households, allowing them to adjust their farm sizes. There is a strong evidence that improving the rental market improves the efficiency of rice farming and increases production, thus increasing farm incomes (Huy, 2013).

Table 7.4. presents an analysis of rice farming in these regencies based on the findings of this study. The largest rice income is in Grobogan Regency, with a revenue/cost ratio of 2,745. This implies that rice farming in Grobogan is economically more profitable than in other regencies of the study areas. From Table 7.3., we can see that Grobogan Regency has the highest percentage of farmers working in off-farm jobs (92%), the highest overall production, and the highest productivity rate. The Grobogan Regency has by far the highest rate of farmers leasing land (both leasing in and leasing out) and the highest productivity. It can therefore be said that farm liquidation in Gorbogan is well developed, while in the other three regencies, farmland liquidation has not developed due to less than optimal off-farm engagements. This finding supports Deininger et al. (2007), who found that off-farm opportunities increase the number of households that lease out their land, opening opportunities for households who are successful in farming to lease in more land. Over time an increase in the supply of farmland available for lease in the market tends to lead to a decrease in transaction costs, hastening the pace of land transfer. In line with expectations, land lease markets improve the productivity of land use by shifting land from less to more efficient producers. It indicates that farmland liquidation can improve the productivity and efficiency of rice farming.

Table 7.4. Rice farming analysis in the study areas.

	Cilacap	Grobogan	Lamongan	Jember
Production (kg/ha/year)	7,564	9,960	6,109	9,929
Production cost (IDR/ha/year)	7,917,122	9,731,409	23,077,086	10,365,984
Production cost per unit (IDR/kg)	1,046.747	977.003	3,777.358	1,044.059
Rice income (IDR/ha/year)	24,591,246	38,756,526	31,356,400	30,587,828
R/C ratio	1,146	2,745	0,927	2,032

Source: Farm Household Survey (2017).

Jember Regency presents different empirical findings. Most of the farmers are full-time farmers with adequate education and professional skills in cultivating their land. Their owned farmland (not lease land) is quite large; therefore, they prefer to operate their own farms rather than lease out their land. As a result, production can be maintained at an optimal level (Muraoka et al., 2014). Indonesia's agricultural sector needs to improve agricultural productivity, particularly rice production, to meet the needs of the rapidly growing economy and ensure food security. In areas where the level of land ownership is inadequate, farm liquidation provides a critical function in transferring land to more efficient producers in order to reach an optimal concentration of land among core productive farmers, which is instrumental for reaping economies of scale (Arimoto, 2011).

Lamongan Regency has the largest farm size among the 4 regencies in the study area, but the lowest productivity and R/C value. This is due to the regency's location in a flood-prone area. During the rainy season, the large rivers in Lamongan often overflow, causing hundreds of hectares of rice crops to fail to reach harvest. Therefore, most rice farmers in Lamongan Regency plant rice only once a year and prefer to cultivate shrimp twice a year. For disaster-prone areas such as Lamongan, it is necessary to apply appropriate risk management to minimize losses and optimize production on farming, focusing on disaster threats rather than land enlargement.

Off-farm jobs play a role in overcoming the labor surplus in rural areas, increasing rural household incomes, reducing poverty, and building rural communities. Once the surplus labor is resolved, the unproductive and inefficient small-scale farmers are willing to lease out land, allowing larger-scale farmers to expand their farming scales with increased cultivated land. An increase in optimal farmland usage will increase rice productivity in many parts of Java, which means an increase in national rice stocks.

Conclusion

Facilitating farm size enlargement is one of the measures to improve the global competitiveness of Indonesia's rice sector. Several policies may be implemented to promote farm size enlargement. Farmland liquidation may improve productivity, thus solving major problems in the agricultural sector (Hirabayashi, 2015). This is an important matter as the Indonesian government has launched a strategic plan for agricultural development, especially in becoming a World Food Barn by 2045.[5] If the expansion of agricultural land outside Java island is not as successful as expected, there will be a need to offer an alternative policy based on the strategy of increasing land liquidation, as has been applied in other countries, to improve national rice production.

A key component of increasing land liquidation is facilitating the development of off-farm jobs in rural areas to properly reduce the surplus labor so that inefficient small-scale farmers would prefer to lease out their farmland. This chapter shows that farmland liquidation in rural Java is well developed in the regency with the highest rate of off-farm employment. When inefficient farmers lease out their land, they can earn revenue while at the same time more efficient farmers who lease in land can expand their operations. Those who earn income from leasing farmland also gain revenue from off-farm jobs. Farm income from small-scale farmers usually has a small contribution to household income due to the small scale of farming. By working in the non-agricultural sector, increased incomes can reduce rural poverty, while providing incentives for more efficient farmers to expand their operations. A number of studies have shown that off-farm jobs play an important role in reducing rural poverty because small-scale farmers receive higher incomes (Godoy and Dewbre, 2010; De Janvry et al., 2005; Babatunde and Qaim, 2009). At the same time, farmland can be utilized at an optimal level due to the consolidation of land into the hands of more efficient farmers. Indonesia should consider the policy implications of this study on farmland liquidation to secure the income of the farmers and at the same time improve production.

---

5   In 2017, Amran Sulaiman, Minister of Agriculture (2014–2019), stated that "Indonesia could become a food barn for the world in 2045" as he expects food production during 2018–2021 to increase 5% annually (*Republika*, 2017). Based on data from the Ministry of Agriculture (2019), food crops production over the past 5 years has increased, except for green bean.

References

Antriyandarti, E. 2015. "Competitiveness and Cost Efficiency of Rice Farming in Indonesia". *Journal of Rural Problems* 51 (2): 74–85.

_____. 2016. "An Economic Study of the Indonesian Rice Sector: Toward Harmonization of Structural Adjustment and Food Security". Dissertation. Graduate School of Agriculture, Kyoto University (unpublished).

_____. 2018. "Constraints of Farm Size Enlargement in the Rice Sector of Central Java: A Case Study". *Bulgarian Journal of Agricultural Science* 24 (6): 949–958.

Antriyandarti, E. and S. Fukui. 2016. "Economies of Scale in Indonesian Rice Production: An Economic Analysis Using PATANAS Data". *Journal of Rural Problems* 52 (4): 259–264.

Anwar, A. and A. Pakpahan. 1990. "The Problem of Sawah–land Conversion to Non-agricultural Uses in Indonesia". *Indonesian Journal of Tropical Agriculture* 1 (2): 101–108.

Arimoto, Y. 2011. The Impact of Farmland Readjustment and Consolidation on Structural Adjustment: The Case of Niigata, Japan. Working Paper Series No. 2011-3. Institute of Economic Research Hitotsubashi University. http://cei.ier.hit-u.ac.jp/English/index.html (accessed October 10, 2017).

Arimoto, Y. and S. Nakajima. 2010. "Review of Liquidization and Concentration of Farmland in Japan". *Journal of Rural Economics* 82 (1): 23–35.

Aulia, A. N. 2008. "Analisis Pendapatan Usahatani Padi dan Kelayakan Usahatani Vanili Pada Ketinggian Lahan 350–800m dpl Di Kabupaten Tasikmalaya". Thesis. Bogor Agricultural University (unpublished).

Badan Pusat Statistik (BPS). 2015. *Distribusi Persentase Produk Domestik Bruto Triwulanan atas Dasar Harga Berlaku menurut Lapangan Usaha, 2000–2014 (persen).* https://www.bps. go.id/statictable/2009/07/02/1207/-seri-2000-distribusi-pdbtriwulanan-atas-dasar-harga-berlaku-menurut-lapangan-usaha-persen-2000-2014.html (accessed January 03, 2018).

———. 2016a. *Luas Panen Padi menurut Provinsi (ha), 1993–2015.* https://www.bps.go.id/dynamictable/2015/09/09/864/luas-panen-padi-menurut-provinsi-ha-1993-2015.html (accessed January 03, 2018).

———. 2016b. *Produksi Padi menurut Provinsi (ton), 1993–2015.* https://www.bps.go.id/dynamictable/2015/09/09/865/produksi-padi-menurut-provinsi-ton-1993-2015.html (accessed January 03, 2018).

———. 2018. *Penduduk Berumur 15 Tahun ke Atas yang Bekerja selama Seminggu yang Lalu menurut Status Pekerjaan Utama dan Lapangan Pekerjaan, 2008–2017.* https://www.bps.go.id/statictable/2016/04/05/1911/penduduk-berumur-15-tahun-ke-atas-yang-bekerja-selama-seminggu-yang-lalu-menurut-status-pekerjaan-utama-dan-lapangan-pekerjaan-2008---2017.html (accessed April 20, 2018).

Badan Pusat Statistik (BPS) Kabupaten Cilacap. 2017. *Kabupaten Cilacap Dalam Angka 2017.* https://cilacapkab.bps.go.id/publication/2017/08/16/d8bcd1fbecc72449ad2af294/kabupaten-cilacap-dalam-angka-2017.html (accessed April 20, 2018).

Badan Pusat Statistik (BPS) Kabupaten Grobogan. 2017. *Kabupaten Grobogan Dalam Angka 2017.* https://grobogankab.bps.go.id/publication/2017/08/16/9c2099cc822b119ebae1557b/kabupaten-grobogan-dalam-angka-2017.html (accessed April 20, 2018).

Badan Pusat Statistik (BPS) Kabupaten Jember. 2017. *Kabupaten Jember Dalam Angka 2017.* https://jemberkab.bps.go.id/publication/2017/08/20/1fa125a3b5ed88703dc88f1a/kabupaten-jember-dalam-angka-2017.html (accessed April 21, 2018).

Badan Pusat Statistik (BPS) Kabupaten Lamongan. 2017. *Kabupaten Lamongan Dalam Angka 2017.* https://lamongankab.bps.go.id/publication/2017/08/16/6f96bc74855cc36c0581d2fa/kabupaten-lamongan-dalam-angka-2017.html (accessed April 21, 2018).

Babatunde, R.O. and M. Qaim. 2009. "The Role of Off-farm Income Diversification in Rural Nigeria: Driving Forces and Household Access". Paper presented at CSAE conference on economic development in Africa, St Catherine's College, Oxford, March 22–24, 2009. http://www.csae.ox.ac.uk/conferences/2009-EDiA/papers/051-Babatunde.pdf (accessed February 18, 2016).

Collier, P. and S. Dercon. 2014. "African Agriculture in 50 Years: Smallholders in a Rapidly Changing World". *World Development* 63: 92–101.

Deininger, K. et al. 2007. Efficiency and Equity Impact of Rural Land Rental Restrictions: Evidence from India. Policy Research, Working Paper 4324. The World Bank.

De Janvry, A. et al. 2005. The Role of Non-Farm Income in Reducing Rural Poverty and Inequality in China. Working Paper No. 1001. Department of Agricultural & Resource Economics, UC Berkeley. http://are.berkeley.edu/~esadoulet/papers/RNF-Nong.pdf (accessed February 15, 2016).

Food and Agriculture Organization of the United Nations. 2016. http://faostat3.fao.org/download/FB/FBS/E (accessed February 24, 2016).

Godoy, D. C. and J. Dewbre. 2010. "Economic Importance of Agriculture for Sustainable Development and Poverty Reduction: Findings from a Case Study of Indonesia". Paper presented at Global Forum on Agriculture on November 29–30, 2010, Policies for Agricultural Development, Poverty Reduction and Food Security. Paris: OECD Headquarters. http://www.oecd.org/agriculture/agricultural-policies/46341215.pdf (accessed February 12, 2016).

Hirabayashi, M. and T. Ono. 2015. "Agricultural Structure of Paddy Field Farming and Core Producers in the Tohoku Region - A Case Study in Hanamaki City, Iwate Prefecture". *PRIMAFF Review* 67: 2–3. www.maff.go.jp/primaff/e/review/pdf/150930_pr67e_02.pdf (accessed January 18, 2018).

Hirasawa, A. 2014. "Frame and Emerging Reform of Agricultural Policy in Japan". Paper presented at International Workshop on Collection of Relevant Agricultural Policy Information and Its Practical Use. June 24, 2014. (COA-FFTC). Taipei, Taiwan. ap.fftc.agnet.org/powerpoint/ppt-257.pdf (accessed October 10, 2017).

Huy, H.T. 2013. "Low Farm Incomes and the Rental Market for Cropland in Vietnam". Thesis. Lincoln University, New Zealand (unpublished).

Ito, J. et al. 2016. "Land Rental Development via Institutional Innovation in Rural Jiangsu, China". *Food Policy* 59: 1–11.

Kementerian Pertanian. 2015. *Rencana Strategis 2015–2019*. Jakarta: Ministry of Agriculture Republic of Indonesia.

_____. 2019. *Production, Harvested Area and Productivity of Rice in Indonesia, 2014–2018*. http://www.pertanian.go.id/Data5tahun/TPATAP-2017(pdf)/00-PadiNasional.pdf (accessed July 24, 2019).

_____. 2019. *Production, Harvested Area and Productivity of Food Crops in Indonesia, 2014–2018*. http://www.pertanian.go.id/Data5tahun/TPATAP-2017(pdf)/01-PalawijaNasional.pdf (accessed July 24, 2019).

Kusakari, H. and S. Nakagawa. 2013. "Optimal Behavior of Rice Farmers in the Imperfectly Competitive Land Lease Market in Japan: With a Focus on Transaction Cost and Uncertain Returns on Land Lease Investment". *Japanese Journal Rural Economics* 15: 1–18.

Li, Y. et al. 2013. "Liquidation of Farmland in Chinese Inland Farming Villages: A Study of Village S, Meishan City, Sichuan Province". *Journal of Rural Problems* 49 (1): 131–136.

Liu, Y. et al. 2017. "Farmland Rental and Productivity of Wheat and Maize: An Empirical Study in Gansu, China". *Sustainability* 9: 1–18.

Ma, X. et al. 2015. "Farmland Tenure in China: Comparing Legal, Actual and Perceived Security". *Land Use Policy* 42: 293–306.

Muraoka, R. et al. 2014. "Land Access, Land Rental and Food Security: Evidence from Kenya". Paper presented at AAEA Annual Meeting, Minneapolis, MN, July 27–29, 2014.

Pearson, Scott et al. 1991. *Rice Policy in Indonesia*. Ithaca: Cornell University Press.

Prayitno, H. and L. Arsyad. 1987. *Petani Desa dan Kemiskinan*. Yogyakarta: BPFE.

Republika. 2017. "Indonesia Set to Become World's Food Barn in 2045." June 5, 2017. https://www.republika.co.id/berita/or2lbx414/indonesia-set-to-become-worlds-food-barn-in-2045 (accessd June 10, 2018)

Takahashi, D. 2012. "Farmland Liquidization and Transaction Costs". *The Japanese Journal of Rural Economics* 14: 1–19.

Tjondronegoro, S.M.P. and G. Wiradi. 2008. *Dua Abad Penguasaan Tanah*. Jakarta: Yayasan Obor Indonesia.

Wang, H. et al. 2015. "Land Documents, Tenure Security and Land Rental Development: Panel Evidence from China". *China Economic Review* 36: 220–235.

World Bank. 2018. *Table Urban Population (% of total)*. https://data.worldbank.org/indicator/SP.URB.TOTL.IN.ZS?locations=ID (accessed April 20, 2018).

Chapter 8
Fiscal Policy and Infrastructure Development:
A Reflection of the Two Decades after the 1997 Financial Crisis

Maxensius Tri Sambodo and Latif Adam

Introduction

Infrastructure is one of the key determinants of accelerated economic development and improved economic competitiveness. The 2018 global competitiveness index ranked Indonesia 45 out of 140 countries, lower than some of its ASEAN neighbors, such as Singapore (2), Malaysia (25) and Thailand (38). In terms of infrastructure performance, Indonesia was ranked 71, which suggests that the development of infrastructure in Indonesia needs to be accelerated to support a significant improvement in its competitiveness. The question that arises is how the government can accelerate the development of infrastructure in a sustainable way, balancing economic gains and social goals across all its regions? The question itself reveals that infrastructure development is critical to achieving social justice. As such, how do fiscal policies in Indonesia support a sustainable approach to infrastructure development?

Basri and Munandar (2008) point to macroeconomic stability and good governance as two important factors that can accelerate infrastructure development. Thus, infrastructure financing, especially from the government budget, needs to be secured. For many years, Indonesia has been dependent on tax revenues to finance infrastructure development. This is risky, however, as economic shocks and natural disasters can suddenly have acute adverse effects on tax revenues, putting the financial resources for infrastructure development in question. At the onset of the 1997–1998 financial crisis, the government intended to maintain infrastructure spending to ensure that existing facilities did not deteriorate. Accordingly, approximately one third of government spending was allocated for development expenditures (in which infrastructure was the main part).

During the financial crisis, development spending reached a crossroads between continuing to spend for physical infrastructure and alleviating the negative impacts of the crisis on the poor and vulnerable groups. The main objective of development spending during that time shifted to job creation, promoting education and health, and providing subsidies for a social safety net program. Because spending was reliant on tax revenue, the government had to select high priority projects, and postpone unnecessary ones. As seen in Figure 8.1., before the 1997–1998 financial crisis, infrastructure comprised about 38% of total government spending. However, after the crisis (2000–2002) the share of the budget allocated to infrastructure declined to about 14.5% of total government spending. Figure 8.1. shows that the central government's budget for infrastructure dramatically decreased in the period immediately following the crisis, and with the exception of a brief period of 2001–2003, continued to decline until 2010, when it began to recover.

It has been noted that developing infrastructure requires strong collaboration among various stakeholders, such as governments, state-owned companies, the private sector, and international agencies. If the central government is too ambitious in developing infrastructure, this can increase budget deficits, which is not sustainable. At the same time, the complex financial, economic, political, technical, environmental, and social dimensions of infrastructure development challenge the government,

Indonesia at the Crossroads: Transformation and Challenges

which can result in failed projects as well as failures of omission (Krueger, 1990).

Against this background, this chapter highlights the trends, obstacles, and prospects of infrastructure investment in Indonesia, by chronologically reviewing two decades of the central government's fiscal policies after the 1997–1998 financial crisis and their relation to the development of infrastructure. Referring to the implementation of public private partnerships (PPP), this chapter also examines the role of non-fiscal policies in accelerating infrastructure development.

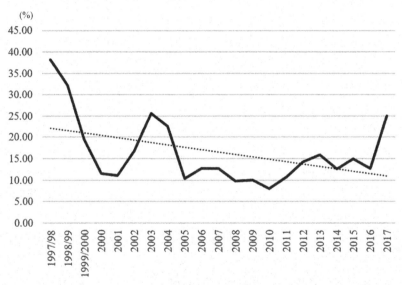

Figure 8.1. Infrastructure spending as a percentage of total central government spending. Note: the dotted line indicates the linear trend. Source: compiled based on budget reports from the Ministry of Finance, Republic of Indonesia.

Policies preceding and during the 1997–1998 Financial Crisis

According to the Indonesian government, the private sector contributed about 77% of total investment in the country in 1995, with the remainder provided by the government (Departemen Keuangan, 1997/1998). However, the 1997–1998 financial crisis revealed that the growing participation of the private sector in the Indonesian economy was fueled by foreign loans (over borrowing) with minimum security and prudence (Sadli, 1999). Three technical factors created the crisis: fixed or quasi-fixed exchange rates, rapidly increasing short-term debt, and a weak financial system (Hill, 1999 as cited by Wie, 2002). Risks in the Indonesian economy at the onset of the crisis also contributed to creating the crises. These included the high inflation rate, the weak structure of the banking sector, a slowdown in the growth of non-oil exports, the widening current account deficit, and the rapidly rising private external debt (World Bank, 1997 as cited by Wie, 2002). Wie (2002) also notes the 'bubble economy' in Indonesia, which was mainly driven by rapid capital inflow, especially huge loans from foreign institutional investors and foreign banks. In addition, Sadli (1999) points to the low quality of Indonesia's institutions, political practices, law enforcement, and bureaucratic procedures.

As a result of the financial crisis, economic growth in Indonesia declined substantially and the economy contracted by 13.1% in 1998. The contraction was the longlest among all other Asian countries, even larger then Thailand. Moreover, the inflation rate in Indonesia reached its highest-ever level, 82.4%, in 1998. The crisis eroded the confidence of investors and creditors in the country's economic performance. The government needed to restore market confidence and play a more active role in stimulating capital investment.

In the early 1980s, more than 70% of fiscal revenue was generated from the oil and gas sector (Departemen Keuangan, 1997/1998). After the price of oil dropped in mid-1986, the government issued many regulations in the tax policy that aimed to improve the collection of tax revenues, both intensively and extensively (Departemen Keuangan, 1997/1998). By the 1995–1996 fiscal year, the share of tax revenues to total government revenues had increased, reaching nearly 68%, while the contribution of the oil and gas sector had decreased considerably to about 21% (Departemen Keuangan, 1997/1998). However, Indonesia had a lower tax ratio compared to other ASEAN countries. In 1995–1996, Indonesia's tax revenue was about 11.8% of its gross domestic product (GDP), while Singapore, Malaysia, and Thailand were 16.2, 33.4, and 16.1, respectively (Departemen Keuangan, 1997/1998).

For the 1997–1998 fiscal year, the government's main concerns were restoring macroeconomic fundamentals, including stabilizing inflation, the exchange rate, foreign exchange reserves, the debt ratio, and the current account deficit. It was understandable that at the time as the government adopted a contractionary fiscal (and monetary) policy, it allocated a large part of its fiscal capacity to restoring the macroeconomic fundamentals. Unfortunately, several studies (see Basri and Patunru, 2006; Adam, 2008) concluded that this effort had a detrimental impact on the development of infrastructure. By allocating a large part of its fiscal capacity to restore macroeconomic fundamentals, the government was left with limited fiscal resources available to improve the quality and quantity of infrastructure.

Statistical evidence indicates that after the 1997–1998 crisis, the growth and contribution of various sectors to the Indonesian economy decreased significantly, with the exception of the electricity, gas, and water supply sectors. For example, after growing by 11.9% per year during 1993–1997, the construction sector contracted by an average of 13% per year during 1997–1999. The share of GDP of the construction sector in the Indonesian economy fell from 8.2% in 1997 to 5.8% in 1999. A similar condition describes the transport and communications sector (Table 8.1.).

Table 8.1. Growth and contribution to GDP by sector in 1993–1999.

	Contribution (percent of GDP)			Growth (percent)	
	1993	1997	1999	1993–1997	1997–1999
Agriculture	17.9	14.9	16.6	2.3	0.9
Mining & Quarrying	9.6	8.9	9.8	5.2	0.3
Manufacturing Industries	22.3	24.8	26.4	10.0	-0.8
Electricity, Gas, and Water Supply	1.0	1.3	1.7	13.6	6.3
Construction	6.8	8.2	5.8	11.9	-13.0
Trade, Hotels, and Restaurants	16.8	17.0	16.0	7.4	-4.8
Transport and Communication	7.0	7.3	7.3	8.1	-2.9
Financial Services	8.5	8.9	6.9	8.3	-10.7
Services	10.1	8.8	9.6	3.3	0.1
GDP	100.0	100.0	100.0	7.1	-2.8

Source: BPS.

For the 1998–1999 fiscal year, the government apparently realized that in order to sustainably strengthen macroeconomic fundamentals, it also needed to address supply-side constraints. Consequently, fiscal policy shifted to improving the effectiveness of development expenditures to support physical and non-physical government projects, particularly to support industries that could promote exports, basic infrastructure, and human resources development. During 1998–1999 the government increased its spending on development from IDR 34,503 billion to IDR 49,392 billion. However, as a percentage of total spending, spending on development decreased from 38% in 1997–1998 to 33.5% in 1998–1999. Five priority sectors received the highest share of development funds: (i) transportation and tourism, (ii) mining and energy, (iii) agriculture and irrigation, (iv) regional development (urban and rural areas), and (v) education and young generation, national culture, and belief in God. However, from 1997 to 1999, almost all these sectors continued to have negative growth. This implies that the government spending did not substantially expand new demand or ease the impact of the financial crisis.

Fiscal Policies after the Crisis

Since the financial crisis of 1997–1998, four presidents have overseen Indonesia's economic development, namely Abdurrahman Wahid (1999–2001), Megawati Sukarnoputri (2001–2004), Susilo Bambang Yudhoyono (2004–2014), and Joko Widodo (2014–present). Each of them has had specific challenges and opportunities in implementing fiscal policy and promoting infrastructure development. President Abdurrahman Wahid, who governed for less than two years, had to consolidate fiscal policy to ensure sustainability and secure budget to protect the poor and other vulnerable groups. He also had to balance fiscal resources while implementing the new decentralization law. During his presidency, the Indonesian economy gradually recovered from the worst effects of the crisis, which brought new hope for increasing the state's revenues (both tax and non-tax). Although President Abdurrahman Wahid did not complete his term, some indicators indicate improvement during his presidency. For example, capital expenditures as a percentage of total expenditures increased from 19 to 36%. Similarly, the tax ratio increased from 8 to 11% by the end 2001. This indicates that the government had more fiscal space to finance its expenditures.

Following Abdurrahman Wahid, Megawati Sukarnoputri was president for three years and three months. During her presidency, Megawati sustained the share of expenditure to GDP at about 19% and the tax ratio increased slightly to about 12%. However, the share of capital expenditure to GDP decreased to about 14%. Similarly, the share of capital expenditures to total expenditures was substantially decreased from 42% in 2002 to about 14% in 2005, as a substantial amount of money was allocated to subsidies and financing interest rates as part of a bank restructuring program.

During Susilo Bambang Yudhoyono's presidency, the share of gross fixed capital formation (GFCF) to GDP increased from 22% to about 33% from 2004 to 2014. However, the share of expenditure to total expenditure and share of total expenditure to GDP both decreased substantially compared to previous presidencies. Similarly, the tax ratio declined slightly. Thus, it seems that Indonesia missed an opportunity to spend on infrastructure during his presidency.

According to some indicators, Joko Widodo's presidency has been similar to that of Susilo Bambang Yudhoyono. However, during the last three years, Joko Widodo has substantially increased the share of total spending on infrastructure to the highest rate that it has been in 15 years. In conclusion, although Indonesia has regained its capacity to develop infrastructure, it still needs more fiscal space and a better tax ratio to sustain infrastructure development through its own endowments. The following section will provide a more detailed analysis for each period of presidency.

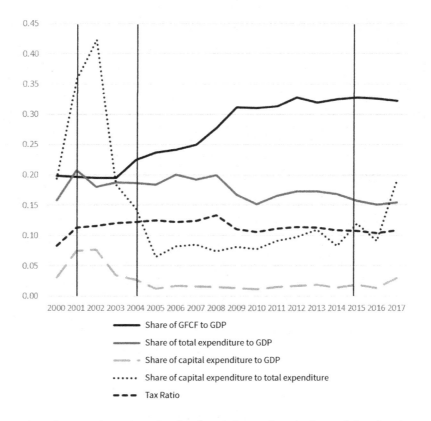

Figure 8.2. Gross domestic product (GDP), capital expenditure, and tax ratio in Indonesia. Note: GFCF and GDP use current market price; Tax ratio = tax revenue divided by GDP; data for year 2017 obtained from Statistic Indonesia and Government budget 2018. Source: Asian Development Bank (ADB), Key Indicators for Asia and the Pacific 2017.

Infrastructure within Fiscal Agenda

Year 2000 marked the early stages of economic recovery, when it was necessary for the government to pave the way and provide a strong economic foundation in order for the country to recover sustainably. To this end, the government needed to maintain macroeconomic stability, enhance bank restructuring, and help the private sector to restructure debt, both domestically and in foreign markets. To support macroeconomic stability, fiscal policy aimed to achieve six objectives. First, government aimed to strengthen fiscal sustainability, by: (i) cutting the fiscal deficit from 6.8% of GDP in 1999–2000 to 5% in 2000; (ii) reducing net foreign borrowing from 4.4 to 2% of GDP in 2000; and (iii) increasing state revenue to reduce foreign debt. Second, it prioritized development spending to provide social assistance for the poor. Third, it provided fiscal support to stabilize the interest rate for bank recapitalization. Fourth, it implemented targeted subsidies to the poor, instead of subsidizing commodities for better allocation. Fifth, it planned to increase the welfare of public servants. Sixth, to support decentralization, the government increased budget allocations to local governments. In 2000, the government allocated 21.1% (or IDR 41,605 billion) of total spending to development expenditures. In 2000, the government budget was used to support programs for job creation, to promote health and education, and to provide subsidies for a social safety net program (Figure 8.3.). The government also increased subsidies for fuel, electricity, food, and medicine. Furthermore, one third of development expenditures were allocated to finance subsidies to the credit program and bank restructuring.

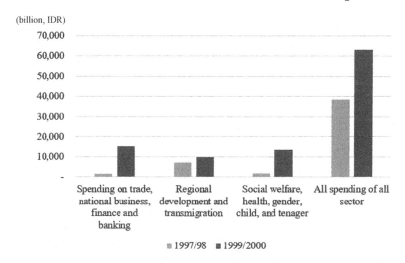

Figure 8.3. Development spending for selected sectors (in billion IDR). Source: Ministry of Finance, Republic of Indonesia (1997/1998; 1999/2000).

The 1997–1998 financial crisis and fiscal decentralization of 2001 increased overall central government expenditures. However, development expenditures as a percentage of GDP decreased from about 4% in 1999–2000 to about 2.7% in 2001. The share of development expenditures to total central government spending decreased from about 22.4% to about 14.5% in the same period. This implies that some development expenditures were decentralized to the local and provincial governments.

Due to a reduction in energy subsidies, the government implemented Program Penanggulangan Dampak Pengurangan Subsidi Energi (Program on Easing the Impact of Energy Subsidies Reduction) in 2001. The program provided rice subsidies for the poor, education assistance for poor students, health services, water access and sanitation, development funds for coastal communities, and subsidies for public transport.

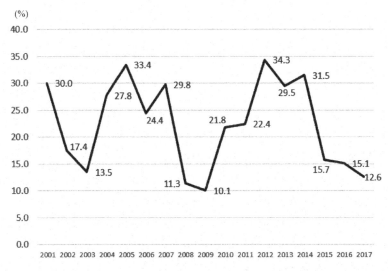

Figure 8.4. Percent of overall central government spending allocated to subsidies. Source: Ministry of Finance, Republic of Indonesia (various issues 2001–2017).

In 2002, the government attempted to allocate budget to support job creation, alleviate poverty, and promote productive sectors at the community level. These allocations amounted to 21.2% (or IDR 52.3 trillion) of the central government's budget for development. The four priority sectors were agriculture, forestry and fisheries; irrigation; transportation; and finance and cooperatives.

In 2003, the government continued to provide a stimulus package to develop different sectors of the economy. The Bali bombing in October 2002 pushed the government to allocate funds to compensate for the decrease in private sector investment due to the tragedy. It allocated IDR 65.1 trillion (25.7% of total state expenditure) to development expenditures. It paid special attention to poverty alleviation and food security, quality of human resource development, financial and economic stability, debt restructuring and privatization, expanding job opportunities, law enforcement and improving the court system, decentralization and community development, the general election in 2004, state unity and general order, maintaining basic economic infrastructure, and pursuing sustainable economic development. Additionally, five sectors received special attention: education, culture, youth and sport; agriculture, forestry, maritime and fisheries; transportation, meteorology and geophysics; defense and security; social welfare, health, and gender. The thematic development programs were broad, covering both unfinished programs from previous years and agenda for the current year. Five years after the financial crisis, the government was still allocating fiscal resources for developing stability in banking and financial sector.

In 2004 the government devoted development expenditure to support nine priority programs: (i) maintaining economic growth as a necessary condition to improve people's welfare, with priority given to developing economic infrastructure; (ii) improving the quality of human resources; (iii) improving poverty alleviation; (iv) securing food security; (v) developing democracy by implementing direct elections for president and parliament; (vi) combating corruption, collusion, and nepotism; (vii) developing defense and security; (viii) speeding regional development, especially in the eastern part of Indonesia; (ix) improving conservation and rehabilitation of natural resources. Government allocated about 27.8% (or IDR 70.9 trillion) of the central government budget to development expenditures. Thus, development expenditure was increased, and the implementation of direct election for the first time was one of the reasons for this increase.

In 2005, the categorization of government spending changed. Initially, the budget was divided into only two types of spending, namely routine and development expenditures. Today the budget specifies spending on a variety of categories, including expenditures for personnel, goods, capital, interest payments, subsidies, grants, social assistance, and others. Capital expenditures are designed to speed up the development of physical infrastructure that can result in multi-year benefits. Capital expenditure includes any spending on land, machinery and equipment, buildings, network construction, and other physical infrastructure. The budget for capital expenditures in 2005 was about IDR 43.1 trillion, representing 16.2% of total central government spending or 2% of the GDP. However, of the IDR 43.1 trillion budget, only about IDR 32.9 trillion of the capital was actually spent, or 24% less than was planned.

A constitutional mandate to spend 20% of the government's budget on education was expected to increase capital expenditures, particularly for school infrastructure, in 2006, and indeed between 2005 and 2006, capital expenditures grew by 81.6%, an increase from IDR 36.9 trillion to IDR 69.8 trillion. There were several reasons for this significant increase. First, the government increased its budget allocation for fuel subsidy compensation such as for education and health. Second, the government increased its budget for rehabilitation and reconstruction in Aceh, Nias, and North Sumatra in response to the tsunami disaster and in Papua and Yogyakarta after earthquakes there. Third, the government was also forced to complete various programs that it had committed to between 2004 and 2006. Fourth, depreciation of the IDR against the USD pushed the government to allocate more funds to repay its debts and foreign grants. This is because not all infrastructure spending is part of capital spending, but also good or services spending. Finally, the government also commenced implementing multiyear programs. In 2006 the government provided special attention to four functions of the government, mainly public services, education, defense, and the economy. To improve the economic function, the government was motivated to develop rural infrastructure, particularly roads, bridges, small ports, irrigation, clean water utilities, and sanitation. It spent about IDR 38.6 trillion to support economic functions.

In 2007 the government's mission was to create job opportunities and accelerate poverty alleviation as crucial and necessary steps to improve the welfare of the people. Nine priority sectors were identified to support the mission: (i) poverty alleviation; (ii) developing job opportunities, investment, and export; (iii) revitalization of agriculture, forestry, and rural development; (iv) improving accessibility and quality of education and health; (v) law enforcement, human rights, corruption eradication, and bureaucratic reform; (vi) improving ability in defense, security, social order, and conflict resolution; (vii) rehabilitation and reconstruction in Aceh,

Nias, Yogyakarta, and Central Java; (viii) acceleration of infrastructure development and (ix) development in border and remote areas. It allocated capital expenditures of about IDR 73.1 trillion. Capital expenditures were intended to support pro-growth, pro-job, and pro-poor policies.

The government's expenditures for economic functions were directed to eleven areas: public service, defense, general order and security, economy, environment, housing and general facilities, health, tourism and culture, religion, education, and social protection. In 2007 the government allocated IDR 51.2 trillion to economic functions. The budget was primarily used to support the development and improvement of roads and bridges, and the management and conservation of rivers, lakes, irrigation, and other related purposes. The government also improved electricity facilities, railways, and sea transportation, and other strategic programs under specific ministries, such as maritime and fisheries, agriculture, and communication and information.

Improving the quality of public services, paying down debt, maintaining price stability for various strategic products, and improving fiscal decentralization were four of the main programs of the government budget in 2008. The priority of fiscal spending was also intended to improve investment, job opportunities, and poverty alleviation; to revitalize agriculture, fisheries, forestry, and rural development; to enhance infrastructure development and energy management; to improve access and quality on education and health; to improve effectiveness in poverty alleviation; to combat corruption and to speed up bureaucratic reform; to strengthen defense ability and national security; to respond to disasters, to minimize disaster risks, and to improve capacity to respond to the avian flu. It allocated about IDR 95.4 trillion for capital expenditures, or 2.4% of GDP. The budget was in large part used to develop infrastructure, to improve access to basic infrastructure, and rebuild infrastructure in disaster areas.

Developing Infrastructure as Top Priority

The fact that government spending was significantly increased to develop infrastructure indicates that infrastructure became a priority target for government fiscal policy intervention. However, it is important to note that although the increase in capital spending was necessary, it was insufficient to improve Indonesia's infrastructure. This suggests that government fiscal policy intervention alone is inadequate and should be complemented by other policies, including infrastructure pricing mechanisms and enforcement of laws and regulations (Adam, 2011). First, the inadequacy of infrastructure to support Indonesia's economic development had been cumulative, and therefore a huge budget allocation was required to address the need. Although government spending on infrastructure (capital expenditure) increased significantly in raw terms, the proportion of GDP (2.4%) remained small compared to before the financial crisis, when it was 6% of GDP (Basri and Munandar, 2008), and still lags far behind the ideal level of 5% recommended by several institutions, including the World Bank (2004) (see Table 8.4.).

Second, the realization of capital expenditure is slow each year and is often delayed. For example, up to September 2008, only around 30% of the total allocated budget (IDR 95.4 trillion) for that year had been spent. The government thus had a mere three months to commit the balance (IDR 66.8 trillion). Unfortunately, infrastructure projects are unlikely to turn out well when the spending process is rushed.

Third, capital expenditure is poorly allocated. A significant proportion of expenditures is allocated for land procurement, consulting services, planning, monitoring, and supervision costs, which reduces direct spending on physical infrastructure. Indeed, Basri and Munandar (2009) argue that only 16% of total capital expenditure is directly used to build new infrastructure. The remaining 84% is allocated to maintain various types of existing infrastructure. Despite this, Adam (2008) found that maintenance expenditures are insufficient to prevent degradation of existing infrastructure. This suggests that capital expenditures for both new infrastructure and maintenance should be increased.

However, unless the government increases its income, it is highly unlikely to increase capital spending. It should therefore change its approach to providing and maintaining infrastructure by introducing a proper pricing mechanism that treats infrastructure as a scarce economic good. By doing so, all infrastructure users would need to, directly or indirectly, pay for it. Pricing infrastructure applies an economic instrument to affect behavior towards maintenance and efficient infrastructure usage, providing incentives for demand management and ensuring cost recovery, ultimately gauging consumers' willingness to pay for additional investment in infrastructure (Queensland Competition Authority, 2003).

The government and several infrastructure authorities have already imposed prices on their consumers. However, lack of recognition of the value of infrastructure resulted in a failure to set the price according to cost recovery principles. Consequently, the government continues to provide price subsidies to consumers. This, in turn, creates a situation in which the imposition of price provides no incentive for the government to increase its infrastructure expenditure on either new infrastructure or maintenance. This suggests that setting the proper price is the first important step to enable the government to increase its infrastructure expenditure.

Fourth, although the government has rules and regulations to maintain the quality of infrastructure, enforcement remains a perennial problem. For example, the government prohibits vehicles over a certain weight from operating on some roads. But in many cases, it has been reluctant to take legal action against vehicles in violation of this rule, leading to continuous over usage. The result is that the roads' quality cannot be maintained.

Developing infrastructure also has implications for labor issues. The demand for infrastructure has shifted from land-based to sea-based, and with more complicated and high technology supports. Indonesia can gain jobs from the creation of infrastructure if the resource and capability of the labor force supports it. The nature of infrastructure projects is different to those twenty years ago. Currently, most infrastructure projects are less labor intensive, and tend to be more capital intensive. This is particularly true for projects that require high-skilled labor. This will bring challenges on labor absorption, especially on low skilled labor.

A Public Private Partnership Program

Due to insufficient capital expenditure, the government has in recent years been focused on encouraging spending by both state-owned companies and the private sector through a PPP program. One infrastructure project assigned to a state-owned company was a fast-track program to supply 10 GW of electricity. This project was mandated by Presidential Regulation Number 71 Year 2006. The government provided a debt guarantee, a manageable supply and stable price of coal, and guarantees in the case of termination or delay of the project. Other projects designated as PPP schemes include the Trans Java Toll Road, the Jakarta Outer Ring Road II (JORR II), and the Monorail; they were set under Presidential Regulation Number 67 Year 2005 and Regulation of the Ministry of Finance Number 38/PMK.01/2006.

In addition, the government set a target of developing 1,600 km of new toll roads and extending the Trans Java by about 913 km by 2018. This project aimed to develop nodes of growth, connect the regions, and increase mobility of both people and goods. To support this project, it collected funds that were managed by Badan Pengatur Jalan Tol (BPJT—Regulatory Agency for Toll Road) to handle land procurement. In the case of JORR II, the government provided a guarantee on political risks and project performance, for example, covering any increases in the price of land beyond the negotiated price. The government also supported the Monorail project by covering costs of shortfalls in the minimum number of passengers (160,000 per day) with a maximum guarantee of USD 11.25 million per year, for five years. Presidential Regulation Number 103 Year 2006 and Ministry of Finance Regulation Number 30/PMK.02/2007 provide the legal basis of this project.

The government used fiscal policy to improve the purchasing power of the poor, and to support the private sector under the PPP model, increasing budget deficits from 0.5% of GDP in 2005 to about 1.3% of GDP in 2007. However, in 2009, it wanted to cut its budget deficit to about 1% of GDP. Meanwhile, it prioritized improving basic services, to enhance the quality of growth and economic resilience with support to agriculture, infrastructure, and energy, and to accelerate corruption eradication, bureaucracy reform, and to improve democratic institutions, and internal defense and security. Planned capital expenditures were increased to about IDR 134.9 trillion in 2008, an increase from 48.2% of the budget in 2005 to about 52.8% in 2008. However, the realization of capital expenditures in 2008 only reached IDR 71.2 trillion (1.5% of GDP). In 2009, capital spending was targeted at IDR 72 trillion (1.4% of GDP). Capital expenditures in 2009 were used to provide financial support for basic infrastructure (such as roads, ports, and power supply), agriculture (irrigation and the optimization, conservation, and reclamation of land to support the food security program), developing infrastructure to ease or to rehabilitate areas impacted by natural disaster such as the Sidoarjo mud flow (in East Java), and supporting multiyear financing projects.

Based on Presidential Instruction Number 5 Year 2008, the government planned to establish an agency that would guarantee an infrastructure fund (the guarantee fund). The aims of the guarantee fund were to help investors settle financial close and to prepare capital costs, and to improve the credit worthiness of infrastructure projects. From the government's point of view, the fund would help improve transparency and accountability, and ease the risks of infrastructure projects. In 2009 the government injected about IDR 1 trillion into the agency.

In 2010, the government implemented a new initiative for capital spending. The new programs consisted of various projects, such as supporting a housing credit facility for low-income families, building prisons, extending domestic connectivity, intensifying construction of the Kualanamu Airport (in North Sumatra), preparing a new system of citizenship administration, building infrastructure for geothermal exploration, and constructing the 2011 Sea Games facilities. Government allocated about IDR 15 trillion for the investment fund, injected capital into several state-owned companies and revolving funds. The amount of state investment was about IDR 3.6 trillion. Of that amount, more than IDR 2.68 trillion was allocated to support a housing credit facility for low-income families. To increase capital capacity and to have better public services, government injected fresh capital to Lembaga Pembiayaan Ekspor Indonesia (Indonesian Agency for Export Financing), PT Sarana Multi infrastruktur (SMI), PT Penjaminan Infrastruktur Indonesia (PII), PT Asuransi Kredit Indonesia (Askrindo), and Perum Jaminan Kredit Indonesia. Furthermore, in an attempt to help PLN develop the 10 GW program, it increased the profit margin that the PLN could enjoy from 3 to about 8%. It also allocated IDR 7.5 trillion for gap financing (viability gap funding). The total injected capital was about IDR 5.8 trillion. Finally, some 5.6 trillion was used for revolving fund.

In 2011, government investment in infrastructure reached about IDR 21.1 trillion. This was a substantial increase, particularly driven by the increase in capital injection to several state-owned companies and the provision of revolving funds. Furthermore, the government guarantee on many infrastructure projects mitigated fiscal risks, especially on contingency liability. In principle, the guarantee aimed to compensate private sector losses incurred because of government actions, such as tariff policy, exchange rate, fuel price, supply of coal, and land capping. The government also provided an interest rate subsidy, such as for constructing drinking water facilities (based on Presidential Regulation Number 29 Year 2009).

Based on the Indonesian Infrastructure Guarantee Fund, on December 30, 2010, the government established PT Penjaminan Infrastruktur Indonesia (PII—Indonesian Infrastructure Guarantee). Presidential Regulation Number 13 Year 2010, Presidential Regulation Number 35 Year 2009, and Presidential Regulation Number 67 Year 2005 formed the legal basis for this agency. It also implemented a single window policy, allowing PT PII to directly evaluate and assess all projects. It secured a land capping fund of IDR 4.89 trillion for 28 toll roads.

In 2014, the government allocated approximately IDR 114 trillion for economic function. However, as a percentage of the total government spending, this allocation represented a drop from about 11% in 2008 to about 8.9%. The government maintained similar targets of economic function, particularly improvement in such areas as the capacity and quality of the transportation network, mobility of people and goods across regions, stability of food prices, stability of imported rice, productivity in the fisheries sector, electrification rates, and the implementation of a green energy initiative.

In 2015, the government set up a new national agenda *Nawacita* that prioritized maritime development, food sovereignty, infrastructure development and connectivity, industrial development of security and defense, and national economic sovereignty. In 2015, the tax ratio was about 12.53%, only a slight increase from 11.8% in 1995–1996. Furthermore, it is important to note that spending on economic function increased to about IDR 216.3 trillion in 2015, a 55.6% increase as compared to spending in 2014. This rapid increase in economic spending was primarily due to re-focusing on national programs and priorities. Developing connectivity was important, especially outside Java. Railways, maritime development, and energy and electricity were among the top priority sectors for infrastructure. Substantial reduction in the energy subsidy from about IDR 341.8 to 137.8 trillion provided fiscal space for infrastructure investment.

In 2015 there was also a substantial capital injection from the government to the 40 state-owned companies. PT SMI received the highest amount, or around one third of the total injection (IDR 20.3 trillion), while PT PII received IDR 1.5 trillion. The government claimed that by providing more capital injection to those companies and agencies, many benefits would be enjoyed, such as an improved capacity to guarantee infrastructure projects under the PPP model, acceleration of infrastructure projects, protecting state budget for any potential claims in PPP projects, expansion of the number of PPP projects that could be guaranteed, improvement in market confidence, and an improvement in the bankability of projects. It also aimed to merge PT SMI and PT PII into one institution to strengthen and improve its support of infrastructure development.

There was a slight decrease in the spending for economic function in 2016. The government still prioritized integrating the transportation system, improving national connectivity and the national logistics system, improving the sovereignty of food and water, rehabilitating the irrigation system, increasing the production of energy, and improving electricity services and increasing electrification rates. In 2017 it increased spending on economic function. This additional spending was basically to support infrastructure development of railways to the Adisumarmo Airport (in Central Java), the Asian Games, to develop the agriculture sector and infrastructure in the border and remote areas and revitalize several traditional markets. In addition, the government has a strong commitment to supporting the development of the LRT system in Jabodetabek. To this end, the government allocated IDR 2 trillion to PT KAI to improve the financial capability of this state-owned company to support the LRT program. However, to maintain its commitment to infrastructure development, it faced a serious problem. As infrastructure expenditures rose, the budget deficit increased from about 2.59% of GDP in 2015 to about 2.92% of GDP in 2017. Debt financing reached the highest level in the previous five years and almost reached 3% of GDP that was the maximum limit of debt financing according to Law Number 17 Year 2003 on the State Finance.

Evaluation of Public Private Partnerships

As noted previously, fiscal policy itself is insufficient to accelerate the development of infrastructure. Currently, one important non-fiscal policy option that the government has selected and implemented to complement fiscal policy is the PPP. Accordingly, it will be relevant to evaluate the implementation of PPP to better understand its achievements and problems.

In 2005 the government launched a new mechanism to develop infrastructure by encouraging private sector participation through PPP. The PPP is an alternative financing program primarily aimed at addressing the government's limited fiscal capacity in developing infrastructure. To carry out this program, it has taken several important actions to reduce the financing risk from the national budget and develop more market-oriented infrastructure projects. It provided a number of financial instruments to facilitate PPP works, such as providing funds for land capping, interest rate subsidies, and a substantial injection of funds to many state-owned enterprises. It also formed institutions, such as PT SMI and PT PII,[1] to strengthen the implementation of the PPP.

Unfortunately, the government's efforts to encourage private sector involvement in infrastructure development have been less successful. Infrastructure projects through the PPP program have been relatively slow to proceed, suggesting a weak response from the private sector to participate. During 2010–2014, the government set its target to offer 79 projects to the private sector. Yet, by the end of 2011, the government was only able to tender five projects (Adam, 2011). Moreover, during 2015–2019, it offered 299 projects (52 priority projects and 247 national strategic projects) to the private sector, but by the end of 2017, it had only succeeded in selling 21 projects to private sector actors.

Adam (2011) identifies various factors that hindered the success of the PPP program. First, Indonesian economic policies for supporting PPP tend to be complicated because of the overlapping function of the multiple government regulations issued. For example, the Geothermal Law Number 27 Year 2003 overlaps with the Protected Forest Management Law. The problem is that almost all geothermal resources are in Protected Forest Districts, while the Forest Law Number 41 Year 1999 forbids

---

1   PT SMI has the following tasks: (1) as a catalyst in accelerating infrastructure development, (2) provide an alternative source of funds for project financing, (3) promote PPP, (4) increase the number, capacity, and effectiveness through partnerships with third parties. Meanwhile, PT PII has the following tasks: (1) provide guarantees for infrastructure projects built through PPP schemes, (2) improve the creditworthiness and bankability of infrastructure projects, (3) improve governance, consistency and transparency in the provision of the guarantee, (4) ring-fencing government contingent liability and minimize sudden shock to state budget.

exploitation within forest areas. As a result, private companies interested in the management and utilization of geothermal energy face high risks, uncertainty, and costs if they are involved in the development of geothermal-based energy infrastructure.

Second, infrastructure development projects are highly likely to be delayed or scrapped due to unexpected obstacles, such as slowness in land acquisition or protests by residents. Unfortunately, government does not provide financial guarantees for delays caused by such problems.

Third, infrastructure projects that are offered to the private sector are not well prepared, because the relevant agencies, including the Penanggung Jawab Proyek Kerjasama (PJPK—the agency in charge of partnership projects), ministry and non-ministerial government agencies, local governments, state-owned enterprises (SOEs), and regionally-owned enterprises, have little experience in preparing projects to offer the private sector. The PJPK has more projects to be funded by Anggaran Pendapatan dan Belanja Negara (APBN—state budget). Therefore, considering the high cost of consultants to conduct feasibility studies, the feasibility studies by PJPK tend to lack technical competence. In addition to technical matters, the private sector also needs information related to legal, economic, and financial risks, the provision of government incentive schemes, and problems that may arise when the private sector is involved in PPP projects. Yet often these are not fully provided.

Fourth, the perception of the private sector is that that the PJPK has a low commitment to maintaining partnerships. Often a partnership between the government and the private sector breaks down when the PJPK diverts its funding away from a PPP to an APBN on a project that is underway. Accordingly, the private sector regards the PJPK to be an unreliable party.

Fifth, in developing infrastructure, the bureaucrats in the PJPK prefer to use the state budget scheme rather than the PPP scheme, because the PJPK has opportunities to earn incentives and fees (whether legal or illegal) from any project financed by the state budget. Accordingly, it is not surprising if the PJPK selects projects with a relatively high rate of return on investment, by using the state budget scheme, while projects with a relatively low rate of return on investment are promoted through the PPP scheme. As the projects promoted through the PPP scheme have a relatively low rate of return on investment, the private sector has been less responsive to engage in the development of infrastructure.

Whether a project is financed by the state budget or promoted through the PPP program ultimately depends on ministerial policy. Therefore, there should be a strong commitment from the ministers to change their policy to carry out infrastructure projects through the PPP program.

Sixth, the PJPK, particularly in local governments, have a limited understanding about the PPP program. Rather than viewing it as a means to build infrastructure, local governments often see the PPP as a source of income in itself and introduce various new taxes and charges on private sector partners. The higher costs in turn deter private sector involvement.

Seventh, overlapping project management across several ministries results in a lack of institutional capacity and disincentivizes the private sector. For example, the Ministry of Public Works has two managerial agencies, the BPJT and Bina Marga. The former is responsible for managing the development of toll roads, while the latter is responsible for managing the development of public roads. The problem is that these two agencies often work in disharmony. Bina Marga will frequently build a public road adjacent to a toll road built by the BPJT, creating unnecessary competition between the toll roads and public roads. This competition has discouraged private sector involvement in the development of toll roads, as it reduces the rate of return on investment of the toll road projects offered by the PPP program. The Sunda Strait Bridge project also highlighted an ongoing row among the Ministry of Finance and other ministries in which the former wants to bring discipline into the system, and the latter tries to short-cut the process. Disharmony among government agencies occurs in many countries. However, unlike many countries, such as South Korea (Clark and Roy, 1997), institutional mechanisms for overcoming disagreements between government agencies in Indonesia have not been well-developed.

Eighth, the private sector is frequently reluctant to follow the tender mechanism involving multiple bidders as a basic principle of the PPP program. The private sector prefers to involve itself in the development of infrastructure through direct appointments, without having to compete with other bidders. Direct appointment is, however, in many cases, determined on the basis of a contract that is not transparent. For example, a partnership between PAM Jaya and Palyja in the provision of clean water resulted in a serious problem when it was revealed that the contract stipulated that the price (tariff) of water would automatically be increased every two years. Resolving this problem is complicated, as Indonesia does not have an arbitration mechanism to resolve business disputes.

The bad example of the partnership between PAM Jaya and Palyja has impeded efforts to accelerate the PPP program. The PJPK is reluctant to establish partnerships with the private sector and is consequently extremely slow in proceeding with the pre-qualification process to determine a short-list of bidders interested in the infrastructure projects offered through the PPP scheme.

The cases of the PAM Jaya and the Sunda Strait Bridge illustrate that the management of tenders requires skills and discipline within government. There will always be people who want to make illegal profits from the process. Therefore, a comprehensive institutional and regulatory framework, with proper enforcement, is required. An arbitration institution is also needed to address any business disputes between the government and the private sector.

The slow response of the private sector to the PPP program forced the government to finance several projects that it initially offered to the private sector in order to maintain the pace of infrastructure development. The government will therefore need to consider the implications of the rapid expansion of infrastructure projects on the state budget. Empirical evidence indicates that the budget deficit has increased and is approaching the maximum level allowed by law. Prioritization and focus on strategic projects are important to increase efficiency. Under resource constraints, the government needs to focus less on profitable projects, and more on those that deliver substantial social benefits, or positive externalities, in other words, emphasize transformative change in budget policy instead of reactive or proactive change. The government needs to seek reforms that extend and integrate the domestic market to increase and sustain productivity and competitiveness (ASH Center, 2013). This strategy can be effective if the government develops gradual reform by recalibrating and redirecting reform efforts while optimizing gains (ASH Center, 2013). Transformative change in turn can provide more space to pursue, and achieve, inclusive and sustainable growth.

Conclusion

Infrastructure is one of the most important basic requirements to support long term and sustained economic growth, and it is a key element to promoting social justice. The challenge is how to provide this basic requirement in a more sustainable way, balancing economic gains and social benefits. Strong macroeconomic stability and good governance are important determinants of accelerated infrastructure development. Indonesia has been dependent for many years on tax revenues to provide financial support for infrastructure development. Thus, the sustainability of infrastructure financing, especially from government budget, needs to be secured.

In the case of Indonesia, economic shocks and natural disasters can have an adverse effect on tax revenues and financial resources for infrastructure development. At the onset of the 1997–1998 financial crisis, the government intended to maintain infrastructure spending to ensure that existing facilities did not deteriorate and to avoid failures of omission. Accordingly, roughly one third of government spending was allocated for development expenditures.

During the financial crisis, development spending reached a crossroads between continuing to spend for physical infrastructure and helping alleviate the negative impacts of the crisis on the poor and other vulnerable groups.

The main objective of the development spending during that time was job creation, promotion of education and health, and providing subsidies for a social safety net program. Because government spending was sensitive to tax revenue, the government had to select high priority projects, and postponed unnecessary projects. The share of infrastructure spending as a percentage of total central government spending declined substantially to about 14.5% of total government spending during 2000–2002 and it has not returned to the pre-crisis level of about 38%.

Between 2000 and 2004, government spending went 'back to basics' to benefit those in the lowest 50% income bracket. Despite development expenditure gradually increasing to about 27.8% of total spending in 2004, it remained lower than pre-financial crisis levels. During that period, Indonesia also implemented a new decentralization law that had significant implications on sharing resources between the central and local governments. This created new challenges to synchronizing capital spending across different levels of government and geographical areas.

Changes to the structure of government spending in 2005 make it difficult to compare development expenditure before and after 2005. However, the best approximation of infrastructure spending can be captured from capital expenditure and economic spending. It seems that after 2005, most spending benefited those in the top 50% income bracket as rapid development of roads, ports, harbors, and airports disproportionately benefited urban residents. This may explain why income inequality in Indonesia increased during 2004–2014. This indicates that fiscal policy on infrastructure has a significant impact on social justice.

Finally, successful infrastructure development depends on four factors: (i) the participation of national banking and synergy among the state-owned enterprises; (ii) expanding the fiscal space for more productive spending; (iii) providing certainty in laws and regulations to stimulate more participation of the private sector; and (iv) isolating the risks of investment projects away from the government budget.

References

Adam, L. 2008. "Prasyarat Dasar" In *Model Peningkatan Daya Saing Perekonomian Indonesia.* Jakarta: LIPI Press.

_____. 2011. "Publik Private Partnership: Sebuah Alternatif Upaya Pemenuhan Kebutuhan Pembangunan Infrastruktur di Indonesia". In *Analisis Model Kebijakan Kerjasama Pemerintah-Swasta dalam Pembangunan Infrastruktur,* edited by L. Adam, pp. 33-45. Jakarta: Pusat Penelitian Ekonomi-LIPI.

ASH Center. 2013. *The Sum Is Greater than the Parts: Doubling Shared Prosperity in Indonesia Through Local and Global Integration.* Jakarta: Gramedia.

Basri, F. and H. Munandar. 2009. *Lanskap Ekonomi Indonesia.* Jakarta: Prenada Media Group.

Basri, M.C. and A.A. Patunru. 2006. "Survey of Recent Developments". *Bulletin of Indonesian Economic Studies* 42 (3): 295–319.

Clark, C. and K. Roy. 1997. *Comparing Development Pattern in Asia.* Colorado: Lynne Rienner.

Departemen Keuangan Republik Indonesia. 1997/98. *Nota Keuangan dan Anggaran Pendapatan Belanja Negara Tahun Anggaran 1997/98.*

Hill, H. 1999. "An Overview of the Issues". In *Southeast Asia's Economic Crisis: Origin, Lessons, and the Way Forward,* edited by H.W. Arnd and H. Hill, pp. 1-15. Singapore: Institute of Southeast Asia Studies.

Krueger, A.O. 1990. "Government Failure in Development". *The Journal of Economic Perspectives* 4 (3): 9–23.

Queensland Competition Authority. 2003. *General Pricing Principles for Infrastructure Investments Made in Response to Extraordinary Circumstances.* Brisbane: QCA.

Sadli, M. 1999. "The Indonesia Crisis". In *Southeast Asia's Economic Crisis: Origin, Lessons, and the Way Forward,* edited by H.W. Arnd and H. Hill, pp. 16-27. Singapore: Institute of Southeast Asia Studies.

Wie, Thee Kian. 2002. "The Soeharto Era and After: Stability, development, and crisis, 1996–2000". In *The Emergence of National Economy: An Economic History of Indonesia, 1800-2000,* edited by Howard Dick, Vincent J.H. Houben, J. Thomas Lindblad, and Thee Kian Wie, pp. 194-243. NSW: Allen & Alwin.

World Bank. 1997. *Indonesia: Sustaining High Growth with Equity.* Washington: World Bank.

PART 3
STRUCTURAL CHALLENGES

Chapter 9
Corruption and Anti-Corruption:
Major Challenges to Reform

Adnan Topan Husodo

Introduction

Scholars have studied the widespread and significant problem of corruption under the Suharto regime (Aditjondro, 1998; Butt, 2012), yet the corruption that was embedded in the New Order political system remains a challenge today.[1] It was assumed that corruption (along with collusion and nepotism) was part and parcel of the authoritarian system and that political reform would rid it from society. Instead, corruption has changed form, becoming more acute within today's democratic government (see Blunt et al., 2012). Among other things, political reforms such as decentralization opened new avenues for corruption to flourish, as local politicians seek advantage. As Setiyono (2015: 239) explains, "[t]he persistence of corruption in Indonesia, however, is not only perpetuated by the inheritance from Suharto's government. It is also a product of incomplete democratic consolidation."

---

1 The notion of corruption in this paper is certainly not limited to the definition that is widely used, namely abuse of authority and public office for personal gain, but also includes bribery, corruption related to state losses, embezzlement, gratuity, conflict of interest on public procurements and fraudulent public procurements. Indonesia's anti-corruption law does not define corruption. The World Bank defines corruption as "abuse of public official for private benefit." See World Bank (1997).

Since the beginnings of democratization in 1998, the international community has praised the implementation of major institutional reforms in Indonesia. Five national elections have been held safely and peacefully without any serious conflicts. Since 2005, Indonesia has also conducted direct local head elections as mandated by Law Number 32 Year 2004 on Local Government. These elections have been executed without significant threat to national and regional economic and political stability.

Nevertheless, a well-regarded electoral democracy does not necessarily produce a clean and accountable government (see Kolstad and Wiig, 2016). Democratic regimes, particularly those evaluated simply on the "success" of elections, seem to be just as fertile breeding grounds for corruption as authoritarian ones. Some argue that corruption in post-Suharto Indonesia has become entrenched in political practice and economic life, and spread to new centers of power, including the parliament, executive branch, judiciary, and local government. A long history of strong patron-client relations seems to contribute to the preservation of corruption. Further, following the implementation of the regional autonomy policy, corruption around local elections has become widespread.[2]

The government has embarked on several major and crucial anticorruption efforts during the reform era. A variety of international donors have funded and continue to fund corruption eradication and good governance projects, most of which require the Indonesian government to follow international anti-corruption standards, implement global best practices, and stress citizen empowerment as the key to successfully eliminating corruption.[3] Several new institutions dedicated to fighting corruption, reforming government, and encouraging citizen participation have been established as a result of legal reforms that emphasized the anti-corruption program. These include the Komisi Pemberantasan Korupsi (KPK—Corruption Eradication Commission), the Anti-Corruption Court,

---

2   On the spread of corruption under decentralization, see Kirana (2014).
3   They include USAID, GiZ, EU, UNODC, the World Bank, and IDLO. For further information, see (1) http://www.tetratech.com/en/projects/usaid-cegah-indonesia, (2) http://ppp.worldbank. org /public-private-partnership/library/indonesia-anti-corruption-action-plans-active-pro jects; (3) https://www.unodc.org/indonesia/en/2013/12/fighting-corruption/story.html; (4) http://www.idlo.int/where-we-work/asia/indonesia.

the Judicial Commission, Komisi Pengawas Persaingan Usaha (KPPU—the anti-monopoly agency), Pusat Pelaporan dan Analisis Transaksi Keuangan (PPATK—the anti-money laundering agency), the Police Commission, the Attorney Commission, the Central Information Commission, and Komisi Aparatur Sipil Negara (KASN—Civil Servant Commission). Indonesia has also participated in many anti-corruption global initiatives since the reform era began. The Indonesian government ratified the United Nations Convention Against Corruption (UNCAC, 2003) in 2006 and has been part of the G20 Anti-Corruption Working Group since 2010. Indonesian parliament chairperson, Fadli Zon from Gerindra party, was chair of the Global Organization of Parliamentarians against Corruption (GOPAC) during 2015–2017.

Notwithstanding the above efforts, however, the effectiveness and the efficiency of corruption reduction remains ambiguous. Although KPK is the most prominent independent anti-corruption agency Indonesia has ever had and has prosecuted corrupt officials in many government agencies, the outcomes of those prosecutions have not had the affect on government institutions expected by concerned civil society organizations. They have had limited impact across government institutions and brought little institutional reform. At the same time, anti-corruption policies alone do not guarantee the efficacy or the future of anti-corruption efforts. Indonesia's score and rank in the Corruption Perception Index (CPI) of Transparency International (TI) indicates that, at least in terms of perception, the country has not made much progress. During the 15 years since the establishment of KPK, Indonesia's CPI score has been unstable, increasing, decreasing, and remaining stagnant. According to TI, corruption persists in four areas, namely the private sector and the judiciary, legislative and executive branches of government, indicating that the ecosystem to promote a clean government has not been well established (*The Jakarta Post*, 2018; *Kompas*, 2018).

This chapter discusses the dynamics of corruption over the past 20 years, focusing on anti-corruption strategies and the obstacles to anti-corruption efforts in post-Suharto Indonesia. It demonstrates how the lack of accountability and transparency of political financing has undermined democratic principles, stimulating new forms and more widespread corruption, and analyzes how the political party system in Indonesia is likely the central root of corruption practices. Various anti-corruption efforts have not been able to fully control corruption, impacting the government's performance and the quality of governance in general.

This chapter argues that the focus on an institutional reform strategy alone cannot dramatically reduce the number of corruption cases in Indonesia. There is a strong indication that corruption has found fertile ground in the electoral democratic system of post-Suharto Indonesia. An unchanged political and economic structure that dis-incentivizes most state actors from taking action to fight corruption—and indeed results in many of them being implicated in corruption practices—is a major obstacle. At the same time, while some good anti-corruption results have been achieved by the KPK, the commission continues to suffer from a lack of support due to the absence of political will. The uncertainty of the anti-corruption agenda in Indonesia has continued under the most democratic government the country has ever seen, the administration of Joko Widodo (2014–present).

Corruption in Post Suharto Indonesia: A Shift in Perpetrators and Practice

To track the recent dynamic of corruption scandals, I use the data of corruption trends reported by Indonesian Corruption Watch (ICW) during 2010–2016. The data reveals that a diverse range of perpetrators across many parts of Indonesia have been prosecuted by law enforcement agencies, namely by the Attorney General Office of Indonesia and the KPK. It also shows that corruption not only involves the political elite, senior public officials, and bureaucrats, but that it also extends to the private sector (see Table 9.1.).[4] This is a shift from the New Order era,

---

4 The data is gathered from online media coverage of corruption investigations and prosecutions conducted by law enforcement officers, as well as official publications from law enforcement offices. It should be underlined that the data cannot be regarded as representing all cases of corruption because (1) it is dependent on the objectivity of law enforcers and therefore does not capture cases that are "overlooked" for personal or other motivations; and (2) it is heavily dependent on law enforcement capabilities, sectoral priorities for handling corruption, and so forth.

when major corruption was mainly perpetrated by family members and those close to Suharto himself.

Figure 9.1. Corruption trend analysis: Suspected and convicted corruption perpetrators in 2010–2016.

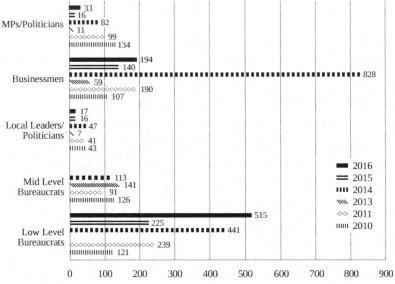

Source: various ICW reports (2010–2016).

As of 2016, 361 politicians, namely governors, mayors, regents, and deputy heads of region, had been convicted of corruption since the implementation of local direct elections in 2005 (Harian Terbit 2016). In addition to local leaders, corruption perpetrators were found in almost all public office levels, ranging from ministers, members of parliament, and local legislators, to law enforcement officials, judges, heads of local government agencies, civil servants, and directors of Badan Usaha Milik Negara (BUMN—State-Owned Enterprises). At the same time, the number of suspects from the private sector has increased dramatically, as businessmen are becoming deeply involved in corrupt behavior.

More recently, new actors have begun to emerge, namely village officials (heads of village), who started receiving cash transfers from the Central Government through the allocation of the *dana desa* (village fund scheme) in 2015 (Harian Terbit 2016).[5] According to an ICW report covering the period 2016–2017, the heads of villages quickly became the second most common actor perpetrating corruption after the cash transfer scheme was implemented, with the number of village head perpetrators reaching 61 people in 2016 and 34 in the first semester of 2017 (ICW, 2017).

In terms of corruption patterns, there is a shift from the corruption during the New Order. During the authoritarian regime (1966–1998), power was concentrated in the hands of Suharto as the single ruler. He successfully integrated the political, bureaucratic, and military forces under his control. To maintain his power, Suharto instituted various policies to prevent any opposition from emerging. He also consolidated power by controlling general elections (both presidential and legislative) and stripping powers from political parties that opposed his rule. Similarly, he controlled civil society groups by requiring any organization to secure approval from the government; those that failed to do so were considered illegal and could be forcibly dissolved and the person in charge could be imprisoned without a transparent or fair trial. At the same time, police institutions, the Prosecutor's Office, and the courts had no independence, as the president appointed all officials. As a result, investigation and prosecution of corruption cases were limited to minor cases that did not involve any of his family members or cronies.

Corruption during the Suharto era was primarily performed through legal means, as Suharto issued numerous presidential discretions that prioritized his family and cronies.[6] For example, he established the Supersemar Foundation through a presidential decree, and stipulated the obligation of state banks to transfer part of their profits to this foundation every year. He, as the president, owned the foundation outright, and there was no accountability regarding use of the foundation's budget.

---

5   Dana desa is meant as a tool of fiscal decentralization to combat rural poverty, however, there is evidence of misallocation and inappropriate spending (see Handra et al., 2017).

6   For example, Presidential Decree Number 20 Year 1992 on the Domestic Clove Production System appointed Tommy Suharto, son of Suharto, as the chairman of Badan Penyangga dan Pemasaran Cengkeh (BPPC—Clove Buffer and Marketing Body). Suharto as the president gave BPPC the authority to monopolize the distribution of clove in Indonesia.

As Suharto centralized his power, corruption became more concentrated among those within his network. Since 1998, corruption has spread beyond a small group of those in power in or near to the central government. Corruption has flowed like water, following the splits in state power as new institutions and positions were created by the decentralization policy of 1999. Today public officials, both at the center and the local levels, have new authority to manage economic resources. New authorities transferred to local governments include managing the state budgets and state revenues and granting various licenses in strategic sectors that were once controlled by the central government, such as mining, forestry, infrastructure, and property. These new authorities fall to the political parties with the most seats, as well as to the directly elected local heads.

Decentralization has also created many new formal rulers, which, unfortunately, have not been separated from the structure and influence of the New Order's power dynamic. Although the *Reformasi* era is the antithesis of the New Order, the means of exercising power has not changed much. As a result, new actors in the executive, legislative, and judicial branches continue to take advantage of opportunities to gain power through corrupt behavior and fail to perform checks and balances or deliver justice.

At the same time, the sudden lack of a single authority to guarantee investments and a predictable pattern of law enforcement created new uncertainties in public affairs. It is no longer enough to bribe one actor to settle one's problem. Instead, it becomes necessary to bribe other (and all) actors to ensure that each has their share, and the desired outcome can be achieved.

Today corruption does not exist only in the collusion between state and private actors, or in the sale of state power to citizens in the form of illegal levies or bribery: it has become a standard practice in the interaction between state actors. In many cases, the executive branch of government must pay legislators to approve budgets, approve certain legislation, or issue specific recommendations. While the practice of paying public officials to pass particular policies might have also occurred during the

Suharto era, there is no law enforcement data to support this conclusion. The practice is becoming more and more straightforward at present.

Anti-Corruption Instruments and their Failure to Create Accountable Government

It can be argued that eradication of corruption in the reform era is ambiguous. On the one hand, corruption eradication efforts have been well structured within anti-corruption policies and instruments, and on the other hand, corruption has increased both in volume and extent. Various laws have been passed to support an anti-corruption agenda. These include the law on the Government Administration that is clean and free from the Corruption, Collusion and Nepotism (Law Number 28 Year 1999), the Corruption Eradication Law (Law Number 31 Year 1999 and Law Number 20 Year 2001), the Corruption Eradication Commission Act (Law Number 30 Year 2002), the Corruption Court Law (Law Number 46 Year 2009), the UNCAC Ratification Act (Law Number 7 Year 2006), the Freedom of Information Act (Law Number 14 Year 2008), the Ombudsman Law (Law Number 37 Year 2008), the Anti-Monopoly and Business Competition Act (Law Number 5 Year 1999), the State Civil Apparatus Law (Law Number 5 Year 2014), the Judicial Commission Law (Law Number 18 Year 2011), and the Constitutional Court Law (Law Number 24 Year 2003). Presidential Instructions, Presidential Decrees, and Presidential Regulations have fortified this agenda.

These laws and regulations have spawned new institutions whose duty is to prevent and prosecute abuse of power and ensure a "clean" government. The Corruption Eradication Commission, the Corruption Court, the Judicial Commission, the Business Competition Supervisory Commission, the Police Commission, the Prosecutorial Commission, Pusat Pelaporan dan Analisis Transaksi Keuangan (PPATK—Financial Intelligence Unit), KASN, and the Ombudsman of the Republic of Indonesia are some of the state pillars essential to controlling abuse of power. In practice, however, these institutions are not very effective in carrying out their role. Some of the elites within the institutions created to curb corruption are instead engaged in corruption themselves (see Table 9.2.).

Table 9.1. Corruption cases of high-ranking public officials from state auxiliary bodies.

No	Institution	Name, Position	Description
1.	KPPU	Mohammad Iqbal, Commissioner	Accepting bribes
2.	Constitutional Court	Aqil Muchtar, Chairman	Accepting bribes
3.	Constitutional Court	Patrialis Akbar, Judge	Accepting bribes
4.	Dewan Perwakilan Daerah (Senator)	Irgam Gusman, Chairman (Senator)	Accepting bribes
5.	Corruption Court	Dewi Suryana, Judge	Accepting bribes
6.	Corruption Court	Heru Krisbandono, Judge	Accepting bribes
7.	Corruption Court	Kartini Juliana, Judge	Accepting bribes
8.	Judicial Commission	Irawady Joenoes, Commissioner	Accepting bribes

Source: various publications.

Meanwhile, supervision of the public financial and bureaucratic administrations attached to Badan Pemeriksa Keuangan (BPK—State Audit Agency), Badan Pengawas Keuangan dan Pembangunan (BPKP—State Supervisory and Finance Agency), the State Administration Institution, and the Inspectorate General are not sufficiently effective in monitoring and controlling corrupt practices. The KPK, for example, has uncovered cases of bribery involving BPK officials evaluating the management of state finance reports (*Kompas*, 2017b; 2017c). Some believe that the alleged corruption involving the state auditor is just the tip of the iceberg. The problem is not limited to the involvement of some audit officials in corruption; the audit function itself is also suspected of being politicized, as the audit and its results serve as political instruments to deflate the power of political opponents or to bring down the reputation of certain public officials (*Kompas*, 2016; *Kontan*, 2016).

299

In addition to the case-by-case approach described above, one of the instruments for measuring anti-corruption outcomes is CPI created by TI.[7] According to the CPI indicator, corruption eradication has been characterized by backward and forward swings, with little progress achieved overall. Table 9.3. provides Indonesia's score and ranking in the index from 2000 to 2016.

Table 9.2. Corruption Perception Index Indonesia in 2000–2016.

Year	Score	Rank	Number of Countries
2016	3.70	90	176
2015	3.60	88	168
2014	3.40	107	174
2013	3.20	114	177
2012	3.20	118	176
2011	3.00	100	183
2010	2.80	110	178
2009	2.80	111	180
2008	2.60	126	180
2007	2.30	143	179
2006	2.40	130	163
2005	2.20	137	158
2004	2.00	133	145
2003	1.90	122	133
2002	1.90	96	102
2001	1.90	88	91
2000	1.70	85	90

Source: Transparency International. https://www.transparency.org/en/.

---

7   Although the CPI does not show evidence of actual corruption (and the ranking may be subject to biases), it helps inform how the general public sees corruption issues and government performances.

With the caveat that the index measures perceptions, it seems to indicate that despite the various anti-corruption instruments adopted by the Indonesian government, eradication has not made significant progress. Only since 2004, when the KPK began operations, has Indonesia's CPI score and rank progressed relatively constantly, albeit at a low level. Why do various anti-corruption instruments fail to achieve results? This question will be discussed in the following section.

Structural Challenges

It is important to analyze the structural challenges in the landscape of the national political economy to understand why the anti-corruption agenda under *Reformasi* has not been fully achieved. It can be argued that the reform era did not change the power structure much. Democratization that brings about changes to combating corruption cannot appear overnight. It must be admitted that elections in Indonesia have become more democratic, despite the challenges of new money politics, which include the manipulation of campaign funds and the mobilization of economic resources to ensure incumbent victories.

The birth of new political parties after the *Reformasi* did not break the power dynamics of the New Order. Groups that benefited from corrupt systems during the New Order era established most of the existing ruling political parties in Indonesia. While a few parties were initially formed by more democratic actors, the middle ground was taken over by non-democratic groups, such as the National Mandate Party, which were related to New Order power in their character and economic-political networks. As a result, the concentration of power and wealth remains in the hands of a small group of people who are capable of influencing public officials' decision making in many respects, especially with regards to the efficiency of bureaucracy and its administrative discretion.

Good governance, as a new buzzword of the *Reformasi*, generally requires government to make its decision-making processes and management of public institutions more transparent. In that way, the interests of the people are served and protected. The oligarchy, on the other hand, undermines accountability and transparent mechanisms. In this context, more corruption takes place, beyond the legal definition, and thus creates systemic obstacles to enforcing anti-corruption measures. Therefore, it is not surprising that in many high-profile corruption cases, such as the Bantuan Likuiditas Bank Indonesia (BLBI—Central Bank Liquidity Assistance) scandal, the main actors remain untouched.

Under the current liberal democracy, spaces still exist for certain interest groups who control economic resources to exert and maintain their political power, especially over political parties. Instead of articulating people's aspirations, political parties have narrowed their actions to serve the interests of a small group of the society. In practice, we see that the anti-corruption agenda has been side-lined in favor of the economic and political interests of political elites.

As the KPK is regarded as the most powerful anti-corruption agency, efforts to undermine it have taken many forms. Political maneuvering to revise the KPK law has been attempted four times. It is just one example of how political groups try to discredit the agency. Revision of the law to decrease enforcement authority, such as cessation of investigation orders, and limit enforcement tools, such as wiretapping, are likely attempts in the same vein, rather than support for the KPK, as politicians claim (see Butt, 2012: 135–139).

There is strong reason to believe that these attempts were sparked by the KPK's intensive investigation of numerous bribery and corruption cases involving members of parliament, political party elites, their cadres, and local leaders. Numerous surveys conducted by various groups in Indonesia, such as TI, Center for Strategic and International Studies (CSIS), the Polling Centre, and *Kompas* newspaper, have shown how corrupt both national and local politicians are in Indonesia. Respondents to these surveys always rank MPs and political parties as the most corrupt public actors and institutions. In a recent survey conducted by the Polling Centre (2017), for example, parliament was regarded as the number one public institution that neglects its responsibility to eradicate corruption (*Kompas*, 2017a; *BBC*, 2017; *Tempo*, 2017; *Tribunews*,2017).

Widespread corruption in the political sector can also be seen in the data reported by KPK, at least since 2010. Local Heads, Vice Local Heads, parliament members, local parliament members, and senior officials of political parties are all involved in corruption, both in relation to the appointment of public officials, the approval and recommendation of certain policies, and budgeting (see Table 9.4.).

Table 9.3. Political corruption cases handled by the KPK in 2004–2017.

Year	2004	2005	2006	2007	2008	2009	2010	2011	2012	2013	2014	2015	2016	2017	Total
MP	0	0	0	2	7	8	27	5	16	8	9	19	23	10	134
Minister	0	1	1	0	1	1	2	0	1	4	9	3	2	0	25
Governor	1	0	2	1	1	2	1	0	0	2	3	3	1	1	18
Mayor/ Regent/ Vice	0	0	3	6	6	5	4	3	3	3	12	4	9	2	60
Total	1	1	6	9	15	16	34	8	20	17	32	29	34	13	

Source: https://acch.kpk.go.id/id/statistik/tindak-pidana-korupsi/tpk-berdasarkan-profesi-jabatan.

The failure of political reform has threatened the effectiveness of the anti-corruption institutions that have been established. Political elites, parliament members, and businessmen collude and use their authority to control the selection process of public officials, particularly for state agencies that have the authority to combat corruption, appointing candidates who are considered weak and willing to compromise.

Based on the ICW's experience of monitoring four selection cycles of KPK Commissioners as an example, the body responsible for selection (Commission III of the House of Representatives) has never chosen the candidates considered superior in integrity, professionalism, or ability to be the five leaders of the KPK. Instead, they consistently choose mediocre candidates in the hopes of controlling the KPK and protecting their interests. For example, the current Commissioners of KPK, Alexander Marwata and Basaria Panjaitan are considered to be weak, both in terms of ability and integrity. It sends the signal that the parliament has preferred to choose them for the chair.

If they fail to control the selection process, politicians use their power instruments, including their right of inquiry into the KPK, to intimidate and politically suppress KPK law enforcement work. Many believe that the right of inquiry into the KPK was granted in response to the E-KTP corruption case investigation carried out by KPK, which named the House Speaker, Setya Novanto, as a suspect.

Another effort that simultaneously dilutes the anti-corruption agenda is the targeting of KPK commissioners for criminal charges. Although the charges are often murky, and the evidence brought by the investigator weak, the police have the power to order an investigation with or without compelling evidence. This is useful because, according to the KPK law, once the police name a commissioner as a suspect in a criminal case, the commissioner must suspend their work (see Butt, 2011). In the history of the KPK, three criminal charges have been brought against commissioners Bibit Samad Riyanto, Chandra M Hamzah, Abraham Samad, Bambang Widjojanto, and Agus Raharjo.

The ambiguous outcomes of the anti-corruption agenda are not unexpected, since the *Reformasi* was not the idea of the state, but rather the result of public pressure. This contrasts to Singapore and Hong Kong, two city-states that successfully eliminated corruption as a result of political will from the power holders (see Quah, 2017; Febari, 2015). While it is true that public pressure also contributed to creating an effective anti-corruption formula in those countries, the state actors responded to the public's demands. In short, political will must be backed by public pressure and vice versa to formulate a successful anti-corruption program.

Indonesia has an abundance of anti-corruption bodies, a complete anti-corruption legal framework, and a long menu of anti-corruption regulations. However, these do not reflect the presence of political will to fight corruption. As Johnston (2005) argues, anti-corruption strategies are not just legal and administrative formulae that must be applied within public institutions; a strong democracy that cultivates lasting political commitment has to be rooted in social institutions as well. Political will, according to Johnston (2005), is the result of intense political contestation among people and groups to reach political settlement, as opposed to sound technical governance per se.

One of the clearest examples of the country's low level of political will to seriously tackle corruption is the stalled discussion over various important rules. For example, the Bill on Asset Recovery has been discussed in the parliament since 2014, without any indication of when it will be become law. Similarly, the provision to adopt the reverse onus clause to streamline corruption eradication has never been alluded to in the drafting of any existing legislation.

At the same time, existing anti-corruption provisions are not consistently implemented. For example, the provision concerning the obligation to regularly report public officials' wealth to the KPK (known as Laporan Harta Kekayaan Penyelenggara Negara or LHKPN) has not been enforced. According to the KPK, many members of the DPR and local parliaments have not submitted their LHKPN (Kata Data 2017). In terms of international standards, Indonesia ratified the UN anti-corruption convention in 2006, obliging it to adopt international anti-corruption principles. As of 2018, however, neither the parliament nor the executive has held any serious discussions on revising the anti-corruption law to be in line with the principles of the UN convention.

From the above examples, it is clear that the corruption eradication agenda in Indonesia does not have a strong political foundation. On the contrary, the main force supporting the anti-corruption movement lies in civil society groups. It can be argued that the ineffectiveness in combating corruption is due in part to the failure of civil society to transfer its anti-corruption agenda to the political sphere (see Setiyono and Mcleod, 2010). This suggests that efforts to eradicate corruption in Indonesia are characterized by a sharp contrast between the interests of civil society groups advocating for a reform agenda and the interests of the political and economic elite doing what they can to maintain the status quo.

Conclusion

Indonesia's *Reformasi* to build a clean government has lasted for about 20 years. Various public sector improvements have been made, both because of international donor initiatives and public pressure. In terms of eradicating corruption, the establishment of numerous regulations and institutions throughout the reform era were expected to accelerate and streamline a good governance agenda. Arguably, however, most of these efforts have failed. This is indicated by Indonesia's consistently low score in the CPI and the persistent quantity and extensiveness of corruption cases that have increased in parallel to the implementation of various state budget allocation policies.

While the KPK was expected to eradicate corruption, in practice it has not been supported due to a lack of political will to combat corruption on the part of the strong vested interests ruling the economy and politics. This reflects a stagnation of the political reform agenda and democratization process throughout the reform period. The trajectory of good governance in Indonesia reveals that a reform agenda that relies solely on an institutional approach is not sufficient to achieve desired outcomes. As political parties block the political aspirations of citizens they claim to represent, reform becomes impossible to maintain, and political contestation becomes an arena open only to the economic and political elite. As such, Indonesia may not be able to expect much from corruption eradication efforts without confronting the political and economic elites who continue to exploit the public's resources.

References

Aditjondro, George Junus. 1998. *Dari Suharto ke Habibie: Guru Kencing Berdiri, Murid Kencing Berlari: Kedua Puncak Korupsi, Kolusi dan Nepotisme Rezim Orde Baru.* Jakarta: Masyarakat Indonesia untuk Kemanusiaan.

_____. 2006. *Korupsi kepresidenan: Reproduksi Oligarki Berkaki Tiga: Istana, Tangsi, dan Partai Penguasa.* Yogyakarta: LKiS.

Anti-Corruption Clearing House (ACCH). 2018. "TPK Berdasarkan Profesi/Jabatan". December 31, 2018. https://acch.kpk.go.id/id/statistik/tindak-pidana-korupsi/tpk-berdasarkan-profesi-jabatan (accessed May 29, 2018).

BBC. 2017. "DPR 'Paling Korup' menurut Persepsi Masyarakat Indonesia". March 8, 2017. http://www.bbc.com/indonesia/indonesia-39189729 (accessed May 29, 2018).

Blunt, P. et al. 2012. "Patronage's Progress in Post-Soeharto Indonesia". *Public Administration and Development* 32 (1): 64–81.

Butt, Simon. 2011. "Anti-corruption Reform in Indonesia: an Obituary?". *Bulletin of Indonesian Economic Studies* 47 (3): 381–394.

_____. 2012. *Corruption and Law in Indonesia.* Oxon: Routledge.

Febari, Rizki. 2015. *Politik Pemberantasan Korupsi: Strategi ICAC Hong Kong dan KPK Indonesia.* Jakarta: Yayasan Pustaka Obor Indonesia.

Handra, Hefrizal et al. 2017. *Village Fund and Poverty Alleviation. Policy Analysis.* Jakarta: Kompak.

Harian Terbit. 2016. "KPK: 361 Kepala Daerah Terlibat Korupsi". August 11, 2016. http://nasional.harianterbit.com/nasional/2016/08/11/67140/44/25/KPK-361-Kepala-Daerah-Terlibat-Korupsi (accessed May 29, 2018).

Indonesia Corruption Watch (ICW). 2017. *Law Enforcement of Corruption Cases Trend Analysis*. Jakarta: ICW.

Johnston, Michael. 2005. *Syndromes of Corruption: Wealth, Power, and Democracy*. Cambridge: Cambridge University Press.

Kata Data. 2017. "KPK: Separuh Lebih Pejabat Negara Belum Lapor Harta Kekayaan". March 14, 2017. https://katadata.co.id/berita/2017/03/14/kpk-anggota-parlemen-paling-tak-patuh-lapor-harta-kekayaan (accessed May 29, 2018).

Kirana, Glenys. 2014. "Decentralization Dilemma in Indonesia: Does Decentralization breed Corruption?". Independent Study Project (ISP) Paper 1984.

Kolstad, Ivar, and Arne Wiig. 2016. "Does Democracy Reduce Corruption?" *Democratization* 23 (7): 1198–1215.

Kompas. 2016. "Kepala BPK DKI Resmi Diganti". February 9, 2016. http://megapolitan.kompas.com/read/2016/02/09/17251231/Kepala.BPK.DKI.Resmi.Dicopot.dari.Jabatannya (accessed May 29, 2018).

Kompas. 2017a. "Jadi yang Paling Korup, DPR dan Partai Politik Seharusnya Malu". March 9, 2017. https://nasional.kompas.com/read/2017/03/09/15054321/jadi.yang.paling.korup.dpr.dan.partai.politik.seharusnya.malu?page=all (accessed May 29, 2018).

_____. 2017b. "KPK Tetapkan Irjen Kemendes dan Auditor BPK Jadi Tersangka Suap". May 27, 2017. http://nasional.kompas.com/read/2017/09/22/17004071/kpk-tetapkan-tersangka-auditor-bpk-dan-gm-jasa-marga-purbaleunyi (accessed May 29, 2018).

_____. 2017c. "KPK Tetapkan Tersangka Auditor BPK dan GM Jasa Marga Purbaleunyi". September 22, 2017. http://nasional.kompas.com/read/2017/05/27/19322131/kpk.tetapkan.irjen.kemendes.dan.auditor.bpk.jadi.tersangka.suap (accessed May 29, 2018).

Kompas. 2018. "Skor IPK Tak Meningkat, Agenda Pemberantasan Korupsi Dinilai Stagnan". February 22, 2018. https://nasional.kompas.com/read/2018/02/22/23550051/skor-ipk-tak-meningkat-agenda-pemberantasan-korupsi-dinilai-stagnan (accessed May 29, 2018).

Kontan. 2016. "Ini yang Beda Audit KPK dan BPK Soal Sumber Waras". June 15, 2016. http://nasional.kontan.co.id/news/ini-alasan-kpk-tak-salahi-pembelian-sumber-waras (accessed May 29, 2018).

Quah, Jon S.T. 2017. "Five Success Stories in Combating Corruption: Lessons for Policy Makers". *Asian Education and Development Studies* 6 (3): 275–289.

Setiyono, Budi. 2015. "Does Governance Reform in A Democratic Transition Country Reduce the Risk of Corruption? Evidence from Indonesia". In *Corruption, Good Governance and Economic Development: Contemporary Analysis and Case Studies,* edited by R.N. Ghosh and M.A.B. Siddique, pp. 217-255. Singapore: World Scientific.

Setiyono, Budi, and Ross H. McLeod. 2010. "Civil Society Organizations' Contribution to the Anti-corruption Movement in Indonesia". *Bulletin of Indonesian Economic Studies* 46 (3): 347–370.

Tempo. 2017. "Survei Ini Membuktikan Partai Politik Paling Tidak Dipercaya". July 27, 2017. https://nasional.tempo.co/read/894871/survei-ini-membuktikan-partai-politik-paling-tidak-dipercaya (accessed May 29, 2018).

The Jakarta Post. 2018. "Editorial: Sluggish Antigraft Drive". February 26, 2018. http://www.thejakartapost.com/academia/2018/02/26/editorial-sluggish-antigraft-drive.html (accessed May 29, 2018).

Tribunnews. 2017. "DPR Lembaga Paling Korup di Indonesia Tahun 2016". March 9, 2017. http://www.tribunnews.com/nasional/2017/03/09/dpr-lembaga-terkorup-di-indonesia-tahun-2016 (accessed May 29, 2018).

World Bank. 1997. Corruption and Economic Development. In World Bank. *Helping Countries Combat Corruption: The Role of the World Bank*. Washington DC.: World Bank. http://www1.worldbank.org/publicsector/anticorrupt/corruptn/cor02.htm (accessed May 29, 2018).

Chapter 10

Beyond the Enclave?

Human Rights Promotion Strategies in Post-*Reformasi* Indonesia

Suh Jiwon

Introduction

It appears that post-*Reformasi* Indonesia is equipped with human rights instruments on many levels. The Indonesian government has a directorate of human rights under the Ministry of Law and Human Rights, which changed its name from the Ministry of Justice in 2001.[1] Since 1998, the Indonesian government has introduced Rencana Aksi Nasional Hak Asasi Manusia (RANHAM—National Action Plans for Human Rights) every five years. In 2010, the Director-General of Human Rights, Harkristuti Harkrisnowo, proudly announced that Indonesia was the only country with local level action plan committees, among twenty-four countries that have similar plans (Hukumonline, 2010).

Post-*Reformasi* Indonesia has ratified eight United Nations (UN) human rights treaties in total, in addition to two conventions that were ratified under Suharto's rule. Now Indonesia is busy participating in human

---

1   Indonesia joined the ranks of countries that promote human rights with a specialized human rights ministry; Angola, Argentina, Benin, Bolivia, Burkina Faso, Chad, the Democratic Republic of Congo (DRC), Ecuador, Iceland, Mauritius, Montenegro, and Peru have a Ministry of Justice and Human Rights like Indonesia, while Brazil, Iraq, and Pakistan have a stand-alone Ministry of Human Rights.

rights treaty bodies, including the Universal Periodic Review (UPR) of the UN Human Rights Council, where each government reports on the progress of the human rights situation every five years.

The human rights promotion strategies of post-*Reformasi* Indonesia have several characteristics. First, Indonesia established new national bodies specialized in rights promotion and monitoring, such as Komisi Nasional Anti-Kekerasan terhadap Perempuan (Komnas Perempuan—National Commission on Violence against Women) and Lembaga Perlindungan Saksi dan Korban (LPSK—Witness and Victim Protection Agency), and Komisi Nasional Hak Asasi Manusia (Komnas HAM—the National Commission of Human Rights), which was established in 1993. I call these specialized bodies "human rights enclaves." These institutions were introduced to improve human rights protection, and they have undoubtedly worked in that direction, often in cooperation with each other. Creating new agencies is a convenient solution, because it is more difficult to reform existing institutions. While these new entities are helpful to demonstrate a commitment to human rights to the international community, if they remain unable to transform the behavior of existing government institutions, such as the Prosecutor's Office, the courts, and the military, they are nothing more than an enclave isolated from the rest of the government.

Second, by introducing new plans, instruments, and institutions, Indonesia is following an identity-affirming strategy for human rights. Indonesian elites promoted the country's new identity as a promoter of human rights and democracy in the region and beyond to resolve its "image problem" in the aftermath of the Asian financial crisis, the bloody referendum in East Timor, as well as riots and communal conflicts. Indonesia supported inserting human rights language in the Association of Southeast Asian Nations (ASEAN) Charter and creating a regional human rights mechanism (Sukma, 2011; Ciorciari, 2012). At the same time, Indonesia embraced the identity of "the third largest democracy in the world" and actively engaged in democracy promotion, launching the annual Bali Democracy Forum in 2008 (Karim, 2017).

This identity-building strategy builds on the New Order tradition of "human rights as foreign policy," which was characterized by two main features: its orientation to the outside and its creation of agencies specializing in human rights, the prime example being the National Commission of Human Rights established by Suharto. Indeed, Indonesian human rights promotion strategies generally originated in the efforts of the Suharto government to counter the international uproar over abuses in East Timor.

Many human rights campaigners and supporters of an "ideational approach" in International Relations believe that by ratifying international human rights treaties, states will eventually acquire a positive, human-rights-friendly identity (Hafner-Burton et al., 2008). If this idea is correct, then simply using the language and label of human rights more often is a meaningful practice.

There are reasons to doubt the effectiveness of carving out human rights enclaves and affirming new labels and identities, however. First, norms and practices can be decoupled. Repressive regimes tend to embrace human rights norms without the burden of adhering to them (Hafner-Burton et al., 2008), just as the New Order regime continued repressive practices despite the existence of the human rights commission. Second, the presence of human-rights-oriented agencies does not guarantee reform of existing institutions. As we will see with how the existing human rights court system has dealt with past human rights abuses, while "enclave" institutions allow human rights abuse cases to be heard, existing institutions, such as the military court (an institution that still plays a role in recent abuses by the security forces), are not significanty affected by their presence. Third, "enclave" institutions may be used to pre-empt more rigorous international intervention.

Fourth, the labels 'human rights' and 'democracy' may conceal meanings that deviate from standard definitions. The Bali Democracy Forum, for example, was often criticized for including countries without a modicum of procedural democracy. While the Forum was presented as an effort to promote democracy, it was not clear what democracy it was promoted. My case study of the *kabupaten/kota peduli HAM* (human rights cities/regencies) program, which certifies "human-rights-friendly" local governments under the auspices of the Ministry of Law and Human Rights, demonstrates that human rights labels can be used without incorporating core human rights values.

Fifth, new confidence acquired from adopting the identity of human rights promoter invalidates the conventional campaign strategy of applying pressure through bilateral channels. As I will show with my fourth case study on the war on drugs, the Jokowi administration proceeded with executions of foreign drug traffickers despite possible tensions in bilateral relations. The executions suggest that the tradition of "human rights as foreign policy" stands at a crossroads after two decades of democratic rule.

Case Studies

The (ad hoc) Human Rights Court

The human rights court system was built to show that Indonesia could "handle" its own human rights abuses. By giving the Komnas HAM authority to compile preliminary reports on cases deemed to have elements of gross human rights violations, the system helped new agencies, such as the LPSK and Komnas HAM itself, generate some victim-oriented policy outputs. Among these, medical aid from the LPSK was perhaps the most useful for aging victims. After the first few years, however, there was no progress in the old, established institutions, such as the Prosecutor's Office and the court itself, whose roles are crucial in making the system work.

At the onset of *Reformasi*, it seemed clear that military perpetrators of human rights abuses should be tried. It was less clear where such cases should be sent. After the bloody 1999 referendum in East Timor, a human rights court system was added to the existing judicial system. In 2000, Law Number 26 on the human rights court was enacted to address the violence in East Timor (Suh, 2015a). The enactment was accelerated to preempt a possible United Nations court hearing. During the nearly two decades since then, only three cases have gone through Indonesia's human rights court system, which imitates the International Criminal Court, borrowing heavily from its Rome Statute. Trials in Tanjung Priok and Abepura (Papua) demonstrated that the products of international pressure could be used for cases that attracted less foreign attention, but the sentences from the trials were disappointing to many observers.

The last time any human rights court opened a case of gross human rights violations was in 2004. Later in the year, the outgoing parliament (DPR, 1999–2004) and President Megawati signed the bill to establish the Truth and Reconciliation Commission (TRC). Many among the political elites regarded the TRC—which President Susilo Bambang Yudhoyono, Megawati's successor, never actually established—as an alternative body that would negate the necessity of the human rights court system. After the Constitutional Court's decision in 2006 to repeal the TRC Law Number 27 Year 2004, the slim possibility of a new commission, based on a future TRC law, continued to promise an alternative to the human rights court (Suh, 2015a). Human rights NGOs were not particularly enthusiastic to campaign for more human rights courts, fearing that light sentences or acquittals would disappoint victims and prematurely "resolve" cases without adequate justice.

Indonesia at the Crossroads: Transformation and Challenges

Table 10.1. Steps taken based on the human rights court law.

Case	Event occurred	Komnas HAM reported	DPR gave recommendations	Presidential Decree	Case in (*ad hoc*) Human Rights Court opened
East Timor	1999	2000	2001 (recommended)	2001	2002
Tanjung Priok	1984	2000	2001 (recommended)	2001	2003
Abepura, Papua	2001	2001	not necessary	not necessary	2004
Trisakti-Semanggi I, II (TSS)	1998, 1999	2002	2001 (not recommended)	pending	pending
1998 May riots	1998	2003	pending	pending	pending
Wasior-Wamena, Papua	2001, 2003	2004	not necessary	not necessary	pending
Enforced Disappearances	1997–1998	2006	2009 (recommended)	pending	pending
Talangsari	1989	2008	pending	pending	pending
Petrus	1982–1985	2012	pending	pending	pending
1965–1966 Communist Purge	1965–1966	2012	pending	pending	pending
Jambo Keupok (South Aceh)	2003	2016	not necessary	not necessary	pending
Simpang KKA (North Aceh)	1999	2016	pending	pending	pending
Rumoh Geudong (Pidie, Aceh)	1989–1998	2018	pending	pending	pending

Source: Author's compilation from various sources.

316

The human rights court system has remained paralyzed, because its older components, such as the Prosecutor General's Office, do not work for the system. In the meantime, new institutions continue to produce victim-oriented policy outputs. Komnas HAM commissioners continue to produce preliminary reports, which are required as the first step for a new case to be sent to the human rights court. The report for the Trisakti-Semanggi case, comprising three incidents of shooting protesters in 1998 and 1999, came out in March 2002; three more—one on the 1998 May riots, another on the enforced disappearances of activists during 1997–1998, and a second Papua case file on killings in Wasior and Wamena—were sent to the Prosecutor General's Office during the 2002–2007 term of the commission. The 2007–2012 commission, headed by Ifdhal Kasim, produced the Talangsari report in 2008 and later announced its decisions on the *penembakan misterius* (petrus—mysterious shootings) killings (the extrajudicial killings of alleged criminals in the 1980s), and the 1965–1966 Communist purge cases before its term expired in 2012. Otto Nur Abdullah (Otto Syamsuddin Ishak), the initial leader of the 2012–2017 commission, helped compile reports on two Aceh cases out of his goal of five in total. The current commissioners (2017–2022) finished a report on one of the Aceh cases, Rumoh Geudong (the torture house) used by the military during the Daerah Operasi Militer (DOM—military operation area) era in 1989–1998.[2]

Many commissioners appointed by Suharto did not leave the body for almost a decade after 1998. It was quite difficult for the commissioners to agree on basic points, such as whether the Buru camp, a forced labor camp that detained alleged Communists without trial for up to ten years, should be regarded as a case of gross human rights violations (Suh, 2016). Recent preliminary reports are follow-up measures to initiatives of the *Reformasi* period that remained uncomplete because of the fragile situation, as in the case of Aceh, or because of internal disagreement in the Komnas HAM, as in the case of the 1965–1966 Communist purge. As the commission has

---

2   The remaining two from the Aceh case file are disappearances in Bener Meriah and a mass killing at the Bumi Flora plantation in East Aceh.

nearly completed its delayed homework, it is not likely that new reports will emerge anytime soon.

In post-*Reformasi* Indonesia, the preliminary reports are the only thing close to official acknowledgement that gross human rights violations occurred in the past. As such, they are used as grounds for related measures. In an initiative imitating policies of Argentina and Chile, the families of thirteen victims of forced disappearance received certificates from the Komnas HAM stating that their missing loved ones were indeed missing.

Later, LPSK—a new institution established in 2008—launched a program providing medical aid for victims of cases recognized by Komnas HAM as having elements of gross human rights violations.[3] During 2012–2018, there were 3,553 beneficiaries of such medical aid. The majority—3,503—were victims of the 1965–1966 Communist purge. Of the remaining fifty recipients, the majority was from Aceh (12 from the Simpang KKA case in North Aceh and 14 from the Jambo Keupok case in South Aceh). Others were victims of the Talangsari massacre (11 recipients), enforced disappearances (8 in total), and the Tanjung Priok killings (5).[4]

The problem with the Komnas HAM reports, however, is that there has been little follow-up to the preliminary inquiries. Few steps are taken outside the like-minded institutions of the Komnas HAM and the LPSK. For example, the DPR recommendation in 2009 to search for the thirteen missing people was never fulfilled by the police or Komando Pasukan Khusus (Kopassus—Special Forces Command).[5] After the 2012 reports on

---

3   The families of the 1998 May riots victims—those who were trapped in the flames while looting—are not eligible for the medical benefits, however. Author's interview with an IKOHI staff member, July 18, 2017. The victims of communal violence in places such as Maluku and Sulawesi are also not eligible, because there is no preliminary report based on the human rights court law (Number 26 Year 2000) for them.

4   The data is from Abdul Haris (2018). I thank Zaenal Mutaqqin for sharing it with me. Talangsari and Tanjung Priok are locations in South Sumatra and Jakarta, respectively, where a government crackdown on Islamists led to killing civilians.

5   This recommendation was made separately from the DPR's support for an ad-hoc human rights tribunal for this case. The activists, already frustrated with the human rights court system, hoped that a search team consisting of related government agencies might help to determine the status of the disappeared even in the absence of an ad-hoc human rights tribunal, to no avail.

petrus and the Communist purge, President Yudhoyono delegated follow-up measures to the Coordinating Ministry of Political, Legal and Security Affairs. Djoko Suyanto, the then Coordinating Minister, was openly and firmly against any official measures, including a TRC, for the Communist purge (*The Jakarta Post*, 2012). The Prosecutor General's Office practice of returning the reports to the Komnas HAM for technical reasons did not change after Suyanto's term. President Jokowi left the matter to the same ministry, and with his frequent cabinet reshuffles, policies for past human rights abuses fluctuated. During Jokowi's first five-year term, many policy proposals were put forward to settle past human rights abuses, but no new moves were made by the Prosecutor's Office or the court.

During Jokowi's first term, it appeared that the Wasior-Wamena case from Papua might lead to a prosecutor's investigation. In 2013, Indonesia began engaging in regional forums with Melanesian and Pacific countries and the UN that supported West Papua's rights. Early in 2017, Coordinating Minister Wiranto ordered the Komnas HAM to revise the 2004 report on the two cases (*Tribunnews*, 2017).[6] Wiranto's predecessor, then Coordinating Minister Luhut Pandjaitan, had revealed a plan to settle abuses in Papua—with the military attacks against villagers in Wasior and Wamena among three priority cases—and invite the ambassadors from Pacific countries to serve as witnesses to the process (*The Jakarta Post*, 2016). Foreign Minister Retno Marsudi announced that the government was preparing the case to be tried in the human rights court at the Universal Periodic Review session of the UN (Kontras, 2017). Talks of a possible human rights court for Papua were another sign that the human rights court is useful in foreign affairs, this time to placate the growing sympathy for West Papuan people from Pacific governments.

---

6   One remaining case was 2014 Paniai shooting, in which four students—aged 16 to 18—were shot dead during protests in Paniai, Papua. The Komnas HAM formed a preliminary inquiry team for this case, but the team just ceased activities, with no results. Luhut's mention of "three" cases is confusing, because at Komnas HAM the attacks in Wamena and Wasior were compiled in the same case file.

The Military Court

The failure of military court reform in Indonesia reflects the difficulty of countering entrenched interests by reforming an existing institution, as opposed to the relative ease of adding a new institution to the existing array. Cases of extrajudicial killings and torture are still being reported and sent to the military court, as in the late New Order period. Meanwhile, the practices of the military court—light sentences for low-ranking soldiers with trials and follow-up measures kept secret—remain largely unchanged. Except that the military court is now officially under the Supreme Court rather than military headquarters, the military justice system has not been reformed in the last two decades (Horowitz, 2013).

The Indonesian public learned about the military court for the first time in 1991, after strong international pressure for justice in the case of the Dili (Santa Cruz) massacre. As a response, the Suharto government sent military officers to an internal honor council, while court-martialing low-ranking soldiers in the military court with charges such as disobeying orders. The military court was used for cases of military abuses throughout the 1990s, even after Suharto's fall. Many of the well-known tragedies of the transitional period—clashes among the police, protesters, rioters, and paid agents on July 27, 1996 at the headquarters of Partai Demokrasi Indonesia (PDI—Indonesian Democracy Party), the shooting at Trisakti university on May 21, 1998, activist kidnappings during 1997–1998, the murder of labor activist Marsinah (1994), the murder of Islamic scholar Teungku Bantaqiah and his pupils in West Aceh (1999), and the murder of the Papuan nationalist leader Theys Eluay (2002)—were sent to the military court or the *koneksitas* court. The latter was used in cases of suspected civilian involvement in the crime, and combined military and civil elements in the trial process. The military court handled less well-known cases of military abuses in various parts of the country as well (Al Araf et al., 2007; Yudhawiranata, 2009).

Advocates of human rights and military reform have criticized the practices of the military court. Soldiers are tried in the military court for all sorts of crimes, including those perpetrated off-duty. The court was responsible to the military hierarchy and was not under the supervision of the public court. The military court is notoriously difficult to monitor, and it has never been clear to the public whether those sentenced to jail actually serve their terms. In some cases, soldiers discharged by the court were later found to have been promoted in the military (Kontras, 2009).

Adding a human rights court on top of the existing court system was a solution to the problem of the military jurisdiction. As we have seen, however, the human rights court had its own problems. Moreover, as the human rights court law defines "gross violations" in almost the same way that the Rome Statute of the International Criminal Court does, only crimes against humanity and genocide could be sent to the court. To achieve justice for victims of "lesser" crimes, reform of the military court had to be pursued separately.

Military justice reform has taken nearly two decades and has not been completed. Although a Majelis Permusyawaratan Rakyat (MPR—People's Consultative Assembly) decree of 2000 underlined the necessity of military justice reform, stating that Tentara Nasional Indonesia (TNI—Indonesian National Armed Forces) personnel should be "subject to the authority of military courts in regard to violations of military law and subject to civil courts in regard to violations of general criminal law" (Crouch, 2010: 170), it was not until the 2004–2009 DPR that debates on the reform really began. While the military was staunchly opposed to any civilian jurisdiction over its members, party politicians agreed to revise the system so that off-duty crimes of soldiers would fall under civilian jurisdiction (Mietzner, 2009). This proposal, however, was eventually stalled by the government.

Abuses by the security forces against civilians continued to be reported until recently. In 2008, land conflict in East Java led to bloody struggles between members of the navy and villagers of Alas Tlogo, resulting in the deaths of four villagers at the hands of navy personnel. Those involved in the incident were sentenced to jail terms of about one-and-a-half years each, and were not discharged from the armed forces.

In 2011, police officers shot at anti-mine protesters in Bima, West Nusa Tenggara, killing at least two of them. The perpetrators received only a few days of detention. In 2010, a "YouTube case"—as the Indonesian government calls it (UN Human Rights Council, 2012)—attracted media attention after a YouTube clip showing Indonesian soldiers torturing two Papuan men shocked the public. Four soldiers received jail terms of five to seven months each (*Tempo*, 2011). While the sentences for human rights abuses from the military court do not match the crime, there are no real alternatives, especially considering the recent record of the human rights court.

Human Rights Cities

The human rights cities program is a prime example of the human rights promotion strategy of identity-building. As abuses by local law-enforcement agencies and mob violence are among the primary sources of human rights violations, law enforcement at the local level is a key to effective protection of human rights. Often with the assistance of global and national advocacy networks, Indonesian cities and regencies now declare themselves to be "human rights cities." A few among these have adopted a full charter or a special regulation on human rights. The Ministry of Law and Human Rights introduced a certifying system for a local administration that wants to be qualified as a human rights city.

It is widely agreed that the idea of human rights cities originated from Henry Lefebvre's idea of "rights to the city." In Latin American countries, the idea of "rights to the city" was used in the struggles of the poor for urban space. Less radical explorations of the links between human rights and local administrations emerged in UN-related agencies. Several cities, such as Barcelona, Montreal, and Rosario (Argentina) adopted their own human rights charters (Kang, 2009; Jung, 2012). The concept of a human-rights-friendly city was propagated in the Asian region through an initiative from Gwangju, a Korean city famous for its 1980 uprising against the incoming military regime (Nurkhoiron, 2017). Every year since 2011, the city administration invites hundreds of participants from South Korea and overseas to its World Human Rights Cities Forum.

In Indonesia, Palu of Central Sulawesi played a leading role by adopting a mayor's regulation in 2013 to implement the national action plan for human rights at the local level. Rusdi Mastura, the mayor of Palu, was committed to reconciliation with victims of the Communist purge in 1965–1966. The regulation thus created a ground on which the city of Palu could provide special services for victims of human rights abuses, including the purge victims. Bandung followed suit, adopting a human rights charter two years later.

Not all human rights cities have specific policy goals as in Palu, however. Overall, the human rights city project seems to be largely based on the belief that projecting a positive identity of a "human rights city" will somehow improve the human rights situation in local communities. In 2015, at a signing ceremony of MoUs on the implementation of Human Rights Cities in Indonesia, a Komnas HAM commissioner said that the title is not for the "best" model cities; a city does not even need to be human rights friendly to be named such, and it is all about the process, rather than achievement (Elsam, 2015). With its supporters focusing on spreading the identity as widely as possible rather than deepening it, it is no wonder that increasing the number of cities, rather than the substance of the certification, is the goal of the project. To this end, the Komnas HAM and Indonesian NGO Forum on Indonesian Development (INFID) at one point planned to contact 100 mayors and regents to convince them to sign human rights city MoUs (*Kompas*, 2017a).

In 2013, the Ministry of Law and Human Rights adopted a regulation on the human rights city too, providing a certification procedure for local administrations. By December 2018, no less than 346 cities and regencies—more than two thirds of all local administrations—had listed themselves as human rights cities (Berita Satu, 2018). The criteria for human rights cities as provided by the Ministry of Law and Human Rights focus on six economic and social rights—rights to health, rights to education, *hak atas kependudukan* (residential rights), rights to work, rights to decent housing, rights to sustainable environment—and rights of women and children. The list seems more like criteria made by a development agency, rather than a ministry for human rights. The measurement for women's and children's rights includes five dichotomous variables that gauge the presence of regulations and programs aimed at protecting both women's and children's rights and two quantitative variables on reported cases of domestic violence and child labor.

It is true that the idea of "rights to the city"—especially its Latin American version—originally emphasized social and economic rights such as housing and poverty eradication. Nevertheless, the absence of civil and political rights in the ministry's criteria is conspicuous. In my view, the absence has more to do with earlier Southeast Asian strategies of promoting human rights in the region in their own way than with the Latin American ideas of "rights to the city." As early as 1993, ASEAN governments expressed commitment to human rights with the Bangkok Declaration. The Declaration was far from embracing core elements of civil and political rights, however. Ciorciari (2012) observes that it emphasized the significance of economic, social, and cultural rights and the "right to development" as a universal right, while expressing concern that existing human rights mechanisms focus on civil and political rights. In other words, ASEAN governments redefined, rather than denied, human rights, to be more compatible with authoritarian rule. The governments also recognized the rights of women and children, believing that these "less controversial" rights should be the first step in human rights promotion in the region (Ciorciari, 2012).

The problem with the human rights city criteria, created in line with the conventional ASEAN human rights promotion strategies, is that nothing prevents a city or regency from receiving the title of a human rights city as long as it has a decent developmental record and some positive programs to promote the rights of women and children on paper, even if the same city or regency has discriminatory local regulations or severe violations of civil and political rights occur. Even the pioneer cities of human rights, regarded as models by Komnas HAM and INFID, are not beyond criticism. An alliance of non-governmental organizations in Bandung has protested the declaration of human rights by its mayor Ridwan Kamil, arguing that the label of a human rights city serves to whitewash the human rights situation in the city, where many cases of rights violations still occur (ASASI, 2016).

It is perhaps too early to discuss the impacts of the human rights cities program on local human rights protection in Indonesia, as the program is quite new. A case from Aceh, however, illustrates how the presence of charters and local regulations of a declaratory nature do not hinder local political elites from adopting discriminatory regulations. On November 8, 2008, the Aceh Charter on Women's Rights was signed by the governor of Aceh and leaders of the provincial parliament, law-enforcement agencies, and non-governmental organizations, including the Islamic scholar council. The next year, the Aceh parliament enacted a *qanun* (provincial bylaw) on the empowerment and protection of women. Although the charter and the *qanun* were praised as "the first charter on women's rights in the Islamic world" and the first bylaw for "gender justice" in Indonesia (Ichwan, 2013), discriminatory measures by local governments aiming to control women's bodies—such as the 2010 crackdown on pants-wearing women in West Aceh and the 2013 ban on women riding motorcycles in a straddling position in North Aceh (Feener, 2013; Suh, 2015b)—were subsequently imposed.

In conclusion, it remains to be seen whether the human rights cities program can cultivate local allies of the existing human rights enclaves. If a local government is committed to specific goals, such as assisting victims of abuse, as in Palu, a local regulation can play a positive supporting role. As long as the program continues to focus on increasing the number of self-proclaimed human rights cities with its problematic criteria, however, it will not improve protection of human rights. Such focus indicates that the program is oriented toward showing the outside world—at the Universal Periodic Review session (UN Human Rights Council, 2017) for example—that Indonesia pays attention to human rights. It does not indicate if, and how, such titles are considered and practiced by those in the local community.

War on Drugs

There is one policy arena where post-*Reformasi* Indonesian governments risk damage to the country's international reputation: executions. Amid widespread domestic support for the execution of drug dealers, President Jokowi issued a controversial order to shoot them on the spot.

While the history of capital punishment in Indonesia dates to the early days of the republic, executions were not common. Under Sukarno's rule, only three executions took place. Thirty-seven people were officially executed during the three decades under Suharto: twenty-two Communists, nine murderers, and six Islamic terrorists.

Post-*Reformasi* governments have already executed more people than that; about 60% of them were drug dealers. Indonesia introduced the death penalty for drug dealers in 1975, along with Malaysia and Singapore. In 2004, weeks before the presidential run-off election, Megawati ordered the execution of an Indian drug trafficker (News.com.au, 2015). The use of capital punishment became more frequent under the Yudhoyono administration. A total of sixteen people—drug traffickers, murderers, and the Bali bombing terrorists—were executed during his first term (McRae, 2013). Ten of the sixteen were executed in 2008, a year before the presidential election. In 2013, five more executions took place.

President Jokowi announced no clemency for those convicted of drug offenses and ordered the execution of eighteen people in eighteen months: fourteen in 2015 and four in 2016 (*Indonesia at Melbourne,* 2017). He did this despite the strong reaction overseas, especially from Australia. Executions of drug traffickers inevitably become a diplomatic issue, because most death row drug dealers in Indonesia are foreigners. Jokowi's execution of the "Bali Nine" drug traffickers in 2015 was the most serious diplomatic incident over the country's capital punishment since the Netherland's reaction to the execution of the G30S[7] prisoners in the 1990s (Berg, 2001). As two of those killed in 2015 were Australian citizens, criticism of the Indonesian government was intense. After the executions, the Australian government temporarily recalled its ambassador in protest. France and Brazil also criticized Jokowi's policies.[8]

Jokowi's war on drugs can be interpreted as an attempt to counter the accusations that he is a weak leader, especially compared to his political rival Prabowo Subianto (Djamin and Adiwena, 2018). In other words, just as his predecessors did, Jokowi used executions to boost his domestic popularity. In 2017, Jokowi even called for a "shooting on the spot" policy for suspected drug dealers. According to Amnesty International, police killed a total of eight foreigners, including three Chinese, and an estimated sixty Indonesians during arrest attempts between January and August 2017 (Amnesty International, 2017).[9] In total, seventy-nine suspects were killed during anti-drug operations in 2017 (*Kompas*, 2017c).

Jokowi's war on drugs reflects Indonesia's new confidence in the face of international pressure over the country's human rights records. However, the war does not mean that Indonesia has abandoned its identity as a human rights promoter altogether. While Coordinating Minister Wiranto boasted that Suharto's legacies of *petrus* killings had become an example for Philippine President Rodrigo Duterte's infamous war on drugs, President Jokowi himself was silent on the point (*Kompas*, 2017b). Moreover, Jokowi stopped executions of death row drug dealers after eighteen executions in 2015 and 2016, before making an extrajudicial turn.[10] While Jokowi wants to fight against drug trafficking and gain popularity at the same time, he does not want Indonesia to be perceived as an outright violator of human

---

7   G30S is an acronym for the *Gerakan 30 September* (September 20 movement), a failed coup attempt in 1965. G30S prisoners who were executed were deemed to have been involved in the coup attempt and were thus tried in a special military court.

8   While the Frenchman was able to delay his execution at the last minute in 2015, the Brazilian was put to death, despite his mental health problems.

9   Amnesty International 2017 also reports that eighteen such killings took place in 2016.

10   In addition, the news on "firm actions" involving extrajudicial killings became rare from the beginning of 2018.

rights, invalidating an identity that the nation's foreign policy elites have carefully built.

Conclusion

The Indonesian human rights policies of the 1990s were formulated under specific international conditions of the post-Cold War era and with intense international pressure on Indonesia over its human rights abuses. The fear of unwanted foreign intervention in domestic affairs was one of the primary motives for Indonesian political elites to carve out human rights enclaves by creating new independent commissions. Commitment to human rights was professed at multiple levels, from the international to the local. The new norms and institutions offered new identities and created some tangible policy outputs, for example the provision of medical aid to Communist purge victims from the LPSK with help from the Komnas HAM, a result of the human rights court system. However, adding new institutions is different from reforming existing ones, and despite numerous human rights training sessions, practices in the rest of officialdom remain problematic, though not as outright repressive as they were under the authoritarian regime.

It is not clear whether the "human rights as foreign policy" tradition will continue. For decades, Indonesian officials have learned how to respond to accusations from abroad. Now they know that a few cases of extrajudicial killings and torture will not invite harsh, if any, reaction from leading powers and major donors. Indonesian officials are also sophisticated enough to redefine human rights as development goals—those social, economic, and cultural rights—as we have seen in the case of the human rights cities program.

So far, Indonesian human rights promotion strategies of establishing a few specialized agencies and claiming a human-rights-friendly identity have been effective to counter international criticism of abuses in places like East Timor and Papua. It remains to be seen, however, whether they can work effectively to address violent persecution of minorities and pervasive impunity for human rights abuses, past and present.

References

Amnesty International. 2017. "Indonesia: At Least 60 Killed as Police Shootings of Drug Suspects Skyrocket". *Amnesty.org*, August 16, 2017. https://www.amnesty.org/en/latest/news/2017/08/indonesia-at-least-60-killed-as-police-shootings-of-drug-suspects-skyrocket/ (accessed September 2, 2019).

ASASI. 2016. "Membangun Kota dengan Konsep Kota/Kabupaten HAM". *asasi.elsam.or.id.* http://asasi.elsam.or.id/membangun-kota-dengan-konsep-kotakabupaten-ham/ (accessed September 2, 2018).

Berg, Esther M. van den. 2001. *The Influence of Domestic NGOs on Dutch Human Rights Policy: Case Studies on South Africa, Namibia, Indonesia, and East Timor.* Antwerpen: Intersentia.

Berita Satu. 2018. "346 Kabupaten/Kota Dapat Penghargaan HAM dari Kemkumham". December 11, 2018. https:// www.beritasatu.com/ nasional/527199/346-kabupatenkota-dapat-penghargaan-ham-dari-kemkumham (accessed September 2, 2019).

Ciorciari, John D. 2012. "Institutionalizing Human Rights in Southeast Asia". *Human Rights Quarterly* 34 (3): 695–725.

Crouch, Harold. 2010. *Political Reform in Indonesia after Soeharto.* Singapore: ISEAS.

Djamin, Rafendi and Wirya Adiwena. 2018. "Death Penalty in ASEAN: No Progress Should Be Taken for Granted." *Thinking ASEAN: From Southeast Asia on Southeast Asia* 31 (January 2018): 2–4.

Elsam. 2015. "Human Rights Cities, Political Awakening Movement of Urban Community". May 4, 2015. http://elsam.or.id/2015/05/human-rights-cities-the-political-awareness-movement-of-city-society/ (accessed November 1, 2017).

Feener, R. Michael. 2013. *Shari'a and Social Engineering: The Implementation of Islamic Law in Contemporary Aceh, Indonesia.* Oxford: Oxford University Press.

Hafner-Burton, Emilie M. et al. 2008. "International Human Rights Law and the Politics of Legitimation: Repressive States and Human Rights Treaties." *International Sociology* 23 (1): 115–141.

Horowitz, Donald L. 2013. *Constitutional Change and Democracy in Indonesia.* Cambridge: Cambridge University Press.

Hukumonline. 2010. "Pemerintah Siapkan RANHAM Periode 2010–2014". February 4, 2010. http://www.hukumonline.com/berita/baca/lt4b6aa27ae0e2f/ranham (accessed September 2, 2018).

Ichwan, Moch Nur. 2013. "Alternatives to Shariatism: Progressive Muslim Intellectuals, Feminists, Queers and Sufis in Contemporary Aceh." In *Regime Change, Democracy and Islam: The Case of Indonesia,* pp. 137-179. Universiteit Leiden.

Indonesia at Melbourne. 2017. "New Hope for Abolition of the Death Penalty?". May 2. 2017. http://indonesiaatmelbourne.unimelb.edu.au/new-hope-for-abolition-of-the-death-penalty/ (accessed September 1, 2018).

Jung, Sung-Hoon. 2012. "The Crisis of Human Rights and the Task of Human Rights City." *Minjujuuiwa Ingwon (Journal of Democracy and Human Rights)* 12 (3): 381–406.

Kang, Hyun-Soo. 2009. "The Evolving Concept of 'the Right to the City' and Related Social Movements". *Gonggangwa* Sahoe *(Space and Environment)* 32: 42–90.

Karim, Moch Faisal. 2017. "Role Conflict and the Limits of State Identity: The Case of Indonesia in Democracy Promotion." *The Pacific Review* 30 (3): 385–404.

Komisi Untuk Orang Hilang dan Korban Tindak Kekerasan (Kontras). 2009. *Menerobos Jalan Buntu: Kajian Terhadap Sistem Peradilan Militer Di Indonesia.* Jakarta: KontraS.

———. 2017. "3 Years Jokowi – Kalla Administration Evaluation: Human Rights Accountability, Worsening, and Neglected Democracy Agenda". Press Release.

Kompas. 2017a. "Komnas HAM-INFID Dorong 100 Kepala Daerah Adopsi Konsep Kota Ramah HAM." May 15, 2017. http://nasional.kompas. com/read/2017/05/15/15475261/komnas.ham-infid.dorong.100. kepala.daerah.adopsi.konsep.kota.ramah.ham (accessed September 2, 2018).

———. 2017b. "Wiranto Ungkap Presiden Duterte Terinspirasi 'Petrus' Di Era Soeharto." August 11, 2017. http://nasional.kompas.com/ read/2017/08/11/13510281/wiranto-ungkap-presiden-duterte-terinspirasi-petrus-di-era-soeharto (accessed September 2, 2018).

———. 2017c "Narkotika: Fokus 2018, Tekan Angka Permintaan". December 28, 2017.

McRae, Dave. 2013. "Yudhoyono's Hypocrisy in U-Turn on Death Penalty". *South China Morning Post,* March 27, 2013. http://www. scmp.com/comment/insight-opinion/article/1200365/yudhoyonos-hypocrisy-uturn-death-penalty (accessed November 3, 2017).

Mietzner, Marcus. 2009. *Military Politics, Islam, and the State in Indonesia: From Turbulent Transition to Democratic Consolidation.* Singapore: Institute of Southeast Asian Studies.

News.com.au. 2015. Reynolds, Emma. 2015. "Indonesia's Bloodthirsty Desire for Crime and Punishment". April 30, 2015. http://www. news.com.au/world/asia/indonesias-bloodthirsty-desire-for-crime-and-punishment/news-story/66ea1528736cb0bb853bbc3e838205d8 (accessed November 3, 2017).

Nurkhoiron, Muhammad. 2017. "Mengembangkan Kota HAM Di Indonesia: Peluang Dan Tantangannya". *Jurnal Pemikiran Sosiologi* 4 (1): 120–147.

Semendawai, Abdul Haris. 2018. "Peran LPSK Dalam Pemenuhan Hak Korban Pelanggaran Ham Yang Berat." Power-point slides.

Suh, Jiwon. 2015a. "Preemptive Transitional Justice Policies in Aceh, Indonesia." *Southeast Asian Studies* 4 (1): 95–124.

_____. 2015b. "Islam, Motherhood, and Participation: A Study of Female Politicians' Identity Strategies with the Case of Illiza Sa'aduddin Djamal, Mayor of Banda Aceh, Indonesia." *Dongayeongu* (*East Asian Studies*) 34 (2): 301–347.

_____. 2016. "The Suharto Case." *Asian Journal of Social Science* 44 (1–2): 214–245.

Sukma, Rizal. 2011. "Indonesia Finds a New Voice". *Journal of Democracy* 22 (4): 110–123.

Tempo. 2011. "TNI Anggap Kekerasan Di Papua Bukan Pelanggaran HAM". January 2, 2011. https://nasional.tempo.co/read/303111/ tni-anggap-kekerasan-di-papua-bukan-pelanggaran-ham (accessed November 3, 2017).

The Jakarta Post. 2012. "Issues of the Day: 1965 Mass Killings Justified: Minister". October 3, 2012. https://www.thejakartapost. com/news/2012/10/03/issues-day-1965-mass-killings-justified-minister.html (accessed November 3, 2017).

_____. 2016. "Papuan Rights Issues Will Be Solved without Deception: Luhut". June 16, 2016. http://www.thejakartapost.com/ news/2016/06/16/papuan-rights-issues-will-be-solved-without-deception-luhut.html (accessed November 3, 2017).

Tribunnews. 2017. "Kasus Dugaan Pelanggaran HAM Di Wamena Dan Wasior Dilanjutkan". January 30, 2017. http://www.tribunnews.com/ nasional/2017/01/30/kasus-dugaan-pelanggaran-ham-di-wamena-dan-wasior- dilanjutkan. (accessed November 3, 2017).

UN Human Rights Council. 2012. "National Report Submitted in Accordance with Paragraph 5 of the Annex to Human Rights Council Resolution 16/21: Indonesia." A/HRC/WG.6/13/IDN/1.

————. 2017. "National Report Submitted in Accordance with Paragraph 5 of the Annex to Human Rights Council Resolution 16/21: Indonesia". A/HRC/WG.6/27/IDN/1.

Yudhawiranata, Agung. 2009. "The Right to a Fair, Open, Free and Impartial Trial: The Difficulty in Bringing Human Rights Violators to Justice." *In Human Rights and the Indonesian Security Sector: 2009 Almanac*, edited by Mufti Makaarim, Wendy Andika Prajuli and Fitri Bintang Timur, pp. 221-241. Jakarta: IDSPS.

Chapter 11
Return Strategy of the State:
Re-taming Private Security Providers in Democratized Indonesia

Okamoto Masaaki

Introduction

In 2006, I contacted the head of a local branch of a rising militant social organization in Jakarta. He told me to meet him near a shopping mall off the highway in north Jakarta. When I got out of the car at the meeting spot, I was surrounded by more than ten muscular men who were dressed in black and holding long wooden sticks and clubs. The branch head asked me to get out of my car and get in his car. With the intimidating presence of the macho henchmen, I thought he had framed me and was going to threaten me for money. This did not come to pass, however. The men had sticks and clubs because they had just finished up dispersing squatters and demolishing their houses in order to "secure" land for one of Jakarta's largest developers. Needless to say, I had an intriguing interview with the branch head and the field commander of that organization.

The guys described above are typically called *preman* in Indonesia, or in English, simply thugs. An influential *preman* usually has both vertical and horizontal networks linked to businessmen, religious leaders, and politicians both at the national and local levels. For example, Yapto

Surjosumarno, the long-time head of the best-known *preman* organization, Pemuda Pancasila (Pancasila Youth), demonstrated his amicable relationship with different power holders by sitting next to both the ex-Army Chief of Staff, Ryamizard Ryacudu, and the chairman of the Corruption Eradication Committee, Antasari Azhar, at a ceremony establishing the Yapto Center in August 2008.

The above two cases suggest that *preman* are used by a wide variety of actors for a range of "security" needs in Indonesia. Private security providers in Indonesia are persons or organizations who resort to or threaten to resort to violence in order to achieve their aims or those of their benefactors. They take different forms and have varying relationships with state security providers (the military and the police). Private security providers include formal ones, such as (registered) security guard companies, and informal ones, such as mafia groups and hooligans. A wide gray zone exists between the two. Private security providers are common in any country or any part of a country, at any period and under any political system. The differences lie in the extent of their political, economic, and social significance, which is often directly related to their relationship with state security providers.

In Indonesia, there has been space for private security providers to flourish since the Dutch colonial period. Both the Dutch colonial state and the Indonesian nation-state have never claimed a "monopoly of the legitimate use of physical force within a given territory" (Weber, 1980). Scholars on Indonesia have produced numerous works on militia, vigilante groups, and thug organizations and their social, economic, political importance as will be mentioned later, but there has not been any trial to see a rather long-term transformation of the relationship between the state and those groups or organizations both at the national and local levels[1].

This chapter aims to fill this gap and argues that the Indonesian state since the New Order has consistently tried to nurture and forge relationships with private security providers for the benefit of the state and has never had any intention of eradicating them. After the unstable democratic

---

1   Wilson's work (2015) excellently describes the transformation of the violent social organizations and their relationship with the (local) state in the Jakarta metropolitan area.

transition in late 1990s and early 2000s, the Indonesian state has started to re-tame the drastically increased private security providers in four ways: professionalizing, cultivating, weeding out, and indoctrinating.

Private Security Providers

Before analyzing the Indonesian case, this section places this chapter in a broader framework of the state and violence. In his classic *Politics as a Vocation*, Max Weber defines the modern state as a human community that (successfully) claims a "monopoly of the legitimate use of physical force within a given territory" (Weber 1980). According to Douglas North et al. (2013: 273), virtually every state assumes that it has a monopoly on violence, but little more than two dozen countries in our time have actually established such a monopoly. The point is not the number of countries with the monopoly on violence, however. Weber's definition has a continued sentence: "all other organizations or individuals can assert the right to use physical violence only in so far as the state permits them to do so" (Weber, 2004). In other words, as long as it is within the limits permitted by the state," certain non-state organizations and individuals can use physical violence without state interference. If this is the case and we call these actors private security providers, it is quintessential to understand the role of private security providers and the relationship between such providers and the state (actors). Private security providers broadly fall into four types from the state's perspective: professional companies, militias, tolerated violent groups, and non-tolerated violent groups.

The typical example of the first type is a private military company (PMC), such as Blackwater of the United States (Scahill, 2008 and Prince, 2013 on Blackwater). Many studies have been produced on PMCs due to the journalistic and academic attention that their increasing number and role in the field of battle since the end of the Cold War has drawn.[2] Private security providers are not limited to PMCs operating in war zones, however. They exist in daily domestic life as well. Professional private

2   The Scopus literature database found 99 articles on PMCs from January 2000 to September 2017.

security companies are also contracted for a variety of security needs such as guarding hotels and factories.

While PMCs are explicitly contracted by the state, militias often engage with the state to provide "security services," sometimes in exchange for the right to hold weapons, special treatment, or certain favors. They are security providers in unstable states. For example, the Myanmar state uses militias to tamp down insurgencies in the border areas (Buchanan, 2016). In the Philippines, the police organize and control militias called Civilian Volunteer Organizations while the Army has Civilian Armed Forces Geographical Units.

Tolerated violent groups have a long history in virtually every country and are dominant security providers in unstable socio-political situations. For example, yakuza groups, organizations, and *gurentai* (hooligan) wielded significant influence in chaotic cities just after World War II in Japan. They had caches of swords, knives, and guns, and competed with each other to maintain and expand their own spheres of influence and profit. They were not always enemies of the state, and while many of their activities were illegal and coercive, the state permitted their existence. Rather than disband such groups, the state (in the form of the police) used them to maintain peace and order in conflict-ridden cities. Some politicians also kept close contact with such groups, protecting them in exchange for their coercive services and financial resources. Similar to many states, a wide gray zone existed between the state security providers and these violent private security providers in post-war Japan. With the recovery of social and political stability, and with the implementation of the Law on the Prevention of Irregularities by Gangsters (Boryokudan) in 1991, however, this gray zone shrank; the police labeled hooligans and yakuza organizations as "antisocial" forces and started to crack down on them harshly. The yakuza was recategorized as a non-tolerated violent groups. This resulted in a drastic decrease in the number of yakuza organizations and in the regular membership of yakuza groups. The state no longer tolerated their existence, aiming to monopolize violence in the literal sense of the word, allowing the existence of security guard companies with limited authority.[3]

Every country has some type of non-tolerated violent groups such as terrorist groups, separatist groups, revolutionary leftist groups or Islam radical groups. As the case of Japan illustrates, however, violent private security providers can be either friends or enemies of the state, depending on the time and situation. They are sometimes used by the state, sometimes they use the state, and sometimes they simply evade the state. Of course, the state is comprised of quite a lot of diverse entities, and thus relationships between the state and violent private security providers comprise networks of different state organs and personnel and different private security provider. The rise and fall of one private security provider, therefore, tends to hinge on how the provider forges relationships with powerful state actors.

Private security providers can also be categorized into four types by their orientation, although the boundaries among the four are blurred. The first is professional-oriented legal groups, specializing in security and crime prevention as a profession or job. Security companies such as Secom and G4S enter into this category. The second is profit-oriented groups with illegality. They are often involved in nightlife and illegal businesses, and therefore dare to use or threaten violence in order to secure, maintain, and expand their business and bailiwick. Typical examples of such actors are mafia and yakuza organizations. Considering the illegal aspect of their business and their threats of coercion, they are often targeted for elimination by the state, but not always. Some state actors benefit from these groups and protect them from state intervention or elimination. The third type is vigilante groups. They include religion-based, ethnicity-based, tradition-based, culture-based, or community-based organizations and groups that justify themselves as security providers and advocate for their religion, ethnicity, tradition, culture, or community; some of them do not hesitate

---

3   This doesn't mean the Japanese police literally monopolized violence. Following the weakening of *yakuza* as a violent force, different types of groups and networks are forming in Japan. They are called *hangure*, comprising an ever shifting and amorphous underground network of criminals which are so flexible that the police cannot deal with them effectively.

to exercise (the threat of) violence. The fourth variety is political-oriented groups. They dare to (or threaten to) use coercion to secure, maintain, and expand the influence of politicians or political families. Every society has private security actors with all four of these orientations, and their roles and significance fluctuate according to the times.

State, Security, and Violence in the Suharto Era

This section describes the relationship between state security providers and private security providers during the 32-year-long authoritarian regime of Suharto. Under the Suharto regime, the military had a strong grip on every aspect of life in Indonesia. The regime not only wielded violence through the official security apparatus—the military and the police; it also controlled non-state violence in three ways, that is, through organizing, detaching, and liquidating.[4] It was both impossible and undesirable for the regime to totally eliminate society's thugs, or *preman*. They were useful in the state's efforts to achieve internal security. Organized thugs have their own territories and strong reasons to secure them from rival organizations. In this way, the goals of the state security providers overlapped with those of private security providers, making it economical and efficient for the state to allow private actors to maintain and secure their own bailiwicks. Furthermore, Indonesia is a multi-ethnic society spread across such a large archipelago that the state could not afford the tremendous political and economic resources required to achieve stability with its own security providers alone. The historical legacy of the role of private security providers, such as militia and vigilante groups, in gaining independence from the colonial Dutch also played a part for the state's willingness to use them.

The military actively gathered juvenile delinquents into violent youth groups and organizations called *organisasi kemasyarakatan* (*ormas*—societal organization) (Beittinger-Lee, 2009: 167). These included nationwide organizations such as Pemuda Pancasila (Pancasila Youth),

---

4   For more on security at the community level during the New Order, see Joshua Barker's pioneering works (1998, 1999).

Pemuda Panca Marga (Panca Marga Youth), and (Forum Komunikasi Putra-Putri Purnawirawan Indonesia (FKPPI—Communication Forum of the Sons and Daughters of Indonesian Veterans). Region-wide *ormas* were also created under the auspices of regional military commands, such as Angkatan Muda Siliwangi (AMS—Siliwangi Youth Force) in West Java Province, Persatuan Pendekar Seni Budaya Banten Indonesia (PPPSBBI— Indonesian Union of Bantenese Men of Martial Arts, Art and Culture) in the Banten area, Angkatan Muda Diponegoro (AMD—Diponegero Youth Force) in Central Java Province, Komando Inti Keamanan (Kotikam— Nucleus Command for Security) in Yogyakarta Special Region, and Ikatan Pemuda Karya (IKP—Youth Force for Works and Deeds) in and around Medan. These groups existed in a gray area between the public and underground spheres. For money, they provided security at nightclubs, bars, karaoke clubs, collected parking fees and debts, controlled the fee collections at bus terminals, and cleared out residents for land expropriation. They were easily mobilized to support the government party, Golongan Karya (Golkar), and to suppress anti-government student and anti-capitalist labor movements. These *ormas* were not only economically motivated but also politically motivated under the aegis of the military.

The most successful *ormas* was and is Pemuda Pancasila (Ryter, 1998; 2014). High-ranking anti-communist military officers established Pemuda Pancasila in North Sumatra to suppress the spread of communism in the late 1950s. It was heavily involved in the 9.30 movement of 1965 in which the army, led by Suharto, was set in motion to crush the rapidly growing communist party. The military mobilized Islamic and *preman* organizations in its mission, resulting in the killing of approximately 500,000 and the arrest of around one million "communists." In North Sumatra, Pemuda Pancasila was at the forefront of the operation. Following 9.30 and the establishment of the Suharto regime, Pemuda Pancasila became influential nationally, particularly after Yapto Surjosumarno became its head in 1981. Feeling threatened by the political and social influence of Ali Moertopo— Suharto's right-hand man with an intelligence background, who cultivated a wide network including the criminal underworld—Suharto strengthened

Pemuda Pancasila under Yapto as a counter force. Suharto trusted Yapto because his father was related to Tien, Suharto's wife, and had a close relationship with the Suharto family (Adijondro, 2006: 20; Janssen, 2015: 270).

Pemuda Pancasila had both formal and informal businesses, collecting security fees from nightclubs and brothels, running protection rackets from stores and street vendors, forcibly collecting debts, and evicting squatters for development projects. Some cadres had their own construction companies and law firms. Pemuda Pancasila established a certain level of order in the underworld and supported Golkar. In return, its members enjoyed the benefits of economic development under the Suharto regime (Okamoto, 2015: 70–72).

The second strategy of the state to control non-state violence was detaching. In December 1980, Awaloedin Djamin, the director-general of the National Police Agency, introduced the *satpam* system, which prohibited private security companies (professional actors) from providing guards to other private companies (Wresniwiro and Dede, 2002: 11).[5] *Satpam* is an acronym for *satuan pengamanan* (security unit) and usually refers to security guards in Indonesia). In other words, the New Order government did not grant any legal status to professional private security companies. The rationale was that such security companies might force small- and medium-size businesses to accept their services and, according to Awaloedin, lead to the penetration of the security business by Japanese Yakuza-like or Italian Mafia-like organizations (Djamin, 1999: 226–227). Instead, each company and institution was to be responsible for its own security by hiring security guards (*satpam*) who were police-registered and trained, and issued with standardized uniforms and identification tags (Djamin, 1995: 240; 1999: 217–218). The *satpam* system thus attempted to detach organized thugs from the "normal" business world. However, army officers opposed the system and operated their own security businesses, dispatching active duty and retired soldiers. The police failed to disband

---

5   Awaloedin is called "Bapak Satpam" (Father of Satpam) (Djamin, 1995: 241).

these companies because the police were a part of the military and were too weak vis-à-vis the army (Djamin, 1995: 240).

Finally, the Suharto regime sometimes liquidated unruly (non-tolerated) private violent groups through the resolute action of killing or jailing thugs and members of organized gangs. From 1983 to 1985, for instance, the military-managed *petrus* killings (a series of mysterious shootings) eliminated over 5,000 suspected criminals (Bourchier, 1990: 177). Suharto justified the killing of thugs in the *petrus* affair, calling the intentional abandonment of corpses in the streets a kind of shock therapy to demonstrate action against criminal activity (Suharto, 1989: 389–390). This killing was seemingly part of Suharto's effort to dismantle Ali Moertopo's underground network (Cribb, 2000). And as mentioned earlier, Suharto used Pemuda Pancasila to strengthen his power in the underworld.

The Fall of Suharto and the Game Changer for State and Private Security Providers

The dominant power of state security providers, especially the military, and the dependency of private security providers on the state during the Suharto period changed significantly as insecurity became more widespread during and after the Asian economic crisis of 1997 and the fall of Suharto in 1998. Racial, religious, and ethnic conflicts and riots broke out in different parts of Indonesia. Criminality in a variety of forms, such as "necklacing" and terrorist bombings, was rampant. The situation had two major impacts on society. First, the ability to control and initiate violence led to increases in the social, political, and economic power of particular actors, as violent entrepreneurs gained influence over various aspects of life. Second, the instability required each segment of society to defend itself by organizing and/or using vigilantes or security groups and organizations.

The fall of Suharto officially changed the state's relationship with private security providers and opened more space for them to operate. The separation of the police from the military during the democratization process of 1999 left the police with primary responsibility for ensuring internal security under Law Number 2 Year 2002 on the police of the Republic of Indonesia. This precipitated changes in the pattern and structure of security-related interests and businesses. As a result, the police were in ascendance and endeavored to weaken military-related businesses.

With democratization came new "rules" for violence and security. Private actors were legally given more opportunities in the security field. These partly stemmed from the state's inability to deter the development of organized security providers, and, more importantly, from the introduction of the concept of "good governance" to the security sector. International donors such as World Bank introduced the "Good governance" concept as a new way of development in developing countries and good governance demands the participation of different stakeholders in development activities; the state is not to be the main actor, but a facilitator of development. With respect to the security sector, this idea dictates that rather than being the sole security provider, the state delegates the role of security to private and social actors. The Suharto regime had delegated some security power to private actors as discussed above, but it did not have any legal foundation except the *satpam* system. The new relationship was codified in Article 3, Law Number 2 Year 2002, which stipulates that the guardian of policing functions is the National Police of the Republic of Indonesia, which is to be assisted by the Special Police, the Investigating Officer of Civil Servants, and vigilante security groups.

The clear acknowledgement by the Indonesian police of vigilante security groups and organizations has allowed private security brokers to emerge and expand. For example, the handling of local security and order by traditional vigilante groups, such as *pecalang* in Bali and *lang-lang* in West Sumbawa, is accepted as suitable for local interests and needs (Wresniwiro and Dede, 2002: 6–8) because these traditional security actors are accepted as legitimate among the community. Consequently, different types of private security providers have proliferated. A clear sign of this has been the birth and rapid increase of security companies. In the late

1990s operating security companies was illegal, and consequently there were just a handful. By 2018 the number of registered security companies had rapidly increased to around 2,200 and the number of security guards reached an estimated 650,000, surpassing the number of police officers (Marketeers, February 2, 2018). Some companies, such as the domestic Sigap and the foreign Secom and G4S, are professional. Others are ambiguous, however, such as the *ormas* Badan Pembina Potensi Keluarga Besar Banten (BPPKB—Agency to Develop the Potentialities of the Bantenese) and the companies of Haji Lulung.

Security Providers for Business, Social, and Political Needs in the Post-Suharto Period

The BPPKB was founded on July 8, 1998, only two weeks after Suharto's resignation.[6] According to the prologue of the BPPKB's platform, it arose from the call of the Independence struggle, was founded on faith, knowledge, and charity, and is infused with the Pancasila philosophy of the nation-state in order to realize national development. This declaration is admittedly quite sweeping and vague; however, the language used is strongly reminiscent of the New Order.

BPPKB activities, as listed in Article 5 of the platform, are as follows:

- Providing security guards, informal workers and staff, *dalam arti kata yang seluas-luasnya* (in the widest meaning of the word);
- Offering general services and legal defense services for the public;
- Cooperating with related organizations and authorities;
- Implementing business and other social activities in the widest meaning of the word.

Noer Indradjaja SH has been the president of the BPPKB since its founding. He has been one of the key persons of the Agung Podomoro Group, Indonesia's largest apartment provider, which controlled 52% of all apartment units in Jakarta in the second quarter of 2016. Noer Indradjaja founded the BPPKB as an ethnic Bantenese-based organization, with the

---

6   The section on BPPKB is mainly from (Okamoto, 2006).

Surgriwas family of local *jawara* (strongmen) as its core. Seven other families from Pandeglang regency in Banten Province initially joined. One of the main aims of the BPPKB is to secure the Agung Podomoro Group and seize land for its operations. The BPPKB is characterized above all by vagueness and opportunism. Indeed, the phrase "in the widest meaning of the word," used in its platform to describe BPPKB activities, reflects this, implying that the BPPKB is ready to do anything if offered an opportunity for profit. Sending security guards to companies or forcing companies to hire security guards from the BPPKB is part of its modus operandi. In 2003, BPPKB successfully sent 130 security guards to the Sukarno-Hatta international airport (Harian Banten, 2003).

The BPPKB has no clear ideological or professional objective other than to generally secure the interests of Bantenese. When asked whether the BPPKB would be on the side of the poor, a BPPKB cadre of the Banten Provincial Branch used the phrase *tergantung suasana* (depending on the atmosphere). In this case, *tergantung suasana* means that BPPKB tends to secure justice for those who benefit BPPKB. It is natural, then, that BPPKB tends to be on the side of political and economic power holders.

The BPPKB will work for any person or organization in any sector to secure its interests. A conflict between two urban parties—often with regard to land seizures or labor strikes—represents a typical opportunity for BPPKB to profit from intervening in the conflict and proposing a solution. Job opportunities and benefits for BPPKB therefore derive from the occurrence of problems. One cadre of BPPKB headquarters said, "The job of BPPKB is problem solving." The organization's indistinct purpose and stated opportunism combine to produce its *rezeki* (income).

The BPPKB maintains a certain distance from politics. Article 5 of the organization's platform states that, "BPPKB, as a Banten people's organization in Indonesia, is a social organization that is independent, self-sufficient, active in the business sector, and in social activities in the widest meaning of the word." President Noer Indradjaja has always claimed that BPPKB is an independent mass-based organization that has no affiliation with any political party: "The purpose of founding BPPKB… is for the benefit of the Muslim community" (Harian Banten, 2003). The BPPKB's Banten provincial branches are careful when accepting business offers to avoid dragging BPPKB or its members into politics.

This does not mean that BPPKB has no relationship with politics, however. Several members of BPPKB are individual members of political parties and local parliamentarians. Organizationally speaking, BPPKB mobilized thousands of members in Gelora Bung Karno to support Megawati Sukarnoputri for president during the 2004 direct presidential election campaign. At an event called Dzikir Akbar,[7] Noer Indradjaja said: "We will pray for Allah to have mercy on Megawati so that she becomes the president of the Republic of Indonesia again" (Gatra, 2004).

However, this statement and the gathering of thousands does not mean that all BPPKB members were ordered to support Megawati Sukarnoputri and pro-Megawati political parties; indeed, BPPKB members backed many other parties as well. The support shown on this occasion for Megawati was symbolic rather than substantial, as the mobilization of BPPKB members at this event seemed to have been at the request and financing (in the form of a donation) of Edi Darnadi, the head of West Java Province police. Legally, of course, the police had to remain neutral about presidential candidates, but in practice they tended to back Megawati because they expected their interests to be better served by her rather than the other candidates. In other words, BPPKB provides the "service" of its membership to various clients.

Another example is H. Lulung Lunggana in Tanah Abang, Jakarta.[8] Haji Lulung is from a Jakarta-native ethnic group called Betawi and became the district head of Pemuda Panca Marga, a Suharto era organized *preman* group. He joined the East Timorese *preman* group led by Rosario de Marshall ("Hercules"), which controlled the Tanah Abang area, the largest textile and garment center in Southeast Asia. When a turf war broke out in Tanah Abang between the Hercules group and the

---

7   *Dzikir* (or *zikir*) is the act of repeating the names of Allah and certain religious formulae as a means of demonstrating piety, or, in the case of mystics, of inducing a mystical trance (Federspiel, 1995: 295).

8   On the rise of Haji Lulung, see (*Tempo*, 2010; *Tirto*, 2017a, 2017b, 2017c).

ethnic-Betawi group led by Bang Ucu over business interests (including protection rackets and the collection of parking fees), Haji Lulung was on the Hercules side even though he was an ethnic Betawi. After Bang Ucu won the war in the late 90s, and Sutiyoso, the Jakarta governor at the time supported the Betawi *preman*, Bang Ucu kicked Haji Lulung out of Tanah Abang. The two eventually reached a truce and Haji Lulung was allowed to join the Betawi *preman* group. Since the fall of Suharto, Haji Lulung has successfully expanded his business, first under Bang Ucu and later by himself. He shrewdly formalized the protection racket and parking fee collection business by establishing his own companies for that purpose, including PT Putraja Perkasa and PT Tirta Jaya Perkasa, among others. He even has his own law firm, Kantor Advokat Haji Lulung, Fendrik & Rekan. He boasts that he has hired 7,000 workers for his companies.

With his economic and violent capital and his companies' workers as voters, Haji Lulung entered politics through the Islamic party Partai Persatuan Pembangunan (PPP), becoming a provincial parliamentarian of Jakarta Province and a vice chairman of the provincial parliament in 2009. He further entrenched his power at the national level by being chosen as the head of Pemuda Panca Marga at the national level in 2011. When Basuki Tjahaja Purnama (Ahok), a reform-oriented governor of Jakarta (2014–2017) tended to depend on the official security providers and tried to weaken *preman*-type *ormas* such as Forum Betawi Rempug (FBR—Betawi Brotherhood Forum) and Forum Komunikasi Anak Betawi (Forkabi—Betawi Children's Communication Forum), Ahok also aimed to cleanse *preman* out of Tanah Abang area. Haji Lulung naturally came into conflict with Ahok and was in danger of losing power. In the gubernatorial election in 2017, therefore, Haji Lulung supported the rival candidate, Anies Baswedan against Ahok, even though his party, PPP, supported Ahok. Anies won the election and Haji Lulung has successfully forged a good relationship with him, enabling him to maintain his political and economic base in Tanah Abang.

As the case of Haji Lulung illustrates, not only have new profit-oriented and/or vigilante security providers such as the BPPKB emerged since democratization, some of the profit-oriented private security providers with illegality nurtured under the Suharto regime have also successfully consolidated their economic power, especially at the local level. The threat of violence has been used to build and reinforce their political prominence. For example, the powerful *ormas* of the Suharto era, Pemuda Pancasila, has entrenched its political power at the local level and also at the national level. According to the West Java provincial branch head of Pemuda Pancasila, Golkar allocated the organization just 24 seats in national and local parliaments in the last election during the Suharto period (in 1997), but by putting its members in different political parties, Pemuda Pancasila rapidly increased its number of seats to 58 in the first free and fair election after the fall of Suharto in 1999 (Okamoto, 2015). In the 2004 general elections, twelve Pancasila Youth members became national MPs, about 115 became provincial MPs, and more than 400 became regency and municipal MPs from Golkar and other parties (Ryter, 2009: 188). In the 2009 general elections, 535 members were elected as MPs at the national and local levels. According to Pancasila Youth cadre Yorrys Raweyai, more than 30 former cadres were serving in the national parliament alone after the 2009 general elections (*Tempo*, 2013).

These security providers reached the local political pinnacles in the Banten and Madura areas. The chairman of PPSBBI in the new Banten Province became the key player of the establishment of the province in 2000 and wielded significant political influence in provincial politics, selecting his daughter as vice governor and then governor, and his family members and henchmen to political and economic positions (Okamoto and Hamid, 2008). In Bangkalan Regency of Madura Island, a violent actor with a well-known religious family background obtained the regency head position two times before passing the position on to his son. Even after his arrest for corruption charges, he retained his socio-political power (Rozaki, 2016).

The post-Suharto era has witnessed a plethora of new violent vigilante groups, too. Just after the fall of Suharto and the start of democratization, the sense of uncertainty and insecurity prompted vigilantism based on religion, ethnicity, tradition, and community. In Jakarta, native Betawi-based organizations emerged, such as FBR and Forkabi (Untung, 2005; Wilson, 2006; Brown and Wilson, 2007; Wilson, 2015). In Minahasa, ethnic-based and/or Christian-based organizations emerged, including the Brigade Manguni, Legium Christum, and the Militia Christi (Jacobsen, 2002; Okamoto, 2015: 180–182). A prominent Islam-based violent vigilante group was Front Pembela Islam (FPI—Islamic Defenders' Front). With the tacit and financial support of the police and the State Intelligence Service, FPI expanded and attacked discos and karaoke pubs as moral enemies of Islam (Wilson, 2015: 152). Because of its demands to turn Indonesian society in a more conservative Islamic direction and its anti-government behaviors, however, the current Jokowi government finally banned FPI in December 2020.

In Bali, a community of customary-law or *hukum adat*-based groups, or *pecalang*, emerged, and the Bali provincial government legalized their existence as traditional security providers for villages in provincial bylaw Number 3 Year 2001 (Suryawan, 2005 and 2006). Bali also has powerful violent profit-oriented cum vigilante actors, such as Laskar Bali, Baladika, and Pemuda Bali Bersatu (PBB—United Bali Youth), which have tacit or explicit support from politicians (Supriatna, 2016). In Lombok, one in four adults have joined community-level vigilante groups (MacDougall, 2007).

In Bandung, Gabungan Inisiatif Barisan Anak Sunda (Gibas—Joint Initiative of the Sundanese sons of Siliwangi), an ethnic Sundanese-based vigilante *ormas* that separated from AMS was established in 2001 and enjoys wide influence. Members of Gibas have helped the city administration resolve many "problems" that could not be solved by legal means, including, for example, the eviction of kaki lima (street vendors) and slum clearance for land development projects. It is also widely believed that the protection rackets of Gibas members in the city's brothels and gambling dens, which amount to more than four hundred, are much more extensive than those of competing preman groups. Both AMS and GIBAS identify themselves as the most effective, committed guardians of the wide-ranging ethnic interests of the Sundanese people, and their local networks are made available to prominent Sundanese brokers (Honna, 2006: 87). In that sense, these groups are profit-oriented with illegality, but also political-oriented vigilante corps.

The Return Strategy of the State

Faced with this rather entrenched power of different types of private security providers, the Indonesian state did little to control them at first. With the further consolidation of democracy (at least as an institution for governance) and the gradual achievement of socio-political stability, however, Indonesia's state security providers began to re-tame private security providers to its own benefit, in four ways: professionalizing, cultivating, weeding out, and indoctrinating. The first strategy is the professionalization of security companies. The police have begun regulating security companies, as well as security guards, by introducing a registration system for security companies and training regulations for guards. In the two decisions of commissioner general of the National Police Agency Number 18 Year 2006 and Number 24 Year 2007, the police instituted a standard uniform for *satpam* again (just after the fall of Suharto, security companies uniforms were similar to military camouflage clothes or Marine Corps uniforms and the police outlawed them because of the confusion it caused). In the new regulations, the police stipulated several key obligations: (1) all new guardsmen/women must receive 232 hours of basic security education, (2) all candidates for security supervisor must receive an additional 160 hours of education, and 3) all candidates for security manager must receive a further 100 hours of training. The police accredit training schools and develop all curricula and training programs themselves. These measures seem to be part of a strategy to force security

Indonesia at the Crossroads: Transformation and Challenges

companies to detach themselves from the military and solicit favors from the police, and is also financially beneficial for the police.

The police also established associations for security companies (Djamin, 1999: 224). On June 28, 2002, the Association of Indonesian Security Managers (AMSI) was formally established to regulate and coordinate the rapidly increasing number of security companies.[9] AMSI's chief supervisor is the director-general of the National Police Agency and three of the four advisory board members are retired police officers; Awaloedin Djamin is the head of the board. While AMSI is a security manager's association, another association for security companies, Asosiasi Badan Usaha Jasa Pengamanan Indonesia (Abujapi—Indonesian Security Service Provider Association), was created in February 2006. Active higher-ranking police officers are on its executive board. All security companies are obliged to join Abujapi to qualify for a police operating permit. Its membership reached 1,700 in 2017 (Jurnal Security, 2017). These associations are expected to serve as a bridge between the state and private security providers and to give the police oversight of professional security providers.

The second strategy is the cultivation of vigilantism. After the police delegated policing power to private and civilian actors with Law Number 2 Year 2002, they began a new project of Pemolisian Masyarakat (Community Policing) and issued an instruction to establish a community policing forum, the Forum Kemitraan Pemolisian Masyarakat (FKPM), under Kepolisian Sektor (Polsek—district level police office) in 2005. FKPM aimed to achieve stability and safety through collaboration between the community and police. The FKPM assumed different names according to local traditions (such as Tuha Peuet in Aceh, Dalihan Na Tolu in Batak, Tungku Tigo Sajarangan in West Sumatra, and Rembug Pekon in Lampung), and involved traditional security providers such as *pecalang* in Bali and *jaga baya* in Java. In Keraton District in Yogyakarta, FKMP was named Paguyuban Seksi Keamanan Keraton (Paksi Katon—Security

---

9   In 1992, a security manager association called APPSI (or APSI) was established, but it was ineffective (Djamin 1995: 240–241; 1999: 223–224).

Section Association for Keraton) after its formal establishment in 2006. Under the strong leadership of Romo Suhud, Paksi Katon has not only developed into a province-wide security provider, but has also assumed the role of protector of Javanese culture and tradition with support from the police and the Sultan (Basrianto, 2016). Paksi Katon is a voluntary security provider that does not collect fees, whose members receive no salary, and that contributes to achieving peace and tranquility in Yogyakarta. In that sense, Paksi Katon has become an ideal partner for the police.

The third strategy is to weed out violent profit-oriented and vigilante groups. The police have now started to wield influence over these actors, and may be able to co-opt, weaken or disband intransigent, unruly, and subversive actors and to support amenable and governable actors. For example, Persatuan Masyarakat Palembang Bersatu (PMPB), a profit-oriented actor based in Palembang city, South Sumatera Province, once had strong influence in the city. It failed, however, to foster a good relationship with the police, and almost collapsed after the candidate it supported lost the gubernatorial election, as the new governor relied on the police for the city's security instead of PMPB.

Another case is the changing stance of the FBR. In 2003, the FBR claimed to provide a neighborhood security service to fill the gap created by an understaffed, inefficient, and corrupt police force (Wilson, 2006: 273). In 2005, after becoming engaged in turf wars with another *preman* organization, and seeing some of its members severely wounded, the FBR changed its position. In an interview with a reporter from a private TV station, one FBR member said, "We will coordinate with the police. We have maintained a good relationship with the police in maintaining peace and order in the Jakarta, Bogor, Tangerang and Bekasi areas."[10] This was a clear indication that the FBR was beginning to adopt state-dependent behavior, and avoiding direct conflict with the police, even while the latter remained understaffed, inefficient, and corrupt.

---

10   Report aired by Liputan 6, SCTV, April 4, 2005. http://www.liputan6.com/view/6,99131,1,0,1184306783.html.

The fourth strategy, indoctrinating, is employed mainly by the military, and relies on "society-on-alert" rhetoric. As mentioned earlier, the police became responsible for internal security after democratization. The military has not totally gone back to the barracks, however. It retains local commands and soldiers stationed in villages. The military has continued its mutually beneficial relationship with profit-oriented actors with illegality and vigilante actors at the local and national levels and has not hesitated to engage in turf wars with the police.

In addition to its day-to-day involvement in internal security and its continuous relationship with private security providers, the military has deepened its role in the internal security sector under the Joko Widodo (Jokowi) government, specifically by beginning in 2014 to propagate "society-on-alert" rhetoric. The fledgling Jokowi government, on bad terms with his own political party, was quite weak, and became more and more dependent on the military to achieve political stability (IPAC, 2016: 1).

Within this political calculus, the military found a golden opportunity to expand its activities. A typical example is the establishment of Program Bela Negara (State Defense Program), started in October 2015. It is a kind of education (or indoctrination) program to raise the loyalty of citizens to the state under the state principle of Pancasila. The defense minister constantly reminds the society to remain alert to the threat of proxy wars, in which a third party (state or non-state) will try to invade Indonesia with an ideology or idea contrary to the Indonesian state. The main enemies in such a proxy war, according to the minister, are communism, drugs, terrorism, and the LGBT community. The military conducts drills with civilians, wearing black-and-blue camouflage uniforms. It is reported that about 1.6 million people had registered for the program by late June 2016 (*Merdeka*, 2016).

The state also mobilizes profit-oriented providers with illegality and vigilante security providers with this alert rhetoric. For example, a well-known *ormas*, Pemuda Pancasila, strongly supports the program and in 2018 signed a memorandum of understanding with the Ministry of Defense on cooperation to promote the program (swaraesi.com 2019). In Bali, the Udayana regional military command has given training to violent profit-oriented actors such as Laskar Bali, Baladika, and PBB (*Tribun Bali*, 2016), suggesting that the program aims to gradually draw these actors to the military's side.

Another component of the society-on-alert rhetoric was the November 2014 creation of the Barisan Patriot Bela Negara (BPBN—Patriot Front for State Defense). The BPBN's uniform is a militaristic black one, and the founder is a businessman in Cianjur Regency, West Java. The headquarters is in the regency. The BPBN began activities on a small scale, to raise patriotism among civilians with the support of active military officers. But it then expanded quite rapidly with the rapid development of the State Defense program. BPBN had 19 provincial branches and 274 regency/city branches, with a claimed membership of 9 million in December 2016. As members of other violent profit-oriented and vigilante groups can join BPBN, this organization might gradually become an umbrella organization for various private security providers with the strong support of the military.

These two society-on-alert strategies are creative ways for the military to return to and deepen its involvement in the internal security field, and to re-establish relationships with private security providers for the military's benefit.

Conclusion

It is crystal clear that the Indonesian state has never had any intention of eradicating private security providers, instead using and to varying degrees controlling them for its own benefit, even in the democratic era. During the Suharto period, the state employed three strategies to deal with private security providers: organizing, detaching, and liquidating. After democratization, the Indonesian state began to adopt four different strategies; professionalizing, cultivating, weeding out, and indoctrinating based on alert rhetoric. These different state strategies correspond to the regimes of the time, from authoritarian government to democratic governance. Realizing that detachment did not work even in the Suharto period, the contemporary police introduced the idea of professionalization and legalized professional security companies. With the idea of governance in the field of security, the state has actively cultivated vigilantism in the community so that peace and order is achieved at the community level in collaboration with police. The state can no longer simply liquidate non-tolerated violent actors as it sometimes did during the Suharto era, and has instead adopted the "weeding out" strategy, a lenient form of Suharto's resolute action. The police remain the major actor in three of the new strategies. Meanwhile, fearful of losing control and power in the internal security sector, and the benefits thereof, the military has implemented its own strategy, using "society-on-alert" rhetoric to indoctrinate citizens and lure violent profit-oriented and vigilante actors to its side.

It is not quite clear if the multitude of strategies suggests disarray between the police and the military and an escalation of tensions between two violent state actors in democratic Indonesia. One thing that is clear, though, is that the return of the state to the internal security sector does not mean that private security providers are losing ground. On the contrary, it can be said that the more state-dependent security providers are, the more socio-economic and political benefits they enjoy, both at the national and local levels simply because the state has no will to eradicate them and has a strong will to utilize them to its own benefit. Making them visible and exposed to the state is the way the state chooses to deal with them.

The main focus of this chapter has been the strategies taken by the state against violent private security providers, but the relationship between the state and providers is complicated as different state actors have different networks with providers and the actual implementation of the state strategies can be quite far from the stratetgies the state envisioned. But one thing to be emphasized is that the constantly changing networks between state actors and private security providers are within the framework of the strategies that this chapter has described and that dependence on a strong state actor is now the key for survival for any violent private security providers in democratic Indonesia.

References

Aditjondro, George Junus. 2006. *Korupsi Kepresidenan: Reproduksi Oligarki Berkaki Tiga: Istana, Tangsi, dan Partai Penguasa*. Yogyakarta: LKiS

Barker, Joshua. 1998. "State of Fear: Controlling the Criminal Contagion in Suharto's New Order". *Indonesia* 66: 7–42.

_____. 1999. "Surveillance and Territoriality in Bandung". In *Figures of Criminality in Indonesia, the Philippines, and Colonial Vietnam*, edited by Vicente Rafael, pp.95-127. Ithaca, NY: Cornell Southeast Asia Program.

Basrianto, Fadel. 2016. "Milisi Tradisi dan Kebangkitan Konservatisme Yogyakarta". Skripsi. Universitas Gadjah Mada (unpublished).

Beittinger-Lee, Verena. 2009. *(Un)civil Society and Political Change in Indonesia: A Contested Arena*. London: Routledge.

Bourchier, David. 1990. "Crime, Law and State Authority in Indonesia." In *State and Civil Society in Indonesia*, edited by Arief Budiman, pp.177-212. Clayton: Centre of Southeast Asian Studies, Monash University.

Brown, David and Ian Douglas Wilson. 2007. "Ethnicized Violence in Indonesia: Where Criminals and Fanatics Meet". *Nationalism and Ethnic Politics* 13 (3): 367–403.

Cribb, Robert. 2000. "From Petrus to Ninja: Death Squads in Indonesia". In *Death Squads in Global Perspective: Murder with Deniability*, edited by Bruce Campbell and Arthur Brenner, pp.181-202. New York: St. Martin's Press.

Djamin, Awaloedin. 1995. *Awaloedin Djamin, Pengalaman Seorang Perwira Polri*. Jakarta: Pustaka Sinar Harapan.

_____. 1999. *Menuju Polri Mandiri yang Profesional: Pengayom, Pelindung, Pelayan Masyarakat.* Jakarta: Yayasan Tenaga Kerja Indonesia.

Federspiel, Howard M. 1995. *A Dictionary of Indonesian Islam.* Monographs in International Studies, Southeast Asia Series Number 94. Athens: Ohio University.

Gatra. 2004. "Asap Politik di Markas Polisi". *Gatra* 32: 24–27, June 26, 2004.

Harian Banten. 2003. "BPPKB Anti Premanisme: Polisi Diminta Tak Ragu Menindak". January 13, 2003.

Honna, Jun. 2006. "Local Civil-Military Relations during the First Phase of Democratic Transition, 1999–2004: A Comparison of West, Central, and East Java". *Indonesia* 82: 75–96.

Institute for Policy Analysis of Conflict (IPAC). 2016. *Update on the Indonesian Military's Influence.* IPAC Report No. 26.

Jacobsen, Michael. 2002. To Be or What to Be – That is the Question' On Factionalism and Secessionism in North Sulawesi Province, Indonesia. Southeast Asia Research Center Working Paper Series No. 29. Hongkong: City University of Hongkong.

Janssen, Hilde. 2016. *Tanah Air Baru, Indonesia.* Jakarta: Gramedia Pustaka Utama.

Jurnal Security. 2017. "Jadi Anggota Asosiasi, Syarat BUJP Bisa Urus Izin Operasional". July 29, 2017. https://jurnalsecurity.com/jadi-anggota-asosiasi-syarat-bujp-bisa-urus-izin-operasional/ (accessed July 30, 2017).

MacDougall, John. 2007. "Criminality and the Political Economy of Security in Lombok". In *Renegotiating Boundaries: Local Politics in Post-Suharto Indonesia,* edited by Henk Schulte Nordholt and Gerry van Klinken, pp. 281-303. Leiden: KITLV Press.

Merdeka. 2016. "Kemhan: Kader Bela Negara Berjumlah 1,5 Juta". June 20, 2016. https://www.merdeka.com/peristiwa/kemhan-kader-bela-negara-berjumlah-15-juta-orang.html (accessd March 13, 2018).

North, Douglas et al. 2013. *Violence and Social Orders: A Conceptual Framework for Interpreting Recorded Human History* (reprint). Cambridge: Cambridge University Press.

Okamoto Masaaki. 2006. "Broker Keamanan di Jakarta: Yang Profesional dan Yang Berbasis Massa". In *Kelompok Kekerasan dan Bos Lokal di Indonesia Era Reformasi*, edited by Okamoto Masaaki dan Abdur Rozaki, pp. 1-19. Yogyakarta: IRE Press.

_____. 2015. *Politics of Violence and Adaptation: Democratization and Local Political Stabilization in Indonesia*. Kyoto: Kyoto University Press.

Okamoto Masaaki and Abdul Hamid. 2008. "Jawara in Power, 1998–2007". *Indonesia* 86: 109–138.

Pinter Politik. 2017. "Potret Negara di Tanah Abang". November 17, 2017. https://www.pinterpolitik.com/in-depth/potret-negara-di-tanah-abang (accessed December 20, 2017).

Prince, Erik. 2013. *Civilian Warriors: The Inside Story of Blackwater and the Unsung Heroes of the War on Terror*. New York: Portfolio.

Rozaki, Abdur. 2016. *Islam, Oligarki Politik & Perlawanan Sosial.* Yogyakarta: Suka Press and Pasca Sarjana UIN Sunan Kalijaga.

Ryter, Loren. 1998. "Pemuda Pancasila: The Last Loyalist Free Men of Suharto's Order?". *Indonesia* 66: 44–73.

_____. 2009. Their Moment in the Sun: The New Indonesian Parliamentarians from the Old OKP. In *State of Authority: The State in Society in Indonesia*, edited by Gerry van Klinken and Joshua Barker, pp, 181-218. Ithaca: Cornell University Press.

_____. 2014. Youth Gangs and Otherwise in Indonesia. In *Global Gangs: Street Violence across the World,* edited by Jennifer M. Hazen and

Dennis Rodgers, pp. 140-170. (eds.). Minneapolis and London: University of Minnesota Press.

Scahill, Jeremy, 2008. *Blackwater: The Rise of the World's Most Powerful Mercenary Army.* New York: Nation Books.

Soeharto. 1989. *Soeharto: Pikiran, Ucapan dan Tindakan Saya: Otobiografi, seperti Dipaparkan kepada G. Dwipayana dan Ramadhan K.H.* Jakarta: PT Citra Lamtoro Gung Persada.

Supriatma, Made. 2016. "Preman Bela Negara". *IndoPROGRESS* (June 17). https://indoprogress.com/2016/06/preman-bela-negara/ (accessed May 3, 2019).

Suryawan, I Ngurah. 2005. "Bisnis Kekerasan Jagoan Berkeris: Catatan Awal Aksi Pecalang dan Kelompok Milisi di Bali". In *Kelompok Kekerasan dan Bos Lokal di Era Reformasi,* edited by Okamoto Masaaki and Abdur Rozaki, pp. 91-114. Yogykarta: IRE Press.

_____. 2006. *Bali: Narasi dalam Kuasa: Politik & Kekerasan di Bali.* Yogyakarta: Ombak.

Swaraesi.com. 2019. "Kemhan dan Pemuda Pancasila Tandatangani MoU tentang Pembinaan Kesadaran Bela Negara". January 10, 2019. http://swararesi.com/article/211268/kemhan-dan-pemuda-pancasila-tandatangani-mou-tentang-pembinaan-kesadaran-bela-negara.html (accessed January 10, 2020).

Tempo. 2010. "Geng Reman van Jakarta". *Majalah Tempo,* November 15, 2010. https://majalah.tempo.co/read/investigasi/135105/geng-reman-van-jakarta (accessd January 22, 2011).

_____. 2013. "Alumni Pemuda Pancasila Jadi Menteri dan Politikus". March 17, 2013. https://metro.tempo.co/read/467526/alumni-pemuda-pancasila-jadi-menteri-dan-politikus (accessed June 3, 2015).

Tirto. 2017a. "Berebut Kuasa di Tanah Abang". November 15, 2017. https://tirto.id/berebut-kuasa-di-tanah-abang-cz5n (accessed December 20, 2017).

_____. 2017b. "Ucu Kambing: Kalau Memang ada Preman di Tanah Abang, Abang yang Bacok". November 15, 2017. https://tirto.id/kalau-memang-ada-preman-di-tanah-abang-abang-yang-bacok-cz5q (accessed December 20, 2017).

Tribun Bali. 2016. "Tiga Ormas di Bali Ikut Pelatihan Bela Negara, Tangkal Radikalisme dan Terorisme". July 29, 2016. https://bali.tribunnews.com/2016/07/29/tiga-ormas-di-bali-ikut-pelatihan-bela-negara-tangkal-radikalisme-dan-terorisme (accessd August 3, 2016).

Untung Widyanto. 2005. "Antara Jago dan Preman: Studi tentang Habitus Premanisme pada Organisasi Forum Betawi Rempug (FBR)". Thesis. Universitas Indonesia (unpublished).

Weber, Max. 1980. *Politics as a Vocation.* Tokyo: Iwanami Shoten (『職業としての政治』).

Wilson, Ian Douglas. 2006. "Continuity and Change: The Changing Contours of Organized Violence in Post-New Order Indonesia". *Critical Asian Studies* 38 (2): 265–297.

_____. 2015. *The Politics of Protection Rackets in Post-New Order Indonesia: Coercive Capital, Authority and Street Politics.* London: Routledge.

Wresniwiro, A. Haris Sumarna and Dede Permana S. 2002. *Membangun Budaya Pengamanan Swakarya: Satuan Pengamanan.* Jakarta: Yayasan Mitra Bintibmas.

Chapter 12
Intelligence Apparatus after Suharto: A Troubled Reform

Muhamad Haripin and Diandra Megaputri Mengko[1]

Reform of Indonesia's Badan Intelijen Negara (BIN—National Intelligence Agency) has lagged behind other security institutions. Reliable information on the country's intelligence agencies is rarely disclosed to the public, instigating great concern over undetected misconduct and violations committed by the agency and the broader security apparatus of which it is a part. Two political factors are salient to defining this situation. First, there is internal resistance to intelligence reform despite strong calls for it from civil society (see Widjajanto, 2006). Second, civilian leadership suffers from a lack of expertise and political support to advocate further democratic control over intelligence affairs (see Gill and Wilson, 2013: 169–170). Literature on intelligence in Indonesia has dealt with these issues since the beginning of *Reformasi* in May 1998. Key problems have been identified and discussed at great length by both Indonesian and foreign scholars focusing on Indonesian politics (see Widjajanto and Wardhani, 2008; Sebastian, 2006; Imparsial, 2005). Nonetheless, we have yet to learn about the state of intelligence activities and the institutional perspective on security threats in the contemporary period: How is Indonesian intelligence adapting to the new landscape of

---

1 Both authors of this chapter contributed equally.

security challenges in the country? How has the rapid shift in the nature of national security threats—from conventional types, such as a foreign invasion, to diverse and trans-national types, particularly terrorism—shaped the strategic views of Indonesia's intelligence community?

This chapter argues that the dynamics of civilian-military and state–intelligence relations are critical in shaping intelligence reform. This is due to the conflicting nature of intelligence and democracy itself, in which the former must operate in secret while the latter requires accountability and transparency. Therefore, finding the most appropriate balance of effectiveness and transparency between the two depends on the continual efforts of civilians as well as intelligence professionals to achieve such a balance. While well-established democracies have relatively well-developed mechanisms to deal with this challenge, young democracies are still in the process of creating them. The challenge of reform is considered even greater in post-authoritarian countries like Indonesia (see Sulistiyanto, 2007: 29).

The legacy of the militaristic culture of previous intelligence institutions, which supported the authoritarian regime, and their relations with the military establishment complicate contemporary institutional measures in establishing democratic control over the intelligence apparatus (see Bruneau and Dombroski, 2006: 153). The authoritarian politics employed by Suharto's New Order politicized and militarized intelligence agencies and structures to an unprecedented degree (see Muqoddas, 2011; Tanter, 1991; Jenkins, 1984; Southwood and Flanagan, 1983). Instead of collecting information and committing counterintelligence against potential hostile foreign and domestic enemies, field agents were heavily involved in monitoring local opposition groups and controlling the flow of information coming in and out of the country. Therefore, once democratic pressure prevailed, and reform aspirations began to sweep military institutions, intelligence reform gradually became one of the main issues advocated for, not only by the student movement and civil society in general, but also by civilian politicians (Haripin, 2013).

This chapter presents a detailed discussion of the latest developments in intelligence reform and their relation to counterterrorism measures in Indonesia. Data for this chapter was generated from open source documents and interviews. We argue that counterterrorism is an important entry point to examine intelligence activities in the democratic period, particularly given the political and economic resources deployed by the state. As we will discuss, the increasing number of terrorist attacks has forced the state to take extra and non-conventional security efforts against alleged radical groups. In tandem with the national police, BIN (Badan Intelijen Negara (State Intelligence Agency)) has been at the forefront of information-gathering activities to uncover terrorist cells and trace their financial transactions. Scholarship on terrorism in Indonesian has been dominated by efforts to disclose the full extent of terrorist networks in the country and examine the use of state resources to contain the threats. Of particular interest is the deployment of the police's counterterrorism special unit Detasemen Khusus Antiteror 88 (Densus 88) (Solahudin, 2013). Terrorism threats have thus determined the process of internal reform and the tactical development of the Indonesian police (Muradi, 2009: 85–96). Unfortunately, however, the relationship between counterterrorism measures and the dynamics of the intelligence community have yet to receive scholarly attention. This chapter therefore attempts to contribute to such important yet overlooked discussion.

Prior to discussing the main topic, two particular events need to be mentioned: (1) the appointment of non-military officers to head the state intelligence agency, which has broken an old pattern of all-military men at the top leadership of the intelligence community, and (2) the promulgation of the Intelligence Law in 2011. The new regulation is the result of a compromised consensus among security stakeholders in the country on how to manage state-intelligence relations in the post-authoritarian period. We will critically examine these two events in the following sections and then correlate them with the ongoing efforts of the post–authoritarian civilian government to impose democratic control over the broader intelligence community.

This chapter consists of three inter-related central components. First, it will discuss terrorist threats in the post-New Order era and how they have proliferated since the Bali bombing in October 2002. The Bali attack was considered a major blow to the security establishment because it exposed structural and technical deficiencies within the intelligence community. Intelligence failed to detect and deter the violence of terrorist groups against civilians, with devastating consequences: hundreds of people were killed and many more injured. Second, to contextualize our discussion about intelligence reform, the chapter will assess the dynamics of civilian-military relations in the post-authoritarian period. Furthermore, it will highlight the growing trend of civilian appointments to BIN and what this situation tells us about current state-intelligence relations. Third, it will examine the intelligence role in counter-terrorism. It argues that gradual reform initiated in the early phase of *Reformasi* required BIN to respond to democratization pressures, but that the emerging threats of terrorism have both enabled and constrained BIN to initiate some important reforms. Finally, the chapter reflects on lessons that can be learned from intelligence reform in Indonesia that might be useful for other new democracies in the region.

Terrorist Threats in Contemporary Indonesia

"Intelligence failure" is a common criticism of the security apparatus when crises and social disturbances erupt. A post-factum analysis of 9/11, a series of attacks in the United States on September 11, 2001 committed by the Islamist radical group Al-Qaeda, describes how the lack of coordination and information sharing within the intelligence community (for example between the Central Intelligence Agency and the Federal Bureau of Investigation) undermined the state's capacity to uphold a sound and rigid early warning system to prevent the terrorists from launching their mission (see Collier, 2010; Lahneman, 2007; The 9/11 Commission Report, 2004: 254–277). A similar lack of coordination among Indonesia's intelligence community was exposed immediately after a series of terrorist attacks in the early 2000s. In the following paragraphs, we will discuss the historical trajectory of terrorism and how it shapes the discourse of intelligence activities and threats assessment in Indonesia.

First, it is important to outline the particular conditions within which terrorist attacks occurred in Indonesia. Prior to the first attacks, the country had just undertaken a massive political shift from authoritarian rule to democratization. A central feature of the transformation was degrading the government's power to maintain public order due to a lack of political legitimacy. B. J. Habibie was unilaterally appointed by former President Suharto as the head of government without public consultation. Several troubling provinces, notably Aceh, Papua, and East Timor openly questioned Jakarta's legitimacy to enforce its power on the regions outside Java. Riots and ethnic and inter-religious conflicts broke out sporadically in—but not limited to—Jakarta, Tasikmalaya, Sambas, Sampit, Ambon, and Poso. In effect, this political instability provided fertile ground for the emergence and proliferation of Islamic radical groups in Indonesia, including Jemaah Islamiyah (JI) (see Vaughn, et al., 2005: 7 and 14.). The group had previously operated underground, away from public view. However, as the conflicts rapidly unfolded, and no viable response was visible on the horizon, JI and similar groups seized the opportunity to extend their networks, gain supporters, and execute violent plots to advance their goals. At that time, the government underestimated the potential devastation of such hostile networks. Terrorism was considered a minor problem compared to other pressing security concerns, particularly separatist movements. When attacks occurred in the first years of *Reformasi* (1999–2001), the security apparatus did not consider them exceptional, but rather criminal acts related to social conflict. Table 12.1. lists the recorded terrorist attacks from 1999 to 2017.

Indonesia at the Crossroads: Transformation and Challenges

Table 12.1. Terrorist Incidents in Indonesia in 1999–2017.

No.	Location	Time	Notes
1.	Al-Istiqlal mosque, Jakarta	April 1999	Explosion, 23 injured
2.	Catholic church, at Jl. Pemuda Medan, Jakarta	May 2000	Explosion
3.	Philippine Embassy, Jakarta	August 2000	Explosion, 2 killed and 21 injured
4.	Malaysian Embassy, Jakarta	August 2000	Explosion
5.	Jakarta Stock Exchange (Bursa Efek Jakarta, BEJ), Jakarta	September 2000	Explosion, 10 killed and 90 injured
6.	12 churches in Batam, Medan, Pekanbaru, Riau, Jakarta, and Mojokerto	December 2000	Explosions, 16 killed and 96 injured
7.	Saint Anna church, Jakarta	July 2001	Explosion, 5 injured
8.	Atrium Senen Mall, Jakarta	August 2001	Explosion (premature), 6 injured
9.	The first Bali bombing	October 2002	Explosion, 202 killed and 300 injured
10.	JW Marriot Hotel, Jakarta	August 2003	Explosion, 12 killed and 15 injured
11.	Australian Embassy, Jakarta	September 2004	Explosion, 9 killed and 173 injured
12.	The second Bali bombing	October 2005	Explosion, 22 killed and 120 injured
13.	JW Marriott and Ritz Carlton hotels, Jakarta	July 2009	Exploded, 9 killed and 53 injured
14.	Cirebon	April 2011	Explosion, 25 injured
15.	Gading Serpong, Jakarta	April 2011	Explosion aborted by the police
16.	Solo	September 2011	Explosion, 1 killed and 28 injured
17.	Solo	November 2012	Aborted by the police
18.	Poso	June 2013	Explosion, killed the perpetrators
19.	Thamrin, Jakarta	January 2016	Exploded, 8 killed and 26 injured
20.	Kampung Melayu, Jakarta	May 2017	Explosion, 5 killed and 10 injured

Source: various public documents.

A series of bomb explosions targeting churches in 2000 finally instilled a sense of emergency among national security stakeholders. The incidents were bigger than mere criminal acts; they were apparently instigated to serve a greater purpose. Nevertheless, due to a lack of reliable information, authorities found it difficult to track down the perpetrators. Only after time-consuming investigations did BIN and military intelligence Badan Intelijen Strategis Tentara Nasional Indonesia (BAIS TNI Strategic Intelligence Agency of Indonesian National Armed forces) gradually begin to piece together a rough sketch of terrorist cells and their areas of operation. Members of JI were monitored by human intelligence (humint). The use of signal intelligence (sigint) and communication intelligence (comint) was minimum, mainly due to budget and technical limitations. However, counter-terror efforts to dismantle JI's network were quite slow. The failure to prevent another bomb attack at Atrium Senen shopping mall in 2001 reflected this problem. Thanks to a tactical error, the bomb exploded prematurely, but its message was well-received by the general public (Conboy, 2004: 212–214). That is Indonesia had become a proxy target of radical cells to establish a non-secular state based on religious values, to fight against Western powers, and to promote their conservative worldview.

The subsequent bombing in Bali on October 12, 2002 prompted the intelligence agencies to ramp up their information gathering and analysis efforts. Intelligence was clearly far behind the terrorist networks, which had cemented their presence and mission not only across the archipelago, but in Southeast Asia more broadly. In this light, some foreign countries expressed frustration about the failures of the Indonesian authorities to prevent such atrocities. United States diplomatic and intelligence officials had reportedly informed their Indonesian counterparts in advance about possible terrorist attacks directed against "Western tourist sites" two weeks before the Bali bombing (*CNN*, 2002). Even more surprising, the director of BIN, A.M. Hendopriyono, admitted that he was aware of the threats ten months prior to the attacks. The problem, he said, was that no one took his concerns seriously (*Liputan 6*, 2002). All of this exposed the weaknesses in coordination between the intelligence agencies and the police. Despite the provision of initial information about JI by domestic and foreign intelligence entities, the Indonesian police began their investigation of the Bali bombing from scratch, with little knowledge about JI and its internal operations (Wachjunadi, 2017: 81–82). It remains unclear, however, whether this was the result of bureaucratic rivalries between security and defense agencies, simply the absence of reliable information-sharing channels, or a lack of political will to share—and follow up—information related to terrorism in the country. We may assume that a combination of these factors is likely.

In October 2002, less than a month after the first Bali bombing, the police arrested the main perpetrators, including Ali Gufron, Ali Imron, Amrozi, and Imam Samudera. More than 200 individuals allegedly linked with the attack were placed in custody in Indonesia and several other countries, including the United States. Indonesian intelligence also deported some key JI members to their home countries. Nevertheless, the extent of JI's capability remained unknown and undeterred, as evidenced by the bomb attacks at the JW Marriott Hotel in Jakarta in 2003. The organization still had sufficient material, personnel, and financial support to undertake a high-level mission in the center of Jakarta's business district (ICG, 2003). The Indonesian National Police explained that they had prior information about the plot; they knew that JW Marriott Hotel was on the terrorists' list, due to its symbolic importance as a Western establishment, but they could not confirm the specifics of how and when the assault was going to be launched. The Jakarta police spokesman stated that the target list was found in Semarang during a police raid against JI members prior to the bombing (*The Guardian*, 2003). BIN officials were hesitant to release any statement regarding the attack and police findings.

By 2004, Indonesia had at least four agencies directly involved in intelligence activities, namely, BIN as the civilian-based intelligence agency, BAIS TNI as the military intelligence, Badan Intelijen Keamanan

Kepolisian Negara Republik Indonesia (Baintelkam Polri) as the police/ security intelligence, and the Detasemen Khusus Antiteror 88 or Densus 88, a newly-established police Special Detachment Unit on Anti-Terror (see Figure 12.1.). The latter has played a significant role in counter-terror measures, including providing tactical intelligence. Equipped with the latest surveillance technology, the police special unit has been able to trace and arrest members of radical cells, some of them highly-trained in bomb-making, for instance Dr. Azahari Husin. Densus 88 has also been involved in various international cooperation efforts with foreign law enforcement agencies (Seniwati, 2014: 563). Densus 88 has had a huge impact on counter-terrorism in Indonesia and in the process, it has helped to strengthen the intelligence gathering process conducted by BIN. This co-development evolved naturally into a division of labor between the police and intelligence: the former deals with tactical intelligence to pursue and arrest alleged terrorists, while the latter is responsible for predicting potential attacks by either home-grown or foreign terrorists on Indonesian soil.

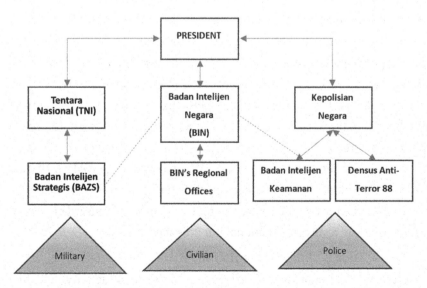

Figure 12.1. Indonesia's intelligence structure 2004–present. Source: various public documents

Despite policies implemented to reinforce the intelligence community, bombings continued unabated. In 2004 and 2005 two major blasts occurred in Jakarta and Bali. In the first, an explosives-loaded minivan killed and injured many local civilians who happened to be on the sidewalks near the security post of the Australian Embassy. Criticism of the intelligence community once again surfaced, questioning the readiness of intelligence in providing necessary information to contain such deadly attacks. Two days prior to the incident, the public was already anxious over the capabilities of the intelligence agencies and the security sector in general. Munir, a prominent human rights activist and lawyer, died on a flight to Amsterdam. The autopsy conducted by the Dutch authorities concluded that Munir had been poisoned using arsenic. Later, the public learned that a high-ranking BIN official was implicated in the murder. Public calls for intelligence reform grew stronger.

The second attack happened in Bali in October 2005. The intelligence response was muddled: instead of providing a clear and sober analysis of the resilience of terrorist networks in Indonesia, BIN suggested that the government's austerity measures—primarily the elimination of fuel subsidies—were the reason behind the attack (Wachjunadi, 2017: 204–205). This speculation was challenged by the police, who found that the same type of explosives used in previous JI operations were used in the Bali attack (ibid.). Commenting on this interpretative discrepancy in 2005, Lt. Gen. (Ret.) Agus Widjojo, the current Governor of Lembaga Ketahanan Nasional or (Lemhanas—National Resilience Institute), noted that the failure lie in institutional factors: the ambiguity of the division of labor among intelligence agencies (BIN, the military's BAIS TNI, and the police's Baintelkam Polri), had created confusion over who should be the leading agency on counter-terrorism, which in turn hindered concerted efforts to create a sufficient national intelligence framework (*Detik*, 2005).

The bombings of the JW Marriott and Ritz Carlton hotels in July 2009 were the first incidents after a brief hiatus in terrorist activity since the Bali bombing in October 2005. For nearly four years, no major incidents happened in Jakarta or other big cities, during which time the police and intelligence agencies continued to pursue terrorist cells and arrest their leaders and followers. Against this backdrop, the second Marriott bombing in 2009 surprised not only the general public, but also officials. It is true that the intelligence apparatus has yet to find a link between Noordin M. Top, a ringleader of JI, and the attack, but at the time nobody seemed to believe that the existing JI network was capable of committing such a high-scale attack. In reality, such assessment turned out to be too optimistic. The director of BIN, Syamsir Siregar, admitted that his agency had no prior knowledge of the terrorist plot. He also stressed that there was no initial information regarding the plan shared among agencies in the region, indicating the lack of capability on the side of fellow foreign intelligences (*Merdeka*, 2009).

The role of BIN in counter-terrorism was once again put to the test in the early 2010s. New unidentified sympathizers of radical teachings and former terrorist convicts proliferated in big cities and were ready to launch attacks unexpectedly. Nevertheless, in terms of magnitude, the series of attacks that occurred in Cirebon (2011), Solo (2011), and Poso (2013) indicated a drastic decline in the capability of terrorist cells. Instead of aiming for major assaults against Western establishments, they were now targeting police officers on duty and state officials in general. Their method of attack had also evolved, from the use of high-grade explosives to low-explosives and guns, reducing the scale of destruction.

Two attempted attacks, one in Gading Serpong, Jakarta in 2011 and one in Solo in 2012, were successfully aborted by the police. Some argue that credit for this must be given mainly to the Densus 88, rather than BIN. The special unit's achievements in arresting terrorist suspects and dismantling their networks are said to be consequential for the development of counter-terror measures in Indonesia (*Tribunnews*, 2011a). Along with the continuing trend of terrorist attacks and other security disturbances, the parliament finally agreed to promulgate a new Intelligence Law in 2001 (Law Number 17 Year 2011 about National Intelligence) that appointed

BIN as the principal coordinator of intelligence in Indonesia. It is hoped that the regulation, by providing more clarity in agency roles, will strengthen intelligence sharing and cooperation.

The rise of the Islamic State of Iraq and Al-Sham (ISIS) in the Middle East presented new challenges for Indonesian intelligence. A small group of former convicted terrorists as well as newly recruited personnel who expressed allegiance to ISIS committed a dramatic assault against police officers and a coffee shop on M.H. Thamrin Road, a main thoroughfare in central Jakarta in 2016. Director of BIN Sutiyoso denied allegations that his agency failed to provide sufficient intelligence of the attacks to the government and police. He said that warnings over potential ISIS-inspired attacks had been looming since mid-2015. BIN was fully aware that the development of ISIS might trigger terrorist incidents in Indonesia (*Kompas,* 2015). Therefore, Sutiyoso implied that false blame should not be used to discredit the intelligence agency. Similar lines of argument reappeared after a bomb explosion at the bus terminal in Kampung Melayu, Jakarta in 2017. Police General Budi Gunawan, Sutiyoso's successor at BIN, issued a statement that the attack was committed by a local radical group affiliated with ISIS (*Detik,* 2017). Nevertheless, there is no record of BIN issuing a warning of the Kampung Melayu bomb.

From the above discussion, we can discern that the rise of terrorism threats generated a new security narrative for Indonesia's intelligence community. Gradually, the target shifted from focusing on public order and maintenance of the New Order regime to defending the post-authoritarian state's national security from internal and external threats. In conjunction with this, the intelligence structure evolved to include the establishment of Polri's Densus 88 and regional intelligence offices (BIN di Daerah or Binda). It is clear that terrorism threats pushed security actors to improve their organizational and coordination capacities. As we will discuss in the next section, such measures have been initiated as part of a broader security sector reform agenda. However, the growth of terrorist threats during the past decade has further complicated the reform process and has exposed the convoluted relationships between intelligence agencies and the police in the post-authoritarian era.

State-Intelligence Relations in Post-Authoritarian Indonesia

This section attempts to provide the political context for intelligence difficulties—and failures—in anticipating terrorist attacks. To provide a better picture, we argue that state-intelligence relations play a significant role in shaping intelligence practices and success rates in counter-terrorism. Furthermore, Indonesia is a compelling case to discuss the challenges of counter–terrorism measures in post–authoritarian states because it still lacks appropriate mechanisms to balance the necessities of secrecy in intelligence and security operations and the democratic requirements of accountability and transparency.[2]

Immediately after 1998, the president was heavily relied upon to provide a civilian counterbalance to the intelligence community; not because of the president's centralized power, but because of the inability of the legislative body to conduct meticulous oversight of intelligence agencies. Meanwhile, civil society only became extensively involved in intelligence reform discourse after the murder of Munir, a prominent lawyer and human rights activist, in 2004. Prior to that, the majority of civil society organizations tended to focus on military reform, neglecting the importance of thorough public deliberation on intelligence reform. These conditions positioned the president, at least until 2004, as the only civilian actor who could exercise authority to monitor the intelligence sector.

---

2   See discussion on the relations of civil and military in democratic countries on Bruneau and Dombroski (2006: 145).

Table 12.2. Director of National Intelligence Agency in post-Suharto Indonesia.

Period	Name	Professional background
May 1998 – November 1999	Z. A. Maulani	Army
November 1999 – August 2001	Arie J. Kumaat	Army
August 2001 – December 2004	A. M. Hendropriyono	Army
December 2004 – October 2009	Syamsir Siregar	Army
October 2009 – October 2011	Sutanto	Police
October 2011 – July 2015	Marciano Norman	Army
July 2015 – September 2016	Sutiyoso	Army
September 2016 – present	Budi Gunawan	Police

Source: various public documents.

Presidents B. J. Habibie (1998–1999) and Abdurrahman Wahid, commonly known as Gus Dur, (1999–2001) were not darlings of the military.[3] As such, the robust legacy of military-dominated intelligence made managing intelligence a constant struggle for both of them. For Habibie, intelligence reform required avoiding any political measures that would put him in a detrimental position vis-a-vis the officers. Focusing on restoring the Indonesian economy, he played it safe by appointing a military man as the director of BAKIN (State Intelligence Coordinating Agency, the predecessor of BIN), Lt. Gen. (Ret.) Z. A. Maulani, one of Habibie's few allies in the military. This decision perpetuated the already strong culture of military supremacy within the supposedly civilian-based

---

3   B. J. Habibie had a problematic relationship with the military. In the final years of New Order, he proposed establishing national defence industries which would have potentially disrupted the military business interests. Meanwhile, Abdurrahman Wahid was known as an activist who never hesitated to criticize the military establishment.

intelligence agency. Given his modest political background, Habibie was also reluctant to direct the agency along democratization lines or to give clear orders regarding internal reform and potential threats to be anticipated (Conboy, 2004: 202). Therefore, it is not surprising that BAKIN failed to fully grasp the early development of terrorism in the post-Suharto period. The terror incidents that occurred in the 2000s were misinterpreted as inter-religion conflicts rather than as a specific and emerging transnational terrorism threat to the archipelago.

Following Habibie's example, President Wahid also appointed a former military man as director of BAKIN, Lt. Gen. (Ret.) Arie Kumaat. Kumaat was the former deputy director of BAIS TNI. The nature of the relationship between these two figures is not clear. However, it seems that Kumaat's Catholic background helped him gain support from Wahid, who aspired to accommodate "the nationalist camp" within the military which had been marginalized in the final years of the Suharto administration.[4] President Wahid spearheaded several breakthroughs in gradually dismantling the militaristic-oriented paradigm that had been entrenched within the intelligence community for years. He issued Presidential Decree 38 Year 2000 to abolish Badan Koordinasi Bantuan Pemantapan Stabilitas Nasional (Bakorstanas—Coordinating Agency for National Stability), the successor of the executive super body Komando Pemulihan Keamanan dan Ketertiban (Kopkamtib—Operational Command for the Restoration of Security and Order), and Penelitian Khusus (Litsus—Special Research), which conducted political "screenings" of public officials as well as private actors. These two agencies were known as Suharto's political machinery and intelligence structure for suppressing opposition groups. In addition, Wahid made a bold move to strengthen civilian intelligence capability by establishing Lembaga Intelijen Negara (LIN—State Intelligence Institute) under the Ministry of Defense, giving it responsibility for overseeing BAIS

---

4   There had been two conflicting factions within the military: the green faction comprising those who established personal links with Islamic figures, and the red-and-white faction (red and white are the colours of Indonesian flag, or the nationalist faction) arguably comprised of non-Muslim officers.

TNI. Finally, he doubled the budget for BAKIN to give the agency more flexibility in domestic operations (Conboy, 2004: 204).

These controversial moves, as anticipated, generated discontent among military officers, and sparked rivalry between civilian and military intelligence. Friction between the president and military was unavoidable, and eventually escalated into a high-level political conflict that cost Wahid his presidency. He was impeached in 2001 by the parliament with support from the military. The appointment of Kumaat, a former military officer, hardly muffled the tension. Against this backdrop, it was hardly surprising when BAKIN accused the military of masterminding bomb threats and terror acts against churches on Christmas Eve in 2000; such security disturbances, it said, were created to delegitimize President Wahid. The accusation turned out to be false, as we have discussed in the previous section: the bombs were planted by JI. However, as Wahid was apparently on the side of BAKIN, the government was reluctant to consider terrorist acts high-priority security threats. Instead, they saw them as the military maneuvering to undermine Wahid's presidency (ibid.).

When Megawati Sukarnoputri replaced Abdurrahman Wahid in 2001, the conditions for civil-military relations were different. Unlike her predecessors, Megawati was widely regarded as a friend of the military and had a long and close association with some high-ranking officers. She appointed A. M. Hendropriyono, her political ally, as director of BIN (the successor of BAKIN). The personal relationship between Megawati and Hendropriyono can be traced back to 1993, when the latter helped the former to win the leadership of Partai Demokrasi Indonesia (PDI—Indonesian Democratic Party). He was also known to have provided protection and support for Megawati to become president (Kingsbury, 2003: 240). Mutual trust between the two should have forged an opportunity for President Megawati to initiate intelligence reform. Nevertheless, she compromised the intelligence function of information-gathering and analysis to benefit her own interests in retaining political power. Moreover, Megawati obscured the distinction between intelligence activities and the decision-making process, which in return helped to shape BIN and Hendropriyono as Megawati's personal intel. It is important to note that studies have found that when intelligence is brought too close to the policy-making process, it is more likely to be corrupted (Bruneau and Dombroski, 2006: 162–164).

Following the first Bali bombing in October 2002, Megawati immediately called a cabinet meeting. From available reports, she seemed to blame the failure on the police rather than intelligence (Wachjunadi, 2017, 86–87). Nevertheless, BIN's internal evaluation suggested that the intelligence agency must be given a mandate to coordinate intelligence activities and to arrest and detain terrorist suspects in order to prevent future atrocities (Sebastian, 2006: 102). In the search for a better framework to contain terrorism, the president signed Peraturan Pemerintah Pengganti Undang-Undang (Perpu—Regulation in lieu of Law) Number 1 Year 2002, which outlined a security, rather than defense-oriented, policy. This regulation was reinforced as the Counter-Terrorism Law in 2003 (Law Number 15 Year 2003 about Combating Criminal Acts of Terrorism). Furthermore, President Megawati signed Instruksi Presiden (Inpres— Presidential Instruction) Number 5 Year 2002 which designated BIN as the coordinating agency of all intelligence activities. According to the Instruction, BIN has the legal standing and political legitimacy to manage information gathering, analysis, and intelligence missions conducted by the police and the military. In practice, however, the opposite occurs (Wise, 2005: 41). Meanwhile, President Megawati seemed to be unenthusiastic about granting arrest and detention authority to BIN. The reason might be political; she did not want risk her position in the eyes of Muslims in the country, since the discourse of terrorism so far had been unfairly discrediting them. Imposing stricter monitoring of the Islamic community might have cost her a large number of votes in the 2004 presidential election.

This raises questions about the impact of political interests on intelligence effectiveness. The extent of JI's network and its terror capability were already identified, so why there was no explicit order or red alert from

BIN to outlaw the organization (Cianflone et al., 2007: 23)? The absence of such recommendations downplayed the imminent threats of terrorism. The intelligence failure to prevent two major blasts, at Jakarta's JW Marriott Hotel in 2003 and the Australian Embassy in 2004, can be seen as a direct consequence of not only technical failures on the part of the government, namely a lack of intelligence coordination, but also the politicization of security threats (*Kompas*, 2002). Intelligence effectiveness was apparently overshadowed by the ruling regime's determination to maintain power. Fear and anxiety over the possible predicament that would befall the Megawati administration if the state extended intelligence activities upon the wider Muslim community hindered the counter-terrorism agenda (Wise, 2005: 47–49).

Susilo Bambang Yudhoyono, elected president in 2004, appointed Maj. Gen. (Ret.) Syamsir Siregar, a former commander of BAIS TNI (1994–1996) and a member of the president's campaign team, to be director of BIN. Yudhoyono removed the BIN director from the cabinet, distancing intelligence from the policy-making process and emphasizing BIN's role as producer of strategic security-related information. Both the president and the newly appointed director shared similar concerns over the threats of terrorism. Nevertheless, the Yudhoyono administration assumed that the evidence of JI involvement in terror attacks in Indonesia was insufficient. It is possible that political considerations played a major role in the formulation of this strategic fallacy, as the rise of Yudhoyono had been largely supported by Islamic groups (Cianflone et al., 2007: 23). This misjudgment, we argue, contributed to the intelligence failure to anticipate the subsequent JI bombings in Bali (2005) and at the JW Marriott and Ritz Carlton hotels in 2009. As mentioned in the previous section, the second Bali bombing was initially assumed to be related to opposition to the government's elimination of the fuel subsidy.

The politicization of intelligence and security threats during the Yudhoyono period was also detrimental to the accuracy of intelligence predictions. From the records available, we learn that Syamsir's appointment had political considerations. He was expected to clear the agency of Hendropriyono's influence. Offering early retirement to existing staff, reassigning personnel who were previously appointed by Hendropriyono, and reducing the number of divisions were among the methods used to accomplish this sensitive mission (Wise, 2005: 51–52). Internally, BIN monitored this situation as the president exercised power cautiously. When the president claimed that terrorist groups wanted to kill him, intelligence reports asserted the ambiguous claim that radicals were targeting him. A photo of him being used as a shooting target indicated that the mission of terrorist groups had shifted from the Western establishment to national leaders (*Liputan 6*, 2009). The photo, however, turned out to have been discovered during the investigation of the Poso conflict in 2004, and the former BIN director Hendropriyono had previously reported it (*Tribunnews*, 2009).

In his second presidential term (2009–2014), Yudhoyono appointed Sutanto, a former Chief of National Police (2005–2008), as the new director of BIN. Sutanto's record on counter-terrorism was stunning; key terror masterminds were arrested by the police during his tenure. The public and the police applauded the appointment as a significant new chapter in BIN development; it had become a civilian-based intelligence agency led by a civilian. Nonetheless, the internal composition of the agency continued to be dominated by the military. Sutanto prioritized strengthening intelligence-sharing between BIN and the police in counter-terrorism operations. He also promoted the notion that intelligence should be applicable as evidence in court (*Tribunnews*, 2011b).

President Yudhoyono replaced Sutanto with Lt. Gen. Marciano Norman, a former Commander of the Presidential Security Unit (Paspamres, 2008–2010) and Jakarta Military Command (Kodam Jaya, 2010–2011), in October 2011. Marciano had a limited intelligence background, but he had maintained close ties with Yudhoyono since the 1990s. His appointment at first generated public criticism about a return of military domination of the BIN. However, Marciano employed Hendropriyono's strategy in harnessing public sympathy, by being open to the media (*The Jakarta Post*, 2011).

Following the Yudhoyono presidency, Joko Widodo, or Jokowi, entered the political scene offering a different style of leadership. In the intelligence sector, he appointed Lt. Gen. (Ret.) Sutiyoso as director of BIN, which can be attributed to Sutiyoso's role as chairman of Partai Keadilan dan Persatuan Indonesia (PKPI—Indonesian Unity and Justice Party), which supported Jokowi in the 2014 election. Sutiyoso's tenure was short-lived, however, and he was replaced by Pol. Gen. Budi Gunawan, deputy chief of the national police. Budi had a problematic track record; prior to being appointed as deputy chief of police, he was under the spotlight for having an unusual amount of money in his bank account. He was also known to be close to Megawati Sukarnoputri, the chairperson of the PDIP. Against this backdrop, Budi's appointment raised concerns about collusion. Indeed, the political context behind this appointment influenced the nature of state-intelligence relations. Even though mechanisms for parliament scrutiny or presidential authority to evaluate BIN's performance were available, both actors exercised it only procedurally rather than substantially, as illustrated by the absence of any thorough evaluation of BIN in the aftermath of the bomb explosions in Jakarta, Thamrin in 2016 and Kampung Melayu in 2017 (*CNN*, 2016).

From the discussion above, we can draw the following conclusions. First, the appointment of the intelligence chief tends to be driven by political considerations rather than merit-based mechanisms and professionalism. This might explain the lack of scrutiny and intelligence oversight by the president and parliament. Additionally, internal evaluations, which mainly promote the need to expand intelligence's authority, are inadequate in providing needed information on how to enhance the professionalism and mission effectiveness of the agency. In sum, the state-intelligence relations in Indonesia during the democratic period have been ambiguous in many respects. Next, we will elaborate these findings in the context of the intelligence role in counter-terrorism.

Indonesian Intelligence in the Age of Terror

Looming terrorist threats have prompted the government to strengthen national intelligence capacities. Given the dim prospect that the intention and skills of terrorist groups to commit violence will retreat, it is important for BIN to have robust human and signal intelligence management (*The Jakarta Post*, 2017). Nonetheless, in this section we argue that the role of intelligence in counter-terrorism remains in the shadows of its earlier role. The agency still suffers from politicization to an extent that hinders the establishment of adequate scrutiny and evaluation mechanisms, thus complicating intelligence activities on counter-terrorism.

Ten days after the first Bali bombing in 2002, President Megawati issued a presidential instruction designating BIN to coordinate all intelligence activities in the country, including those conducted by the military (ICG, 2002; Republik Indonesia 2002). At the same time, the national police was urged to immediately investigate the attacks, search out the perpetrators, dismantle their networks, and establish a better institutional arrangement to deal with emerging threats. Meanwhile, the military took the initiative to mobilize personnel at the village level, through the Babinsa (Bintara Pembina Desa), to identify terrorist groups and improve intelligence-gathering (Honna, 2013: 192). Despite these efforts, significant concerns remained about the availability of reliable information on the Bali bombing perpetrators, specifically the identity of terror group members and their operational coverage. As confirmed by the police account, Polri itself did not have adequate and reliable data on such important information; this suggests the attacks came as much of a surprise to officials as they were for the public in general (Wachjunadi, 2017). Chief of National Police Pol. Gen. Da'i Bachtiar (2001–2005) was particularly in the spotlight for failing to give a convincing account of the nature and extent of terrorism in the archipelago. Furthermore, a sense of panic was rising, not only in Indonesia, but across the regional. Less than a month after the Bali bombing, on November 3, 2002, the Association of Southeast Asian Nations (ASEAN) issued a Declaration on Terrorism, which in effect further pushed the national effort to urgently tackle terrorism (ASEAN, 2012).

The regulation President Megawati issued was an important stepping stone for the national intelligence agency, BIN, to reinvigorate its internal cohesion and external coordination. The government argued that a decentralized and highly-compartmentalized intelligence apparatus was a major problem that hindered the development of an integrated and well-connected early warning system among agencies to detect and deter terrorist attacks. Thus, the role of BIN as national intelligence coordinator and provider of strategic information needed to be revitalized. Being given such a strong mandate by the president, Director Hendropriyono went further, requesting the authority for BIN personnel to arrest and detain alleged terrorist suspects. He argued that the existing authority of collecting, analyzing and distributing information, without direct involvement in operations, was inadequate for the agency to properly fulfil its role in combating terrorism. Nevertheless, such aspirations have never been realized due to public criticism and tacit rejection from fellow security actors that opposed an expansion of BIN's role. In this regard, the government also seemed to be unaware of the unexpected consequences of centralizing intelligence; instead of a better-coordinated counter-terrorism effort, it led to excessive surveillance of society. At the same time, it emboldened the military to promote territorial commands (komando territorial, koter) as a domestic/security intelligence instrument (Haripin, 2017).

Aside from the rather contentious proposal above, Hendropriyono introduced much less controversial institution-building initiatives. To fulfil the urgent need of personnel, Sekolah Tinggi Intelijen Negara (STIN—National Intelligence College) was established to provide BIN with highly-skilled personnel who could creatively extract information from reliable sources and conduct covert operations in challenging circumstances. President Yudhoyono signed a presidential regulation to affirm STIN in 2009, even though the college had already been in operation for four years (Republik Indonesia, 2009). Responding to the aspiration for public engagement in intelligence affairs, a number of experts and relevant figures were invited to join Board of Strategic Analysts (Dewan Analis Strategis or DAS), a so-called internal think-tank to support the director of BIN in formulating intelligence policy. Growing threats of terrorism prompted the agency to expand its network outside traditional intelligence circles. One notable member of DAS was Muhammad AS Hikam, Minister of Research and Technology during B.J. Habibie's presidency. Hikam was the editor of "Toward 2014–2019: Strengthening Indonesia in a Changing World," a book on Indonesia's strategic overview released by BIN after the promulgation of the Law on Intelligence in 2011 (Hikam ed., 2014: 107[5]). The book reflects BIN's assessment of current and future political and strategic trends that will impact Indonesia and lists terrorist threats as one of the most pressing issues facing the archipelago. Following the standard exposition about the network of radical groups and their rising capability, it is interesting to note that the book also asserts the importance of effective counter-terrorism in Indonesia. The prospects of democratic consolidation will be greatly threatened if the state apparatus fails to take extraordinary measures to urgently tackle terrorism (Hikam, ed., 2014: 107). Thus, according to the authors, the role of BIN in domestic and foreign intelligence gathering is paramount to ensuring the success of democratization.

The appointment of Syamsir Siregar as Hendropriyono's successor signified an interesting development in the relationship between BIN and counter-terrorism. After his inauguration, Syamsir said he would prioritize internal capacity building and the fight against terrorism (Haseman, 2005: 28). The job apparently was not easy. Counter-terrorism has become a collective effort, positioning Polri as the leading force. BIN was expected to supply detailed analyses and substantial inputs that would help the counter-terrorism special detachment carry out its mission. Intelligence and police

---

5   This book is written by a group of scholars and officials working under the auspices of the Board of Dewan Analis Strategis, Badan Intelijen Negara (DAS, BIN—Strategic Analyst, National Intelligence Agency). For a short review of the document, see (Noor, 2014).

reportedly established a mutual collaboration (authors' interview with the former Deputy Director of BIN, 29 April 2015; Haseman, 2005: 29). The results can be seen in a series of arrests and raids against terrorist suspects successfully undertaken after the first Bali bombing on October 12, 2002. As the role of intelligence in counter-terrorism was acknowledged, pressures for internal reform and democratic oversight over BIN activities increased. As discussed in the previous section, the murder of Munir, a prominent human rights activist, on September 7, 2004 on a flight to Amsterdam which implicated BIN operatives forced the agency to take into account public concerns about intelligence abuse of power. Interestingly, the BIN establishment did not explicitly demonstrate a meaningful effort to neutralize this political brouhaha, even though the judicial process of the Munir case compromised their counter-terrorism agenda.

Domestic security deteriorated rapidly following the major bombings that occurred throughout 2003–2005. JI proved to be resilient despite some of its key leaders being detained by the police. The problem was how to dismantle the radical networks and prevent future attacks. BIN argued that they needed extrajudicial authority to arrest, detain, and wiretap individuals allegedly connected with terrorist networks. They requested expanded power through formal regulation, thus obtaining necessary justification to broaden their role in counter-terrorism missions. The Yudhoyono administration was particularly interested in this notion. Against this background, the government tried to embark on the strenuous task of combining a reform agenda, which would be oriented towards establishing a democratic intelligence system, and a pragmatic program of strengthening intelligence's counter-terror capability. Both public concerns and long-term strategic necessities had informed the decision makers that BIN should undertake internal reforms in order to enhance its tactical effectiveness against terrorist networks. Similar to the typical institutional engineering implemented to the post-authoritarian intelligence agency, for instance the initiatives of Hendropriyono and Syamsir to establish economic intelligence as well as information technology divisions, BIN proposed establishing local intelligence offices, which was approved by the president. Since BIN had been designated to coordinate intelligence activities among the military, police, immigration, and attorney general offices, it was argued that the agency would be better able to carry out its mission if it had local reinforcements that could collect and analyze information promptly. The first regional intelligence office was eventually built in Bali, the location of two major bomb attacks in 2002 and 2005 (*Tempo*, 2005).

Further intelligence fiascos that resulted in the terrorist assaults at the JW Marriott and Ritz Carlton hotels in 2009 in Jakarta strengthened BIN's plan to greatly expand its function. President Yudhoyono and Syamsir reiterated the importance of strengthening BIN by granting it arrest, detention, and wiretapping authority on the premise that field operatives sometimes obtain crucial information that leads to the location of perpetrators and their networks, which needs to be responded to as soon as possible, and coordinating with other agencies takes time that put operations at risk. This happened, for instance, when the alleged key actors behind the second Bali bombing learned of the plan to raid their hiding place (Al A'raf, 2015: 243). This failed ambush was believed to be the result of information leakages and uncoordinated efforts between the police and BIN. Thus, the effective division of labor among security stakeholders underpinning mission effectiveness was argued to be an urgent task for the government. One way to achieve this objective was to delegate arrest and wiretapping authority to BIN personnel.

Throughout the final years of Yudhoyono's first presidency, the government made great efforts to expand BIN's authority to collect information. The draft Intelligence Law detailed the method and elucidated the role and objective of the intelligence agency. Civil society did not endorse this draft. A significant objection was that BIN would not need court approval to conduct disturbing methods of intelligence gathering. People worried that this could obstruct the broader agenda of establishing a democratic intelligence system and society; court rule, they argued, should determine whether BIN's proposal to arrest and wiretap alleged terrorist suspects was justifiable. Nevertheless, the Intelligence Law was promulgated in 2011. It stipulates that BIN is allowed to conduct wiretapping to collect intelligence from reliable sources. The Law also underlines the operational scope of BIN's authority in *penyelidikan* (investigation), *pengamanan* (counterintelligence), and *penggalangan* (covert action). This indicates that Indonesia is adopting an integrated intelligence system rather than a differentiated or rigid separation of intelligence activity and policy. The continuing threat of terrorism has certainly been one of the main considerations in submitting such provisions into the law.

Conclusion

We have discussed the dynamics of the role of intelligence in counterterrorism in the post-1998 political context of Indonesia. The country had previously experienced unexpected security turbulence instigated by armed groups, but never before had it suffered impacts as severe as those of the Bali bombing on October 12, 2002. Both the state and society were caught off guard by the existence, extent, and capabilities of terrorist networks. Prior to the 2002 bombing, violent incidents had used similar methods, but on a much smaller scale. Intelligence has identified some of the alleged masterminds behind the terror attacks. Nevertheless, due to a lack of an early warning system, BIN failed to provide and share necessary information that might have prevented the assaults. Threats, and acts, of terrorism have loomed in Indonesia ever since. A set of new regulations was introduced to launch counter-terror measures: BIN was given a crucial role as the coordinator of national intelligence, responsible for supplying reliable dossiers on anything related to the proliferation of terrorist cells, including their international links and sources of funding.

We have proposed how the discussion of intelligence and counterterrorism should be located within a framework of state-intelligence relations in the post-authoritarian period. Although is is a civilian-based institution, for more than three decades the country's main intelligence agency has been dominated by uniformed military officers (especially, from the army). Following the *Reformasi* movement, the notion of professional and demilitarized intelligence entered the policy agenda of security sector reform. President Wahid, for instance, abolished the extra-judicial intelligence body Bakorstanas, in effect reducing the state's overreaching tentacles into public life. Nevertheless, Wahid and his predecessor, Habibie, failed to transform BIN into a civilian agency, appointing former high-ranking military officers to direct it. Megawati continued this tradition with the appointment of Hendropriyono. Yudhoyono tried to introduce a new tradition by appointing former head of the national police Sutanto to head the intelligence agency, but subsequently returned the directorship to the military. Joko Widodo adopted a similar strategy, appointing his own political supporter as head of the intelligence agency. What does this tell us? First, that patronage politics has greatly undermined the development of intelligence reform and second, the expansion of BIN's role in counterterrorism remains problematic.

Greater threats invite greater interest in strengthening intelligence capacity in Indonesia. The BIN establishment seriously attempted to expand its roles, seeking authority for its operatives to arrest, detain, and wiretap suspicious individuals, criminals, and members of terrorist cells. In this context, the Yudhoyono administration also tried, with little success, to connect the intelligence reform agenda in which demilitarizing became the primary objective, to strengthening intelligence capability for the counter-terror mission. However, the alleged involvement of high-ranking BIN officials in the murder of a prominent Indonesian activist and public concerns about private obstruction have hindered political and tactical advancement. The intelligence community then proposed less-controversial initiatives, notably the establishment of a new education institution and internal think-tank that would strengthen internal capability and external coordination. The promulgation of a new Intelligence Law in 2011 marked the government's latest effort to give BIN adequate mandates to undertake investigations, counter-intelligence, and covert operations. BIN retained authority to conduct wiretapping, but was restrained from arresting and detaining alleged terrorist suspects.

Taking all this into consideration, this chapter has shed light on the complicated process of counterterrorism measures in contemporary Indonesia. We see how the threat of terrorism has dominated the discourse of intelligence reform after *Reformasi*. Despite the threats, the intelligence community responded ambiguously. The legacy of military domination has yet to be erased, which contributed to shaping the "clash of interests" among security stakeholders. Literature on security sector reform argues that such behavior is quite normal in post-authoritarian settings (see, for instances, Bruneau and Dombroski, 2006; Gill and Wilson, 2013; Organization for Economic Cooperation and Development, 2005). Intelligence agencies need time and institutional adjustment to adapt to democratic ideas and arrangements and to respond to democratic pressures, which are often hostile. The Indonesian experience is a clear example of these intricate political dynamics.

References

Al A'raf. 2015. "Menjaga Kesimbangan antara Keamanan dan Kebebasan dalam Kebijakan Penanggulangan Terorisme". *Jurnal Keamanan Nasional* 1 (2): 225–249.

ASEAN. 2002. "Declaration on Terrorism by the 8th ASEAN Summit Phnom Penh, 3 November 2002". *ASEAN*, October 17, 2002. http://asean.org/?static_post=declaration-on-terrorism-by-the-8th-asean-summit-phnom-penh-3-november-2002-4 (accessed March 9, 2018).

Bruneau, Thomas and Kenneth R. Dombroski. 2006. "Reforming Intelligence: The Challenge of Control in New Democracies". In *Who Guards the Guardians and How: Democratic Civil-Military Relations*, edited by Thomas C. Bruneau and Scott D. Tollefson, pp. 145-177. Austin: University of Texas Press.

Cianflone, Matt et al. 2007. *Anatomy of a Terrorist Attack: An In-depth Investigation into the 2002 Bali, Indonesia, Bombings*. Pittsburgh: Matthew Ridgeway Center.

CNN. 2002. "US Warning of Bali Threat". October 17, 2002. http://edition. cnn.com/2002/WORLD/asiapcf/southeast/10/16/bali.bombings/ (accessed March 1, 2018).

———. 2016. "Nuansa Politis Kepala Badan Intelijen Negara". September 9, 2016. https://www.cnnindonesia.com/nasional/ 20160909095550- 20-157 196/ aura- politis-kepala-badan-intelijen-negara (accessed March 9, 2018).

Collier, Michael. 2010. "Intelligence Analysis: A 9/11 Case Study". In *Homeland Security and Intelligence*. Santa Barbara: Praeger.

Conboy, Kenneth. 2004. *Intel: Inside Indonesia's Intelligence Service*. Jakarta: Equinox.

Detik. 2005. "Masih Transisi, Intelijen Gagal Deteksi Bom Bali". October 4, 2005. https://news.detik.com/berita/454887/masih-transisi- intelijen-gagal-deteksi-bom-bali-ii (accessed March 8, 2018).

———. 2017. "BIN: Serangan Kampung Melayu Strategi ISIS Tunjukkan Eksistensi". May 28, 2017. https://news.detik.com/berita/d-3513313/ bin-serangan-kampung-melayu-strategi-isis-tunjukkan-eksistensi (accessed March 3, 2018).

Gill, Peter and Lee Wilson. 2013. "Intelligence and Security-Sector Reform in Indonesia". In *Intelligence Elsewhere: Spies and Espionage Outside the Anglosphere*, edited by Philip H. J. Davies and Kristian C. Gustafson, pp. 157-179. Washington, DC: Georgetown University Press.

Haripin, Muhamad. 2013. *Reformasi Sektor Keamanan Pasca Orde Baru: Melacak Pandangan dan Komunikasi Advokasi Masyarakat Sipil* [Security Sector Reform in Post-New Order Indonesia: Exploring the Perspective, Communication, and Advocacy of Civil Society]. Tangerang: Marjin Kiri.

———. 2017. "Military Operations Other Than Warfare and Problems of Military Professionalism in Democratizing Indonesia". Thesis. Ritsumeikan University (unpublished).

Haseman, John. B. 2005. "New Intelligence Chief is Well-connected". In *Asia-Pacific Defence Reporter.*

Hikam, Muhammad AS (ed.). 2014. *Toward 2014–2019: Strengthening Indonesia in a Changing World.* Jakarta: Rumah Buku.

Honna, Jun. 2013. "Security Challenges and Military Reform in Post-authoritarian Indonesia: The Impact of Separatism, Terrorism, and Communal Violence". In *The Politics of Military Reform: Experiences from Indonesia and Nigeria,* edited by Jürgen Rüland, Maria-Gabriela Marea, and Hans Born, pp.185-199. Heidelberg: Springer.

Imparsial. 2005. *Evaluasi Kinerja BIN di Masa Transisi dan Catatan untuk Reformasi.* Jakarta: Imparsial.

International Crisis Group (ICG). 2003. "Jemaah Islamiyah in Southeast Asia: Damaged but Still Dangerous (Report No. 63/Asia)". https://www.crisisgroup.org/asia/south-east-asia/indonesia/jemaah-islamiyah-south-east-asia-damaged-still-dangerous (accessed March 9, 2018).

_____. 2011. "Indonesia: Debate over a New Intelligence Bill". *Update Briefing,* July 12. https://www.crisisgroup.org/asia/south-east-asia/indonesia/indonesia-debate-over-new-intelligence-bill (accessed March 12, 2018).

Intisari Online. 2017. "Menguak Misteri Sekolah Intelijen, Tempat Para Calon 'James Bond' Indonesia Ditempa Secara Rahasia". November 21, 2017. http://intisari.grid.id/Unique/Fokus/Menguak-Misteri-Sekolah-Intelijen-Tempat-Para-Calon-James-Bond-Indonesia-Ditempa-Secara-Rahasia?page=all (accessed February 14, 2018).

Jenkins, David. 1984. *Suharto and His Generals: Indonesian Military Politics, 1975–1983.* Ithaca, New York: Cornell Modern Indonesia Project, Cornell University.

Kingsbury, Damien. 2003. *Power Politics and the Indonesian Military.* London: Routledge Curzon.

Kompas. 2002. "Membenahi Kerusakan, Mengisi Kekosongan." October 20, 2002.

_____. 2015. "Sutiyoso Sebut ISIS Ganti Strategi setelah Alami Sejumlah Kekalahan". July 6, 2015. http://megapolitan.kompas.com/read/2016/07/06/17480741/sutiyoso.sebut.isis.ganti.strategi.setelah.alami.sejumlah.kekalahan (accessed January 17, 2018).

Lahneman, William. 2007. "U.S. Intelligence Prior to 9/11 and Obstacles to Reform". In *Reforming Intelligence: Obstacles to Democratic Control and Effectiveness*, edited by Thomas C. Bruneau and Steven C. Boraz, pp.73-95. Austin: University of Texas Press.

Liputan 6. 2002. "BIN Telah Mengendus Rencana Bom Bali". November 6, 2002. http://news.liputan6.com/read/44504/bin-telah-mengendus-rencana-bom-bali (accessed March 4, 2018).

_____. 2009. "SBY Sasaran Tembak Teroris". July 17, 2009. http://news.liputan6.com/read/237379/sby-sasaran-tembak-teroris (accessed February 17, 2018).

Merdeka. 2009. "Bom Marriott Tak Terdeteksi BIN". July 17, 2009. https://www.merdeka.com/peristiwa/bom-marriot-tak-terdeteksi-bin.html (accessed January 15, 2018).

Muqoddas, M. Busyro. 2011. *Hegemoni Rezim Intelijen: Sisi Gelap Peradilan Kasus Komando Jihad*. Yogyakarta: Pusham UII.

Muradi. 2009. "The 88th Densus AT: The Role and the Problem of Coordination on Counter-Terrorism in Indonesia." *Journal of Politics and Law* 2 (3): 85–96.

Noor, Farish A. 2014. "A Guide to Indonesia's Trajectory for Next 5 Years". *The Nation*, December 27, 2014.

Organization for Economic Co-operation and Development. 2005. *Security System Reform and Governance*. Paris: OECD.

Republik Indonesia. 2002. Instruksi Presiden Republik Indonesia Nomor 5 Tahun 2002 tanggal 22 Oktober 2002 tentang Koordinasi Intelijen oleh Badan Intelijen Negara.

_____. 2009. *Peraturan Presiden Republik Indonesia Nomor 14 Tahun 2009 tentang Sekolah Tinggi Intelijen Negara.*

Sebastian, Leonard C. 2006. *Realpolitik Ideology: Indonesia's Use of Military Force.* Singapore: Institute of Southeast Asian Studies.

Seniwati. 2014. "The Role of Australia in Countering Terrorism in Indonesia". *Australian Journal of Basic and Applied Sciences* 8 (5): 558–563.

Solahudin. 2013. *The Roots of Terrorism in Indonesia: From Darul Islam to Jema'ah Islamiyah.* Sydney: UNSW Press.

Southwood, Julie and Patrick Flanagan. 1983. *Indonesia: Law, Propaganda and Terror.* London: Zed Press.

Sulistiyanto, Priyambudi. 2007. "The Politics of Intelligence Reform in Post-Suharto Indonesia". *The Journal of the Australian Institute of Professional Intelligence Officer* 15 (2): 29–46.

Tanter, Richard. 1991. "Intelligence Agencies and Third World Militarization: A Case Study of Indonesia, 1966–1989, with Special Reference to South Korea, 1961–1989". Dissertation. Monash University (unpublished).

Tempo. 2005. "Badan Intelijen Buka Kantor di Bali". December 30, 2005. https://nasional.tempo.co/read/71503/badan-intelijen-buka-kantor-di-bali (accessed April 1, 2018).

The Guardian. 2003. "Indonesia Knew Hotel Area was Bomb Target for Terrorist". August 7, 2003. https://amp.theguardian.com/world/2003/aug/07/indonesia.johnaglionby (accessed May 1, 2018).

The Jakarta Post. 2017. "Extraordinary Measures Needed to Root Out Terrorists: BIN Chief". May 28, 2017. http://www.thejakartapost.com/news/2017/05/28/extraordinary-measures-needed-to-root-out-terrorists-bin-chief.html (accessed March 28, 2018).

The 9/11 Commission Report. 2004. *Final Report of the National Commission on Terrorist Attacks Upon the United States.* New York: W.W. Norton & Company.

Tribunnews. 2009. "SBY Dibohongi Foto Teroris". July 22, 2009. http://surabaya.tribunnews.com/2009/07/22/sby-dibohongi-foto-teroris (accessed August 17, 2018).

_____. 2011a. "Pujian Semu Sidney Jones Soal Teroris di Indonesia". August 9, 2011. http://www.tribunnews.com/tribunners/2011/08/09/pujian-semu-sidney-jones-soal-teroris-di-indonesia (accessed October 5, 2019).

_____. 2011b. "BIN Minta Informasi Intelijen Jadi Dasar Hukum". September 27, 2011. http://www.tribunnews.com/nasional/2011/09/27/bin-minta-informasi-intelijen-dasar-penegakan-hukum (accessed July 12, 2018).

Vaughn, Bruce et al. 2005. *Terrorism in Southeast Asia. CRS Report for Congress.* https://fas.org/sgp/crs/terror/RL31672.pdf (accessed November 11, 2018).

Wachjunadi, Arif. 2017. *Misi Walet Hitam 09.11.05-15.45: Menguak Misteri Teroris Dr. Azhari.* Jakarta: Penerbit Buku Kompas.

Widjajanto, Andi, ed. 2006. *Negara, Intel, dan Ketakutan.* Jakarta: Pacivis UI.

Widjajanto, Andi and Artanti Wardhani. 2008. *Hubungan Intelijen–Negara, 1945–2004.* Jakarta: Pacivis UI and Friedrich Ebert Stiftung.

Wise, William. 2005. *Indonesia's War on Terror.* Jakarta: USINDO.

Concluding Remarks

Jafar Suryomenggolo and Okamoto Masaaki

This book discusses Indonesia's transformation during the past twenty years, from an authoritarian country to a democratic one, from a lower-middle income country to a promising and ambitious upper-middle income country, from a country with a predominantly rural population to a country with a high urban population density, and from a society that was drowning in state propaganda to a nation that promotes human rights. These changes have touched many and various spheres that no single study can fully assess. This book does not propose a single common view based on a certain theoretical perspective when examining Indonesia's transformation. Instead, it has offered a wide range of views on certain key areas to illuminate the changes and how various actors have contributed to make democracy work in Indonesia. In this conclusion, we wish to provide an overview of the main themes of the discussion and locate them in a general context to understand Indonesia's transformation from a comparative perspective.

Part 1: Governance and Social Dynamics discusses how changing social conditions have shaped state-society relations, with a focus on four issues: the governance of ethnic diversity, the right to participate in the urban landscape (with a case study of Yogyakarta), the state's ineffectiveness in tackling violence against a religious minority group (the Shia community in Madura), and problems with the affirmative policy to support Papuans in the political sphere. These four issues illustrate the social dynamics of reform that have forced the state to abandon or rebrand outdated policies of the previous authoritarian regime and yet continue to challenge the state to effectively respond to the demands of the society. Although the state was slow to respond to the changes, since the consolidation of democracy in 2004, it has finally come to grips with the realities of managing Indonesia's diversity.

Part 2: "Paths to Equality" highlights Indonesia's macro-economic situation after 1998 by looking closely into four separate yet related issues: the ambiguous nature of education outcomes as part of the decentralization program since 1999, the anatomy of how metropolitan poverty (in Jabodetabek) correlates to educational attainment, the challenges of farm liquidation in Java where land ownership is highly valued, and the importance of financial backing for infrastructure development. Two key points emerge from these issues in regard to Indonesia's quest to reduce poverty and tackle inequality. First, although education reform has been one of the cornerstones of Indonesia's transition, strong and high-level educational outcomes remain elusive. As such, rather than simply enlarging the education budget at the regional level, policy makers need to rethink a national education policy that ensures open access for all and considers the diversity of local conditions. Although one of the five major agendas of the administration of Joko Widodo and Ma'ruf Amin (2019–2024) is social investment in human development, it is not yet clear how this will develop education policy and expand the skilled labor pool to meet industry's needs.

Second, due to increasing urbanization during the last two decades, Indonesia's rural areas have to adapt to changing agricultural and social landscapes, including the threats of an aging population among farmers and environmental degradation. Indonesia is facing a set of typical challenges similar to other middle-income countries where agricultural transformation fails to bring economic gains, instead creating more agrarian conflicts. Farm liquidation may provide an alternative solution to enhance agricultural growth, and infrastructure development to reduce regional disparity. We have yet to see how the current administration will develop policy to prioritize rural development beyond reliance on foreign investment.

Part 3: Structural Challenges discusses four crucial challenges that impede Indonesia's democracy amid major institutional reforms: the acute problem of corruption, human rights violations, the ideological return of the military, and the troubled reform of the intelligence apparatus. In all four of these issues, we note how civil society organizations (in general, the social movement) have played important roles in monitoring the implementation of on-going reforms, educating the public, and suggesting further reforms. Indonesia does not yet have an active and robust social movement to balance the powerful interests of various elite social and political actors. Nonetheless, there is hope that Indonesia's civil society will continue to grow, as the younger generation is more aware of these issues and more articulate in promoting democracy ideals. They understand that democracy provides a space to foster their freedom and future, too.

Indonesia's experience of reform and its six-year process of consolidating its democracy may offer an interesting case in Southeast Asia, where democracy is contested and often fails to take root. Unlike Thailand and Myanmar, where democracy has experienced a setback since the military *coup d'etat*, Indonesia is moving toward a more stable democracy with a civilian government and functioning parliament, despite institutional weakness. Political reforms in Malaysia (since 2018) are moving toward consolidating democracy, but the pace of reform has been slow as the old political guard continues to loom large and dictates the course of change.

As a country with a Muslim-majority population, Indonesia's experience of democracy shows that a secular government is a prerequisite to maintain the course of reform. The rise of political Islamism may become a concern in the changing democratic landscape. However, unlike Turkey and Egypt, successive governments of Indonesia have navigated its security approach well enough to monitor and contain the threat of violence (and terrorism) from Islamist radicals and intolerant groups. While Indonesia is still troubled by religious-based violence, it promotes respect for pluralism in the society by developing a pragmatic approach to religious tolerance (under the banner of "Islam Nusantara").

Democracy in Indonesia is far from perfect, but the majority of political actors have adopted it as the "only game in town" because it provides an open-for-all platform to advance their interests within the political system. This adoption is mainly (though not solely) buoyed by the country's economic growth. The politics of economic growth binds the nation together in democracy. Although Indonesia is not the best performing economy in the Southeast Asian region (or among middle-income countries), its economic indicators have been steadily improving since 2004. Beyond infrastructure development, there are calls to improve the environment for (foreign) investment and further deregulations, including revising labor laws. A PwC projection report lists Indonesia in the world's top five economies by 2050—a forecast that is warmly welcomed by the country's ruling elites and the Ministry of Finance (Hawksworth, 2018). This is also in line with the general ambition to escape the middle-income trap by 2045,[1] despite major hurdles to accomplishing that target, as discussed in this book. Whether the target will be reached or not, and whether Indonesians are willing to bear the social costs, Indonesia's story continues to be written.

References

Hawksworth, John. 2018. "The World in 2050: The Shift of Global Economic Power and the Challenge of Automation". Seminar presentation on December 6, 2018. https://fiskal.kemenkeu.go.id/aifed/seminar-files/4/Docs_20181206_the_world_in_2050__the_shift_of_global_economic_po.pdf (accessed July 16, 2019)

---

1 *Nikkei Asian Review* (2019) reported that Joko Widodo is confident that Indonesia will be among the world's top 10 economies by 2030, and top four by 2045.

Nikkei Asian Review. 2019. "Jokowi Vows to Invest in Tech Skills for an Indonesian 'Golden Age'. *Nikkei Asian Review,* July 3, 2019. https://asia.nikkei.com/Spotlight/The-Big-Story/Jokowi-vows-to-invest-in-tech-skills-for-an-Indonesian-Golden-Age (accessed July 16, 2019)

Index

A

Abdurrahman Wahid (Gus Dur) 110

Adam Malik 115

Adat 112, 123, 128, 133, 142, 143, 145, 146

Ahmadiyya 87, 96, 100, 102

Aliansi Nasional Anti-Syiah 102

Al-Malikiyyah (Hai'ah Ash-Shofwah Al-Malikiyyah) 93

Anggaran Pendapatan Belanja Negara 286

Angkatan Muda Diponegoro 340

Angkatan Muda Siliwangi 340

ASEAN 259, 262, 312, 324, 329, 381, 382, 388

Asian financial crisis 2, 312

Australia 4, 6, 32, 50, 114, 120, 326, 392, 406, 407

B

Badan Intelijen Keamanan Kepolisian Negara Republik Indonesia (Baintelkam Polri) 368

Badan Intelijen Strategis Tentara Nasional Indonesia (BAIS TNI) 367

Badan Kesatuan Bangsa dan Politik 95

Badan Pembina Potensi Keluarga Besar Banten 344

Badan Pengatur Jalan Tol 275

Badan Silaturahmi Ulama Pesantren Madura 93

Bali bombing 269, 326, 364, 366, 370, 377, 378, 381, 384, 385, 386

Bali Democracy Forum 312, 313

Bangkok 213, 232, 324

Banten 11, 41, 171, 174, 177, 180, 207, 212, 217, 340, 344, 348, 357

Bappenas 8, 38, 39

Barisan Ansor Serbaguna 103

Barisan Patriot Bela Negara 354

Basuki Tjahaja Purnama 12, 87, 347

Bhinneka Tunggal Ika 31

Bina Marga 282

Buddhist 1

C

China 197, 241, 242, 250, 256, 331

Chinese Indonesians 44, 53

Christian 1, 44, 77, 86, 349

Cilacap x, 18, 240, 243, 245, 246, 248

Confucian 1

Corruption Perception Index viii, 293, 300

COVID-19 xi, 13, 22

D

Decentralization 23, 195, 297, 308

Democratization 14, 16, 19, 23, 24, 53, 106, 301, 308, 358

Detasemen Khusus Antiteror 88 (Densus 88) 363

Development vi, x, 8, 26, 30, 38, 39, 77, 84, 100, 126, 134, 142, 145, 150, 156, 158, 184, 194, 232, 266, 268, 286, 307, 309, 310, 323, 388, 391, 406

Dewan Adat Papua 124

E

East Timor 312, 328, 329, 365

Education v, vii, 84, 88, 92, 97, 144, 149, 155, 162, 188, 189, 194, 204, 220, 222, 223, 230, 233, 309

Egypt 396

Environment 142, 232, 233, 330

environmental degradation 215, 395

environmental protection 9, 21

F

Farmland vi, vii, x, 235, 239, 240, 241, 245, 249, 250, 253, 254, 257, 258

Farmland liquidation vii, 239, 240, 249, 250, 253

Fiscal vi, 233, 259, 265, 267

fiscal decentralization 18, 153, 268, 272, 296

Forum Betawi Rempug 347, 360

Forum Kemitraan Pemolisian Masyarakat 351

Forum Komunikasi Putra-Putri Purnawirawan Indonesia 340

Forum Rekonsiliasi Masyarakat Irian 111

Forum Ulama Ummat Indonesia 102

G

G20 3, 293

Gerakan Pemuda Ansor 103

Gerakan Pemuda Ka'bah 77

Gereja Kristen Indonesia 30

Grobongan 18, 240, 243

H

Hindu 1

Human rights 315

Huria Kristen Batak Protestan 30

I

Ikatan Pemuda Karya 340

Indonesian Corruption Watch
(ICW) 294

Indonesian NGO Forum on
Indonesian Development
(INFID) 323

Inequality 25, 198, 199, 234, 256

Infrastructure vi, x, 9, 259, 261,
267, 273, 277, 280, 284, 286

infrastructure deficit 8

infrastructure development 8, 9, 16,
18, 72, 259, 265, 266, 272, 278,
395, 397

intelligence x, 21, 94, 95, 97, 340,
361, 396

Islam 12, 13, 23, 29, 30, 43, 48, 53,
79, 87, 88, 92, 94, 97, 100, 102,
103, 105, 330, 338, 349, 357,
358, 392, 397

Islamic State of Iraq and Al-Sham
(ISIS) 372

Islam Nusantara 397

J

Jabodetabek v, vii, x, 17, 210, 279,
395

Jakarta 12, 17, 24, 25, 37, 44, 50,
75, 84, 86, 87, 90, 96, 101, 119,
122, 126, 142, 211, 275, 286,
293, 318, 334, 335, 344, 346,
347, 349, 352, 365, 368, 370,
378, 379, 380, 381, 385, 394

Japan xi, xii, 5, 6, 24, 25, 234, 240,
242, 254, 257, 337, 338, 406,
407

Jaringan Damai Papua 133

Jemaah Islamiyah 365, 390

Jember x, 18, 99, 190, 240, 243

Jogja Mural Forum 60

Joko Widodo 6, 8, 9, 10, 101, 265,
266, 294, 353, 380, 387, 395,
397

K

Komnas HAM 19, 312, 314, 316,
323, 325, 328, 331

Komnas Perempuan 312

Komunitas Intelijen Daerah 95

Korea 5, 6, 52, 196, 282, 323, 392,
407

L

Lamongan x, 18, 240, 243, 244,
245, 247

Land vi, 111, 119, 143, 145, 198,
232, 235, 239, 240, 256, 257,
258

Laskar Bali 349, 354

Lembaga Pembiayaan Ekspor Indonesia 277

M

Majelis Rakyat Papua 123, 144

Majelis Ulama Indonesia 96, 106

Makassar 92, 231

Malaysia 9, 44, 45, 54, 55, 219, 234, 259, 263, 326, 396

Manila 213

Megawati Sukarnoputri 110, 118, 120, 121, 265, 346, 376, 380

Merauke Integrated Food and Energy Estate 132, 143

Minority 105

Muhammadiyah 30, 44, 79, 100

Multiculturalism v, 29, 32, 49, 50, 53, 54

Myanmar 337, 396

N

Negara Kesatuan 31, 49

New Delhi 214, 234

New Order 1, 3, 7, 10, 18, 20, 21, 26, 29, 37, 43, 44, 46, 56, 65, 94, 291, 294, 296, 297, 301, 313, 320, 335, 339, 341, 344, 356, 360, 362, 364, 372, 374, 389

Nigeria 215, 232, 256, 390

O

Off-farm income 248

Off-farm jobs 241, 250, 252

Orang Asli Papua 112, 122, 144

P

Paguyuban Seksi Keamanan Keraton 351

PAM Jaya 283

Pancasila 75, 335, 339, 348, 353, 358, 359

Papua vii, ix, 12, 15, 16, 31, 41, 53, 110, 170, 174, 176, 181, 193, 271, 315, 328, 365

Papua Barat 126, 144

Partai Demokrasi Indonesia-Perjuangan 42, 121

Partai Golongan Karya 121

Partai Kebangkitan Bangsa 90, 121

Partai Persatuan Pembangunan 77, 100, 347

Pemekaran 138

Pemuda Panca Marga 340, 346, 347

Pemuda Pancasila 335, 339, 348, 353, 358, 359

Penanggung Jawab Proyek Kerjasama 281

Persatuan Masyarakat Palembang Bersatu (PMPB) 352

Persatuan Pendekar Seni Budaya Banten 340

Philippines 8, 48, 221, 232, 337, 356

Plural Society 53, 54, 144

Potensi Desa (Podes) 195

Poverty v, vii, x, 189, 197, 199, 210, 212, 215, 232, 256, 307

Poverty rate 189, 217

Prabowo Subianto 327

Preman 359, 360

Presidium Dewan Papua 120

Program Penanggulangan Dampak Pengurangan Subsidi Energi 268

R

Reformasi v, vi, xi, 3, 10, 16, 21, 22, 30, 40, 56, 58, 64, 75, 78, 79, 82, 84, 86, 107, 110, 138, 235, 237, 242, 297, 301, 304, 306, 311, 312, 314, 317, 318, 326, 358, 359, 361, 364, 365, 387

religious violence 89, 104

Rencana Aksi Nasional Hak Asasi Manusia 311

Rice production x, 238, 239

Rio de Janeiro 214, 215, 233, 234

S

Satpam 341

Shia v, 15, 86, 91, 394

Singapore 23, 45, 105, 106, 145, 259, 263, 286, 304, 309, 326, 329, 331, 392

Solo 244, 366, 371

Sri Lanka 8

Suharto vi, viii, 1, 16, 23, 24, 25, 31, 84, 86, 92, 95, 110, 112, 115, 116, 118, 119, 123, 124, 133, 144, 160, 161, 171, 291, 292, 307, 311, 313, 317, 320, 326, 327, 332, 339, 342, 346, 354, 361, 362, 365, 374, 375, 390, 392

Sukarno 1, 47, 110, 114, 118, 119, 326, 345

Surabaya 88, 92, 95, 96, 98, 100, 101, 106, 231

Susilo Bambang Yudhoyono 3, 30, 100, 265, 266, 315, 378

T

Tentara Nasional Indonesia 321, 367

Thailand 9, 10, 259, 262, 263, 396

Theys Eluay 124, 126, 320

Transparency International 293, 300

Turkey 396

U

Urban v, 9, 56, 82, 199, 220, 226,
    232, 258, 329

Urbanization 9, 232, 234

urban landscape 14, 56, 57, 58, 65,
    66, 71, 79, 81, 82, 394

urban poverty 219

V

Vietnam 153, 214, 233, 257, 356

Violence v, 23, 24, 55, 86, 88, 106,
    144, 234, 312, 339, 356, 358,
    360, 390

W

World Bank xi, 9, 25, 30, 150, 152,
    155, 156, 158, 160, 184, 194,
    200, 210, 213, 232, 233, 234,
    242, 256, 258, 262, 273, 287,
    291, 292, 310, 343

Y

Yakuza 341

Yayasan Pesantren Islam 88, 92

Yogyakarta v, ix, 14, 56, 61, 105,
    146, 178, 207, 258, 271, 272,
    307, 340, 351, 352, 356, 391,
    394, 406, 407

Authors

Abdul Wahid Fajar Amin works for the Ministry for Finance, in Jakarta. He holds a Ph.D. in Public Policy from the National Graduate Institute for Policy Studies (GRIPS), Japan.

Adnan Topan Husodo is the Coordinator of Indonesia Corruption Watch (ICW), in Jakarta. He holds a Master of Development Studies from the University of Melbourne, Australia.

Asep Suryahadi is Senior Research Fellow at The SMERU Research Institute, in Jakarta. He holds a Ph.D. in Economics from the Australian National University (ANU).

Brigitta Isabella is a member of KUNCI Cultural Studies Center, in Yogyakarta and a member of the editorial collective of a new peer-reviewed, scholarly journal *Southeast of Now: Directions in Contemporary and Modern Art in Asia,* published by NUS Press.

Cecilia Marlina is a former researcher at The SMERU Research Institute, in Jakarta. She holds a Master of Management from International College of Management Sydney, Australia.

Diandra Megaputri Mengko is researcher at Center for Political Studies, Lembaga Ilmu Pengetahuan Indonesia (LIPI—Indonesian Institute of Sciences), in Jakarta. She holds a Master of Defense Management from Indonesian Defense University.

Ernoiz Antriyandarti is Senior lecturer at Faculty of Agriculture, Universitas Sebelas Maret, in Surakarta. She holds a Ph.D. from Kyoto University, Japan.

Kayane Yuka is Assistant Professor at Faculty of Humanities and Social Sciences, Tsukuba University. She holds a Ph.D. from Kyoto University, Japan.

Latif Adam is senior researcher at Economic Research Center, LIPI, in Jakarta. He holds a Ph.D. in Economics from the University of Queensland, Australia.

Maxensius Tri Sambodo is senior researcher at Economic Research Center, LIPI, in Jakarta. He holds a Ph.D. from the National Graduate Institute for Policy Studies (GRIPS), Japan.

Muhamad Haripin is Coordinator of the National Politics Research Group at the Centre for Political Studies, LIPI, in Jakarta, and Research Coordinator of Intelligence Reform and National Security in the same institution. He holds a Ph.D. from the Graduate School of International Relations, Ritsumeikan University, Kyoto, Japan.

Okamoto Masaaki is Professor at Center for Southeast Asian Studies (CSEAS), Kyoto University. He holds a Ph.D. from Kyoto University, Japan.

Rosita Dewi is researcher at the Center for Political Studies, LIPI, in Jakarta. She holds a Ph.D. from Kyoto University, Japan.

Suh Jiwon is Associate Professor at Department of Asian Languages and Civilizations, Seoul National University, South Korea. She holds a PhD. from Ohio State University, United States of America.

Jafar Suryomenggolo is associate member of Centre Asie du Sud-Est (CASE), Paris, France, and Visiting Research Fellow at the Institute for Southeast Asian Studies, Jeonbuk National University, South Korea.

Susi Wuri Ani is lecturer at Faculty of Agriculture, Universitas Sebelas Maret, in Surakarta. She is a Ph.D. candidate at Universitas Gadjah Mada, Yogyakarta, Indonesia.

Thung Ju Lan is senior researcher at the Research Center for Society and Culture, LIPI, in Jakarta. She has a Ph.D. from La Trobe University, Melbourne, Australia.